'94

Van

London

SPACE AND PLACE:
Theories of Identity and Location

SPACE AND PLACE

Theories of Identity and Location

EDITED BY
Erica Carter, James Donald
and Judith Squires

LAWRENCE & WISHART
LONDON

Lawrence & Wishart Limited
144a Old South Lambeth Road
London SW8 1XX

First published 1993 by Lawrence & Wishart

Cover design by Jan Brown Designs
Photoset in North Wales by
Derek Doyle & Associates, Mold, Clwyd.
Printed and bound in Great Britain by
Redwood Books, Trowbridge, Wiltshire.

Contents

Introduction   vii

A. HOME AND EXILE

Dave Morley and Kevin Robins
No Place Like *Heimat*: Images of Home(land)
   in European Culture   3

David Kazanjian and Anahid Kassabian
Naming the Armenian Genocide   33

Elizabeth Grosz
Judaism and Exile: The Ethics of Otherness   57

Glenn Bowman
Tales of the Lost Land: Palestinian Identity and the
   Formation of Nationalist Consciousness   73

Renata Salecl
National Identity and Socialist Moral Majority   101

Peter Hulme
Islands of Enchantment: Extracts from a Caribbean Travel Diary   111

McKenzie Wark
Vectors of Memory ... Seeds of Fire: The Western Media
   and the Beijing Demonstrations   129

B. ENGLISHNESS AND IMPERIALISM

Iain Chambers
Narratives of Nationalism: Being 'British'   145

v

CONTENTS

James Donald
How English Is It? Popular Literature and National Culture   165

Gail Ching-Liang Low
His Stories? Narratives and Images of Imperialism   187

Benita Parry
The Contents and Discontents of Kipling's Imperialism   221

Gail Ching-Liang Low
White Skins/Black Masks: The Pleasures and Politics
   of Imperialism   241

C. CITY SPACE

Victor Burgin
Chance Encounters: *Flâneur* and *Detraquée* in Breton's *Nadja*   269

Donatella Mazzoleni
The City and the Imaginary   285

Kevin Robins
Prisoners of the City: Whatever Could a Postmodern
   City be?   303

Peter D. Osborne
Milton Friedman's Smile: Travel Culture and the
   Poetics of a City   331

Kristin Ross
Rimbaud and Spatial History   357

Meaghan Morris
Metamorphoses at Sydney Tower   379

Notes on Contributors   397

Introduction

The articles in this book were first published in the journal *New Formations* between 1987 and 1991, the first five years of its life. *New Formations* was launched in, and assuredly against, the full ideological flood of Thatcherism and Reaganism. It took as its focus questions of culture and politics. For, after decades of post-war consolidation, the very fundamentals of both were subject to radical theoretical and practical contestation. By 1991 however the political and cultural context in which the contributors wrote was very different. The neo-liberal experiment was falling apart, the map of Europe had been redrawn by the revolutions of 1989, the old Communist regimes in Eastern and central Europe had collapsed. These traumatic political events rendered old certainties obsolete in both East and West – the would-be and the so-called liberal democracies – and an anxious new search began for theoretical frameworks with which to understand and engage in these developments. In the academies of the West this was manifest in the search for new modes of radical cultural analysis and political imagination. It is this flux that formed the backdrop against which the journal's authors were writing.

In this collection, we have drawn together articles which reflect this turmoil through questioning notions of identity and location. The presumed certainties of cultural identity, firmly located in particular places which housed stable cohesive communities of shared tradition and perspective, though never a reality for some, were increasingly disrupted and displaced for all. 'Places', argue David Morley and Kevin Robins, 'are no longer the clear supports of our identity.'[1]

For many peoples, displaced and exiled from their homelands, places have long since ceased to provide straight-forward support to their identity. Yet, though the 'homes' which ground and house identities can be denied people physically by enforced exile or lost through chosen migration, they still continue to resonate throughout the imaginations of displaced communities. The ways in which 'home and exile' impact upon identity are addressed in various form by the contributors to the first section.

The second section focuses on those for whom, until recently, the relation between place and identity at least appeared to be more stable and less challenged. The construction of Englishness as an identity has involved not only a celebration of the geographical integrity of the nation-state, but also an assertion of its opposition to other communities and identities, through narratives of empire and exotic others. These imperial narratives and cultural artifacts shape not only the colonisers' perception of the colonised, but also their perception of self.

If the easy alliance of place and identity was never a reality for all those who experienced the enforced displacement of diaspora and exile, it has recently been disrupted for very different sorts of people. The forces of new technologies, globalization and 'time-space compression' have together created a sense of information flows, fragmentation and pace replacing what is now perceived to be a previous stability of homogeneity, community and place. Yet, this time-space compression has not been experienced by all in the same way: whilst some initiate its operation others are constrained by it.[2]

This is seen nowhere more clearly than in the contemporary city. As the distinct history and heritage of certain places becomes increasingly difficult to maintain amidst the flux of contemporary capital, there is a sense that if the cities are to act as locations for identity once again, they must be 'reimagined' as such. This is the concern of the third section.

IDENTITY

The concern with questions of identity over recent years may at first sight seem surprising, for the consistent logic of modern social and cultural thought has been to undermine the notion of individual identity. Sociologists and Marxists have insisted on its social determinations; Freud's account of the unconscious showed the inherently split, and so non-identical, nature of the self; Saussurean linguistics posited the self as the product rather than the author of symbolic codes and systems; Foucault and others point to the processes of subjectification operated by cultural apparatuses and technologies. So why the return of identity as a theoretical topic and a political project?

INTRODUCTION

The logics of universalism and, more recently, modernization and globalization have sought to represent localised identities as historical, regressive characteristics, and have worked to undermine the old allegiances of place and community. But the burgeoning of identity politics, and now nationalism, reveal a clear resistance to such universalising strategies. Difference and particularity will not be wished away by the language of universal rights or international brotherhood; nor are they fully repressed – as some versions of political economy might suggest – by the forces of international capital. Old divisions and loyalties based around class and geographical community may have been undermined by the globalization of markets, communications networks, networks of power and capital flows: but in their place – paradoxically both as a resistance to, and at the same time a product of those global forces – we see the development of new communities of interest and belief. Feminism, lesbian and gay activism, black political and cultural movements have all arisen in some way from a redrawing of the boundaries – geographical, socio-symbolic, psychic – of identity and community: and, in asserting the reality of cultural differences and the affective investments they solicit, all have posed unmistakable challenges to the universalist democratic discourse of rights.

Against the traditional assertion of essential group difference and hierarchical social orders, the Enlightenment brought with it the claim that all people were equal in their capacity to reason and therefore entitled to equal political rights. The state should therefore express rights only in universal terms, applying equally to all. Differences, though they did not cease to exist, were claimed to be irrelevant to one's political status, role and rights. They were now argued to be of relevance only within a private realm of partiality and caring, and not the proper concern of the public realm of universality and justice. This ideal of justice, still articulated in the most recent attempts to restate the liberal position[3] understands liberation and 'fairness' as the transcendence of group difference. Differences are excluded from the public sphere and forced into the shadows of the private. The norms and procedures of the public realm are then claimed to be neutral and equally accessible to all. It is not that differences are denied by this strategy, but they are located in a private sphere, claimed to be beyond the scope of politics and negotiated consensus. Thus difference actually comes to be understood as essential. Groups are claimed to have distinct natures, and ignorance and distance ensure that these myths of otherness live on.

Whereas the universalist, humanist claims of identity and neutrality mark only oppressed groups as different, as other to the norm, a more fluid and relational notion of difference allows for the recognition of cultural specificity and heterogeneity as the touchstone against which *all* political claims are assessed, embraced and/or contested. In other words, to assert 'identity' in this *relational* form as a basis for politics is to challenge the universalist ideal. It is to display 'difference' forcibly in the public sphere and challenge the claimed neutrality of the procedural mechanisms of justice as fairness.[4]

These identities are shaped by embodied and embedded narratives, located in particular places and times. They need neither to be assimilated to a neutral norm, nor essentialised as absolute other: they are fluid, migratory identities, which if recognised fully in a political sphere would demand a more heterogeneous conception of the public sphere than was ever accommodated within liberal political structures as classically conceived. It is this notion of relational group identity politics which has mobilised against the neo-liberal assertion of atomistic individualism.

Of course, not all claims to identity politics take this relational form. A more dichotomous notion of difference has regularly been mobilised to legitimate cultural and political exclusion, and to assert the dominance of the norm. Such has certainly been the case in the history of British national identity, whose cultural contours and pathologies are explored in this collection 'from the inside' (uncomfortably) by James Donald and Iain Chambers, and by Gail Ching-Liang Low and Benita Parry through the prism of colonialism.

The themes of cultural belonging, the comforts and costs of affiliation are also explored in Section A in a more global perspective. The important point about these articles is not whether they endorse the political claims associated with any one national identity, but rather the way they explore, in Morley and Robins's words, 'the role of the stories we tell ourselves about the past in constructing our identities in the present' – stories often rendered as a national literature or cinema. That is not to say that we are dealing merely with a textually conjured dream-world. The trauma of Armenian and Jewish genocide, and the difficulties and incompleteness of German attempts to work through guilt and mourning for the Holocaust, underline the brutal reality of events that spark the need for such stories. David Kazanjian and Anahid Kassabian see this narrativization of events as an uncertain and inescapably textual quest for truth, for 'truth in historical discourse'. As young Armenians living in the United States, they perceive that the search for a 'homeland' – never an innocent utopia – may be a material quest, but is 'yet certainly emotional, a space to feel, and feel justified.'

That experience of diaspora, or even exile, is echoed – another paradox – in both the Palestinian and the Jewish experience. The ambivalent position of the migrant, the refugee, the exile, the foreigner, or simply the child of someone who once came from somewhere else, can be both painful and powerful. Painful, because, as Elizabeth Grosz, for example, observes: 'The Jew strives to be part of culture, to conform to its laws and customs, while at the same time, remaining an outsider, estranged and alienated the more he/she is included. Represented as a perennially landless, homeless wanderer, an exiled nomad, the Jew is both familiar with, yet excluded (and estranged) from the cities, the cultures, and the communities within which he or she circulates.'[5] And yet also powerful, because this alterity, as we have already remarked of the postcolonial perspective on Englishness, allows a conception, and again an experience, of otherness which is not reduced to a projection or inversion of the self same. Or at least potentially powerful for a dispersed population like the Palestinians, Glenn Bowman argues. For them the memory, the ideal and the image of 'the land' from which they have been exiled can be a potent symbolic force in the struggle for national recognition.

Such nuanced perspectives begin to reveal the important issues often elided by the lazy invocation of 'identity politics'. They underlie the point that the quest for identity cannot be separated from the experience of division.[6] As Grosz argues in her account of Levinas: 'The other is prior to any identity, even to the distinction between subject and object'.[7] Once we jettison fundamentalist versions of identity politics, once we accept that the belonging ascribed to us is structurally both exorbitant and unsatisfying, then we can begin to ask how the narratives and claims of ethnos actually impinge on individual subjectivity and agency. How, in other words, do we live in the symbolic space of home or exile?

This leads again to the idea that the constitutive other of national or communal identity is neither an ontological nor an epistemological entity, but is integral to, and definitive of, a psychical geography. As Renata Salecl suggests in her account of national identity in the post-Communist states, 'the fact that the nations of Eastern Europe are seeking new enemies, obsessively reviving old national hatreds, demonstrates quite clearly that the Other is always the Other within us and that hatred of the Other is in the final analysis hatred of one's own enjoyment.'[8]

The articles in the first two sections of this book take the questions of identity, community and belonging seriously. In doing so, they necessarily have a sceptical and uneasy relationship to any communal Subject that acts as the authority for, or guarantor of, a political project. They reveal the techniques and dynamics through which the narratives, symbolic spaces and collective fantasies of communal identity are produced and regulated. This radical critique of identity opens up opportunities to write a new political agenda, one no longer constrained by the claims of essentialised identity.

LOCATION

If places are no longer the clear supports of our identity, they nonetheless play a potentially important part in the symbolic and psychical dimension of our identifications. It is not spaces which ground identifications, but places.

How then does space become place? By being named: as the flows of power and negotiations of social relations are rendered in the concrete form of architecture; and also, of course, by embodying the symbolic and imaginary investments of a population. Place is space to which meaning has been ascribed. In his article on the postmodern city, Robins quotes Doreen Massey: 'Instead, then, of thinking of places as areas with boundaries around, they can be imagined as articulated movements in networks of social relations and understandings.'[9]

As Bernard Rose's horror film *Candyman* (1992) has revealed, both spaces and places are constitutive of the city. Rose plays with these two ways of representing the city. On the one hand, the film is punctuated by aerial shots of freeways, amphitheatres and housing projects which show the city as a space of geometric designs, the embodiment of social planning and public life. On the other hand, at street level, the people who live in those projects make sense of the city's irrationality in terms of urban myths and sub-cultural legends. These two styles of imaging of the city echo the theoretical distinction drawn by Michel de Certeau between the 'concept city' of rational, urbanist discourse and the resourceful, often dream-like tactics which people use to make sense of the city, and to survive it. Victor Burgin takes up this dual mapping to explore André Breton's surrealist readings of urban space in his novel *Nadja*. 'Breton's city,' he observes, 'is a stage for the encounter with the marvellous in the everyday. Breton is actor-director and general manager. Brilliant illusions are conjured on this stage, but they are imposed on a space whose co-ordinates are fundamentally Cartesian, whose geometries are Euclidean.'[10]

As with the rethinking of identity and community, what begins to emerge in this discussion of the city is an account of space that gives full weight to the symbolic and the imaginary without reducing these aspects to the functionalism of ideology. Donatella Mazzoleni underlines the *purely* conceptual nature of de Certeau's Concept. The modern (or postmodern) metropolis, she argues, cannot be seen as a whole and so loses the identity, the coherent profile of a place. It therefore has to be intuited in more aesthetic and psychical ways. In the words of Mazzoleni:

> 'In the metropolitan aesthetic the eye fails in its role as an instrument of total control at a distance: once more the ears, and then the nose and skin, acquire an equal importance. The sensory field of the metropolis is ultra- and infra-visual: it is the field of a total aesthetic. The mutation does not only concern perceptive behaviour, but also deeply involves the modalities of appropriation and symbolization of space – since it reaches the horizon, the metropolis is a habit without a 'somewhere else'. It is, therefore, a total interior.'[11]

For some social theorists, this emphasis on the city as an imaginary institution might be interpreted as a retreat from politics. But Kevin Robins argues that, on the contrary, to understand this transformed nature of ascribing social significations to space is a prerequisite for any effective politics of the city. This is so, not least, because this change acts back on the very fabric of the city; 'This imaginary institution of the city defines the scope – the possibility and their limits – within which, at any particular time, we can imagine, think and experience city life; it defines the aesthetic and the intellectual field within which cities will be designed, planned and engineered.'[12]

Robins therefore criticises much recent work on civil society and the public sphere which ducks this issues, and opts instead for a nostalgic appeal to an older imaginary, that of Enlightenment urbanity. For these are public spaces conceived from the universality of the 'logic of identity', the willing away of difference, and they do not allow for the positive contestation which will arise from the recognition and acceptance of radical difference rather than simply liberal diversity.

'The new urban sensibility that is emerging may be more about not liking what it sees in the modern city than about really imagining an alternative vision.'[13] As with the critique of identity articulated in terms of community and tradition, the point here is not to deny the force of such fictions but to show how and why they are so powerful as a prelude to acting on them. Thus the rethinking of space calls for a public politics that acknowledges the partiality and violence of any rationalist Concept imposed on the space (and population) of the city and calls instead for a heterogeneous public, sensitive to local rhythms and dynamics of urban life. Such a heterogeneous public stands, as we have suggested above, in opposition to both the liberal and the communitarian vision of the public sphere; populated neither by atomistic individuals nor cohesive communities, this public sphere will be the site of contestation between groups of distinct, located (physically and culturally) identities. This requires, as Kevin Robins argues, 'tougher public spaces'.

TRAVEL

One theme, and also a style of writing, that has featured in many issues of New Formations has been that of travel: the negotiation not of familiar spaces, but of strange places. These distant places can now confront us in our everyday lives as mediatized information and images (as McKenzie Wark illustrates in his account of the Beijing demonstrations of 1989). But the encounter with other cultures, other places, and new ideas continues to provide both an occasion and a motif for the production of cultural studies: here, for example, in the self-reflective, inquisitive travels of Peter Hulme in the Caribbean or Peter D. Osborne in Columbia. These accounts attempt to avoid the exoticising tendency of much travel-writing. The distinction is analogous to one drawn by Kristin Ross. Whereas French ideologists of the newly formed nineteenth century discipline of geography saw space in abstracted, conventional terms of landscape, Ross suggests, Rimbaud imagined and represented it always as social space.

As an early issue of New Formations (number 3, Winter 1987) took as the theme of its editorial Edward Said's 'travelling theory', so this volume too, in some sense, offers theories of travelling and travelling theories. In his original essay Said was concerned with the locatedness and mobility of theory. He wandered 'whether by virtue of having moved from one place and time to another an idea or a theory gains or loses in strength, and whether a theory in one historical period and national culture becomes altogether different for another period or situation.' The virtue of ideas from elsewhere is that they can unblock intellectual and cultural formations. The danger is that theories which had been adversarial and oppositional in the place and time of their first formation can become, when transplanted, insidiously dogmatic. In contrast to this, the articles in this volume are characterised by a welcome restlessness. In their lively engagement with theoretical issues, they show both a sensitivity to the claims and demands of cultural traditions and also an alertness to the uniqueness of places and events. Together, they form a contribution to an emerging social and symbolic geography which is one of the most exciting aspects of today's cultural studies.

Erica Carter, James Donald and Judith Squires
July 1993

NOTES

[1] David Morley and Kevin Robins 'No Place Like *Heimat*: images of home(land) in European culture' in this collection p5.
[2] For development of this argument see Doreen Massey 'A Global Sense of Place' in *Marxism Today* June 1991, pp24-9.
[3] For the primary advocate of this liberal position see John Rawls 'Justice as Fairness: Political Not Metaphysical', in Shlomo Avineri and Avner de-Shalit (eds) *Communitarianism and Individualism* (Oxford University Press, Oxford, 1992).
[4] For discussion of this argument see Irish Marion Young *Justice and the Politics of Difference* (Princeton University Press, 1990) pp170-172.
[5] Elizabeth Grosz, 'Judaism and exile: the ethics of otherness' in this collection. p60.
[6] This point is made by Lefort...
[7] Elizabeth Grosz op cit p65.
[8] Renata Salecl, 'National identity and socialist moral majority' in this collection p103.
[9] Doreen Massey quoted by Kevin Robins in this collection p325.
[10] Victor Burgin, 'Chance encounters: Flâneur and detraquée in Breton's *Nadja*' in this collection p279.
[11] Donatella Mazzoleni, 'The City and the Imaginary', in this collection pp297-98.
[12] Kevin Robins, 'Prisoners of the city: whatever could a postmodern city be?' in this collection p315.
[13] Kevin Robins op cit p.313.

A.   Home and Exile

heima

No Place Like *Heimat*: Images of Home(land) in European Culture

David Morley and Kevin Robins

Our story is the old clash between history and home. Or to put it another way, the immeasurable, impossible space that seems to divide the hearth from the quest.

(Jeanette Winterson, 'Orion')

Evey country is home to one man
And exile to another.

(T. S. Eliot, 'To the Indians who died in Africa')

Everybody needs a home, so at least you can have some place to leave, which is where most folks will say you must be coming from.

(June Jordan, 'Living Room')

INTRODUCTION

Our concern here is with questions of identity and memory in the construction of definitions of 'Europe' and 'European Culture'. It is in this context that we address the centrality of the metaphor of Heimat ('home/land'). We take as a particular instance the debates opened up in the Federal Republic of Germany by Edgar Reitz's *Heimat*, with its focus on the opposition of Heimat:Fremde ('homeland/foreignness'). Our specific focus is on the relations between European and 'other' cultures in the post-war period and, more particularly, on the question of the representation of the European past as constructed through the American and the German media. Our argument is that we see played out here, in these debates over who holds the franchise on the representation of the past, an illuminating pre-echo of contemporary debates as to who (the Germans? the Allies?) has the right to determine Germany's future. This is, of course, no local matter, but is crucial to the future of Europe as a whole, as the franchise rights on the past are clearly intermeshed with the franchise on the future. We take the 'German story' to be both a symbolic condensation of many of the most problematic themes of the European past and to be clearly a central issue in the contemporary *realpolitik* of Europe.

If Germany, the past (somehow) reconciled, is to be united, and Europe no longer divided by the 'iron curtain' then the question arises, inescapably, as to where 'Europe' ends (what is the status of 'Mitteleuropa' or 'Eastern Europe'?) and against what 'other' (besides America) 'Europe' and 'European Culture' is to be defined, if not against Communism. Our argument is that, if America continues to supply one symbolic boundary, to the 'west', there is also, implicit in much recent debate, a reworking of a rather ancient definition of Europe – as what used to be referred to as 'Christendom' – to which Islam, rather than Communism, is now seen to supply the 'eastern' boundary. Our concern is with identifying some of the threads from which this pattern is being woven – the better, hopefully, to unravel it.

BRINGING IT ALL BACK HOME

'Modern man', Peter Berger and his colleagues argue, 'has suffered from a deepening condition of "homelessness" ': 'The correlate of the migratory character of his experience of society and of self has been what might be called a metaphysical loss of "home".'[1] To be modern, writes Marshall Berman,

> is to find ourselves in an environment that promises adventure, power, joy, growth, transformation of ourselves and the world – and, at the same time, that threatens to destroy everything we have, everything we know, everything we are. Modern environments and experiences cut across all boundaries of geography and ethnicity, of class and nationality, of religion an ideology; in this sense, modernity can be said to unite all mankind. But it is a paradoxical unity, a unity of disunity; it pours us all into a maelstrom of perpetual disintegration and renewal, of struggle and contradiction, of ambiguity and anguish.

4

The project of modernity is then 'to make oneself somehow at home in the maelstrom'.[2]

It is this image of home that interests us. Home in a world of expanding horizons and dissolving boundaries. Anthony Giddens draws attention to the implications of modernity for ontological security, for the confidence we have 'in the continuity of [our] self identity and in the constancy of the surrounding social and material environments of action'.[3] In pre-modern times, he argues, this sense of trust and security was rooted in kinship systems, in local community, in religious beliefs, and in the continuity of tradition. The effect of the great dynamic forces of modernity – what Giddens calls the separation of time and space, disembedding mechanisms, and institutional reflexivity – has been to 'disengage some basic forms of trust relation from the attributes of local contexts'.[4] Places are no longer the clear supports of our identity.

modernity

If anything, this process of transformation has become accelerated, and time-space distanciation has come to be ever more intense. It is through the logic of globalization that this dynamic of modernization is most powerfully articulated. Through proliferating information and communications flows and through mass human migration, it has progressively eroded territorial frontiers and boundaries and provoked ever more immediate confrontrations of culture and identity.[6] Where one it was the case that cultures were demarcated and differentiated in time and space, now 'the concept of a fixed, unitary, and bounded culture must give way to a sense of the fluidity and permeability of cultural sets'.[7] Through this intermixture and hybridization of cultures, older certainties and foundations of identity are continuously and necessarily undermined. The continuity of identity is broken too. 'There are *lieux de mémoire*, sites of memory', writes Pierre Nora, 'because there are no longer *milieux de mémoire*, real environments of memory.... We speak so much of memory because there is so little of it left.'[8] Indeed, we speak so much of memory, and also of place and community. As Michael Rustin argues, there is an increasingly felt need for 'some expressive relationship to the past' and for attachment to particular territorial locations as 'nodes of association and continuity, bounding cultures and communities'.[9] There is a need to be 'at home' in the new and disorientating global space.

Home, homeland, Heimat. It is around the meaning of European culture and identity in the new global context that this image – this nostalgia, this aspiration – has become polemically activated. It is associated, particularly, with Gorbachev's appeal to a 'common European home':

> Europe is indeed a common home where geography and history have closely interwoven the destinies of dozens of countries and nations. Of course, each of them has its own problems, and each wants to live its own life, to follow its own traditions. Therefore, developing the metaphor, one may say: the home is common, that is true, but each family has its own apartment, and there are different entrances, too.[10]

This notion of a single Europe, from the Atlantic to the Urals, has an obvious appeal. But what does it really amount to? What kind of community does it offer? Perhaps Susan Sontag is right. Where once Europe symbolized empire and expansionism, the new idea of Europe is about retrenchment: 'the Europeanisation, not of the rest of the world, but ... of Europe itself'.[11] This is a defensive identity, a fortress identity, defined against the threat of other cultures and identities (American, Japanese, Islamic, African, or whatever). What this reassertion of European cultural identity amounts to is a refusal to confront the fact of a fundamental population shift that is undermining 'the little white "Christian" Europe' of the nineteenth century. As Neal Ascherson argues, 'we are living in a new America which is reluctant to admit the fact; in a continent which the poor of the outside world are beginning to choose as a destination'.[12] The European Heimat invokes the past grandeur of Europe as a bastion against future uncertainties. This is a Europe that divides those who are of the Community from those who are *extracommunitari* and, effectively, extraterrestrial.[13]

There are those, however, who are less committed to this vision of a European home.[14] They are, to appropriate Gorbachev's metaphor, more interested in the different apartments than in the common home. For them, a faceless europeanism is inimical to the rich diversity of national cultures and identites that are, supposedly, the basis of a more authentic sense of belonging: it is only in the sense of nationhood that one can feel truly 'at home'. Throughout Europe, we can now see the rekindling of national and nationalist sentiments. It is more apparent in central and eastern Europe where national aspirations of sixty or seventy years ago are currently being reactivated through the reassertion of ethnic, religious and cultural differences. But also in western Europe, particularly in the context of German reunification

(*Deutschland, einig Vaterland*), national allegiance is a powerful way of belonging. As Ian Davidson argues, 'western reactions to the prospect of German unification show that the civilised advances of European integration are very recent compared with the old reflexes of nationalism; and that despite 45 years of reconciliation, there are primitive national feelings which lie only millimetres below the skin'.[15]

As an alternative to continental Europeanism and to nation-statism, there is yet another kind of 'homely' belonging. This is the identity rooted in the Heimat of regions and small nations. According to Neal Ascherson, the 'melting away' of the European nation states 'may allow other entities, smaller but more durable, to replace them'. He evokes the rich pluralism of regional traditions, languages, dialects and cultures as the true basis for authentic identities. The European community, Ascherson argues, 'will travel from the western Europe of nation-states via the Brussels superstate to the Europe of Heimats'.[16] This 'small is beautiful' ideal of a Europe of the regions clearly seems to offer a richer and more radical way to belong. There is a romantic utopianism in this celebration of small nationalism and regionalism, a utopianism of the underdog. 'The Irish, the Basques, the Corsicans, the Kurds, the Kosovans, the Azerbaijanis, the Puerto Ricans, the Latvians', writes John Berger, 'have little in common culturally or historically, but all of them want to be free of distant, foreign centres which, through long bitter experience, they have come to know as soulless'. All of them 'insist upon their identity being recognised, insist upon their continuity – their links with their dead and the unborn'.[17]

Yet Heimat is an ominous utopia. Whether 'home' is imagined as the community of Europe or of the national state or of the region, it is drenched in the longing for wholeness, unity, integrity. It is about community centred on shared traditions and memories. As the German film director Edgar Reitz puts it:

> The word is always linked to strong feelings, mostly remembrances and longing. Heimat always evokes in me the feeling of something lost or very far away, something which one cannot easily find or find again.... It seems to me that one has a more precise idea of Heimat the further one is away from it.[18]

Heimat is a mythical bond rooted in a lost past, a past that has already disintegrated: 'we yearn to grasp it, but it is baseless and elusive; we look back for something solid to lean on, only to find ourselves embracing ghosts'.[19] It is about conserving the 'fundamentals' of culture and identity. And, as such, it is about sustaining cultural boundaries and boundedness. To belong in this way is to protect exclusive, and therefore, excluding, identities against those who are seen as aliens and 'foreigners'. The 'other' is always and continuously a threat to the security and integrity of those who share a common home. Xenophobia and fundamentalism are opposite sides of the same coin.[20] For, indeed, Heimat-seeking is a form of fundamentalism. And, like all fundamentalist beliefs, it is built around what Salman Rushdie calls 'the absolutism of the Pure'. The 'apostles of purity', he argues, are always moved by the fear 'that intermingling with a different culture will inevitably weaken and ruin their own'.[21] In contemporary European culture, the longing for home is not an innocent utopia.

COMMUNICATIONS, MEMORY AND IDENTITY

In our view these questions – of identity, memory and nostalgia – are inextricably interlinked with patterns and flows of communication. The 'memory banks' of our times are in some part built out of the materials supplied by the film and television industries. It is to the role of these industries in the construction of memory and identity that we now turn.

Elsewhere[22] we have directly addressed the debates concerning the role of new communications technologies (satellite, cable, etc.) in the creation of 'electronic spaces' transcending established national boundaries and in the reconfiguration of European culture. As argued there, that dynamic involves two poles – pressures both towards globalization and centralization and towards the localization and regionalization of cultures. We take the position that most current perspectives on these issues are inadequate in so far as they operate with a (technologically) determinist model of the communication process. Within this prevailing framework cultural identities can only ever be responsive and reactive to the controlling stimulus of communications technologies. What is needed is a better formulation of the problem, one that takes questions of cultural and national identity as problematical and central categories.

One of the first questions concerns how we are to understand the 'national' as a process of 'remembering, a pulling together and reassemblage of its members'[23] and what the role of institutions such as television and cinema is in the construction of national identities. To

8

take first the institution of cinema: as Andrew Higson notes, the concept of national cinema has almost invariably been mobilized 'as a strategy of cultural (and economic) resistance; a means of asserting national autonomy in the face of ... Hollywood's international domination'.[24] In that context, *art* cinema has played a central role 'in the attempts made by a number of European countries both to counter American domination of their indigenous markets in film and also to foster a film industry and film culture of their own'.[25] The discourses of 'art', 'culture', 'quality' and 'national identity/nationhood' have thus been mobilized against 'Hollywood' and used to justify various nationally specific economic systems of support and protection for indigenous cinema-making.

The role of the state is crucial in this respect, in so far as state policies have often determined the parameters and possibilities of various 'national cinemas', in the context of governmental recognition of 'the potential ideological power of cinema ... as a national cultural form, an institution with a "nationalising" function'.[26] Given that nationhood is always an image constructed under particular conditions, and drawing on Benedict Anderson's concept of history as 'the necessary basis of national narrative',[27] Stephen Heath has suggested that, just as nationhood is not a given but 'always something to be gained' so 'cinema needs to be understood as one of the means by which it is "gained" ...'.[28] The same points would apply in relation to EEC policies designed to mobilize television in the production of European identities. This is, necessarily, a contentious business. Thus definitions of British cinema always involve the construction of an 'imaginary homogeneity of identity and culture ... apparently shared by all British subjects'; a process of inclusion and exclusion whereby one definition of 'British' is centralised and others are marginalised, in a process which Higson refers to as one of 'internal cultural colonialism'.[29]

It is a question of recognizing the role of the stories we tell ourselves about our past in constructing our identities in the present. One key issue concerns the power of the idea of the 'nation' to involve people in a common sense of identity and its capacity to work as an inclusive symbol which provides 'integration' and 'meaning' as it constructs and conscripts public images and interpretations of the past 'to re-enchant a disenchanted everyday life'.[30] In this fashion 'the rags and tatters of everyday life take on the lustre of the idealised nation when they are touched by its symbolism. There is therefore no simple replacement of "community" by "nation" ... but rather a constant ... redemption of its unhappy remains',[31] as the idea of the national past is constantly reworked and represented within the historical experience of a particular nation-state.[32]

The 'struggle for the past' has been a central issue at different stages in a number of European countries in recent years. Thus, in France in particular, the mid-1970s saw the emergence in the cinema of the 'retro style' (*Lacombe Lucien*, etc.) with films aiming to articulate a new, post-Gaullist concept of French history and French identity, specifically with reference to the role of the French Resistance movement (the 'emblem' of French identity at that point) under Fascism.[33] As Foucault noted at the time these films represented an attempt to 're-programme popular memory' through film and television, to recover 'lost, unheard memories' which had been denied (or buried) by the dominant representations of that past. So identity, it seems, is also a question of memory, and memories of 'home' in particular.

In this context that we address the centrality of the metaphor of Heimat (or 'home'): principally with reference to the specific debates opened up in the Federal Republic of Germany by Edgar Reitz's film/TV series of that name. The 'Heimatfilm', is, of course, a well established genre in Germany. One obvious question concerns whether one *can* work within this traditionally reactionary genre and yet give the material new and different meanings. Reitz's attempt to do so has to be seen in the context of the political revitalization of the rural 'Heimat' tradition in West Germany in the 1970s – as an attempt by a coalition of ecological and anti-nuclear groupings to reclaim these traditions for the left, via the rediscovery/revaluation of regional/folk traditions, dialect poetry, etc. in an anti-centralist (and anti-urban) political movement.[34] This turn in ecology represents an important shift, and in this context Adolf Muschg has noted that 'in the face of the steady destruction of the environment "homeland" has ceased to be a dirty word'.[35] More cynically perhaps, just as Raphael Samuel[36] has noted the resurgence of a concern with 'roots' and 'tradition' in contemporary Britain, Baudrillard observes that 'when the real is no longer what it used to be, nostalgia assumes its full meaning. There is a proliferation of myths of origin ... and authenticity.'[37] Heimat then is a place no one has yet attained, but for which everyone yearns. Reitz notes that 'Heimat, the place where you were born, is for every person the centre of the world' and yet recognizes that the concept is not simply territorial, but rather invokes a 'memory of origin' and inevitably involves a notion of an 'impossible return' to (imaginary or real) roots or origins.[38] The question is *which* 'roots' and to whom they, and their 'heritage' are seen to 'belong'.

TELEVISION, FILMS AND POPULAR MEMORY

An ABC Network newspaper advertisement boasted in February 1983 'more people relived the war than fought it' when its eighteen-hour mini series *The Winds of War* achieved the distinction of becoming one of the highest rated programmes in television history, reaching, according to ABC projections, virtually every American over twelve.[39] In much the same way, millions of Europeans have 'experienced' the Vietnam War through the lens of films such as *Apocalypse Now* or *The Deer Hunter* (see p14). As Anton Kaes argues, 'these films interpret national history for the broad public and thus produce, organise and homogenise public memory ... swiftly spreading identical memories over the earth.'[40]

This is no new process. As Anthony Smith pointed out in his review of Koppes and Black's *Hollywood Goes to War*,[41] at times, the role of national cinema in the representation of others (as allies, enemies, good, bad, etc.) is quite transparent. Koppes and Black quote the head of the US War Department's public relations section (Office of War Information) in this period as reporting that 'No matter what we want from Hollywood, we get it – and quick. We do not even have to ask – Hollywood comes to us', in a context where the Hollywood chieftains were revelling in the new role they had acquired, of orchestrating and manipulating popular images of the participants in the drama of World War Two. As Koppes and Black demonstrate, the content and scripts of movies were explicitly manipulated so as to mobilize American public opinion, firstly to support the war, and secondly to accept each changing situation and shifting military alliance, as the war proceeded. Thus the Office of War Information prevailed on the studios to tone down their mockery of the English class system expressed in their 'castle and caste' picture of Britain and to stress the country's 'stubborn resistance' after Dunkirk. More problematically, but with a notable degree of success, the studios were also prevailed on, when it became politically necessary, to transform their depiction of the Soviet Union. As Smith notes 'here a whole history had to be turned around and a series of pro-Soviet films created, to explain how Russians came to be fighting alongside Americans and their Allies in a just war'[42] – a process which involved 'humanising' the representations of Russians in general, presenting Stalin as a normal and balanced personality, and turning Russia into the perfect ally.

Our sense of 'others' has long been mediated by such processes. When the American-produced TV series *Holocaust* was shown in West Germany in 1979 it was watched by more than 20 million Germans, who were confronted with this version of their history in their own living rooms. Very large proportions of the West German TV audience (25 to 50 per cent) watched both *Holocaust* and, later, *Heimat* and both these series acquired the status of 'TV events' – a 'critical mass' at which it was simply necessary for people to watch the programme if they were to be able to participate effectively in the public debates that were generated in daily conversation. Thus when *Heimat* was shown in the Federal Republic of Germany, in the autumn of 1984, it was much more than a TV series – it was a 'media event' which provided the focus and stimulus for a wide-ranging debate on German identity and history, with the popular press proclaiming, for instance, that 'Germany's theme this fall is Heimat'.[43] As Thomas Elsaesser puts it:

> The move of some filmmakers (Reitz, Lanmann) ... to undertake projects whose scale can generate TV events can be seen as an attempt to use film and cinema as release mechanisms for a discursive activity that crosses the boundaries of entertainment, and even of the arts. When a documentary film makes it from the review pages to the front of newspapers or becomes the subject for late night talk shows it demonstrates television's potential for creating something like an instant public sphere.[44]

The question then, is that of who has the power to construct the discourses which structure and dominate this 'instant public sphere'.

In this connection Heinz Hone argues in *Der Spiegel* that:

> an American TV series, made in a trivial style, produced more for commercial than for moral reasons, more for entertainment than for enlightenments, accomplished what hundreds of books, plays, films ... documents and the concentration camp trials themselves have failed to do in the three decades since the end of the war: to inform Germans about crimes against Jews committed in their name so that millions were emotionally touched and moved.[45]

Reitz, of course, explicitly conceived *Heimat* as the German 'answer' to this American series. For Reitz, *Holocaust* was a 'glaring example (of an) international aesthetics of commercialism (for which) the misery produced by the Nazis is nothing but a welcome background spectacle for a sentimental family story.'[46] Reitz was concerned that German filmmakers should establish their right to their own history, reclaiming it from the hands of the Americans. For Reitz the real scandal was 'German history – Made in Hollywood' (hence his subtitle to *Heimat*: 'Made in Germany'). In Reitz's view the issue was that the Americans, with *Holocaust* 'have stolen our history ... taken narrative possession of our past.... I watched the crocodile tears of our nation and I saw how it was all taken seriously and how the question of guilt in German history was being discussed by all the great German intellectuals on the basis of this travesty'.[47] The further point is that, when shown in America, many critics responded negatively, deeming the series to be a dangrous whitewash of German history. Clearly, a history that unleashed a world war does not belong to any single nation. Our argument, as stated in the introduction to this article, is that we see played out here, in these debates over the politics of the representation of the German past, a pre-echo of the contemporary political debates as to who (the Germans? the Allies? the EEC?) has the 'right' to determine Germany's future.

HOW GERMAN IS IT? AN IMPOSSIBLE HISTORY

> Everyone is passionately in love with outdoors, in love with what they refer to as Natur, and the splendid weather is an added inducement to put on their Lederhosen and spend several hours serenely tramping through the woods.
>
> (Walter Abish, *How German is it.*)

In his commentary on Adorno's essay 'On the question: What is German', Thomas Levin notes that 'In order to say just what is the German language, one must be able to establish the identity, limits and character of a natural idiom.'[48] Adorno argues that the character or specificity of a natural idiom can best be ascertained by reference to those of its terms which cannot successfully be translated. Thus:

> Every language draws a circle around the people to which it belongs, a

circle from which we can only escape in so far as one at the same time enters another one.[49]

The very form of the question 'What is German?', argues Adorno, 'presupposes an autonomous collective entity – "German" – whose characteristics are then determined after the fact'. However, he argues, in reality, it is quite 'uncertain whether there even is such a thing as the German person or specifically German quality or anything analogous in other nations'.[50] These concerns inevitably take us back into questions of stereotyping and collective narcissism. In this process the central dynamic is one in which 'the qualities with which one identifies onself – the essence of one's own group – imperceptibly become the Good; the foreign group, the others, the Bad. The same thing then happens, in reverse, with the image the others have of the German.'[51] For our present purposes, the key issue concerns the way in which the images and identities of 'Germany' and 'America' have been (and continue to be) defined in relation to each other. Our initial stress is on the distinction between the signifier and the signified, in each case.

As Wim Wenders notes, 'America always means two things: a country, geographically, the USA, and an "idea" of that country which goes with it. (The) "American Dream", then, is a dream of a country in a different country that is located where the dream takes place.... "I want to be in America", the Jets sing, in that famous song from West Side Story. They are in America already and yet still wanting to get there.'[52] Similarly, Buruma notes the necessity to distinguish between 'Germany as a legal and political entity, a Reichsstaat, and "Germany" as a romantic ideal, a "Heimat", devoid of politics, a land of pine forests, lonely mountain tops and dreamy Wandervogel anxiously searching for identity.'[53]

Moving to the central term in our argument, Heimat, Wenders notes a crucial difference between the meanings of the term 'home' in American, as opposed to German culture.

> They have that in America: 'Mobile Homes'. 'Mobile' is said with pride and means the opposite of 'bogged down' ... (or) 'stuck'. 'Home' means 'at home', 'where you belong' ... (whereas) ... what *makes* makes it a home in the German language is the fact that it's fixed somewhere.[54]

In the context of the German debate, one of the crucial dimensions along which the term 'Heimat' is defined is by contrast to all that is foreign or distant: 'America' in particular, becomes the very antithesis

14

of 'Heimat'. Thus the characteristics of the traditional Heimat film genre, according to Rentschler, include 'a conflict between the stable world of the "Heimat" and the threatening assault of the "Fremde" (foreign) ...'.[55]

Reitz's film *Heimat* follows exactly this pattern, in so far as it is structured around a central contrast between those (principally women) who stay in the village (*die Dableiber*) and those (men) who represent a culture of emigrants, who left home (*die Weggegangenen*). As Anton Kaes notes,[56] a pervasive anti-Americanism recurs in *Heimat*, from the first mention of the United States as the 'land of the electric chair' (*sic*). In Reitz's own production notes for the series, one of the central characters, Paul, is described as having 'become a real American ... a man without a home, without roots, a sentimental globetrotter'.[57] To this extent, Reitz seems to fall into what Duncan Webster has described as a 'standard image of Americanisation ... drawn from American horror films, the invasion of the alien, the replacement/transformation of the local, the community (viewers, consumers) becoming mindless zombies'.[58]

Throughout the series, Kaes argues, *Heimat*'s sympathetic treatment of the pre-war period and the focus on the destruction of 'Heimat' in the post-war period, means that the weight of its critique falls on the Federal Republic of Germany which, the film implies, has lost all trace of its identity – in the course of its Americanization. Thus as Michael Geisler puts it:

> With *Heimat* working to reconcile the German left ... with its own country, 'America' seems to have taken the place formerly occupied by 'Deutschland' ... Reitz ... is projecting ... a mythical 'America', country of the perennially homeless ... a land of loneliness, without history, without culture.... As the German left is trying to renegotiate their traditional stance towards their 'Heimat', the exclusionary mechanisms find a new target in 'America'.[59]

Against this kind of perspective, Webster[60] points out that when one of Wenders' characters, in *Kings of the Road* says that the 'Americans have colonised our subconscious' it should be noted that the 'our' in question has a double resonance – 'we Germans' and 'we post-war consumers of popular culture' – and these resonances mark the site of intersection of generational, cultural and national identities. What is at stake here is something more than any simple 'invasion' of other cultures by America: what Wenders poses is, rather, the *specific* appeal of American culture to a generation growing up in post-war Germany (Wenders was born in 1945), with what Webster describes as a 'schizophrenic response to history, a double bind of remembering and forgetting fascism ... (where) ... one way of dealing with this was an involvement with other cultures'.[61]

In similar vein, Gabriele Kreutzner[62] argues that, as a result of this history, intellectuals on the German left have taken on the heritage of an over-determined hostility toward popular phenomena of German culture. At the same time, she notes that it is common practice for the German left to supply its public events with music from the third world (South America, Africa, etc.). Kreutzner suggests that this 'celebration of traditional music not only signifies a (romantic) desire for an "authentic" popular culture. It also suggests that the search for popular phenomena with which they can identify leads the German intellectual outside of her or his immediate cultural context.'[63] It is only the 'popular' phenomena of other lands which are thus felt to be free of an ideological taint.

Thus the appeal of American culture has to be seen in the context of Germany's 'profound mistrust of sounds and images about itself', its post-war greed for foreign images: 'I don't think that any other country has had such a loss of faith in its own images, stories and myths as we have.'[64] As Wenders puts it:

> In the early Fifties or even the Sixties, it was always American culture.... In other words, the need to forget 20 years created a hole, and people tried to cover this, in both senses, by assimilating American culture much more than French or Italian or British people did. The only radio I listened to was American Forces Network. But the fact that US imperialism was so effective over here was highly favoured by the Germans' own difficulties with their past. One way of forgetting it, and one way of regression, was to accept (or indeed, embrace – DM/KR) the American imperialism.[65]

Rock 'n' roll might have been 'foreign' but at least it had nothing to do with fascism.

A close parallel can be made between this contemporary analysis and Adorno's comments on the significance of 'foreign words' (*Fremdwörter*) in the German language. Adorno recounts how, as a child, he delighted in the 'exterritorial and aggressive' character of these terms, which provided, for him, a refuge from the increasingly unavoidable German chauvinism of the period. Thus, for him 'the *Fremdwörter* formed tiny cells of resistance against the nationalism in the First World War'.[66] The Nazis, not surprisingly, systematically eliminated the *Fremwörter* from the culture, in so far as they were able, in order to protect the 'purity' of the mother-tongue.[67] In a similar way, Kaes notes that the term 'Heimat' was a synonym for race (blood) and territory (soil) – a deadly combination that led to the exile or annihilation of anyone who did not 'belong'. Under the National Socialists 'Heimat' meant the murderous exclusion of anything 'un-German'.[68]

Reitz has argued that 'The problem with us, in Germany, is that our stories are blocked by … history. In 1945 everything started happening from scratch, erasing all that had gone before. It's like a gaping hole in people's memories and feelings.'[69] As he puts it:

> It is our own history that is in our way. In 1945 the nation's 'zero hour' wiped out and created a gap in people's ability to remember … an entire people has been 'unable to mourn' … unable to tell stories, because out memories are obstructed … we are still afraid that our personal stories could recall our Nazi past and remind us of our mass participation in the Reich....[70]

Thus, it is argued, 'Deutschland' became, in the post-war period, an entity which it was impossible to represent:

> Nazism, the war … the defeat and its aftermath … produced a homelessness … in the feeling of a loss of 'right' to a homeland … even language no longer provided a 'home'. Even the image of Germany in the post war period was part of this uprootedness. America (was) represented, for example, by the White House, England by Buckingham Palace … France by the Arc de Triomphe … Germany, however, (was always) represented by its division, above all by the Berlin Wall, marking the absence of certainty about home: separation, expulsion, exile.[71]

Prior to the success of *Heimat*, it could be argued that the West German audience for art cinema (in its enthusiasm for Bertolucci's *1900* or the Tavianis' *Padre Padrone*, for example) had compensated for the lack of an acceptable image of its own history and peasant culture by over-identifying in a plainly nostalgic way with that of its neighbours.[72] The other side of this coin was that:

Hollywood had a wonderful time after 1945, because they had limitless possibilities for showing evil Nazis, whereas before they'd had to content themselves with a limited repertoire of (stereotypical) villains. But in reality, the personification of evil doesn't exist. The Nazi people were as ordinary as everyone else: in special moments ... they acted as Nazis.[73]

In this process 'Nazi Germany' or 'Deutschland' readily becomes a cipher for an undefined, only superficially historicized evil – a diabolical entity: thus the real horror of the war was 'contained' and, in a sense, defused.[74] As Enzensberger has noted, this is 'yet another transfiguration of the attribute "German" into a metaphysical entity – only this time it carries a negative charge (i.e. simply the inversion of a Nazi ideology – DM/KR).... Instead of Good, as before, it is now the absolute Evil, which is defined along biological or racial parameters.'[75]

WHERE IS EUROPE ANYWAY?

The debates around the concept of 'home' and 'homeland' occasioned by *Heimat* have now, of course, also to be seen in the transformed context of President Gorbachev's call for the construction of a 'common European home' to transcend the cold war division of Europe which found its most dramatic expression in the division of Germany. As argued above, the debates around the question of who should hold the franchise rights over the telling of the story of the German past have many parallels in the debates as to who should have the right to determine Germany's future. Current debates concerning the reunification of Germany have a necessary centrality to our argument: not least in so far as in the context of *perestroika* and *glasnost* the very concept of 'Europe' now becomes geographically less distinct. If Europe no longer has a de facto boundary at the 'Iron Curtain', where does it end? What is the status of 'Mitteleuropa' or of 'Eastern Europe'? And if this boundary has fallen, what is to replace it? As argued below, it would seem that, implicitly, religion may be becoming the new criterion – or rather, that what is implicit in much recent debate is, in fact, a rather ancient definition of Europe – as what used to be referred to as 'Christendom', to which Islam supplies the boundary.

As argued in an earlier paper,[76] we are committed to a perspective in which identities are understood to be necessarily constructed as relational, through processes of boundary-drawing and exclusion, where the 'I' or 'we' can only be defined in relation to the Other, from whom it is distinguished. Given this premise, one part of our concern is with tracing the process through which these boundaries have been drawn and thus with the various others (Americans, Soviets, Muslims, Blacks) against whom Europe has been, and is being defined.

'Mitteleuropa' has recently asserted itself as the true repository for European civilization: 'they are desperately trying to restore the past, the past of culture, the past of the modern era. It is only in that period, only in a world that maintains a cultural dimension, that Central Europe can still defend its identity, still be seen for what it is.'[77] The drama of Central European identity, with its 'long meditations on the possible end of European humanity', evokes a fundamental insecurity:

> Thus it was in this region of small nations who have 'not yet perished' that Europe's vulnerability, all of Europe's vulnerability, was more clearly visible before anywhere else. Actually, in our modern world where power has a tendency to become more and more concentrated in the hands of a few big countries, *all* European nations run the risk of becoming small nations and of sharing their fate. In this sense the destiny of Central Europe anticipates the destiny of Europe in general, and its culture assumes an enormous relevance.[78]

The same vulnerability is apparent in the responses of the European nations to the great America (Satan) of anti-culture. Here, too, there is a fight against 'the subtle, relentless pressure of time, which is leaving the era of culture in its wake'.[79] America, the future, is counterposed to the values and traditions by which Europeans have understood themselves and identified themselves as european. Here, too, European industry must come to terms with the sense of threat and loss.

The real issues concern European identity in a changing world, and 'America' can be a vehicle for defensively containing, rather than resolving, these issues. Change and disruption are projected onto an imaginary America[80] and, in the process, tradition and conservative ideals of European and national identity are reinforced. This strategy is akin to what is described by psychoanalysts as projective identification. An aspect of European identity is split off and projected outwards. This can take the form of a 'benign defence which simply wishes to postpone confrontation with some experience that cannot yet be tolerated', or it can take a more trenchant form that 'aims really to *disavow* identification, and perhaps would be better called projective *dis*identification'.[81] The consequence is that the crisis of European culture is never directly confronted. And 'America', as the container of that 'experience that cannot be tolerated', assumes a fantasy dimension as that which always threatens to 'contaminate' or overwhelm European cultural integrity.

THE LOUDEST SILENCE: QUESTIONS OF RACE AND RELIGION

A number of useful parallels can be drawn between the debates surrounding Heimat and the filmic representation of 'Vietnam' in the USA. Here again we see the pertinence of Patrick Wright's[82] argument that the representation of the past is very much a question of active processes in the present – as the Vietnam war continues to be waged symbolically on television, in bookshops and at a cinema near you.[83] The historical Vietnam war, a specific set of conflictual events, policies and conditions has been transformed into a symbolic 'Vietnam' just as with the German (and thus the European) past: *Holocaust/Heimat*. In the case both of *Heimat* and of the Vietnam films we have the questions not only of loss and of mourning but, more problematically, the blockage created by questions of guilt and how *that* is to be represented. In both cases we also have the question of the (im)possibility of attempts to construct a progressive reappropriation of patriotic sentiment and the further issue of the potential usurpation of the role of victim by the perpetrators of the initial violence.[84] And then, of course, we have the question of the silences in these discourses – on the one hand, the marginalization of the Holocaust itself in *Heimat*'s sixteen hours, on the other, the almost total absence of anything other than caricature representations of the Vietnamese themselves in Hollywood's 'Vietnam' films.[85]

The subtext of both *Heimat* and the 'Vietnam' films is, of course, the question of race and racism: it is precisely in relation to this question that the metaphor of 'home' and 'homeland' (*for whom?* cf. Lanzmann, quoted earlier) acquires such power. The question of race is of course central to the definition of 'Europe' and 'European culture'.[86] Our primary concern here is with a differently focused question – that is the centrality of Christianity in the definition of European culture, as the Iron Curtain crumbles and the boundary of Europe shifts from the east to the south. If Germany, the past (somehow) reconciled, is to be united, and Europe is no longer to be divided as it has been since the end of World War II, then the question arises, inescapably, as to where 'Europe' ends and against what 'Other' European culture is to be defined, if not against Communism.

In this context the debates generated by Turkey's application to join the EEC offer a number of interesting insights into the issues at stake. At one level, the issue is simple. On the one hand Turkey, on account of its membership of NATO, its possession of a small but important triangle of land on the European side of the Bosphorus, and the modern secular framework of institutions bequeathed by Kemal Atatürk has a strong *prima facie* case for membership of the EEC. On the other hand, there is a complex set of questions concerning trade barriers, the potential impact of cheap Turkish agricultural (and increasingly, electrical) products on existing EEC countries, and, of course, the continuing question of Turkey's record on human rights.

However, we would want to suggest that, at base, something far more fundamental is at stake: and that is the question of whether in contemporary debates 'Europe' is being defined as coextensive with what used to be called Christendom. Or, to put it the other way round, can an Islamic (albeit a partially secularized) state be fully accepted as part of Europe, given that historically (through the Crusades, and the Moorish and Ottoman empires' invasions of Southern Europe) 'The Turk' and 'The Moor' have always provided key figures of difference, or 'threat' (and indeed, dread) *against* which 'Europe' has defined itself? Edward Mortimer reminds us that Today's EEC was founded by Christian bureaucrats (indeed, Catholics) across Europe; historically it was the fact that they professed Christianity and saw themselves as threatened by 'the Turk' that first gave European nations a sense of common purpose and identity.

The point is that if 'Europe' as a concept really is another word for 'Christendom', then the maintenance of the distinction between it and the world of Islam (or in Muslim terms, the continuing division of the world in to Dar-el-Islam – the realm of the true faith – and Dar-el-Harb – the realm of war) is central to its identity, and the Sword of Islam will remain Europe's (not so) private nightmare.

Certainly, in recent years there has been a marked increase in the anxiety and suspicion with which many Europeans view the Islamic world. Across Europe we can see an emerging pattern of racial hostility towards Islamic peoples – dramatized in complex ways by the Rushdie affair in Britain, by violence and hostility to Turkish immigrant workers in Germany,[87] and to North African immigrants in France and in Italy. One could argue that the oil crisis of the 1970s, images of PLO terrorists and Lebanese hostage-takers and the growth of Islamic fundamentalism throughout the Middle East have been aggregated in the popular media to produce a greater sense of an 'Islamic threat' to Europe than at any time since the seventeenth century. The French mass circulation news magazine *Le Point* recently headlined a story about Islamic fundamentalism in Algeria – 'The Holy War at our Gates' – a story full of references to the Muslim 'danger' and its 'threat' to French national identity.[88] Jean-Marie le Pen, the French far-right National Front leader, claims Joan of Arc as his inspiration. Sefyi Tashan, director of the Turkish Foreign Policy Institute in Ankara, puts it quite simply: 'In Europe, many people see us as a new version of the Ottoman empire, attacking this time in the form of guest workers and terrorists'.[89]

Certainly it can be argued that Islam (in the shape of the Muslim populations of North Africa, Turkey and the Indian subcontinent) is now the primary form in which the Third World presents itself to Europe and that the North–South divide, in the European context, has been largely inscribed onto a pre-existing Christian–Muslim division. However, there is more to it than that, in so far as the relation between these two terms, or rather, the significance of this relation, has itself been shifted by the current transformation of East–West relations.

As Mortimer argues,[90] the deep-seated anxieties about 'European identity' (and the centrality of Christianity to that definition) were, for a long period driven underground by the Cold War, during which Stalin's empire provided Europe with a de facto eastern frontier: whatever was not 'communist' was, by contra-distinction 'western' (i.e. European). To this extent, as a member of NATO (and a strategically crucial one, at that) the 'European' credentials of Turkey were therefore long accepted, without much question. Certainly many Turks now regard their membership of NATO as 'proof' of their 'western' status. But now, suddenly, it seems the Iron Curtain has gone (or is crumbling) and Eastern Europe is reasserting its identity, in large part, as a Christian one – which means that Europe has now to re-establish its boundaries anew (and especially its eastern one). In this process of redefinition, it is of course the question of who is to be excluded (and in contra-distinction to whom or what 'European' identity is to be defined) which moves to the centre of the contemporary historical stage.

There is it seems, after all, no place like home – or rather, perhaps, no place in that home for some who wish to dwell there. Our common European home remains to be built: but the stories we tell ourselves about our common (and uncommon) past are already shaping our understanding of how it should be constructed, how many floors it should have (a basement for the servants?), which way it should face (what price a south-facing garden?) and who should have the keys to the door.

THE BORDER RUNS RIGHTS THROUGH MY TONGUE

Our discussion has, at various points, focused on Germany because of its particular strategic and symbolic importance in the contemporary transformation of Europe. Germany, once again the question mark of Europe. Germany has been divided against itself, and this divide has also marked the separation of the eastern and western halves of Europe. Now the dividing wall has been deconstructed: what was protectively solid has apparently melted into air. 'Germany is stretching its limbs', wrote Jens Reich shortly before the 9 November:

> The Federal Republic is shedding its geopolitical hair-shirt like a dried skin. The GDR is bursting its ideological corset, supposedly all that can give its existence legitimacy. Reunification or confederation, annexation or single cultural nation? – it is all equally alarming. The neighbours are on the qui vive and look for ways to keep the two components of the poison in their separate vessels. The pressure on the valves grows.[91]

Now the two components have come into direct contact. What compound mixture is being distilled in the process? If Germany had until recently been seen as a kind of 'post-national' society, questions of national culture and identity are once again on the political agenda. What does it mean to be German today, after forty years of division? What is 'German' now? The border ran right through German identity and now it has been dissolved and Germany re-encounters itself, across space and also across time. Ralf Dahrendorf describes a kind of historical 'doppelgänger' effect; West Germans must now see their past, their history, reflected back at them; and East Germans have the dislocating and disorientating experience of confronting their future.[92] Who now are 'we the people'?

The tragedy will be if reunification provokes a defensive and exclusivist form of nationalism. The defeat will be if German identity is refounded in terms of a closed community, with boundaries drawn between those who belong and those who do not. 'Germany is one' and 'we are one people' were the slogans chanted outside the opera house in Karl Marx Square. One people. One homeland. For Edgar Morin, nationalist sentiments are akin to infantile attachments to the family. The nation, he argues, is both mother and father: 'It is maternal-feminine as the motherland (mère patrie) that its sons should cherish and protect. It is paternal and virile as the just and commanding authority that calls them to arms and to duty.' this complex allegiance, this 'matri-patriotism', expresses itself, Morin argues, in a strong sense of rootedness, of belonging to a home and a homeland ('un sentiment très fort de la patrie-foyer (*Heimat, home*), toit, maison').[93] One people, one family, one homeland: belonging together, with common origins. 'We the people' defined against the 'others' who do not belong, and have different origins.

The question of a German home, as we have argued at length, has been a central motif in recent cultural debates in the Federal Republic. At the heart of the New German Cinema the problem of identity and the quest for origins have centred on the theme of the family, the damaged relation to the (absent) father, and the fixation on the mother figure.[94] For many, this has been about trying to find a way home. It has been about becoming reconciled to German culture and identity. The romantic utopia of Heimat, with all its connotations of remembrance and longing has been about reconnecting with a national heritage and history. For others, however, the issue is far more complex. National integrity is a vain ideal; one people, a false utopia. The cinema of Wim Wenders, particularly, has been about the state of homelessness that seems to be a necessary expression of the condition of modernity. Wenders evokes 'a world of surfaces increasingly deprived of memory or self-reflection, where fantasy and reality have become so confused and the notion of self-identity so diluted that it no longer seems possible to tell one's story.'[95] In his films there is no easy recourse to the security of origins, rootedness and authenticity. As Thomas Elsaesser has argued, Wenders is concerned with journeys, with crossing borders, with exile, with the relation between inside and outside. What he seeks to explore, particularly through his relationship to 'America', are the realities of difference, otherness and estrangement. For Wenders, there is no utopia of home and homeland:

The idea is that, not being at home [my heroes] are nevertheless at home with themselves. In other words, not being at home means being more at home than anywhere else.... Maybe the idea of being more oneself when one's away is a very personal idea.... Identity means not having to have a home. Awareness for me, has something to do with not being at home. Awareness of anything.[96]

Being away, not being at home, is what Wenders aspires to. Not being at home is, of course, the permanent destiny of so many people and peoples ('involuntary cosmopolitans') in the modern world. It is the condition of those millions of *Ausländer* or *Gastarbeiter* who live precarious and unsettled lives in the German homeland itself. As Ruth Mandel emphasizes, 'Germany has a long history of confronting a salient other. The incorporation of "others" into the German *Volksgemeinschaft* has long been troublesome, as it has challenged the underpinings of German notions of identity': *Überfremdung* (over-foreignization) has been perceived as a threat to national integrity and culture.[97] Now it is the 1.5 million Turks living in Germany who have become the salient and disturbing 'other'. 'We the people' are now defined, in Germany, against the Islamic 'other'. The question is whether Germany can come to terms with this 'Islam within', or whether the new nation will be imagined on the basis of an exclusive and excluding racism. The question is whether Germany can understand that it is not one, can never be one, because it is multiple, because it contains many peoples, Germans of different ethnicities.

What must be seen is that, if Germany is a home for some, then it is at the same time exile for others. What must be understood is the relation between Heimat and Fremde. If Heimat is about security and belonging, Fremde evokes feelings of isolation and alienation. Fremde is a 'synonym for separation, hardship, privation, homesickness, and the loss of a sense of belonging'.[98] Germany – the real, rather than the imaginary, Germany – is at once Heimat and Fremde. Is it possible to come to terms with this relational truth, rather than taking refuge in the comforting absolute of Heimat? Is it possible to live with this complexity and ambivalence? In his poem 'Doppelmann', Zafer Senocak writes of his Germany:

I carry two worlds within me
but neither one whole
they're constantly bleeding

the border runs
right through my tongue.[99]

It is this experience that is fundamental to questions of German – and also European – culture and identity today. It is out of this tension – between homelessness and home – that we might begin to construct more meaningful, more complex, identities. As Zafer Senocak writes: 'The split can give rise to a double identity. This identity lives on the tension. One's feet learn to walk on both banks of the river at the same time.'[100]

Our discussion has been about images of home and homeland, and it has arrived at the reality of homelessness. If it has focused particularly on the idea of a German home, it has done so to illuminate the powerful appeal of Heimat throughout a changing Europe. Whether it is in terms of a national home, a regional home, or a common European home, the motivating force is a felt need for a rooted, bounded, whole and authentic identity. And yet Heimat is a mirage, a delusion. As Edgar Reitz recognies, 'Heimat is such that if one would go closer and closer to it, one would discover that at the moment of arrival it is gone, it has dissolved into nothingness.'[101] It is a dangerous delusion. Heimat is rooted in that intolerance of difference, that fear of the 'other', which is at the heart of racism and xenophobia.[102]

The crucial issue that now confronts European culture, we would argue, is whether it can be open to the condition and experience of homelessness. The questions posed by Wim Wenders are at the heart of the matter. Can we imagine an identity, an awareness, grounded in the experience of not having a home, or of not having to have a home? Can we see home as a necessarily provisional, always relative, truth? Writing of modern Irish culture and identity, Richard Kearney describes its multiple complexities and paradoxes:

> It is striking how many modern Irish authors have spoken of being in transit between two worlds, divided between opposing allegiances. They often write as *émigrés* of the imagination, conveying the feeling of being both part and not part of their culture, of being estranged from the very traditions to which they belong, of being in exile even while at home.[103]

It is this experience of transit that is fundamental to the culture. 'The contemporary sense of "homelessness"', Kearney argues, 'which revivalism sought to remedy by the reinstatement of a lost homeland, becomes for modernism the irrevocable condition not only of Irish culture but of world culture.'[104]

There can be no recovery of an authentic cultural homeland. In a world that is increasingly characterized by exile, migration and Diaspora, with all the consequences of unsettling and hybridization, there can be no place for such absolutism of the pure and authentic.[105] In this world, there is no longer any place like Heimat. More significant, for European cultures and identities now, is the experience of displacement and transition. 'Sometimes we feel that we straddle two cultures', writes Salman Rushdie of his own experience, 'at other times we fall between two stools'.[106] What is most important is to live and work with this disjuncture, what Paul Willemen calls 'this in-between position'.[107] Identity must live out of this tension. Our feet must learn to walk on both banks of the river at the same time.

NOTES

[1] Peter L. Berger, Brigitte Berger and Hansfried Kellner, *The Homeless Mind: Modernisation and Consciousness* (Harmondsworth: Penguin 1974), 77.

[2] Marshall Berman, *All That is Solid Melts Into Air: The Experience of Modernity* (London: Verso 1983), 15, 345.

[3] Anthony Giddens, *The Consequence of Modernity* (Cambridge: Polity 1990), 92.

[4] *Ibid.*, 109.

[5] Peter Emberley, 'Places and stories: the challenge of technology', *Social Research*, 56, 3 (Autumn 1989), 755-6.

[6] Kevin Robins, 'Global Times', *Marxism Today* (December 1989).

[7] Eric R. Wolf, *Europe and the People Without History* (Berkeley: University of California Press 1982), 387.

[8] Pierre Nora, 'Between memory and history: *Les lieux de memoire*', *Representations*, no 26 (Spring 1989), 7.

[9] Michael Rustin, 'Place and time in socialist theory', *Radical Philosophy* no 47 (Autumn 1987), 33-4.

[10] Mikhail Gorbachev, *Perestroika: New Thinking for our Country and the World* (London: Collins 1987), 195.

[11] Susan Sontag, 'L'idée d'Europe (une élégie de plus)', *Les Temps Modernes*, no 510 (January 1989), 80.

[12] Neal Ascherson, 'Europe 2000', *Marxism Today* (January 1990), 17.

[13] See Ed Vulliamy, 'Carnival "joke" turns out to be a nation's tragedy', *Guardian* (13 April 1990).

[14] For example, Enoch Powell, 'My view of a Common European Home', *New European*, 2, 4 (Winter 1989/90); Ferry Hoogendijk, 'There is no "European House" ', *European Affairs*, 4, 1 (Spring 1990).

[15] Ian Davidson, 'Old European ghosts return to haunt Germany', *Financial Times* (22 March 1990). See also, Richard Evans, 'Promised Land?', *Marxism*

Today (April 1990).

16 Neal Ascherson, 'Little nations hang out their flags', *Observer* (1 October 1989).

17 John Berger, 'Keeping a rendezvous', *Guardian* (22 March 1990).

18 Franz A. Birgel, 'You can go home again: an interview with Edgar Reitz', *Film Quarterly* (Summer 1986), 5.

19 Berman, *op cit*, 333.

20 See Eric Hobsbawm, *Nations and Nationalism since 1780* (Cambridge: Cambridge University Press 1990), 168.

21 Salman Rushdie, 'In good faith', *Independent on Sunday* (4 February 1990).

22 See D. Morley and K. Robins, 'Spaces of Identity', *Screen* vol 30.4 (Autumn 1989); D. Morley and K. Robins, 'Non-tariff barriers' in Gareth Locksley (ed.) *The Single European Market* (London: Belhaven Press 1990).

43 Sean Cubitt, 'Over the borderlines', *Screen* vol 30.4 (Autumn 1989), 2.

44 Andrew Higson, 'The concept of national cinema', *Screen* vol 30.4 (Autumn 1989), 37.

25 Steve Neale, 'Art cinema as institution' *Screen* vol 22.1 (Spring 1981), 11.

26 Higson, *op cit*, 43.

27 Benedict Anderson, quoted in Higson, *op cit*, 44.

28 Stephen Heath, quoted in Higson, *op cit*, 44.

29 Higson, *op cit*, 44.

30 Patrick Wright, *On Living in an Old Country* (London: Verso 1985), 24.

31 Wright, *op cit*, 24.

32 In his review 'The Age of Dead Statues' (*New Society*, 6 December 1985) of David Lowenthal's *The Past is a Foreign Country* (Cambridge University Press 1985) Patrick Wright argues that, far from being merely archival, the past exists as an accomplished social and cultural presence – a *modern* phenomenon which owes its shape and meaning largely to the present society which saves, evokes and retrieves it. Memory, of course, is the guarantor of identity, and ideas (indeed celebrations) of our past (vide the present debate over the content of the 'A' level history syllabus) have played a vital role in the last few years of British politics.

33 See, for example, 'History/Production/Memory' *Edinburgh TV Festival Magazine* no 2, 1977.

34 See Richard Gott, 'The Green March' (*Guardian* 17 March 1989) for a review of Anna Bramwell's *Ecology in the Twentieth Century* (New Haven, Conn.: Yale University Press 1989) which identifies the extent to which, in Gott's words 'In Germany the Greens are clearly a German nationalist movement. They fill the vacuum inevitably left blank since 1945.'

35 Adolf Muschg, quoted in Martin Chalmers 'Heimat: Approaches to a word and a Film', *Framework*, no 26-7 (1984), 91.

36 Raphael Samuels, 'Exciting to be English' in R. Samuels (ed), *Patriotism: the making and unmaking of British National Identity* (London: Routledge 1989).

37 Jean Baudrillard, quoted in Martin Chalmers, *op cit*, 91.

38 Reitz, quoted in Anton Kaes *From Hitler to Heimat* (Massachusetts and London: Harvard University Press 1989), 163.

39 Kaes, *op cit*, 195.

40 *Ibid*, 196.

[41] Anthony Smith, 'In wartime the movie is the message' (*Sunday Times* 7 February 1988), review of Clayton R. Koppes and Gregory Black *Hollywood Goes to War* (London: I. B. Tauris, 1988).

[42] Smith, *op cit*.

[43] Quoted in Kaes, *op cit*, 183.

[44] Thomas Elsaesser, 'National Cinema and International Television: the death of New German Cinema', in Cynthia Schneider and Brian Wallis (eds), *Global Television* (New York: Wedge Press 1988), 133.

[45] Quoted in Ian Buruma, 'From Hirohito to Heimat', *New York Review of Books* 26 October 1989, 40.

[46] Quoted in Kaes, *op cit*, 184.

[47] Miriam Hansen, 'Dossier on Heimat', *New German Critique* no 36 (Fall 1985), 9.

[48] Thomas Y. Levin, 'Nationalities of Language', *New German Critique* no 36 (Fall 1985), 111.

[49] Theodor Adorno, 'On the Question: "What is German?" ', *New German Critique* no 36 (Fall 1985), 117.

[50] Adorno, *op cit*, 121.

[51] *Ibid*, 121.

[52] Wim Wenders, 'The American Dream', in his *Emotion Pictures* (London: Faber 1989), 117-18.

[53] Buruma, *op cit*, 43.

[54] Wenders, *op cit*, 144.

[55] Quoted in Hansen, *op cit*, 10.

[56] Kaes, *op cit*, 190.

[57] Michael Geisler, '*Heimat* and the German Left', *New German Critique* no 36 (Fall 1985), 63.

[58] Duncan Webster, 'Coca-Colonization and National Cultures', *Over here* vol 9, no 2 (Winter 1989), 65.

[59] Geisler, *op cit*, 65.

[60] Webster, *op cit*.

[61] Webster, *op cit*, 67.

[62] Gabrielle Kreutzner, 'On doing Cultural Studies in Western Germany', *Cultural Studies*, vol 3, no 2 (May 1989).

[63] Kreutzner, *op cit*, 245.

[64] Quoted in Webster, *op cit*, 69.

[65] *Ibid*, 67.

[66] Levin, *op cit*, 115.

[67] *Ibid*, 118-19. Thus Adorno's chilling aphorism: '*Fremdwörter* are the Jews of language'.

[68] Kaes, *op cit*, 166. The point is made most forcibly by Claude Lanmann, in his discussion of the history of European anti-semitism, as documented in his film *Shoah*. As Lanzmann puts it. 'Initially it was "you cannot live among us as Jews"; then it was "you cannot live among us"; then it was "you cannot live" '.

[69] Reitz, quoted in Don Ranvaud, 'Edgar Reitz at Venice', *Sight and Sound* vol 54.2 (Spring 1985).

[70] Reitz, quoted in *City Limits*, no 176 (15 February 1985), 12.

[71] Chalmers, *op cit*, 93.

[72] cf. Hansen, *op cit*.

[73] Reitz, quoted in *City Limits*, no 176 (15 February 1985).

[74] cf. Geisler, *op cit*.

[75] Hans Magnus Enzensberger, quoted in Geisler, *op cit*, 32.

[76] Morley and Robins, 1989, *op cit*,.

[77] Milan Kundera, 'A kidnapped West – or – Culture bows Out', *Granta* no 11, 1984, 119.

[78] Kundera, *op cit*, 109.

[79] *Ibid*, 118.

[80] See Duncan Webster, *Looka Yonder: the imaginary America of populist culture* (London: Comedia 1988).

[81] J. Grotstein, *Splitting and Protective Identification* (New York: Jason Aronson 1981).

[82] Wright, 1985, *op cit*.

[83] Webster, 1990, *op cit*.

[84] See Webster, 1990, *op cit*, on Richard Nixon's view of the USA as a 'pitiful, helpless giant' in South East Asia. See also Webster's comments on Stallone's representation of that 'beefcake vulnerability' in his film roles; cf. also some of the debates in Germany about the post-war generation as 'victims' of the Nazi past.

[85] cf. conversely, the telling detail in Michael Herr's *Despatches*, of a map of the Western United States with the shape of Vietnam reversed and fitted over California.

It is also, finally, a question of the difficulty of 'bringing it all back home' (the experience of the returning 'Vets', their sense of rejection 'at home', the impossibility of their reassimilation) and of the difficulty of representing any post-traumatic 'Heimat'. On this see Walter Benjamin (quoted in Kaes, *op cit*, 257): 'Didn't we notice at the end of the ... (first world) ... war that people came back from the front mute? Not richer, but poorer in their ability to communicate their experience.' Similarly, see Bobbie Ann Mason's *In Country*, where the 'Vet' explains to his niece, desperate to understand 'what happened' – 'You can't learn from the past. The main thing you learn from history is that you can't learn from history. That's what history is.'

[86] See, *inter alia*, Yasmin Alibhai, 'Community whitewash', *Guardian* (23 January 1989); Paul Gilroy, *There Ain't No Black in the Union Jack* (London: Hutchinson 1987); Edward Said, *Orientalism* (Harmondsworth: Penguin 1985) and 'Identity, Negation and Violence', *New Left Review* no 171, 1988; S. Sassen-Koob, 'Issues of core and periphery' in J. Henderson and M. Castells (eds), *Global Restructuring and Territorial Development* (London: Sage 1987); A Sivanandan, 'The new racism' *New Statesman and Society* (4 November 1988); M. Walker, 'A pigsty without frontiers', *Guardian* (15 November 1988).

[87] See *New German Critique* no 46 (Winter 1989), for a collection of articles addressing this issue.

[88] R. W. Johnson, in *Independent on Sunday* (20 May 1990).

[89] *Newsweek* (21 May 1990).

[90] Edward Mortimer, 'Is this our frontier?', *Financial Times* (3 April 1990).

[91] Jens Reich, 'Germany – a binary poison', *New Left Review*, no 179 (January-February 1990), 122.

[92] Ralf Dahrendorf, 'Europe's vale of tears', *Marxism Today*, (May 1990), 23.

[93] Edgar Morin, 'Formation et composantes du sentiment national', *Cosmopolitiques*, no 16 (May 1990), 30.

[94] See Thomas Elsaesser, *New German Cinema: A History* (London: British Film Institute/Macmillan 1989), ch 8.

[95] Richard Kearney, *The Wake of Imagination* (London: Hutchinson 1988), 324.

[96] Wim Wenders, quoted in Thomas Elsaesser, 'Germany's Imaginary America: Wim Wenders and Peter Handke', in Susan Hayward (ed), *European Cinema* (Modern Languages Department, Aston University 1985), 48.

[97] Ruth Mandel, 'Turkish headscarves and the "foreigner problem"': constructing difference through emblems of identity', *New German Critique*, no 46 (Winter 1989), 37.

[98] Heidrun Suhr, '*Ausländerliteratur*: minority literature in the Federal Republic of Germany', *New German Critique*, no 46 (Winter 1989), 72.

[99] Quoted in *Ibid*, 102.

[100] *Ibid*, 103.

[101] Birgel, *op cit*, 5.

[102] See Stephen Frosh, 'Psychoanalysis and racism', in Barry Richards (ed), *Crises of the Self* (London: Free Association Books 1989).

[103] Richard Kearney, *Transitions: Narratives in Modern Irish Culture* (Dublin: Wolfhound Press 1988), 14.

[104] *Ibid*.

[105] See Stuart Hall, 'New ethnicities', in *Black Film, British Cinema* (London: Institute of Contemporary Arts 1988); Paul Gilroy, *There Ain't No Black in the Union Jack* (London: Hutchinson 1987), ch 5.

[106] Salman Rushdie, 'Imaginary homelands', *London Review of Books* (7-20 October 1982), 19.

[107] Paul Willemen, 'The third cinema question: notes and reflections', in Jim Pines and Paul Willemen (eds), *Questions of Third Cinema* (London: British Film Institute 1989), 28.

frontière

Naming the Armenian Genocide
The Quest for 'Truth' and a Search for Possibilities

David Kazanjian and Anahid Kassabian

In the 1890s, Sultan Abdul Hamid, with the help of Turkey's German allies, extended the tradition of understanding Armenians as second-class citizens to its 'logical' extreme: he began a policy of small-scale, local exterminations. Estimates indicate the death toll to have been over 100,000 within the space of a few years. By early 1915, the Committee of Union and Progress (the Young Turks, who had come to power in the 1908 revolution) had enacted a sweeping extermination policy of their own. Young men and community leaders were taken from towns and cities and executed; women, children, and older men were marched into the desert until they died of starvation, dehydration, or exhaustion; in all 1.5 million Armenians were killed.

This is history as we know it, or rather, part of the Armenian history we know. The other significant part is our families' stories. Each of us has in our own families sole survivors of their families. For one of us, that sole survivor's stories and a name are the only connection to Armenian identity. For the other, Armenian identity is a complex field of music, food, dance, politics, a rusted first language, and family identity, including having been the first in the family to marry a non-Armenian. For both of us, the intersection of these histories and our Anglo-American educations requested (and continues to request) examination.

The last substantial revisions were made to this article in August 1988: that is, before the earthquake and the imprisoning of members of the Karabagh Committee.

33

We shall begin our discussion with an analysis of two documentaries: *The Forgotten Genocide* (1975) and *An American Journey* (1988). Both of these documentaries are quests; they set out to establish, to make convincing (for whom?), to narrativize, a history which holds, on some level, a shaky position. The quest, then – and the shaky position is related to this – is for truth, *truth in historical discourse*. The recognition these quests seek to gain involves a certain narrative position of historical truth, which corresponds to specific political issues that recognition will allow – for example, reparations (perhaps material – a 'homeland' – yet certainly emotional, a space to feel, and feel justified). This quest, however, the discourse these documentaries engage in, involves a specific approach that reveals certain interests; the 'specific' approach becomes implicated with these interests – it narrativizes them. What this approach looks like and what these interests might be are our concerns in this article.

We think and speak about these documentaries differently. Our interests are the same in many ways; we would like to resituate the issues addressed in these documentaries, critique (in vulgar terms) most of the means and a few of the ends, while salvaging others. Our approaches are much the same as well; it is our relationship to the issues which is different.

Throughout the article, we are engaging in a dialogue with each other, not because we want to lay some authorial claim on specific statements (each of us has, in fact, 'put words in the other's mouth'), but because we want to insist that subject positions organize the way we think about these issues. Moreover, the dialogue format allows us to consider the complex interconnections among the issues involved in ways that traditional linear essay form prevents. These issues, while rarely discussed in the specificity of the Armenian context presented here, connect with more general debates. Questions of 'name', 'gender', 'history', and 'identity' create the highly charged atmosphere within which questions of representation are raised. While these terms may appear separately (along with the term 'genocide', here equally charged) part of our commitment to the dialogue format involves *resisting* their separation. We are using this format and the specific issue of 'the Armenian question' which (is one among many that) concerns us personally to explore the topoi on which these terms vibrate.

Naming the Armenian Genocide

I ANALYSIS

DK   Since throughout this discussion we will situate ourselves in relation to names, to namings, and take up some questions of history, or truth, as I begin a double bind emerges for me by virtue of this name I hold. Named Kazanjian, partially, I am far from culturally constituted as, and far from the trade of, coppersmith, which it means in a foreign language. But (not only) legally, it is my name. I am concerned with the same truth these films are beginning with, the truth of a genocide, which I hold because of stories (though stories that certainly exist in a somewhat 'exotic' place in my childhood memories) related to my name. Thus by constructing some distance between this truth, the interest I will work within, and the 'specific' approach of the films, I am allowing myself a stance from which to begin to read, critically and interestedly.

AK   *The double bind of my name is a slightly different one. It is in my first name, the one I call myself and by which I am known to friends and family. It is 'Anahid', a name which to me is both common and unusual: common among the Armenians I know, and yet unmanageable by virtue of its strangeness to most non-Armenians. I live with mispronunciations and stumblings over my name. And so do I stumble over it, but for different reasons. 'Anaid, the protectress of the land, was the most closely bound up with Armenian religious consciousness.... Miraculous healing powers were ascribed to her, the embodiment of fertility in man and beast, and she was worshipped as the provider of life-giving water.'[1] The responsibility that comes with the name my parents gave me is no small one: how can I protect the land when I've never seen it? How can I bear more than twenty-five hundred years of history – my name is that old – that I don't know? How can I say what I must say here about these stories when the stories are told in my name (in the name of protecting the land)?*

Perhaps I can begin by noticing what has replaced the 'land' my name protects. In both documentaries, as in most discussions and representations of the Armenian genocide, the western model of 'nation' has been taken on as the means to the end of 'identity'. While it's clear from the most cursory reading of even a picture-book history of Armenia that there has been an Armenian 'nation' for at most two years (1918-1920), there is no indication in these texts of consciousness towards this strategic catachresis (term with no adequate literal meaning/reference).[2] In other words, while 'nation' has no meaning as

35

a description in an Armenian history, it is used unselfconsciously as the privileged concept in representations of Armenian history. The use of the name 'nation' may be the necessary 'mistake' which makes narratives about genocide possible; the grounds for claiming identity must be found, and nationality and religion are the likely candidates.[3] If no identity can be claimed, genocide cannot be claimed.[4]

The unwillingness to acknowledge the use of the name 'nation' as a strategic manoeuvre rather than an historical truth, however, makes many problematic representations possible. One can suggest, as Forgotten Genocide *does, that* nationalism *rather than* religion *or* economics *was the reason for murders, the latter having been simply pretences, erasing the connection between nationalism and economics. One can claim an 'Armenian national spirit' which is kept alive by the church* (An American Journey).

The name 'nation', then, is in the place of the stall at the beginning: it makes 'beginning' possible by positing itself unproblematically as a truth, and by ignoring the problems of beginning a history-as-narrative. In other words, 'nation' covers over inconvenient history, it makes identity, it makes possible the claim to genocide. Naming then becomes an interesting thematic in these documentaries. In The Forgotten Genocide, *the experts are named with their individual names – Senator Tip O'Neill, Professor Richard Hovanissian, etc. – as are the eyewitnesses with professional credentials – a German doctor/missionary, Ambassador Henry Morgenthau (speaking through his grandson). The non-professional eyewitnesses, those who were in danger, the Armenians, are called simply 'Survivor from Ourfa', 'Survivor of Musa Dagh', etc.; they are representatives of the people of a 'nation', unnamed or named as survivors to signal both their typicality as Armenian victims and their difference from those who did not survive. Similarly, Mariam Davis is chosen for* An Armenian Journey *for two reasons: she has photos and documents, and hers is a 'typical tragic tale'. (No mention is made, of course, of her non-Armenian name, or her unusually fluent, relatively unaccented English in comparison to other Armenians of her generation.)*

DK The first name I want to discuss is just emerging, the name of 'genocide'. In the middle of *An Armenian Journey* a Turkish historian (Professor Justin McCarthy), the only voice of 'opposition' allowed in either film, began his objection to the historical claim for the Armenian genocide by casting doubt on this name; it is an emotional name, McCarthy said, one he prefers not to use; it brings up emotions that are usually felt in relation to difficult times, but that cloud the historicity. Emotion clearly fits into a neat place in western discourse. It is usually in devalued opposition to logical, rational truth, and yet this particular Armenian truth, this genocide, as the historian pointed out, cannot be separated from its highly charged emotion. It is precisely the history with this emotional charge contained in the name genocide which is in some way the strategic mistake to hold on to. It violates traditions of historical objectivity enough to enable the possibility of a self-consciously interested historiography. On one level there needs to be a shift here away from standards of consistent truth in history and towards an interested truth that could free up this quest to follow other agents of this history, other 'subjects'. We will undoubtedly come back to some of these other subjects later, but for now I want to stay with the name 'genocide'.

The Forgotten Genocide begins by stating the facts of genocide: 1.5 million Armenians killed in less than three years (1915-18), wiped off their lands, lands which we are shown visually. The voiceover, that of Mike Connors as we are told in the opening credits, adds at the end of this introduction, 'My grandparents were among them.' The importance of stories, and of personal connection to this genocide, is presented immediately here. This is an example of violating traditions of historical objectivity, quite overtly, in the interest of preserving the important charge of genocide.

AK *Let me interrupt your for a second. I don't know if you remember him, but Mike Connors was the star of* Mannix, *the TV detective show.* The Forgotten Genocide *was made in the mid-70s, at the height of his popularity; he was used as a legitimating tool by virtue of his television stardom. And, as Bill Todd pointed out to us,* Mannix's *secretary was a black woman, and some* Mannix *episodes raised racial issues, as well as one or two episodes based on Connors's Armenian heritage.*

DK I wasn't aware of that – at that age, I think I was still watching *Sesame Street.*

Anyway, after the introduction, *The Forgotten Genocide* breaks into a series of interviews with interested parties; the first an Armenian male priest, the second and third Armenian male lawyers. All these men clearly occupy seats of authority and interest – the lawyers are wearing suits, sitting in their offices, framed by shelves of books, the priest, wearing his collar, is also framed by an office of books. They each speak of a different connection to the genocide, and yet all relate personal connections and an interest in the telling of this story. The next interview is with an Armenian man speaking Armenian. He is, as you said, identified just as a survivor from Ourfa and is not given a name as the other interviewees were. A bit of what he says is translated, again concerning his personal connection to the genocide. He is then followed by another named man in an office of books, Professor Gidney from Kent State. Professor Gidney is presumably not Armenian (he refers to 'their moral claim to the land'), and he confirms the historicity of the genocide as a moral claim to the Armenian homelands.

The methodology in this series of interviews is quite important. The personal and emotional claims set up by 'genocide' as an act, by Mike Connors's grandparents, and by the unnamed survivor work as an undercurrent of personal, 'genocidal' reality, while the named and 'authorized' men become a privileged foreground. They represent the discourse of truth – of religion, law, history, (as well as 'success in America' – all are identified by location as well as by profession and name), although they too speak of being tied personally to this genocide; except, that is, for the 'neutral'-historian from Kent State. Clearly they also represent the voice of man (we must wait a while for the first woman to appear in the film), as connected to this discourse of truth.[5] The unnamed survivor, however, seems to share a certain peripheral or background position with the women interviewees we encounter later; in this opening segment he and his stories act as a highlight, a connection to one part of 'genocide', but not the part that is really threatened, the historical, which is the subject of this film's quest.

AK   *Let's stay just for a moment with the gender representations in the films. The women in both documentaries are relegated to the position of representing women, children, family life, affective values, while the men represent 'Armenians'. In* The Forgotten Genocide, *two female 'survivors' speak: one describes the constant threat of rape by the soldiers, and the other explains that the women fought alongside the men. The survivors who discuss hiding their language, fighting battles, any general non-gendered issue are all male. In* An Armenian Journey, *there is again a clear division of labour: the male narrator/journalist represents the objective quest for knowledge and truth (along with Dr Bardakjian), while Mariam represents the affective quest for family and a past. Of course, this division of labour is not only an Armenian formation, but one we know all too well from other places.*

DK   I think this masculist code cuts deeply into the narrative of both films as they develop. In *The Forgotten Genocide*, a traditional story-line history of Armenia leading up to the genocide works to establish an Armenian 'claim' to 'historical territories' by documenting 'the high level of Armenian civilization in literature, art and architecture'. We are told that Armenia was a deeply faithful Christian nation, and we see shots of black-robed and bearded Armenian male priests spreading incense and blessings. These privileged images of authority, here connected to 'culture' and 'the nation', resonate with the authority images of the opening interviews. Furthermore, Armenia is brought in line with a western concept of nationhood – patriarchial nationhood – thereby grounding the claim, which Mike Connors makes a number of times, for 'their historic territories' in a familiar western discourse. The storyline quite clearly presents a consistent and wondrous state, using western historical terms such as 'golden age', leading up to what is referred to as the eve of that day of genocide. Civilization is privileged in terms of 'splendour' (with images of gilded documents, crowned kings on thrones, cities, fortresses), 'advancement', and 'education' (images of the 'advanced Armenian Alphabet', and of mathematical drawings of complex geometric figures). The historic Muslim-Christian conflict is also played out in the privileging of Christianity against Islamic others. In these ways (all) Armenians become in the film the (sole) cultivated and educated intelligentsia of Turkey by the time of the genocide.

AK *David, I'm sorry, let me just take us away from the documentaries for a moment. The privileging of Christianity against Islamic others is an important part of western news coverage of the current situation in the Soviet republics of the Caucasus, which makes it clear this this conflict is overdetermined. On the one hand, a tradition of western discursive formations means that we understand Christianity to be more 'secular' (more industrialized, more modern) than Islam, and all Islamic nationalism to be religious fundamentalism (and thus less progressive), making most of us complicit with the Armenian story. On the other hand, it is impossible to determine whether the 'ancient hostilities'[6] between Armenians and Azeris are ethnic or religious in origin, or even whether the Armenians began their recent efforts in Nagorno-Karabagh as a target of opportunity to raise nationalist issues. And a demonstration in Tblisi, Georgia which protested the potential destruction of a monastery, the oppression of 'the Meskhi, a small Georgian Muslim minority', and the building of a railroad[7] is even more inaccessible to 'originary fictionalization'.*

DK Yes, but I have to point out the obvious, which is that narratives as *we know them* require an origin, one which serves the narrative's interests. We can see this in the second video. *An American Journey* is structured around the quest of its narrator, an Armenian-American journalist, to settle the 'intolerable discrepancy between Armenian and Turkish accounts' of what Armenians call a genocide. He begins with a brief historical account of Armenia which follows the unified-civilized-Christian nation story-line of *The Forgotten Genocide*. He too calls upon Christian/Muslim antagonisms and refers to the Armenians' 'Christian faith' and 'Muslim aggressors'. This faith is underscored, as in *The Forgotten Genocide*, by prolonged shots of the patriarchal image of Armenian priests. The historical summary of Armenia is shorter and less extensive in *An Armenian Journey*, but there is a similar use of traditional historical discourse to establish an Armenian nation which will then be violated and thus have an historical claim. The historical validity, this nation-being, seems to be a point without which the history of Armenia would be unimaginable, or would not be justified.

AK *The question of strategic exclusions (exclusions made, whether intentionally or otherwise, in the service of making linear representation possible) is extremely interesting here. At the beginning of* The Forgotten Genocide, *a German doctor/missionary describes the Armenians as cultural and educated in comparison to the Turks, who he says had no interest in education. If we take Kumari Jayawarden's* Feminism and Nationalism in the Third World *as one text with other interests, we find a different set of exclusions. (This is not to suggest that Jayawardena is representative of all, or even a certain 'type' of, scholarship on Turkey, but rather to take one textual example that has different interests – interests with which we are also concerned – from the Armenian ones under consideration here.) She says:*

> *This period [1908-19] also witnesses renewed intellectual and cultural activity among the Turkish intelligentsia. The journal* Türk Yurdu *('Turkish Homeland'), edited in 1912 by Ziya Gokalp, became the rallying point for Turkish nationalists. Associated with this, the* Türk Ocaği *('Turkish Hearth') movement was formed in 1912 to 'advance national education and raise the scientific, social and economic level of the Turks, who are the foremost people of Islam, and to strive for the betterment of the Turkish race and language'.[8]*

You see, then, what comes of putting these texts – the documentaries and Jayawardena – next to each other: the Turks themselves made the German doctor's representation of them as vulgar possible, by calling for European forms of education in the name of Turkish nationalism. I am, of course, by no means suggesting that educational reform in Turkey was not necessary, nor that the Turks as a group were or were not educated: I have no idea what the state of education in Turkey was before the Committee of Union and Progress (the Young Turks) came to power. I am simply suggesting that this early form of Turkish nationalism had a hand in making representations of itself as vulgar and backward possible.

Actually, cross-reading Jayawardena and the documentaries yields other interesting points as well. But here I must also include historical accounts from other sources. The Armenian history I learned from an international Armenian nationalist organization contains many pieces which are absent from both the documentaries and Jayawardena's account of Turkey in the period of modernization. She states: 'The great powers of Europe, which had contemptuously referred to Turkey as 'the sick man of Europe', took this opportunity to dismember the Ottoman Empire. They not only attacked Turkey but also fomented revolts among its non-Turkish elements.'[9] This is the only sentence in the chapter on Turkey which might be a reference to the 'Armenian problem', and it not only erases the killings, but also the history of Armenian revolutionary groups. It is that second piece of history that is also absent from the documentaries, and which I learned: the training Armenian intellectuals got in St Petersburg and other academic centres of Russia in the mid- to late 1880s with anarchist groups such as Narodnaya Volya, and the establishment of at least two Armenian revolutionary groups in the late 1880s (the Tashnags and the Hnchags).[10] (It would, of course, be interesting to examine the exclusions in the history I learned as well; for example, what was the role the 'great powers of Europe' played in 'foment[ing] revolts among … non-Turkish elements'.) Jayawardena's exclusions are in service of presenting Turkey as the victim of imperialism; the exclusions in the documentaries are in service of constructing the Armenians as victims of the Turks. Two very different representations, in other words, require the same exclusions.[11]

DK   This is the question of what 'history' is left out in the use of this account of history as 'culture' and 'civilization'; what is smoothed over. Do 'we' want to stake the claim of genocide on this nation-history discourse? The point, however, is not to deconstruct this account in order to 'de-struct' it, for the *ways* in which this narrative is complicitous are not necessary, I think, to its documentation of genocide.[12] In other words, the continuation of the story of unified nation, civilized culture, and consistent history is reactionary because it is part of and in support of the discursive formation of history-as-objective, and because that history has been implemented in the interests of neo-colonialism. We ought to look for ways out of this historiography in making this historical claim of Armenian genocide.

As I said earlier, I think this 'way out' is actually a 'way in' (recognizing full well that the amusement of the pun might gloss its phallic imagery) to other subjects. Jayawardena's work on women in Turkey is an example of this. As she says of her book,

> One has to remember that [revolutionary] women often belonged to left-wing movements which, in many of these countries, were crushed by repressive governments. The history of such movements has often been suppressed, and thus the history dealing with women in such movements also disappeared.[13]

The histories in these films can participate in this suppression/ disappearance move within their truth-quest narratives because women's histories have never been important to such a quest. But Jayawardena constructs some of this women's history and thereby shifts historical narrative just a bit. She presents lists of women, tells of women's roles of leadership in and exclusion from the Young Turks period and the Kemalist Revolution. But what is really interesting to note about her lists of activist women is the inclusion of two Armenian women, Varsenika Kasparova, 'a Bolshevik militant', and G. Nasarbekowa. As you pointed out, this is the only specific mention of Armenians in the whole book. Thus in her historiography and her move towards inclusion she implicates herself in a huge exclusion, of Armenians from the history of women's emancipation in Turkey. We might wonder when she says things like 'Kemal's ideas about the position of women in society were quite advanced',[14] and '[under the Young Turks] women participated in the gatherings on terms of equality with men and for the first time were able to speak on a public platform and in amateur dramatics',[15] what Armenian women's rights changed and what access to speech they had in various contexts.

This is not meant to nullify Jayawardena, because first I am treating her history for my purposes, and second we never can escape implicating ourselves in this way: even if it were possible to avoid making strategic exclusions *within* a (hi)story, making the necessary mistake which replaces the stall at the beginning[16] necessarily involves strategic exclusions. In addition, I want to note that Jayawardena's historiography imparts a 'subject-effect'[17] to Turkish women, even while excluding Armenian women, whereas the videos do not treat their (predominantly male) subjects with this 'subject-effect'.

The other important move Jayawardena makes is to consider the case of Turkish women's education, recognizing simultaneously its problems and merits. She presents the history of education as tied to western and bourgeois values, and yet sees its involvement in helping free women from patriarchy. While 'the education provided was a very basic one, mainly religious in orientation, with the aim of creating good Muslim wives and mothers',[18] she also speaks of the first women writers, who went through this educational system, as being revolutionary voices. Again we might wonder about Armenian women's literature, absent from both the films and Jayawardena. Finally, to add to this matrix of exclusions, Jayawardena's depiction of 'the Turkish intelligentsia'[19] displaces *The Forgotten Genocide*'s claim that Armenians were the intelligentsia of Turkey. Ultimately all this problematizes the organic notions of 'identity' and 'nation' by stressing the heterogeneity of 'nation' subjects, or rather suggests all the unspoken heterogeneity of subjects in historical discourse.

AK *You know, those mentions of Armenian feminists in Jayawardena's introduction really threw me. Not only had I never learned about them, but it occurred to me that I had never even thought to ask if there had been any that no one was telling me about. This makes the whole question of strategic exclusions even more loaded. The information in the documentaries – the genocide – is absent from her story. The history I learned, however, is directly contradictory with Jayawardena's account – she says revolts among Turkey's non-Turkish elements were 'fomented' by the 'great powers of Europe' around the First World War, while I learned that the Armenians had been organizing for fifty or more years. Yet they both make the same exclusion.*

But now the question of 'nation' and recognizing it as a catachresis returns as well. Jayawardena's account of feminism in Turkey depends on the western model of 'nationhood',[20] as do the documentaries and my 'revolutionary' history. By not recognizing 'nation' as a catachretical naming, accounts of Armenian nationalism and accounts of Turkish nationalism are complicitous with each other: they form an 'unholy alliance' through their acceptance of the western model of history which does not apply to them.

DK Picking up on this name 'nation' again, there is a line in *The Forgotten Genocide* in which Mike Connors calls the Armenians a 'subject people'. Now this immediately constructs, in the interest of the name of an Armenian nation, a clear Turkish-Armenian power dynamic. My question is, weren't the Armenians 'subject' only to the Turkish power elite, to the sultanate and not to the Turkish people?

AK *Right, no Armenian 'propaganda' says that there were areas where Armenians and Turks lived together for a long time, and that only with the rise of the Ottoman Empire did the Armenians become ruled in some organized way by Turks. They write instead a catachretical linear history: what they say is 'Armenian nation – Armenian nation – Armenian nation – subject people'. Not only is the name 'nation' unexamined, but they make no real account of how such a radical break could happen, and what made them all of a sudden a 'subject people'. This is not to say that Armenians were not oppressed: they paid huge extra taxes, they could not bear arms, and their testimony in courts was not officially recognized.[21]*

DK No, of course, but the point of this is that such a clear binary power dynamic does construct a sense of an Armenian nation, but only against Turkish dominance. More importantly, it 'clarifies' the history such that other class, race, and gender hierarchies *and* cross-class, race, and gender solidarities are erased. This is a problem with hegemonic, 'clear' names that pretend to operate uncatachretically.

AK *And the exclusion of power hierarchies which cross ethnicity (or whatever you want to call it) makes for some interesting exclusions in the representations as well. In* The Forgotten Genocide, *one of the 'survivors' explains that they were forced to stop speaking Armenian and speak Turkish instead. As he is telling the story, he tells the Turkish parts in Turkish and the Armenian parts in Armenian, never hesitating as he switches back and forth. And yet, no mention is made of this: the translation moves along as if the whole story were in Armenian, and there would be no way for someone who speaks neither language to tell.*

DK I feel like I have stayed away from *An Armenian Journey* for a while now. I would like to consider Mariam specifically because in some ways her role in that film works into what we have been saying and in some ways it does not.

Mariam came across to me at first as the emotional tie to the name 'genocide'; now I think this can be both problematic and useful. Considered in opposition to the rational, historically minded journalist (his voice borders on monotone, and in his recounting of facts and of aspects of his quest he reminded me of Spock on *Star Trek*), she becomes dominated by images of her crying, and thus works as a 'feminine' symbol of the victimized and the emotional.

She is, however, much more than this. Mariam is the being of 'genocide' in some way. Her proof, her 'genocide', exists in her reactions, in her emotion, in her memories of stories and in pictures (which we are told she has); as she says herself at one point, 'I saw it.' These histories are exactly what McCarthy, the Turkish historian in the video, rejects as suspect, as ahistorical. Her opposition to this historian in useful here when her 'genocide' is valued against the historian's, or against the one the journalist is seeking to 'establish'. Mariam's 'genocide' is multiple. It is one of closure in Turkey, as she puts the flowers on the river where her mother died, and one of re-membering (remembering and reconstructing) as she walks back through the town she lived in as a street orphan. It is one of re-establishing connections as she recalls the family members who helped her, and the Turkish priest and Turkish shopkeepers who took care of her – again, here, an 'unclear' solidarity. But it is also one of eternal pain and fracture, as she recalls the image of putting her brother's arms and legs back into his grave after it was dug up by dogs, and as she said, 'I don't know how to express it, say it, feel it. I feel just dead.' This 'genocide' seems in every way a name of heterogeneity, of inconsistencies, of history. Mariam, an Armenian woman with a partially Armenian name living in Mexico, is subject *of* this history. And yet, familiarly, it is objectified and subjected *to* the master-narrative of the journalist's quest, as his last statement establishes; upon considering the unfilfilled part of his quest, the historical proof of the Armenian genocide, he says:

> [However] I did find the strength, the immortality of an Armenian Spirit that has endured despite all challenge and denial. In my search I found another truth that could not be denied. In a living people scattered across the globe, I found a nation.

AK *You know, the question you began to get at of Mariam's function in* An Armenian Journey *in terms of narrative and subject positioning is a very interesting one. This is a big question in feminist film theory, and* many theorists have argued that subject positions are not available to women in narrative. (Others, such as Tania Modleski, argue that subject positions are less binary and more complex, but these theories are also not without problems.[22]) In general, I find these analyses need further development; for now, these important insights have become somewhat like painting yourself into a corner: you work so well that you have no way out, and that's just politically unacceptable. In other words, the arguments mainly suggest that women in film and women as spectators cannot be granted subjectivity (by whom – who grants subjectivity?), and the most common solution proposed is a Brechtian one, with the ante upped a bit, as it were: we should give up traditional narrative structures since they make no positions available to women, and break them (up) instead. Of course, I have some sympathy with that argument, but since I work with dominant American film, this is not a viable answer. It's unlikely that you will get people to go see movies that look like 'art films'. But if this kind of rupture is not the answer, what is?

So, then we look at Mariam, who is granted a certain degree of subjectivity, or perhaps a partial one. She can tell her story, she has (in Jurij Lotman's terms) freedom with regard to plot-space,[23] she may or may not be the agent of the trip to Turkey (it's never clear who suggests the trip, but certainly she could have said no). And yet, in the bigger narrative, the framing one, the narrative of historical truth (which is partially abandoned), she is absent. She fills the space of waiting, of non-action for the narrator, with her actions (they go to visit the scenes of her story while he is waiting for documents to be translated). But still, within her piece of narrative, she asks the questions and moves the story-line forward, and she provides herself with a kind of narrative closure she needs: she puts the flowers on the water where, as a child, she found her mother's body.

She is the subject of her narrative, and (one of) the object(s) of his. No matter how I look at this, though, I think the fact that she has a partial subjectivity is important. It is without question a problem that women are erased from or forbidden access to the big narratives, but they are ugly narratives anyway. For me, Mariam's piece of narrative is the only one I want to identify with.

Finally, now, I can make sense of my responses to these two documentaries. When I first saw them, An Armenian Journey made me cry, while The Forgotten Genocide made me feel like a National Geographic aborigine of some sort. I cried during An Armenian

Journey, *I think, because it was the first time I could connect all of this historical truth stuff with the suffering my family must have felt. Because Mariam's narrative is personal, in the present, and encourages identification with a woman subject, I could feel things I haven't felt before. Then, watching* The Forgotten Genocide *two days later, I was drastically distanced from this historical narrative which discourages identification in the name of truth and objectivity, so I was the American student me watching something about the second generation Armenian me as an object of study.*

II POSSIBILITIES

DK Now that we've said all this, we still have not suggested any alternative. In other words, since neither of us wants to let the deaths of a large number of Armenians go ignored, what do we do? Do we work at writing better history, and so stay within the questions of representation? Or are there other possibilities? Maybe a way into this alternative is to interrogate the question of value and how it's produced. Now that we've thought about how these notions of nation and genocide are being presented in the documentaries, and we can identify the catachreses of their arguments, we want to see how to work within the existing mode(s) of production of value (i.e. what produces value, and how, within certain ideological-philosophical systems) more effectively.

AK *I think that's a key point here. It seems to me that the claim of right to land in terms of modes of production of value is the 'way in'. The claim is made by suggesting that victimization confers moral rectitude, which in turn somehow confers the right to land. This, I think, is the exchange being suggested by the documentaries; the problem is that it doesn't fit into any currently operative mode of production of value.*

DK Right, it doesn't work today (if it ever did) to speak of 'land for victimization', where land means 'nation' and victimization means 'genocide'. This should be obvious, not only for Armenians: it hasn't worked, for example, for Native Americans either. This doesn't mean abandoning the concept-metaphors 'identity' or 'land' ...

AK *No, of course not. That's not something I'm willing to do either. It does mean, though, that we have to find exchanges that work within modes of production of value which are legitimated in the current situation. For example, I think that basing the claim to land on the right*

47

to self-determination is somewhat more viable, although we're still stuck with the fact that Turkey is strategically important for NATO. It will be interesting to see if that importance lessens as strategic arms reductions talks continue.

DK I think the question of land in Turkey is a real problem. And anyway, I don't see any way around the problematic exchange we just spoke about there, at this point in time. There are other demands to be made in that context. The most significant and problematic one revolves around 'genocide', were I started.

AK *OK, how do you say something happened and needs to be recognized as having happened without participating in the whole package of historical truth? Maybe this is simply a moment to make another 'mistake', to go forward as Mariam did, without ever questioning the event.*

DK Yes, and as an aside, I *do* think there is a way to do the historiography differently from the films. To establish genocide, you don't have to value 'nation' even in the western context as 'civilized', the 'people' as 'law-abiding', the 'oppressors' as homogeneously oppressive. Mariam's story showed that especially, that genocide is just as fractured as 'nation' or 'people'. But what about what you were saying about self-determination?

AK *Well, self-determination is at least produced in the liberal humanist (co-dependent on the bourgeois capitalist) mode of production of value. It belongs to 'Taxation without representation is tyranny', etc. So at least you make the claim on their terms, recognizing that that's what you're doing, and pointing it out when it won't hurt your cause.*

DK But then how is that different from the 'land for victimization' argument?

AK *There's only one important difference, and that's in that I suspect 'land for victimization' no longer belongs to any currently operating mode of production of value. In other words, land as 'reparations', while also part of the capitalist mode of production of value – the idea that there is a general equivalent through which violation of rights can be exchanged for land – may well have been 'written out' of that mode of production of value since the establishment of Israel. At least self-determination is still an operative 'principle'. But there has to be some way to make the argument for land, or even for recognition, stand up to the current geopolitical situation and work within a current mode of production of value.*

DK Well, in terms of recognition, I don't have any problem with taking up the 'morally right' line. If you do the history differently from the way the films did, recognition has to come from the powers that be, so you have to speak to them with their own rhetoric.

AK *I agree, wholly, but it doesn't seem to get anywhere. That's been going on for twenty plus years now. One way might be to suggest that a Christian nation in the middle of rising Islamic fundamentalism would be useful to the west, but that's too complicitous for me.*

DK Yes, for me, too. What if we look at a mode of production of value we're less familiar with – Soviet Armenia?

AK *Well, my first response is that the Soviet Armenians are on the right track. For the first time, they're making an attempt to push their issues more within the operative mode of production of value. They're not asking for independence, but for all Soviet lands predominantly populated by Armenians to be in the same Armenian Soviet Socialist Republic. The problem is that the Soviet socialist mode of production of value is inconsistent on this topic: on the one hand, there is recognition of national minorities in the existence of the republics, but on the other hand, nationalism is ideologically unacceptable. So, everyone's stuck; the Politburo can't say identity as a national minority is not permissible because it's already institutionalized, because they (the Communist Party of the Soviet Union) had expected these 'tendencies' to die away.*

DK But there are pieces of 'identity' that are not hooked up with 'nationalism', don't you think? The Soviet Armenians seem to be pushing the Soviet socialist mode of production of value as far as it will go, especially under *glasnost*, and that seems to have something to do with what identity means for them. I think it would be really interesting to know who is really involved and what they're doing. The line we seem to be getting from the press is the same as the line Guha critiqued in 'The prose of counter-insurgency':[24] the Armenians are revolting, and Soviet repression is implied, and a whole anti-communist line is activated. For example, the *New York Times* reported in February 1988 on the Armenian 'nationalist furore'. Typically, the report spoke of the protests first as a threat to Mikhail Gorbachev, and, except for a few mentions of 'the Armenian Party Central Committee', the issue was depicted as 'tens of thousands of Armenians reported march[ing] again through the Soviet Armenian capital' or 'The demonstrations began in Nagorno-Karabagh two weeks ago and spread to Yerevan a week ago'.[25] It seems that in these reports the whole issue is reduced to a very simplistic 'worried leadership/threatening masses' scenario. Clearly it's the 'Armenian

Central Committee' that represents Armenian agency, and it's the *demonstrations* that spread, thereby erasing the Armenian rebel subjects' agencies. Maybe if we knew the agendas of the rebelling 'subjects', how much freedom they have or want, how they view the Soviet mode of production economically, how Soviet Armenian women view their position, their roles in a patriarchal environment – that kind of information would really help us to envision some Armenian concerns in an active situation. While Guha thought it important to consider Indian peasants in the nineteenth century as heterogeneous, conscious subjects of history, and I agree, I think it's also important and more politically charged to consider present-day rebels as conscious subjects.[26]

AK   *It's important here to note again that there are two versions of the same question being posed. Because the two pieces of land, the Armenian Soviet Socialist Republic and the 'Armenian' lands in Turkey, operate within two different modes of production of value, or two different sets of modes of production of value, there are two different pieces of argument going on. The one about Turkey is being done badly, because it's resting on an old mode of production of value that is no longer operative (or perhaps never really was), and on the other piece of land there are signs of the Soviet Armenians learning to function within a different mode of production of value, but not wholly.[27]*

The Soviet Armenian situation is interesting to look at, and look to, but we're still not any further with the question of recognition here and now. And in some ways, the spellchecker we ran earlier on the word processor seems to me to be the perfect metaphor for the problem. It recognized 'Turkey', 'Turkish', and 'Sultanate', but it didn't recognize either 'Armenia' or 'Armenian'. And if the administration doesn't recognize them, why should the spellchecker? And if no one recognizes Armenians (us? them?), then how can anyone recognize them (us?).

DK   The problem replicates itself. But we're obviously not satisfied with this.

AK   *OK, let's go through this again. The question is: how do you get recognition? Maybe it's not tactics that are wrong; it's not wrong to lobby senators to pass resolutions. Maybe what's wrong is what you say when you lobby. While I wholeheartedly believe that one should not be able to kill with impunity, much less kill millions of people, maybe the moral claim is not the one that's going to work at the moment.*

DK   Especially because it hasn't.

50

AK *Obviously, for the government, the religious moral rhetoric is catachretical; otherwise, how do you invade Grenada, and support the Contras, and sustain the Reagan administration policy in the Persian Gulf? So maybe it has to be another way.*

DK OK, but we still can only work with what we have. I mean, we're not going to find a new discourse to put it in, and then everybody will say 'Ahhh, of course'; we're going to need to wrench some things around.

AK *Well, what makes sensational journalism? Maybe what's necessary is that kind of publicity. But that's how you end up doing terrorism – you look to get front page space, or any kind of space, or television time. That's, at least in my experience, what makes people think of doing that; it has almost nothing to do with the people they're proposing to kill. The question is: how do you make something newsworthy and compelling without being violent? Terrorism is not the right answer, at the very least because it gets bad press.*

DK Well, it's especially not the right answer for Armenians. I'm thinking that in South Africa, it's one of the right answers, because it doesn't get the same bad press, and it is a real revolution, as in 'We're going to overthrow the government', that they want. It's one thing to kill people who are killing you, and quite another thing to start killing the grandchildren of people who killed your grandparents.

There's another thing here, which is: within the capitalist mode of production of value ('the west'), do we know what the question of recognition is? Whose recognition are we asking for, and why? Is it the US government, or the Turkish government, or the UN?

AK *Good, so then the question is 'What should be asked for?' rather than 'What is to be done?' And it's a very interesting question. A long time ago, when I was still doing Armenian organizing, I said to someone that if the Turkish government were smart, it would recognize the genocide. They could say, 'Yes, you're right, what the Young Turks did was a horror, and we're terribly sorry, and you're welcome back anytime you like.' If they said that, the whole question would be over, and then what do you ask for? Recognition has been achieved, and on what grounds do you argue the need for self-determination?*

This is, of course, not something Armenian activists are likely to take well. But it is exactly the issue of the anxiety inherent in all political action. If you succeed in what you're asking for, you become irrelevant, or you become something else. Who wins, loses.

DK And that loss is a really anxiety-producing loss of *identity*, because in so many ways Armenian identity means subject of genocide, and thereby victim. I wonder what happens to identity then? **AK** *Well, let's take apart the sentence I just said: 'If you succeed in what you're asking for, you become irrelevant, or you become something else.' Now I would say, you not only become irrelevant, but in fact you become something else. You become irrelevant according to the old system of naming, because exchange is no longer possible on those grounds (victimization); exchange is no longer possible because you've lost identity (victim, subject of genocide), because you become something else (not simply victim, and not not victim). Once you lose victimization as a foundational term, you can't make equal or equatable, or equi-valent (having equal value)[28] what is different – that is, Armenians. Since many Armenians don't speak Armenian, we live in diaspora, in many different cultures, and many who consider themselves Armenian don't even have Armenian names,[29] what would make identity, or equi-valence? Whatever the mode of production of value was which was coded into that identity, there is no obvious candidate for a different mode of production of value to produce similar results.*

DK Right, there is no context for, no contact with a new name which would produce value as 'identity', or 'identity' as value. And what excites me about this is, that becoming something else, I wonder what that is? That's really interesting.

AK?*And bizarre – but yes, exciting; since these questions continue endlessly, so does the challenge before us as analysts and teachers, in and out of institutions.*

NOTES

We would like to thank Gayatri Chakravorty Spivak for her endless help in developing these arguments, as well as Regenia Gagnier, William Todd, and Patrica Ticineto Clough for their helpful comments on early drafts of this article.

The political situation in the former Soviet Armenia has, of course, changed dramatically since we wrote this article in 1988, and those changes have had a multitude of contradictory effects on the discourses and practices of diasporic Armenian nationalism and demographics. In a forthcoming article in *Armenian Review* we made a first attempt at analysing these changes, and we intend to continue working in this area.

[1] E. Bauer, *Armenia Past and Present*, trans. F. A. Leist (Lucerne: Reich

Verlag and New York: Armenian Prelacy, 1981), 52.

[2] For a discussion of nation as catachresis and postcoloniality, see G. C. Spivak, 'Postcoloniality as the field of value', in P. Collier (ed), *Literary Theory Today* (Cambridge: Polity Press, forthcoming).

[3] Presumably nationality comes from the transition to capitalism, i.e. the establishment of the nation-state, but it is also intimately related to imperialist discourse. Religion seems older than that to me, a sedimented alibi from an older mode of production of value. For a further enquiry into this question of the grounds for claiming identity, see part II of this article.

[4] 'Genocide' was coined to describe the Nazis' mass murder of the Jews; in that case, is strategically excluded the murders of communists and Catholics. Here, its use by Armenians allies us with the Jews, even though the historical facts are dissimilar – the most significant similarity being mass murder. In many ways an analogy between the 'Palestinian question' and the 'Armenian question' makes more sense, given the current agendas of each group.

[5] Presumably, one could imagine a video made in the interest of denying the Armenian genocide that would feminize these men. Here, they speak with the patriarchal authority of truth because genocide as truth is assumed. In the hypothetical video, however, genocide would be emotional overreaction, which could easily be represented as a feminizing quality, whereas truth (patriarchal objectivity/masculinity) would reside, for example, in Justin McCarthy's narrative.

[6] *New York Times*, 22 September 1988, A1.

[7] *New York Times*, 23 September 1988, A12.

[8] K. Jayawardena, *Feminism and Nationalism in the Third World* (London and New York: Zed Books, 1986), 32-3.

[9] *Ibid*, 31.

[10] The next sentence in Jayawardena is 'Under the Treaty of Sèvres (1920), Turkey lost all its European and Arab possessions, while the Dardanelles and the Bosphorus were internationalized.' What happened between this sentence and the former is also erased: the establishment of an independent Armenian Republic from 1918 to 1920. The Treaty of Sèvres 'had promised the Armenians their own state under the protection of the League of Nations' (Bauer, *Armenia*, 150). For a brief version of the history of Armenian revolutionary groups which I learned, see, for example, C. J. Walker, *Armenia: The survival of a nation* (New York: St Martin's Press, 1980), 68-9, 177-8, and 351-5.

[11] Obviously, this is the peculiarity of much of contemporary alliance politics: one glaring example is the alliance of some women's groups with some fundamentalist Christian groups to protest the publication and sale of pornography. In other words, overdetermination makes possible an issue-oriented politics which seeks to exploit it, without forcing the analysis of such politics and of overdetermination itself.

[12] This is not to posit a space free of complicity, but rather to look toward other complicities, other ways of adding to this account that bring up some other names. I also want to credit the affirmative deconstruction argument here to Gayatri Spivak, 'A view from outside', *The Statesman* (Calcutta), *Supplement on Forty Years of Independence*, 15 August 1987.

[13] Jayawardena, *Feminism and Nationalism*, 19.

[14] *Ibid*, 36.

[15] *Ibid*, 33.

[16] This 'mistake' is best explained by Spivak in 'A literary representation of the subaltern: a woman's text from the Third World', in *In Other Worlds: Essays in Cultural Politics* (New York and London: Routledge, 1988), an essay on Mahasweta Devi's '*Stanadayini*': 'Most rhetorical questions, such as the cook's "What's there to tell?" imply a negative answer: "Nothing." Jashoda's story tells itself by (mis)understanding the question as literal and answering: "This." Such would be the morphology of "affirmative deconstruction", which says "yes" to everything, not as a proper negation which leads to a strategically exclusive synthesis, but by way of an irreducible and originary "mistake" that will not allow it to totalize its practice. This affirmation is not the "yes" of pluralism or repressive tolerance, which is given from a position of power. "Stanadayini" as *énonciation* might thus be an example of an ever-compromised affirmative deconstruction' (308, n 81).

[17] 'A subject-effect can be briefly plotted as follows: that which seems to operate as a subject may be part of an immense discontinuous network ("text" in the general sense) of strands that may be termed politics, ideology, economics, history, sexuality, language, and so on. (Each of these strands, if they are isolated, can also be seen as woven of many strands.) Different knottings and configurations of these strands, determined by heterogeneous determinations which are themselves dependent upon myriad circumstances, produce the effect of an operating subject.' (Spivak, 'A literary representation', 204).

[18] Jayawardena, *Feminism and Nationalism*, 28.

[19] *Ibid*, 32.

[20] It is unclear whether or not (or to what extent) Jayawardena is self-conscious about this use of 'nation'. She states: 'The resistance, which used the paradoxical strategy of adopting Western models in order to combat Western aggression, reinforce cultural identity and strengthen the nation, took various forms.... In this agitation, which took on a bourgeois democratic form, the bourgeoisie had to assert the national cultural identity in the form of patriotic appeals intended to unite and arouse the consciousness of the people' (*Ibid.*, 3-4). Is this a recognition of a model taken on from western political philosophy? I would suggest that this is partly the case, but that 'nation' as a concept remains unquestioned here.

[21] R. Hovanissian, as cited in A. Z. Hajian, 'Turkish Denials', author's manuscript, 1988, 4.

[22] T. Modleski, *The Women Who Knew Too Much* (New York and London: Methuen, 1988).

[23] J. Lotman, 'The origin of plot in the light of typology', trans. J. Grafy, *Poetics Today*, 1, 1-2 (Autumn 1979), 161-84.

[24] R. Guha, 'The prose of counter-insurgency', in R. Guha and G. C. Spivak (eds), *Selected Subaltern Studies* (New York and Oxford: Oxford University Press, 1988), 45-86. Along with this discursive analysis of reporting on the Armenian demonstrations in Soviet Armenia, the consistent ellision of the Armenian and Estonian efforts bears noting. In many reports, both in print and broadcast, both in Europe and America, these efforts are mentioned together.

[25] *New York Times*, 27 February 1988, 1.

They are, however, quite different, in so far as (according to the western press) the Estonians have been seeking 'independence' while the Armenians have been seeking reunited lands. Both efforts rest (to different extents) on the notion of 'self-determination', but operate within different modes of production of value. Consequently, closer examination might unpack the assumptions behind, and the history of, the use of the notion 'self-determination'.

[26] In the context of this discussion, heavily informed by American media coverage, it is interesting to note a conversation I had, after we originally wrote this article, with a Soviet-Russian journalist. He had recently left his job with *Pravda* to write for a new, glossy, full-colour Soviet magazine. When I asked him about the great concern Mikhail Gorbachev must be harbouring over the situation in Armenia he responded, quite matter-of-factly, that 'the Armenian situation' did not have to be a serious problem for the Soviet government. In the context of his general feeling that *perestroika* was not moving fast enough for his or for Gorbachev's taste, he said that were Soviet Armenia and Azerbaidjan more solidly under Gorbachev's control, rather than under the control of more conservative factions of the party, Gorbachev would press to have the republics' borders realigned to satisfy the Armenian demands. Given that this is rarely mentioned as a possibility in mainstream American press analyses, and given that this journalist made his comments three weeks before Gorbachev moved to solidify his power during the Communist Party Congress in the fall of 1988, it might be interesting to see future Soviet policy decisions concerning 'ethnic disturbances' in light of this bit of personal, opinionated, and unofficial news.

[27] I would, however, question their timing, since it has become clear that the Armenian demonstrations could bring *glasnost* to crisis.

[28] 'Equi-valent' is not my own; this particular use of 'equivalent' as 'making or being of equal value' was suggested by Gayatri Chakravorty Spivak in a recent conversation.

[29] It is not only Mariam Davis for whom this is true. The two Armenian women Jayawardena mentions (p85 of this text), for example, have 'Russified' names; their names are Kasparova and Naserbekowa, not the Armenian Kasparian and Nasarbekian. This is not at all unusual; many Armenians in Turkey changed the 'ian' to 'oghlu', and in the USA many have dropped the 'ian' (which means 'from the family of') altogether.

homogeneity

Judaism and Exile: The Ethics of Otherness[1]

Elizabeth Grosz

> First I thought I was a writer. Then I realized I was a Jew. Then I no longer distinguished the writer in me from the Jew because one and the other are only torments of an ancient world.
>
> Edmond Jabès

I would like to use this opportunity to explore the ways in which the lived experience of Jewishness contributes to understanding that position of social marginality or exile which the Jew shares in common with other oppressed groups. This position cannot be either excluded from or really incorporated into a cultural centre or pyramid. This marginalized position is both perilous and enabling, providing a locatable target for systems of oppression and social domination, in this case, anti-semitism; and at the same time, it may provide a site for the positive production of strategies and resources for survival and struggle, tools of resistance which can be utilized to insinuate a flaw, rift or crack in dominant systems to help facilitate social transformations. All social marginals, all exiles, are splayed between these two poles or extremes – one a tendency towards death, the other a positive movement towards self-production, critical resistance and transformative struggle. There seem to be a number of broad similarities between various forms of exile and marginalization: but my major concern here will be the differences and specifying features of different forms of oppression.

Before I begin, I would like to point out some limitations in my focus, some of the issues I will *not* be discussing: first, I have not had a thorough or scholarly training in Judaic thought, so, although I refer to this major tendency in the constitution of Jewish identity, I do not do so as an expert. I refer to religious themes, rituals and practices only in so far as they feed into socio-cultural and political representations of the Jew. Second, I do not enter into a central debate in the self-definition and self-identification of the Jew, centring on whether a Jew is defined by religion or by race/ethnicity. (This debate is itself, to my knowledge, quite unique to Judaism. Religious and racial persecutions frequently go together, but nowhere else it is undecidable whether persecution is based on racial or ethnic characteristics (membership of a group) or beliefs and religious convictions. Indeed the idea of a 'Jewish atheist' is not contradictory in the way an 'Anglican atheist' is.) Third, although I intend to refer to and rely on notions of the Jew as an historical image and figure, I will not be tracing the history of the notion of the Jew. Such a history is vital to understanding the notion of exile in general, and the particular case of Jewish oppression. Nevertheless, this is not the place to elaborate such a history, and in any case, I am not trained as an historian of Judaic culture. (We should note in passing the dilemma of producing an autonomous history of the Jew: Jewish history cannot be seen as self-contained and autonomous for, even in its own terms, this is a history of oppression, suffering, persecution, a history imposed on the Jew by others; nor can this history simply form a coherent narrative of perpetual oppressions – for this effaces any notion of Jewish activity or agency. Any Jewish history would have to be, in some sense, a counter-history, a subordinated history, a history produced by yet subversive of received Hellenic/Christian histories. This dilemma is the same as that facing the Third World intellectual: such a person cannot afford politically to accept the 'truths' provided by colonial history, for this is a history written by oppressors from the First World; nor is there any longer an indigenous, native discourse and intellectual position, given the history and impact of colonialism on the colonized, and given that the Third World is now a resistant and resisting effect or projection of the First World. The problem is how to speak a language of the colonizer which nevertheless represents the interests and positions of the colonized? If the subaltern can speak, what language is able to articulate, to speak or adequately represent the subaltern's position?)

So far, I have spelled out what I will *not* discuss in any depth: a specific and detailed knowledge of the history and culture of Judaism. My article will address a more limited and abstract issue, the *concept* of the Jew which informs a personal sense of Jewish identity and plays a subversive role in the assessment and transformation of prevailing paradigms of knowledge. I will look at the ways in which Judaic thought has fed into and helped deflect a prevailing series of assumptions and theories developed in western thought since ancient Greece. In oppposition to an historically dominant tradition that places the growth of knowledge in an uninterrupted line of progress from Hellenic thought to modern western philosophy and science, I will instead claim that since Classical Greece if not before, the Judaic has provided a counter-tendency within this intellectual history which continually threatens to undermine or subvert the pretensions of self-creation, self-reflection and self-refinement made by Hellenistic (or, in Derridean terms, 'logocentric') thought. This repressed but subversive tradition provides a history that is uneven, scattered, a series of interruptions, irruptions, outbreaks and containments – an intellectual history of skirmishes in an undeclared conceptual war.

I   JUDAISM AND FRENCH THEORY

In spite of the cultural dominance of the Hellenic tradition in contemporary thought, there exists among a number of contemporary French theorists a desire to undermine and transform this heritage so that new kinds of questions can be asked, new knowledges produced, and new criteria of intellectual assessment developed. This critical goal has prompted many of these theorists to develop new orientations or to seek out older, sometimes repressed traditions latent within Hellenism which may provide methods and models on which to base alternatives. This may explain why there is, in spite of the overwhelming Catholicism of the country as a whole, nevertheless a strong sense of *Jewishness* that pervades many of the texts and positions of French theory. This position of 'Jewish subversiveness' is a function of two conflicting forces: one a wide-ranging and personally experienced *anti-semitism*, that produces a force, a movement to oppose, to rebel, to set oneself up against the dominant Christocentric values of culture – a negative, oppositional position; and the other, a more positive identity based on shared narratives and history, and a mode of identification with certain stories derived from Jewish history (stories which, incidentally, lean towards interpretive rather than athletic or military skills). These heterogeneous, incompatible forces breed a tension that both affirms and annihilates Jewish identity. Together, their tense relations may induce the position of the marginal, exiled, or alienated – a simultaneous cultural or national detachment (or exclusion) *and* an attempted engagement in and contribution to cultural values (the position of the Jew today in the diaspora). The Jew strives to be part of culture, to conform to its laws and customs, while at the same time, remaining an outsider, estranged and alienated the more he/she is included. Represented as a perennially landless, homeless wanderer, an exiled nomad, the Jew is both familiar with, yet excluded (and estranged) from the cities, the cultures, and the communities within which he or she circulates.

The concept of the Jew has, then, exerted a certain fascination for post-war French theory, with a number of unexpected theorists taking up the notion of the Jew as outsider, the alien, an emblem of self-chosen exclusion in so far as the Jew is more-or-less indistinguishable in terms of appearance from others, but remains fundamentally different, almost as if by wilful choice. The Jew has often served as a metaphor or emblem for a more universal (even an ontological) alienation and estrangement. I hope to explore the use of the Jew as a figure of universal oppression (as, for example, it is in the work of Sartre); and of the Jew as concrete subject (in the work of Levinas), exploring the differences between these two approaches.

Sartre develops an intensive, detailed study of the relations between the Jew and the anti-semite in his important text, *Anti-Semite and Jew*. For him, anti-semitism is an exemplar of the evasion of human freedom he calls 'bad faith'. The anti-semite cannot be seen as an otherwise fair-minded and reasonable citizen who holds only one set of mistaken or prejudicial beliefs on a single issue, that concerning Jews; rather, he holds on to a complete system of beliefs and values in bad faith, which affects all his relations to the world. He holds onto a system of unshakeable prejudices, to which he clings independently of, indeed before, any empirical observation. For the anti-semite, the Jew is unalterably, unassimilably other, alien, the personification of evil. Sartre's elaborate and convincing exposé of the cowardice, mediocrity and conformity of the anti-semite (or the racist) is a powerful denunciation of that oppression; yet his reading of the Jew, as I will further discuss, is entirely problematic in so far as he ignores the weight of Jewish experience and counter-history in constructing his notion of Jewish identity.

The Judaic has been more satisfactorily discussed in the works of Edmond Jabès, Emmanuel Levinas, and more recently, Jacques Derrida and Jean-François Lyotard, who, in their different ways, use the concept of the Jew to represent alterity. Rather than seeing Judaism in simply religious, sociological or historical terms, these theorists are primarily interested in the Judaic in so far as it represents a tradition of textuality – of writing, reading interpretation, commentary – that challenges while existing alongside the dominant Hellenic/Christian/ Logocentric canons of truth, logic, authority and knowledge.

Within this French intellectual tradition, the Judaic is thus connected to two related interests: the first is a politico-ethical concern regarding alterity: how to think the *otherness of the other* without assuming the other is merely a version of the self-same? In what terms, from what positions, with what characteristics, is this otherness to be understood and addressed? The second concern involves an exploration of alternative models of textuality, reading and interpretation, challenging the limits of coherence imposed on discourse by dominant paradigms: how to speak differently, without falling into silence or non-sense; how to engage in a dialogue which both connects with but also challenges dominant discourses and speaking positions? These two interests are of course related: we can only adequately think otherness if different modes of discourse, representation and language are developed. And conversely, discourses themselves will be unable to sustain their subversive positions unless they are taken up by and are of use for those characterized as 'other', put to use in socially subversive activity.

2   JUDAISM AND ALTERITY

The Jew has functioned as a figure or trope of *alterity*, occupying the position of *perennial other* for millennia. The strangeness of Jewish religious rituals, the apparent mysticism and literalism of the Jewish faith, the adherence to a set of autonomous scriptural and interpretive practices mark the Jew as different from and unassimilable to the traditions and loyalties of a citizen to a nation and class and community. As *radically heteronomous*, the Jew represents a resistance to the norms governing the citizen, the neighbour, and the (Hellenic/Christocentric) subject. Informed by a knowledge, indeed by a text radically different from any other, bound by a morality that differentiates the Jew in every aspect of day-to-day life (from eating to love-making to clothing); by a commitment to a collective narrative based on a paradoxical passivity *and* strength (the Jew *endures* all types of oppression, represented as an eternally oppressed other who yet survives throughout history), the Jew is marked as an *eternal foreigner*, dispossessed, the other. At home in no land, exiled from national identity, the Jew is well positioned to represent *alien otherness*, an otherness which confirms and ensures the gentile's identity, his right to belong. Even if the Jew mimics the gentile's sense of propriety, sense of allegiance to country and community, this remains gestural, superficial, a dissimulation. This indeed is the strength of Sartre's analysis, for the anti-semite *is* to a large extent responsible for bestowing on the Jew this position of otherness. The otherness of the Jew, like women's cultural otherness, is not self-chosen – it is always an effect of power relations (one is always a subject for oneself unless one has thoroughly internalized another's view of oneself).

> The true Frenchman, rooted in his province, in his country, borne along with a tradition twenty centuries old, benefiting from ancestral wisdoms, does not *need* [Jewish] intelligence. His virtue depends upon the assimilation of the qualities which the work a hundred generations has lent to the objects which surround him; it depends on property. It goes without saying that this is a matter of inherited property, not property one buys....[2]

If the other is the repressed or subordinated precondition of self, identity and sociality, for a number of contemporary French theorists (including Foucault, Deleuze, Derrida, Kristeva, Irigaray etc.) alterity has been identified with a position of social, political and intellectual marginality. It becomes what the subject, the self, is unable to tolerte and thus refuses to recognize: it is the threat posed by blacks for the racist; by woman, for the male chauvinist; and by the Jew for the anti-semite. Alterity must be dissimulated, reduced to a version of the same, structurally identical with the self. The self that cannot abide its non-mastery of the world fears and hates the other for concretizing its own specificity and limits, and seeks to reduce otherness at every opportunity to a form of sameness and identity modelled on itself. Sartre, for example, claims that the anti-semite fears the loss of national identity, a sense of belonging, a solid impregnable identity problematized by (his image of) the Jew. If not for his imputation of pre-given evil to the Jew, the anti-semite would be forced to confront his own freedom, and to take responsibility for his place and value in culture:

The anti-semite is afraid of discovering that the world is ill-contrived, for then it would be necessary for him to invent and modify it, with the result that man would be found to be the master of his own destinies, burdened with an agonizing and infinite responsibility. Thus he localizes all the evil of the universe in the Jew.[3]

For Sartre, then, the Jew is the projected evil double of the anti-semite, what the anti-semite cannot accept about himself and his possibilities. In this sense, Sartre claims, the anti-semite *makes* the Jew. All the negative qualities the anti-semite attributes to the Jew, he makes true through his very persecution of the Jew:

Today we reproach the Jews for following unproductive activities, without taking into account the fact that their apparent autonomy within the nation comes from the fact that they were originally forced into these trades by being forbidden all others. Thus it is no exaggeration to say that it is the Christians who have *created* the Jew in putting an abrupt stop to his assimilation....[4]

Yet while his analysis of anti-semitism is astute, Judaism itself still mystifies him: its specificity escapes his grasp. For him, the Jew remains a Jew, an outsider, in so far as his situation is one provided by anti-semitism. He analyses specific Jewish 'attributes' and stereotypes as effects of the anti-semite's persecution. He takes the caricature of the Jew as money-loving: he does not dispute it but explains it in terms of the anti-semitic prohibition on property ownership. The Jew's taste for money is an effect of the appeal exerted by universality and abstraction, the non-discriminatory nature of money:

Appropriation by purchase does not depend on the race of buyer; it does not vary with his idiosyncrasies. The *price* of the object is set with reference to *any* buyer.[5]

Sartre cannot recognize any positive or self-chosen history or identity for the Jew: he only understands the Jew as a figure who strives, in the absence of anti-semitism, to assimilate into and be absorbed by the community. Judaism is reactive, a secondary effect of the primary activity of anti-semitism: (this may be an effect of his negative ontology, in which the other is always an adversary). As he claims,

... it is not the Jewish character that provokes anti-semitism but, rather, it is the anti-semite who creates the Jew. The primary phenomenon therefore is anti-semitism....[6]

His underlying belief is that the Jew will ultimately strive for assimilation, for self-annihilation rather than annihilation by the other. Indeed his 'solution' to the problem of anti-semitism betrays his own (anti-semitic) refusal to recognize any autonomous or self-chosen identity. The problem of anti-semitism will be solved by the removal of class antagonisms through the socialist revolution!

Sartre's analysis is contemporary with the work of the philosopher and Judaic scholar, Emmanuel Levinas, who is arguably the most articulate and eminent theorist of alterity, providing both inspiration and a concrete direction for recent French theory with his analyses of an ethics of alterity in over twenty texts. His interest is, he professes, motivated by the aftermath of Auschwitz, where he was interned in the War. Levinas refuses to romanticize the Jew by granting him the position of universal otherness, for he writes from the position of a self-conscious Jewish subject (the subject cannot be other to himself without also being a subject, contra de Beauvoir). Levinas takes the position of the Jew as exemplary, not of alterity, but of the necessity of ethics in the face of an encounter with otherness, the otherness of God. He proposes an analysis of an ethics appropriate to the full cognizance of alterity. Such an ethics would be based on the responsibilities and reactions the other summons up in the subject. If the subject is not a self-formed and self-contained subject, and if the other, others, are not simply replicas, versions of the same, then one of the constitutive questions raised for subjectivity is the ethical question of the relation between the subject and the other.

Levinas' conception of alterity has four defining characteristics: first, alterity is a form of *externality*. It always exerts itself outside of and unforeseen by the subject. (It is what surprises and astonishes.) Second, alterity is an *excess*, an unabsorbable remainder or residue, a 'force' that exposes the subject's limits. Third, alterity is an *infinity*, it exceeds all bounds, it is beyond any limit imposed by the subject on it. And fourth, alterity is an *activity*, in relation to which the subject is passive. The other initiates actions, encounters, approaches which summon, call for or demand the subject's responses. The subject is called upon, is passive in the face of the other.

Alterity, in short, solicits and commands, appeals and contests; it extracts responsibility from the subject. The subject is *exposed* to, and opened up by alterity, the origin of the subject's openness to the world. Alterity is not itself open to the subject: it opens the subject up to/for the other, opens things, entities and elements, the world, to the subject. It is a non-reciprocal relation, a relation in which the other's alterity is prior and primary to the subject's identity. Alterity entails that *another* meaning, use or value is always an open possibility for all things.

By contrast, Levinas seeks to ground ontological and epistemological commitments governing Hellenic thought in an ethics conceived as anterior to identity, prior to knowledge and being. Where the Christian-Hellenic tradition derives its ethics and politics (the 'ought') from ontology and epistemology (the 'is'), Levinas posits the ethical as primary and derives an onto-epistemology from it. Time, space and objects, as well as knowledge, find their possibility only in the encounter with alterity. Alterity is always a *prior* condition and ethics is the necessity of a response to the other's call. The other is prior to any identity, even to the distinction between subject and object. Levinas seeks to problematize Hellenic/Christocentric philosophies by devising an ethics from the Judaic image of 'the Chosen', the ones called upon, burdened, by the needs of the other.

3 JUDAISM AND TEXTUALITY

Like Levinas, Derrida also traces his point of departure from logocentric traditions in his quest for an alterity that is closely related to reading and textual interpretation and is heavily reliant on an openly acknowledged Hebraic tradition.

This may explain why, in positioning his own work in the tradition of the Torah, Derrida signs his name, his signature, anagrammatically as 'Reb Rida',[7] and as 'Reb Derissa'[8]; here, there is a different play: here it does not simply, through difference, retrace the letters of his name; now it actively inscribes the Hebraic ('Reb' = (congregationless) rabbi) onto a Nietzschean frame: 'risa', from '*rire*', '*risée*', 'to laugh', 'laughing': he is now the 'laughing rabbi', not altogether opposed to the 'dancing philosopher' (one of his most revealing interviews is called 'Choreographies').

In *Glas*,[9] he also plays on his name: 'Reb Derissa' is also the transposition of the phrase, 'derrière les rideaux', beyond the veil, unveiling, beyond (ontologically grounded) Truth:

> In Algeria, in the middle of a mosque that the colonists had changed into a synagogue, the Torah once out from *derrière les rideaux*, is carried about in the arms of a man or child.... Children who have watched the

pomp of this celebration, especially those who were able to give a hand, perhaps dream of it long after, of arranging there all the bits of their life.[10]

To arrange one's life in terms of the Book, the Scroll, is, in a sense, the millennial dream and hope of the Jew. It is the wish of the homeless people of the Book to be assimilated into a secular culture, to speak its language; yet also to retain the history and the *scripture* of the text that marks their unassimilable history, their perennial difference. Behind the veil, (the curtain covering the sanctified arc, the home of the Torah in the synagogue) is not Truth, but the Text. The text is that through which Derrida's name, and his 'autobiography' (in *Glas*) are inscribed.

It is not fortuitous that 'écriture' (writing), one of Derrida's names for his deconstructive project, and for the object of deconstructive reading, also means 'scripture'. Behind the veil, then, is the Word, the Torah. But here it is not the word as the Greek *onoma* (the name, name as distinct from the thing it names), but as the Hebraic *davar*, the word *and* thing, the name *and* reality. The word, the text, the Hebrew Torah is both word and life, representation and reality, whereas the Greek *onoma* is instrumental sign, the sign not of the thing, but the Form. In the Greek tradition, the name is able to represent only through imitation; it is a mimetic copy of the thing: 'A name is ... a vocal imitation of any object and man is said to name an object when he imitates it with the voice.' (Plato, *Cratylus*: 423b). By contrast, for the rabbis and Talmudic commentators within Judaism, the text does not re-present: instead, it generates and creates, ensuring further writing(/scripture)/reading/interpretation *ad infinitum*:

> The Jew ... will not abandon Scripture for Logos. The Jew approaches divinity through ever more intense concentration on the text – not through a transcendent vision of the spirit that ends the labours of interpretation. The text, for the Rabbis, is a continuous generator of meaning, which arises from the innate logic of the Divine language – the letter itself. Meaning is not sought in a nonlinguistic realm external to the text. Language and the text, to use Derridean terminology, are the place and play of differences; and truth as conceived by the Rabbis was not an instantaneous unveiling of the One, but a continuing process of interpretation which God himself participates in, learning what the Rabbis have to say.[11]

4 THE JUDAIC AND THE HELLENIC

The major divergences between the Hebraic and the Hellenic traditions can be crudely summarized in the following, which will indicate some major differences between the Judaic and the Hellenic pretensions to identity, objectivity, truth and knowledge:

1 Where the Hellenic seeks out the *origin* of terms (in the Forms), a paternity, which explains their essence, the Hebraic is an undoing or continual displacement of an 'original'. It is the continual rewriting of paternity, and the father. For Levinas, paradoxically, it is the *absence* of God (an absence that would clearly be heightened by the Holocaust experience), the God whose face cannot be seen, that underpins faith. Theirs is not a logocentric philosophy of presence, but an enigmatic concept of endless rewriting, remaking, interpretation and reinterpretation.

2 The Hebraic tradition forbids representation. Iconography, similitude, the correspondence between image and thing, are idolatrous. This is not because, as Plato suggests, the representation is a replica of the thing, liable to be mistaken for it, but precisely the opposite. The visual is never adequate; its adequacy, however, is not measured by its correspondence with the real, but to the verbal. The specular, the image, representation, are pagan literalizations of a primarily verbal metaphor. The eyes must close on the sacred image – or rather, the Divine image is *invisible*, unseeable. Sight does not reveal the other, nor command the subject's response. On the contrary, the look or gaze objectifies, it reduces the subject to the position of object. The subject is called as such only by the voice: 'Hearing is the way to perceive God.... Hearing is the knowledge – abolishing all distance – of knowing oneself encountered, of recognizing the claim of him who speaks.'[12] This aversion to privileging the visual has major implications not only for modes of representation and depiction available to the Jew but also for notions of knowledge, which, in the Hellenic tradition have been so reliant on metaphors derived from the privilege of vision – 'insight', 'reflection', 'enlightenment', 'clarification'. These imply a knowledge that is 'seen', 'regarded' as tangible correspondence, the correspondence between word and thing – very different from the disputational and insecure status the Jew accords to knowledge as 'interpretation'.

3   The privileging of vision corresponds to a denigration of the other senses, particularly the auditory/invocatory and the tactile. Where the Jew disdains the literal definiteness of the visual, by contrast, the word is elevated to (quasi-)divine status. The word not only defines a very different structure of knowledge; it also sets up a model of ethical responsibility quite different from the Hellenic/Christian tradition, which is so heavily dependent on 'revelation'. The word is spoken, and the subject is called upon to listen and respond. One cannot *not* respond.

The Graeco-Christian tradition depends on an incarnation or manifestation of presence through visual resemblance. The Christian doctrine of spirit too is resolutely anti-linguistic: '... the letter kills, but the Spirit gives life' (2 Cor: 3:6). signs are thus sacramental; they are mediated representations of a divine presence. To be *called*, to be commanded, has a different imperative force. One cannot block one's ears as one can shut one's eyes. The call of the other for a response cannot be blocked out or ignored. The Jew is chosen not as a privilege but as a burden, chosen by the other to hear and obey.

4   Where the Hellenic demands a clear separation of truth from fiction, and a clear characterization of the propositional forms in which truth is expressed – where discourse is subordinated to truth or meaning – the Judaic tradition refuses the distinction between the textual and the real. The relation cannot be one of correspondence; the question of truth cannot be raised. Instead of a correspondence between discourse and the real, the Judaic tradition sees a contiguity, a continuous web of interpretations, with no certainty, objectivity or truth, no original or derivative, simply an endless rewriting. The written Torah is itself mediated, a 'translation' of God's own name, the name no mortal being can utter. This name is encrypted in the Holy text, which differentialy plays on it. Writing/scripture is a play of permutations on God's name, augmented by the Midrashic and Talmudic interpretations of the commentators. Like poetry itself, God's name has no meaning but provides the conditions for all meaning. This emphasis on the divinity of language radically ruptures the idea of totality and identity: the Torah is composed essentially of fragments – fragments of God's words, intermixed with fragments of commentary. Always incomplete, open-ended, opening up new interpretations rather than confirming old ones, interpreting interpretations *ad infinitum*. Signs do not collapse into icons (as they do for the pagan) nor into indices (as they do for the Greek). They are irreducibly autonomous and productive. The sign

produces reality in/as its image.

5 CONCLUSION

Judaism, then, contrary to Sartre's assertions, is not simply the product or effect of anti-semitism, just as women and femininity are not simply the consequences of male domination. While it is true that certain features which characterize oppressed and marginalized social groups are a direct result of oppression (forbidding Jews access to the position of property owners or women positions of authority and power does indeed breed a series of sometimes contradictory characteristics and strategies), is is also true that each oppressed group also has self-defined and historically specific features and attitudes which it self-consciously chooses to include in its self-representations (whether these originate from an oppressed context or not). One gives all sorts of meaning to one's own position and the history of that position; this is what is to be an historical, concrete subject. This is not only true of exiles but of all oppressed groups. In the case of the exile – whether national refugee, cultural outsider, social outcast, linguistic foreigner or rejected convert – the production of a self-definition is considerably more difficult than that facing the citizen or the one who belongs, who can find his ready-made. Besides producing a positive history of oneself (one that is necessarily selective and to some extent arbitrary, as are all histories and self-representations), the outsider, the exile, the Jew, must not only survive but actively resist cultural attempts at homogenization on the one hand and total rejection or expulsion on the other. To be homogenized, absorbed into the *status quo* is to be neutralized, to be disconnected from the history of one's oppression; yet to be expelled or ejected from culture is to leave the ejecting culture intact; and at the same time to abandon all hope of a positive self-definition because it is to abandon any position. Without a position there can be no identity, no speaking position, no point of view or self-interests. The borderline position of the exile – not at home in one place or another, nomadic, meandering, indirect, yet not necessarily lost and abandoned – has, in spite of its difficulties, some strengths and qualities which the exile may be reluctant to give up. The marginalized position of the exile, at the very least, provides the exile with the perspectives of an outsider, the kinds of perspective that enable one to see the loopholes and flaws of the sytem in ways that those inside the system cannot. The position of the exile automatically has access to (at least) two different kinds of discourse and history, one defined by exclusion from a social mainstream; and one provided autonomously, from its own history and self-chosen representations. This is a position uniquely privileged in terms of social transgression and renewal.

NOTES

[1] Two different versions of this paper were delivered at the 'Politics of Exile' Conference, organized by the Performance Space in Sydney, Australia in September, 1989; and at the 'Displacements. Identities/Migrations' Conference organized by Cultural Studies at the University of California, Santa Cruz, March-April, 1990.

[2] J.-P. Sartre, *Anti-Semite and Jew* (New York: Schocken 1961), 23-4.

[3] *Ibid*, 40.

[4] *Ibid*, 68.

[5] *Ibid*, 126.

[6] *Ibid*, 143.

[7] See his paper on Jabès in J. Derrida, *Writing and Difference*, trans. Alan Bass (London: Routledge & Kegan Paul 1978).

[8] In *Ibid*, 'Ellipsis'.

[9] J. Derrida, *Glas* (Paris: Editions Galilée 1974).

[10] Translated in G. Spivak, 'Glas-Piece: A Compte Rendu', *Diacritics* 7 (1977), 23.

[11] S. Handelmann, 'Jacques Derrida and the Heretical Hermeneutic', in M. Krupnick (ed), *Displacement, Derrida and after* (Madison: University of Wisconsin Press 1983), 106.

[12] Rudolf Bultman, quoted by J.-F. Lyotard in 'Jewish Oedipus', *Genre* 10 (1977), 395-411.

BIBLIOGRAPHY

R. A. Cohen (ed), *Face-fo-face with Levinas* (New York: SUNY Press 1986).

J. Derrida, *Glas* (Paris: Editions Galilée 1974).

——, *Of Grammatology*, trans. G. Spivak (Baltimore: Johns Hopkins University Press 1976).

——, *Writing and Difference*, trans. Alan Bass (London: Routledge & Kegan Paul 1978).

——, *La Carte Postale* (Paris: Flammarion 1980).

M. Foucault, *The Uses of Pleasure* (New York: Pantheon, 1985).

S. Handelmann, *The Slayers of Moses. The Emergence of Rabbinic Interpretation in Modern Literary Theory* (New York: SUNY Press 1982).

——, 'Jacques Derrida and the Heretical Hermeneutic', in M. Krupnick (ed), *Displacement, Derrida and after* (Madison: University of Wisconsin Press 1983).

L. Irigarary, *Le Corps-à-corps avec la mère* (Montreal: La Pleine Lune 1981).

——, *L'Ethique de la différence sexuelle* (Paris: Minuit 1984).

——, 'The Fecundity of the Caress', in R. A. Cohen (ed), *op cit.*

J. Kristeva, *Powers of Horror: An Essay on Abjection* (New York: Columbia University Press 1982).

E. Levinas, *Quatre lectures talmudiques* (Paris: Minuit 1968).

——, 'To Love the Torah more than God', *Judaism* 28 (1979), 216-37.

——, *Existence and Existents*, trans. A. Lingis (The Hague: Martinus Nijhoff 1979).

——, *Totality and Infinity: An Essay on Exteriority*, trans. A. Lingis (The Hague: Martinus Nijhoff 1979).

——, *Otherwise than Being or Beyond Existence*, trans. A. Lingis (The Hague: Martinus Nijhoff 1981).

——, 'Dialogue with Emmanual Levinas', in R. A. Cohen, *op cit.*

A. Lingis, *Libido. Six Existential Thinkers* (New York: SUNY Press 1985).

J.-F. Lyotard, 'Jewish Oedipus', *Genre* 10 (1977) 395-411.

J.-P. Sartre, *Anti-Semite and Jew* (New York: Schocken 1961).

G. C. Spivak, '*Glas*-Piece: A Compte Rendu', *Diacritics* 7 (1977).

71

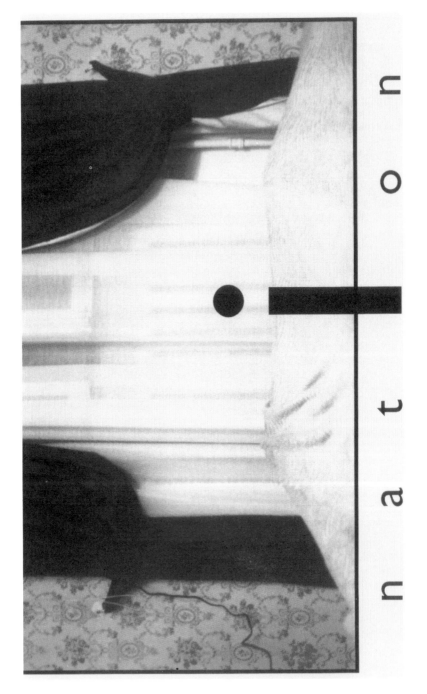

Tales of the Lost Land
Palestinian Identity and the Formation of Nationalist Consciousness[1]

Glenn Bowman

Yitzhak Khayutman, an Israeli national, asserted during a conference on Middle Eastern cities that Palestinians, if they wanted to return to their homeland, should retrospectively 'declare themselves Israelites'. Sari Nasr, a Palestinian sociologist born in the Jerusalem suburb of Lifta but resident since 1958 in Amman, Jordan, replied:

> I am a Palestinian, I was born in Jerusalem, I started out to be a Palestinian, then they started calling me someone who does not have a country. They called me a refugee. After that I was stateless. Then I was called a Syrian, a Lebanese, a Jordanian, what have you. Then they started called me a terrorist. Today I learned from Professor Khayutman that I am originally Jewish.[2]

Nasr's response raises issues central to the matter of Palestinian identity by stressing not only the difficulty non-Palestinians face in 'placing' a people displaced from their origins, but also the struggles Palestinians must engage in to assert their own senses of identity and territoriality against history's dislocations and the dislocating effects of others' discourses. As Edward Said suggests in his elegiac *After the Last Sky*, the idea of 'Palestine' is so loaded with significance for others that it is impossible for Palestine's indigenous inhabitants to assert their claims to the land without self-consciously having to contend with a plague of counter-claims. The Palestinians, in engaging the discourses in which those counter-claims are couched, are forced into territories where their actual existence, as well as any possible claims that existence might merit, is denied.[3]

Such counter-claims are not only Zionist; non-Jewish westerners have consistently presented Palestine as 'a land without a people'. A representational programme highlighting the land and erasing its inhabitants was generated in the early days of Christianity, and has continued to operate, in various modalities, through to the present day. Since the first decades of the fourth century western pilgrims have mentioned local inhabitants (Jewish, Christian, and, later, Islamic) only as impediments to pilgrims' free access to 'their' own holy places. This programme is easily translated from the rhetorical into the practical. Thus, in the twelfth century William of Tyre, a native of Jerusalem who became Archbishop of Tyre and a noted chronicler of the Crusades, observed of pious visitors to the city of his birth that 'the pilgrims [who] reached the city most carefully and boldly killed the citizens' before rushing blood-soaked into the Holy Sepulchre to celebrate Mass.[4]

Seven hundred years later the local inhabitants of the Holy Land were still most present to others in the observer's felt need for their effacement. Yeshayahu Nir's study of early Holy Land photography shows that for twenty years after photography's introduction to Palestine (in December 1839), the technique was used solely to portray a landscape rich in monuments and denuded of inhabitants, whereas in Europe during that period, photography was commercially developed as a medium of portraiture (Nir refers to Jerusalem in the calotypes of the 1850s as a 'ghost city'). Eventually, and largely because of the influence of growing messianic fundamentalism in the Christian west, local people were permitted to crawl from behind the rocks and into the pictures. Even then the only ones allowed to appear as themselves were those whose rights to be there were sanctioned by the Bible's prophecies of the re-establishment of the kingdom of Israel. Thus, from the late 1860s on it was common practice for western photographers such as Frank Mason Good, Felix Bonfils, and G. Eric Matson to photograph immigrant and local Jews fulfilling the prophecy of the 'Return' by praying at the Wailing Wall or gathering for the Sabbath in their settlements. Palestinian Arabs, on the other hand, were permitted to stand before the cameras only when costumed and stage-managed to look like ancient Israelites.[5]

It took the popular resistance of the Arab Revolt (1936-9) to produce a more general western awareness of the presence of a contemporary indigenous non-Jewish population in Palestine. By then, however, that presence was well on the way to being eradicated by the (sometimes uncomfortable) co-operation of western governments and Zionist forces. Within a decade of the revolt's suppression the process of

74

defining a Palestinian became problematic for non-Palestinians; after the 1948 creation of the state of Israel and the subsequent expropriation by Egypt and the Hashemite kingdom of Jordan of what remained of Mandatory Palestine, a Palestinian could no longer be defined as an inhabitant of a land called Palestine. The dispossessed and displaced were subsequently described in terms of what they had been transformed into by the loss of their homeland – 'refugee', 'Israeli Arab', 'Jordanian', 'Egyptian', 'Lebanese', 'fedayeen', 'fanatic', 'terrorist'....

post 1948

I am not primarily concerned here, however, with the way others see Palestinians – with what one could call the 'identification' of Palestinians – but with how Palestinians see themselves – with Palestinian 'identity'. None the less, much of the initial process of constructing a sense of one's group identity lies in the activity of rejecting the appropriateness of definitions others attempt to impose, arguing that those characterizations do not coincide with experiences and desires one has oneself and that one senses are shared with a wider community. This process of formulating identity, and of formulating national identity in particular, is manifest in a struggle of symbolic formulations, and the Palestinian, in order to say who or what he or she is, must be able to undermine and counter what Zionists, Europeans, Americans, and the nationals of other Middle Eastern states claim to identify as 'Palestinian'. Sari Nasr's ironic act of self-assertion partakes of two gestures: one the diacritical (and implied) statement of what he is not – 'I am not Syrian', 'I am not without a country', 'I am not Jewish', 'I am not Jordanian'; the other the positive expression of what he is – 'I am a Palestinian, I was born in Jerusalem.'

In this process of symbolic formulation and reformulation certain elements of the concerned group's cultural repertoire are given a somewhat overdetermined significance. Language (Arabic), items of clothing (the *kūfiyya*), village and place names (particularly those renamed in Hebrew by the Israelis), combinations of colours (the green, red, black and white of the outlawed Palestinian flag) and other 'bits' of Palestinian experience become themselves emblems of the whole experience of being Palestinian. None the less, such symbols of identity are not semantically fixed. Whilst standing in for Palestine they at the same time function as elements of everyday life. As such they have different meanings in different contexts. Markers which seem best to distinguish a group from others in some situations will function, in other situations, to obscure or deny precisely the boundaries whose drawing seems so important. Therefore identifying characteristics used in some contexts to exclude members of what are perceived as other groups, will be underplayed in other contexts where they would instead be seen to assert affiliations either not felt or not seen as appropriate.

In Israel and the Occupied Territories the Arabic language is used to distinguish between Hebrew-speaking occupiers and the Arabic-speakers who suffer their occupation. Palestinians, who have often learned Hebrew in state-run schools, or, for business reasons, in *ulpans* (Israeli language classes), will rarely use the language when speaking with Israelis. They will instead use English, which, in a land which was previously occupied by the British, now serves as a politically neutral *lingua franca*.[6] Similary, 'Oriental Jews', – Israelis whose original provenance was within the Arabic-speaking Middle East – will refuse in public to use the Arabic they will speak with their families at home for fear that they might be thought to be 'Arabs'.[7] In the different context of contacts between members of the several Middle Eastern nations, Arabic is not treated as an essential feature of Palestinian identity precisely because it confuses Palestinians with other Arabic-speaking national groups. Only when national identity is subordinated to the desire to forge bonds between members of the 'Arab Nation' does the issue of the shared language again rise to prominence.

For similar reasons, qualifications are imposed on certain group-marking characteristics where their unqualified usage might compound identities best kept separate. Hence, in the Palestinian instance, territoriality, a central focus of group identity, is qualified both historically (by using pre-1948 Palestine as the territorial locus of Palestinian identity) and semantically (by distinguishing in name between the two homelands – Israel and Palestine – which occupy the same geographical space) so that the identity Palestinians (both in their diaspora and within historic Palestine) derive from the land they claim is kept distinct from and antipathetic to that which the Israelis drive from the land they occupy.

Markers of national identity are mobilized and manipulated in certain situations to suit the strategies appropriate to the contexts. One could suggest, then, that national identity is both semantic and situational. It distinguishes a national group form others by defining one set of 'national' characteristics and placing a boundary between that set and all others. It also, when various situations demand, modifies both the boundaries and the salient characteristics determining them so as to assimilate or exile other persons or groups. These diacritical functions serve various ends: they can provide a sense of solidarity, be used to express oppositions to contiguous communities, generate symbols with which to mobilize groups of people and so on. National identity is, in other words, a rhetorical device used by different persons and groups in different ways in different contexts for a multitude of ends; it is not in itself a particular form of nation-creating practice.

I have described national identity in this manner in order to draw an important distinction between its general form and a particular modality of it called nationalism. Ibrahim Abu-Lughod, considering the rise and decline of the idea of the 'Arab Nation', succinctly expresses the difference:

> We should, at the outset of our discussion, distinguish two types of group consciousness which have often been confused. The first is a group's consciousness of itself, of its heritage, of its traditions and other bonds which it members might share. The type of political system in which the group happens to exist has no bearing on this form of consciousness.... The second type is a group's consciousness of being a community in terms of language, traditions, history, ethnicity and the like, but in this case the members insist on living together and conducting their lives as one political community independent of all other polities.[8]

National identity, in other words, is a fairly diffuse recognition of various forms of cultural continuity shared by certain individuals and not shared by others; it can be asserted, and mobilized, in a number of different ways. Nationalism, on the other hand, is a particular assertion of national identity which mobilizes, organizes, and transforms a sense of shared identity into a political programme designed to realize, territorially and politically, the idea of community which underlies it.

This distinction and its implications have not been well charted by theorists of nationalism; most write as though the struggle for national existence is a foregone conclusion once the idea of national identity has arisen. Thus Benedict Anderson's *Imagined Communities* inquires into the preconditions of a national sense of identity – the decay of cosmology, the collapse of dynastic rule, the development of print culture, and the familiarization of indigenes with the constraints of colonial administrative networks – but does not consider the processes which might transform the resultant potential nationalism into a specifically political form of identity.[9] Ernest Gellner's several meditations on nationalism offer a stimulating theory of the way industrial development disrupts the traditional segmentary organization of societies, thereby promoting a cultural homogeneity capable of suppporting the new mythologies of nationalism.[10] The actual mobilization of this new sense of potential community into political activity is not, however, analysed; he seems to assume that the transformation of national consciousness into political consciousness is determined by the same materialist forces which establish its preconditions. Clifford Geertz, in 'After the revolution: the fate of nationalism in the new states', mentions four phases of nationalism: the initial development of national consciousness out of more particulate ethnic and territorial awarenesses, the struggle to overcome colonialist opposition, the formation of the new state, and the subsequent effort to create a functioning national ethos capable of linking individual identity with the national destiny the state claims to represent. Geertz's interest in the final phase causes him to give fairly short shrift to the preceding stages, yet he suggests that the initial phase, the development of 'a painfully self-conscious concept of political ethnicity', is motivated by opposition to the domination of colonial forces. Such opposition leads, through an almost-Bakuninesque revolutionary ferment, to a 'popular rallying behind a common, extremely specific political aim.... Nationalism [comes] to mean, purely and simply, the desire – and the demand – for freedom.'[11] The complex dynamics which link the growth of community identity with perceptions of domination by others not of that community, and hence give rise to long processes of political agitation which may or may not lead to decolonization, are here reduced by an idealist reification of the 'will to freedom' into a moment of revolutionary alchemy wherein slaves are transmuted into free men and colonial territories take on the bright aura of nationhood.

The assumption, more or less explicit in these theories of nationalism, that perceptions of subordination or restriction of opportunity will create in people a sense of national identity necessarily giving rise to political nationalism causes the theorists in large part to disregard forms of national identity which do not bear fruit in explicit nationalisms. I would suggest, however, that even when a potentially nationalist community has developed national consciousness, there is no necessity for that population to develop politically separatist programmes. There are other routes for it as a whole to follow – into assimilationist ameliorism, into revolutionary internationalism, or into despair, fragmentation, and anomie.[12] Furthermore, different groups within the 'national' entity may, because of different sets of experiences, follow divergent paths towards national fulfilment. In South Africa, for example, the range of potential forms of national realization articulated and acted upon by different groups within the black communities is, at present, dividing a potential nationalist struggle into an internecine contest of black against black.

Only when it is realized that the transformation from national into nationalist consciousness is problematic can the social theorist began to apprehend, and analyse, the failure, or the long latency, of many potential nationalisms. Writers on nationalism will often cite – in part – Ernst Renan's statement in *Qu'est-ce qu'une nation?* (1882) of the preconditions of nationhood. In Anderson, for instance, we find: 'Or l'essence d'une nation est que tous les individus aient beaucoup de choses en commun, et aussi que tous aient oublié bien de choses.'[13] Eugene Kamenka refers as well to this first requirement for nationhood, but he proceeds by paraphrasing Renan's second prerequisite along with the first, and the addition is telling:

> According to Renan, a nation is based on two things. First, it must have a sense of common history, particularly a memory of common sufferings which seem more important than the conflicts and divisions also to be found within that history. Secondly, the people concerned must have a will to live together: 'To have done great things together, and the will to do more, these are the essential conditions for a people.'[14]

It is the formation of that 'will to live together' that is problematic, and without the memory of having 'done great things together, and the will to do more' people who share a sense of national identity are unlikely to develop the mechanisms to transform cultural identity into nationhood.

An examination of the conditions and constraints of the formation of a will to nationhood will not only have to inquire into the creation and promulgation of a symbolic repertoire (examining its particular emblems and interpretations of history as well as the channels through which these signs of community are disseminated). It will also need to study the ways various groups who are potentially parts of the nation interpret these symbols and the community to which they relate. The Palestinian situation is a particularly apt locale for an examination of the way national identity connects with nationalism because, unlike most situations where nationalist movements develop out of a community's sense of national identity, it lacks a continuous territorial setting. Usually nationalism developes in a shared landscape; the strong degree of contiguity a continuous territory provides makes for intensive interaction in social, economic, and political domains and thus for a strong sense of who makes up the collective in which each member envisages a place. Renan's concept of having done great things together foregrounds the idea of the domain in which the members of a group have shared central experiences.

The fact that, in the Palestinian instance, there are several discrete locales of Palestinian life (in Israel and the Occupied Territories, in the Middle Eastern refugee camps, in the bourgeois diaspora) which do not often (if ever) come into unmediated contact, means that there is potential for the evolution of several different kinds of national identity. These different forms will have different political impacts. Some may simply serve as diacritical markers, enabling the Palestinian, in certain instances, to differentiate him/herself and his/her community from the members of other surrounding social groups. Other conceptions may work for the interest of the particular Palestinian communities concerned without regard for Palestinians in different situations. Others may actually serve to foment nationalist movements oriented towards the creation of a Palestinian national entity to be shared by all persons who claim Palestinian identity. An examination of these several forms of identity, and of the sorts of collective activity they promote, will show not only that national identity and nationalism are not necessarily continuous, but also what sorts of community structures and perceptions are likely to develop forms of national identity which will in turn generate nationalist movements.

There is, however, a significant difference between the idea of a 'land' as the ground on which a nation can be built and a land as an expanse of continuous territory. A topographically unbroken landscape can be shattered by the representations of several groups which may mutually inhabit it yet which envisage themselves as discrete and discontinuous communities. A striking example of this is set out in Raymond Williams's *The Country and the City* where, in discussing Jane Austen's rural landscapes, Williams demonstrates that for the agrarian aristocracy the distances between one country house and the next were seen as unpopulated territories despite the dense inhabitation of those lands by the rural peasantry.[15] In this instance, as in that of the pre-state Zionist declaration that Palestine 'is a land without a people for a people without a land', it is clear that the recognized population is made up of groups and individuals with whom the definers see themselves sharing common interests and projects. The state of Israel has displayed its own recognition of this principle of the formation of the 'imagined community' in its attempts to obviate Palestinians' recognition of shared national interests through the promotion of specific village and clan interests.[16]

For a 'land' to serve as a ground on which to build nationhood it must be more than a geographical setting. It must be as well a domain of the imagination wherein persons can locate others, many of whom they will never meet, with whom they see themselves as sharing a present situation as well as a future nation. Although a fertile ground for nationalist movements is provided by a literal landscape populated by a people who share in a situation they perceive as one of occupation and who imagine a future liberation from that state, the national community need not be 'in place' on national ground to become nationalist. Religio-nationalist Armenians and Jews, dispersed beyond the borders of the lands they conceive of as their national territories, are none the less able to imagine themselves as nations awaiting reconstitution on national territory. Each community engages in frequent religious gatherings in which it liturgically celebrates itself as a national entity constituted in eternity and working towards historical reconstitution on the land on which it, and its religion, was formed. 'Israel' and 'Armenia' are, after their historical loss, represented in a liturgical landscape, and 'standing on' that sacred ground prefigures returning to the actual lost territories. Diasporic Jews or Armenians, while engaged in such ritualized reminiscences in spaces which symbolically participate in the territories of Israel or Armenia, are able to see themselves as part of a world-wide community of others who share both their exile and their projects of recuperation.

For Palestinians, the 'land of Palestine' is the correlate. In a sense, however, 'Palestine' was constituted as an imaginable entity at the moment of its loss, and there were few explicitly national traditions for its members to carry in to exile. The inter-factional feuding of the political élite of pre-1948 Palestine as well as the localized interests of the Palestinian peasantry meant that identity was tightly tied to local, factional, or class interests rather than to some idea of national or nationalist solidarity. Resistance to Zionist encroachment was couched by the various concerned groups in terms either strictly regional – focused on resistance to land loss – or broadly international – pan-Islamic or pan-Arabist.[17] Consequently there was no existing vehicle (either secularly or religiously nationalist) which could be mobilized to create, in the exile, a sense of national simultaneity and a promise of territorial re-establishment in the way the Armenian Orthodox liturgy was able to do for the Armenians or the way 'that mixture of folklore, ethical exhortation and nationalist political propaganda that we call the Bible' was mobilized for the Jews.[18]

Palestinians have memories (or traditions of memories) of the land before the 1948 and 1967 expulsions and they have their various experiences of exile – whether within or outside the borders of historic Palestine. The problem, in terms of the development of a cohesive nationalist movement, is that the memories from before the disaster invoke experiences specific to particular village, faction, or class groups; the experiences specific to particular village, fraction of the Palestinian diaspora with which the individual shares exile. 'Palestine' will be imagined differently by Palestinians in different situations; a Palestinian in the occupied territories, seeing before his other eyes the transformations brought about by Israeli 'development', will conceive of 'Palestine' as a very different place, in past, present, and future tenses, than the land imagined by Palestinians exiled in New York, or in Beirut. These variations in perception, and in imagination, may create real problems when it comes to propagating, and maintaining, 'a will to live together'. There is little question that the Palestinian people are suffering, but differences in the forms of that suffering and in its perceived causes may make the conflicts and divisions found within contemporary Palestinian history more significant than the memory of the common suffering that gave it birth.

MEMORIES AND STRATEGIES

Such differences in the way both a Palestinian identity and also the appropriate strategies of redemption are envisioned are strikingly exemplified in three texts – Fawaz Turki's *The Disinherited: journal of a Palestinian exile* (1974), Edward Said's *After the Last Sky: Palestinian lives* (1986) and Raja Shehadeh's *The Third Way: a journal of life in the West Bank* (1982).[19] Their differences clearly reflect the very different experiences of living in the Lebanese refugee camps, of being a Palestinian university lecturer in New York, and of practising as a solicitor in Ramallah on the Occupied West Bank. But the books do share at least two outstanding characteristics. First, all three were written and published in English. Secondly, all three authors describe who they and their people are very largely by describing their enemies. Thus the act of identifying the self is engaged in before the gaze of an Other and through a process of struggling against an Other (in part made up of the audience and in part a fully other Other) whose project is perceived to be the obliteration of the self and its community. The importance of the enemy in defining the friend remains a significant problem for the growth of a pan-Palestinian nationalist movement because the diverse communities of the Palestinian nation face different enemies in their different locales. As a result, the friends the members of these communities recognize may not be each other.

THE DISINHERITED

Fawaz Turki states in the first pages of *The Disinherited*: 'If I was not a Palestinian when I left Haifa as a child, I am one now' (p8). Although born in Haifa, Turki left at an age that ensured that his childhood memories came from the squalid Beirut refugee camps in which he was raised rather than the Palestinian city from which his family was driven. The 'Palestine' he did not remember was, none the less, ever-present in the murmurings of older Palestinians who gathered in tight knots to re-create compulsively every detail of the lives which had been so suddenly wrenched from them:

> The moths would gather around the kerosene lamps and the men would mumble between verses '*Ya leil, ya aein*' (my night, my mind – they have fused). It is a typical Palestinian night, Palestinian mind. And we would know we were together in a transplanted village that once was on the road to Jaffa, that once was in the north of Haifa, that once was close to Lydda. (p45)

Such obsessive re-creation of the past is not unusual in persons who have been brutally separated from their previous ways of life. Similar reactions have been found among Greek Cypriot villagers driven from their lands by the Turkish invasion, and displaced peoples' compulsive memorialization of the past has been likened to the neurotic reactions of family members who cannot accept the loss of a loved one.[20] For Palestinian peasants, who made up the overwhelming majority of people in the camps, village life had provided the frame of reference for all experience, and the loss of that frame effectively led to the disintegration not only of the world but of their conceptions of self as well. Thus Rosemary Sayigh, who had done extensive work within the Lebanese camps, writes:

> The village – with its special arrangements of houses and orchards, its open meeting-places, its burial ground, its collective identity – was built into the personality of each individual villager to a degree that made separation like an obliteration of the self. In describing their first years as refugees, camp Palestinians use metaphors like 'death', 'paralysis', 'burial', 'non-existence', etc.... Thirty years after the uprooting, the older generation still mourns.[21]

Such nostalgia does not, however, provide a foundation for national identity since in large part the collectivities being imagined in the villagers' reminiscences are their own obliterated village communities (which were, where possible, demographically reconstituted in the new settings of the camps).

Fawaz Turki and his generation did not learn what it was to be Palestinian from these dreamers. Instead, they learned their identity through suffering intolerance and harassment at the hands of their unwilling hosts – initially the Lebanese authorities but later, as migrant labouring forced them to travel through the Middle East, the business and state personnel of the entire Arab world. Turki's generation were taught that to be Palestinian is to be cursed, exploited, and imprisoned by powers who despite the lumpenproletariat generated by their treatment of the camps. For the younger camp Palestinians, the enemy eventually ceases to be he who drove their people from Palestine and becomes instead first the 'Arab' and then everyone who exploits them in their exile:

> To the Palestinian, the young Palestinian, living and growing up in Arab society, the Israeli was the enemy in the mathematical matrix; we never saw him, lived under his yoke, or, for many of us, remembered him. Living in a refugee camp and going hungry, we felt that the causes of our problem were abstract, the causes of its perpetuation were real.(p53)[22]

84

Just as the enemy is given the features of the particular tormentors of the camp Palestinians, so too the population of the imagined 'land' of Palestine becomes those who share the camp Palestinians' experiences of being 'Palestinian rather than those who are descended from persons who lived in Palestine. At first this population is made up of all Arabs who suffer under the unjust leadership of reactionary Arab states – 'The revolution is Palestinian in its origin and Arab in its extension' (p103) – but in time, as the drift of diasporic life introduces Turki to the world-wide extension of reaction and corruption, the Palestinian community is redefined as 'a commonwealth of peoples heavily laden, heavily oppressed' (p54). The struggle for the homeland becomes the struggle to constitute a ground on which human beings can have integrity, and thus

> the liberation of Palestine, in a sense, becomes the liberation of [all] men and women.... Palestine is not a struggle that involves only Palestinians. It is Everyman.... [We are] confronting the whole mosaic or racist mythology in the West and in Israel that essentially claim[s] that certain races are inherently cowardly, inferior, backward, and incapable of responding to the fierce exigencies that press on the human spirit. (p176)

The Palestinians created by camp life in the *ghurba* grew up with no links to a past and with few non-oppressive connections to the present. The experience turned a number of them, like Turki, into revolutionaries working within internationalist, rather than nationalist, parameters:

> We grew up in a vacuum. We belonged to no nation. We embraced no culture. We were at the bottom. The only way for us to go was up.... We had nothing to lose. We lived on the edge of the desert. On the fringe of the world. We had little to risk.... We made common cause with the oppressed. The oppressors made common cause against us. (p154)

AFTER THE LAST SKY

The bourgeoisie, who for the most part managed to flee Palestine just before the 1948 catastrophe, were not, like the peasantry, hurled into a vacuum, but were welcomed into an established and well-to-do expatriate community.[23] From the mid-nineteenth century on, the urban élite of Palestine had established settlements throughout the

The former mayor of Jerusalem and his wife in exile in Amman, Jordan, 1984
[Photograph: Jean Mohr]

Middle East, Europe and the Americas where their children could go for cosmopolitan educations and where they themselves could move to escape the Ottoman draft, the British taxation, and the depredations caused by Zionist penetration.

Although the bourgeoisie of the *ghurba* has always been socially and economically assimilationist,[24] its members have nevertheless maintained a strong sense of Palestinian identity. This reflects to some degree the importance to social and business relations of family ties and loyalties based on place of origin. But it also has a significant role in maintaining a feeling of 'rootedness' – a fixity if identity – for individuals scattered across a number of continents, integrated into a multitude of culturally heterogeneous societies, and subject to numerous radically different economic, social, political, and confessional influences.

The loss of the homeland exaggerated the bourgeois's already-present sense of displacement and severance by making it impossible for him literally to 'go home' – to perform in the flesh the pilgrimage he constantly made in the imagination to remind himself of who he was and where he came from. Cut off from that past, the bourgeois found himself inescapably immersed in the anomie of the post-industrial world:

> where no straight line leads from home to birthplace to school to maturity, all events are accidents, all progress is a digression, all residence is exile.... stability of geography and the continuity of land – these have completedly disappeared from my life and from the life of all Palestinians. (pp20-1)

This world, unlike that of the camp Palestinians or that of the Palestinians of Israel and the Occupied Territories, is one in which individuals, alone or hived off in nuclear families, live in relative isolation from extended Palestinian communities. Here the connections between wider networks of Palestinian families and friends are not constantly rehearsed in daily life but instead run sporadically along telephone lines or scheduled air flights.

In such a context national identity is a fragile thing maintained not so much through contemporary patterns of action and affiliation as through fetishized links to a common past:

Intimate mementoes of a past irrevocably lost circulate among us, like the genealogies and fables severed from their original locale, the rituals of speech and custom. Much reproduced, enlarged, thematized, embroidered and passed around, they are strands in the web of affiliations we Palestinians use to tie ourselves to our identity and to each other. (p14)

This Palestine, embodied in objects, images, and gestures, cannot constitute an imagined simultaneity of like persons dreaming of (and working towards) a future state. The diversity, and the isolation, of the members of the diaspora's bourgeoisie is too great to allow them to imagine Palestine as anything more than a past moment in which all the now-scattered people of their homeland were once together. The rituals of remembrance serve therefore to provide a touchstone, like a memento from childhood, offering sensed continuity to lives almost wholly defined by the practices and the rituals of the surrounding communities in which the Palestinian bourgeois is immersed. Only in the domestic shrines which Jean Mohr photographs are these individuals able momentarily to make contact with an island of identity afloat in the sea of their difference.

Edward Said's writings illuminate not only the experiences of the Palestinian bourgeoisie in exile but also those of other Palestinian communities both inside and outside historic Palestine. They appear to transcend the constraints to nationalist vision that I have described above. But if one compares the place of the 'enemy' in defining identity in his writings with the role played by Arab oppressors in forming Turki's Palestinianism, then, I think, Said's work can be seen to be aligned with its bourgeois context. If the core of identity for the displaced bourgeoisie is memory and its mementoes, then the chief enemy of their form of national identity is the corrosive impact of time and misinformation. Years and miles bring about a gradual blurring and smearing of the contours of a remembered land – a gradual destruction aggravated by the systematic misrepresentation of Palestinian history by Zionist and pro-Israeli manipulators of the media. Said's projects, which range from explicit attacks on the media's anti-Palestinian calumnies and obfuscations to philosophical-literary disquisitions on the question of how to begin to tell a story when one is always already *in medias res*, approach from various directions the question of how forms of representation can be true to the objects they claim to represent.[25] The structure of Said's recent *Blaming the Victims*, a collaborative effort with Christopher Hitchens, exemplifies this. A series of ten essays, all describing the mechanisms by which Palestinian history and the Palestinian people have been and are being misrepresented, leads up to a long piece entitled 'A profile of the Palestinian people' which 'sets the record straight' by describing in detail the subject distorted by the previously discussed presentations.

After the Last Sky, with its profiles and its portraits, is a similar attempt to represent a fragmented subject. However, the diasporic experience of the bourgeoisie determines the character of the entity Said reconstitutes in that the Palestinian nation Said senses is, like the Palestinian community of which he is a part, a group composed of individuals tenuously tied together by what is lost rather than by what is held in common:

> To be sure, no single Palestinian can be said to feel what most other Palestinians feel: ours has been too various and scattered a fate for that sort of correspondence. But there is no doubt that we do in fact form a community, if at heart a community built on suffering and exile.... We endure the difficulties of dispersion without being forced (or able) to struggle to change our circumstances.... Miscellaneous, the spaces here and there in our midst include but do not comprehend the past; they represent building without overall purpose, around an uncharted and only partially surveyed territory. Without a centre. Atonal. (pp5-6; 129).

There is little room in such a presentation for the revolutionary internationalist programme of a Turki or the stolid solidarity in suffering evident in the people described by Shehadeh. Said's 'Palestinian' is a composite of the Palestinians he knows, and these are persons who, caught in the web of exile amidst the anomic mileux of the late capitalist world, find occasional but brief respites from alienation in the celebration of an identity set off against that world.

Finally, however, like most people caught up in that dynamic yet decentred world, their identity is always elsewhere and their knowledge, like ours, is made up of the central fact that wherever they are it is always away from home:

> Whatever the claim may be that we make on the world – and certainly on ourselves as people who have become restless in the fixed place to which we have been assigned – in fact our truest reality is expressed in

the way we cross over from one place to another. We are migrants and perhaps hybrids in, but not of, any situation in which we find ourselves. This is the deepest continuity of our lives as a nation in exile and constantly on the move. (p164)

Although Said's 'Palestine' can occasionally be seen in the 'exhilaration and energy and pleasure … [the] cheerfully vulnerable triumph' which flashes in the eyes of a Palestinian child and reminds the watcher that 'movement need not always be either flight or exile' (p165), that glimpse is always momentary and epiphanic. This nationhood, sensed in a moment lost by the time it is recognized, is a ground for redemption, but it is a redemption promising integrity to the unrooted individual and not one promising political re-establishment to a fragmented community.

THE THIRD WAY

Said's cosmopolitan humanism and Turki's revolutionary interna-tionalism seem to share little common ground on which an allied nationalist movement could be built. The strategies their two readings of the situation suggest are at odds, and the populations to be brought together by those strategies would probably be unwilling to abide with each other within shared boundaries. This divergence is in large part the consequence of the Palestinian dispersion. The international bourgeoisie and the camp Palestinians (groups differently constituted since well before the disaster) have developed in isolation from each other and have consequently cultivated their respective images of the Palestinian past, present, and future under very different sets of influences.

The situation within the borders of historic Palestine is different. There, a heterogeneous Palestinian population has shared the burden of Israeli domination. This is not to say that all social groups within these borders have been influenced in the same ways by the Israeli occupation.[26] Nevertheless, since the Palestinian populations of the Israel established in 1948 and those of the territories occupied in 1967 were brought into contact, there has been, throughout the occupied land, a continuous Palestinian population with an awareness of itself as a community opposed to and oppressed by the Israeli state.

The old adage, 'The enemy of my enemy is my friend', does reflect a situation in which a common foe can unify traditionally opposed groups: but this will happen *only if* that enemy is recognized as shared. A traditional opposition, like that between Christian and Muslim Palestinians in the Old City of Jerusalem, will be maintained as long as the context out of which it has grown remains pertinent. When life is sufficiently disrupted to throw the relevance of old categories into doubt, people are able to subordinate old oppositions to the need for new alliances.[27] The radical transformations of traditional life brought about by the Israeli occupation – massive expropriation of agricultural lands, militarization of vast areas, development of a migrant labour market to serve newly developed industrial and service sectors, intensive inculcation of western capitalist culture, full-scale political repression, and so on – have forced the majority of Palestinians to recognize the inadequacy of old confessional, factional, and territorial divisions and to look for new ways of forging a strong national awareness out of the fragments.[28]

This is not to say that there is a united Palestinian nationalist movement operative in historic Palestine at the present time, but that the distinct borders within which national identity develops (borders drawn both territorially and by widespread recognition of membership in a group opposed to a common and clearly visible enemy) provide the necessary knowledge of who will be fighting against whom, and for what. There is in Palestine a demographic foundation on which a heterodox population is building a will to live together.

Furthermore, and perhaps most importantly, the image of the nation of Palestine held by Palestinians within historic Palestine is a contemporary image, not one frozen in a shadowy past or burning brightly in a distant and somewhat millenarian future. Palestinians on the land have watched that land being transformed from what it was before the occupations, and can see not only what it has become but also the forces that have effected that transformation. The land for them is alive; not an object of fantasy and reverie but a field for work and struggle.

Raja Shehadeh's *The Third Way* locates itself within a nation in the process of becoming aware of its present situation and the possibilities that situation provides. Shehadeh's narrative, although centred on the experiences of a West Bank lawyer based in Ramallah, draws on a wide range of Palestinians in describing the state of the nation. The 'nation' that Shehadeh claims is drawing together in the face of a common enemy is evoked in his descriptions of the strength of the women's groups; of peasants' growing awareness that land expropriations threaten the homes on which their traditional 'my-home-is-my-castle' attitudes have been built; of professional and academic lives distorted and blocked by state and racialist interventions; of the degradations brought on by touristic development. His image of the population of 'Palestine' is neither as expansive as Turki's nor as isolating as Said's. It is made up of vignettes of land stories from people he has met and worked with during his activities within a shared set of borders and under a shared set of restraints.[29] Shehadeh calls up in concrete images a diverse community bonded together by the common experience of oppression.

Shehadeh's historical awareness and his constant contact with the actual transformations of historic Palestine enable him to treat the development of the contemporary situation as a coherent process rather than as an abrupt shifting of images from the idyllic to the demonic. Instead of sketching an opposition of perfect past to perfidious present, he lays out for critical examination those aspects of past Palestinian lives which lent themselves to the production of the alienated present. He analyses, for instance, the structures of authority and of trust that were developed in pre-Zionist days and sees in them a major contribution to the loss of the land and the subsequent muting of political activism: 'No effort is needed to control a society so geared to paternalism that it barely matters who the authority is which does the ordering' (p29). He also discusses how past structures can be transformed into tools of present resistance, examining, for instance, the way women are remobilizing their traditional solidarity to resist new enemies:

> Sometimes I think that those few women who manage to survive this are the strongest of all *samidin* and it is they who will finally lead the revolt. They have the least to lose and no ego to be pampered, hurt, or played on by the Israeli rulers. You see them fearlessly head demonstrations and shout at soldiers at road blocks. They have been used to brutal oppression by men from the day they were born, and the Israeli soldiers are not a new breed of animal to them. (p115)

Shehadeh's image of 'the land' has a real population, present and future,[30] as well as a temporal location which permits him to conceive of the present growing out of the past and a future (or a number of futures) growing out of the present.

As an observer of the land and its people in the process of their

92

transformations, Shehadeh is able to describe not only the genesis and growth of a national consciousness but also the processes by which that growth engenders unity out of diversity. He considers the losses – as well as the gains – involved in the development of a 'pornographic' relation to the land wherein desire is rooted in an imagery of Palestine rather than in a concrete relationship with the land's literal body. While discussing with an Israeli friend the approach to the land of Zionists raised outside Palestine on a nationalist imagery derived from Palestine, he brings up the alienation from and violence towards the real land implicit in that 'pornographic' approach:

> When you are exiled from your land ... you begin, like a pornographer, to think about it in symbols. You articulate your love for your land in its absence, and in the process transform it into something else.... When Jews came to settle here this century, they saw the land through these symbols. Think of the almost mystical power that names of places here have for many Zionists.... As for what it really looked like, they tried to transform it into the kinds of landscape they left in Europe.... It is like falling in love with an image of a woman, and then, when meeting her, being excited not by what is there but by what her image has come to signify for you. You stare at her, gloating, without really seeing her, let alone loving her. (p86-7)

Shehadeh is aware, none the less, that the Palestinians, exiled from their land while still on it, are themselves being placed in a pornographic relation to it by the experience of having that which they know and love taken away piece by piece. He watches himself transforming the land he had known intimately and unselfconsciously into a symbol of what he must join with others to struggle for. He finds himself resenting the process even as he accepts its inevitability if the object of desire is to be regained:

> Sometimes, when I am walking in the hills ... unselfconsciously enjoying the touch of the hard land under my feet, the smell of thyme and the hills an trees around me – I find myself looking at an olive tree, and as I am looking at it, it transforms itself before my eyes into a symbol of the *samidin*, of our struggle, of our loss. And at that very moment, I am robbed of the tree; instead there is a hollow space into which anger and pain flow. (p87)

Shehadeh realizes, though, that this 'hollow space' now exists in the heart of all Palestinians under occupation. The anger that fills it is what lifts those people out of the isolation of their previous experiences of living on their own private lands. It makes them citizens of a common land – even if that land is one that is forfeit and must be redeemed.

Before the occupation there was no national symbolism and cohesion specifically connected with the West Bank.... [Now] even Abu-'Isa, who always thought of himself and his house as a separate kingdom, is beginning, through the threat of an Israeli incursion, to extend his horizons.... Although I am glad that this is happening – we could not hope to fight off the Israelis without it – I cannot but allow myself a moment of anger and regret. I feel deep, deep resentment against this invasion of my innermost imagery and consciousness by the Israelis. (p88)

Here and elsewhere in *The Third Way* Shehadeh provides a striking phenomenological account of the transformation of diverse individual experiences into the material of a national identity.

This process is, of course, not dissimilar to the way in which Palestinians in the diaspora invest cultural imagery with national references. The difference, which is crucial, is that here the reference which turns the olive tree from a tree into an emblem is to the *samidin*, a collectivity dedicated to 'stay[ing] put, to cling[ing] to our homes and land by all means available' (pvii). The stance of *sumud*, of steadfast perseverance in the face of occupation, is proto-nationalistic in that it refers to a distinct land (historic Palestine), a distinct people (the Palestinians resident within its borders), and a distinct adversary (those who would erase that land and its occupants). Its territorial boundedness makes it demographically inclusive *and* exclusive while its policy of confrontation defines a distinct enemy and demands an (as yet undefined) political programme. *The Third Way* describes a people who, having come to recognize their national identity, are on the verge of transforming that into a nationalist programme.

National identity, as I have stressed above, does not necessarily express 'a will to live together' with other members of the national collectivity. It can serve to provide individuals with distinct identities in the midst of cultural homogeneity, or its development can be, as it is for Turki, the first stage of a movement into wider, distinctly non-national movements.[31] The Palestinian identity set forth in *The*

94

Third Way, however, does represent a community's will to live as a national unit, even while that will is prevented from developing into an active nationalism by uncertainty about how Palestinians under occupation should move to overthrow foreign rule. The stance of *sumud* is, none the less, a positive response in the circumstances, since it keeps alive the idea of a complex and dedicated Palestinian nation until historical circumstances and political innovations throw up strategies for moving the people into a more active struggle.

BLANK BANNERS, INVENTED TRADITIONS

Edwin Ardener designates as 'blank banners' those emblems of an identity not linked to a specific programme which hold together groups of persons without directing them towards any set ends. Similarly, Eric Hobsbawm's 'invented traditions' refer to a set of practices, perhaps developed out of traditional practices, which serve, in new situations, to signify membership in a group without imposing on that group specific and restrictive rights and obligations.[32] They too provide cultural emblems which distinguish one group from others without obliging that group to enact anything but a celebration of identity. 'Blank barriers' and 'invented traditions' exist within every group that uses cultural emblems to differentiate its members from those of other groups. It is, however, in the way that the body of localized experience rushes in to fill those empty spaces, that the national identities of groups spread over a wide range of social and topographical domains take on different, and often antipathetic, senses of who they – and the citizens of their nation – are.

Emblems and rituals of Palestinian identity will, in the diaspora, serve as foci of identity for peoples whose memories and experiences have already caused them to differentiate themselves from those who surround them. But although their memories of a common origin (however reconstituted these might be) give them a ground, and a symbolic repertoire, for identity, it is their experiences which will provide references for those symbols and a landscape for that ground. These experiences are specific to particular positions in class and social structures. Because of the degree to which 'Palestinian' groups in the diaspora have been integrated into wider non-Palestinian societies, they tend to be constituted as fractions (proletariat, bourgeois, and so forth) of whole societies.

The experiences of the occupants of historic Palestine are different from those outside. The people who will align themselves around the 'blank banners' and 'invented traditions' of the Occupied Territories represent a wide range of classes, types of employment, and expectations. The recognition of their communality as Palestinians will here draw together a multitude of persons who, outside, have little chance – or desire – to engage in dialogue. The fact that their banners are as yet blank means that each of the fractional groups can, as the occupation continues to change the face of the physical and the social landscapes, both re-evaluate its own positions and programmes and attempt to align its interests with those of other groups.[33]

It may be, as one Palestinian leftist in *al-Quds* (Jerusalem) told me in 1985, that the Palestinians of historic Palestine 'have two battles to fight; the first is the war of national liberation, and after that is the revolution'. For now, however, the right and the left, the workers and the aristocracy, the peasants and the petit-bourgeoisie have discovered a common identity in their shared oppositon under Israeli occupation to that which would destroy them all as 'Palestinians'. Their knowledge of common suffering is at present sufficiently powerful to overcome awareness of the conflicts and divisions which have split Palestinian society in the past and will most likely fragment it again in the future. Their strengthening will to live together is a pragmatic recognition that to survive at all as a people is to struggle as an allied movement against the enemy they all share. In time, when and if the disruption that is the occupation has ended, Palestinian identity in Palestine is likely to become problematic and multi-factional as various groups within that society break with consensus to assert their particular readings of their rights. At this moment, however, the struggle in the land that was Palestine is a struggle to discover the means of creating a nation for a population that recognizes itself as a people, and it is there – in Occupied Palestine – that the Palestinian national can become a Palestinian nationalist.

NOTES

The original version of this article was presented as a paper to the British Society for Middle Eastern Studies (BRISMES) Annual Conference, 12-15 July 1987.

[1] 'A tale of the lost land' is the title of the manuscript enclosed within Samuel Clemens's (Mark Twain's) *A Connecticut Yankee in King Arthur's Court*

(1889). It recounts the Connecticut Yankee's story of the brutal collision of a feudal society with the technological power of the industrial world.

[2] Abdulaziz Y. Saqqaf (ed), *The Middle East City: ancient traditions confront a modern world* (Proceedings of the Second Annual Conference of the Middle East Chapter of the Professors' World Peace Academy) (New York: Paragon House, 1987), 186, 192.

[3] Edward Said, *After the Last Sky: Palestinian lives* (London: Faber, 1986), 40. Salman Rushdie, in conversation with Said at the Institute of Contemporary Arts (London) in September 1986, remarked that 'one of the problems of being Palestinian is that the idea of interior is regularly invaded by other people's descriptions, by other people's attempts to control what it is to occupy that space – whether it be Jordanian Arabs who say there is no difference between a Jordanian and a Palestinian, or Israelis who claim that the land is not Palestine but Israel'. (Edward Said and Salman Rushdie, 'On Palestinian identity', *New Left Review*, no 160 [1986], 66.)

[4] William of Tyre, *A History of Deeds Done Beyond the Sea*, ed Emily Babcock and A. C. Krey, vol 1 (New York: 1943), 372.

[5] Yeshayahu Nir, 'Phillips, Good, Bonfils and the human image in early Holy Land photography', *Studies in Visual Communication*, 8, 4 (1982), 33, 36.

[6] See Jonathan Webber, 'The status of English as a lingua franca in contemporary Jerusalem' (Oxford: D.Phil. thesis, 1979).

[7] See Kenneth Brown, 'Iron and a king: the Likud and oriental Jews', *Merip Reports*, no 114 (1983), and Kenneth Brown and Jean Mohr, 'Journey through the labyrinth: a photographic essay on Israel/Palestine', *Studies in Visual Communication*, 8, 2 (1982).

[8] Ibrahim Abu-Lughod, 'Arab nationalism: sociopolitical considerations', in U. Davis, A. Mack, and N. Yuval-Davis (eds), *Israel and the Palestinians* (London: Ithaca Press, 1975), 71.

[9] Benedict Anderson, *Imagined Communities: reflections on the origin and spread of nationalism* (London: Verso, 1983).

[10] Ernest Gellner, *Thought and Change* (London: Weidenfeld & Nicolson, 1964); Ernest Gellner, 'Scale and nation', in *Contemporary Thought and Politics* (London: Routledge & Kegan Paul, 1974); Ernest Gellner, *Nations and Nationalism* (Oxford: Basil Blackwell, 1983).

[11] Clifford Geertz, 'After the revolution: the fate of nationalism in the new states', in *The Interpretation of Cultures* (New York: Basic Books, 1973 [1971]), 239.

[12] On the 'quasi-nationalism' of ethnic minorities in modern western societies, see Eugene Kamenka, 'Political nationalism – the evolution of the idea', in E. Kamenka (ed), *Nationalism: the nature and evolution of an idea* (Canberra: Australian National University Press, 1973), 19; on revolutionary internationalism, see my analysis of Fawaz Turki below; on fragmentation, see Peter Marris, *Loss and Change* (London: Routledge & Kegan Paul, 1974).

[13] Anderson, *op cit*, 15.

[14] Kamenka, *op cit*, 12.

[15] Raymond Williams, *The Country and the City* (London: Chatto & Windus, 1973), ch 11.

[16] See Ian Lustick, *Arabs in the Jewish States: Israel's control of a national*

minority (Austin: University of Texas Press, 1980); Salim Tamari, 'Factionalism and class formation in recent Palestinian history', in R. Owen (ed), *Studies in the Economic and Social History of Palestine in the Nineteenth and Twentieth Centuries* (London: Macmillan, 1982), and Salim Tamari, 'In league with Zion: Israel's search for a native pillar', *Journal of Palestine Studies*, vol 13 (1983).

[17] Nels Johnson, *Islam and the Politics of Meaning in Palestinian Nationalism* (London: Kegan Paul International, 1982); I. Abu-Lughod, 'Territorially-based nationalism and the politics of negation' and Rashid Khalidi, 'Palestinian peasant resistance to Zionism before World War I', both in Edward Said and Christopher Hitchens (eds), *Blaming the Victims: spurious scholarship and the Palestinian question* (London: Verso, 1988).

[18] Kamenka, *op cit*, 4. Benedict Anderson (*op cit*, 39) illustrates 'simultaneity' – central to his ideas of the 'imagined community' – with the modern 'ceremony' of reading the newspaper: 'each communicant is well aware that the ceremony he performs is being replicated simultaneously by thousands (or millions) of others of whose existence he is confident, yet of whose identity he has not the slightest notion.... What more vivid figure for the secular, historically-clocked, imagined community can be envisioned?' A parallel, in terms of the practices being discussed here, would be the knowledge of the communicant in an Armenian Orthodox liturgy that throughout the diaspora there are hundreds of thousands like him or her 'simultaneously' sharing in the same activities and the same desire.

[19] Fawaz Turki, *The Disinherited: journal of a Palestinian Exile*, 2nd edn (London: Modern Reader [Monthly Review Press], 1974); Said, *op cit*; Raja Shehadeh, *The Third Way: a journal of life in the West Bank* (London: Quartet Books, 1982). Page references will be given in the text.

[20] Peter Loizos, *The Heart Grown Bitter: a chronicle of Cypriot war refugees* (Cambridge: Cambridge University Press, 1981); Marris, *op cit*.

[21] Rosemary Sayigh, *Palestinians: from peasants to revolutionaries: a people's history* (London: Zed Press, 1979), 107.

[22] The Israelis may well figure more in the demonology of camp Palestinians as their role in the persecution of Lebanese Palestinians becomes more overt. The increasing participation of Israelis in the inter-communal strife of the Lebanon through the 1970s culminated, in the early 1980s, in the occupation of significant parts of the country. Just as the 1967 Israeli occupation of new territories of historic Palestine led to a sense of solidarity between 'Israeli Arabs' and the Palestinians of the Occupied Territories, so it might be hoped that eventually the Palestinians of Lebanon might grow more empathetic towards the Palestinians of Palestine who share with them Israeli occupation.

[23] On the nature an extent of this exodus, see Tamari, 'Factionalism and class formation', 180 and Lustick, *op cit*, 40.

[24] Recent restrictions on Palestinian economic influence in the Middle East in general and the Gulf States in particular may cause interesting redefinitions of position.

[25] In the former strand of Edward Said's work would be *Orientalism* (London: Routledge & Kegan Paul, 1978), *The Question of Palestine* (London: Routledge & Kegan Paul, 1989), *Covering Islam: how the media and the*

experts determine how we see the rest of the world (London: Routledge & Kegan Paul, 1981), and Said and Hitchens, *op cit*; and example of the latter is *Beginnings: intention and method* (New York: Basic Books, 1975).

[26] On Israeli strategies of occupation within 1948-67 Israel, see Lustick, *op cit*; on the occupation of the West Bank and Gaza, see Jan Metzger, M. Orth, and C. Sterzing, *This Land is Our Land* (London: Zed Press, 1986); on the experience of the West Bank peasantry, see S. Tamari, 'Building other people's homes: the Palestinian peasant's household and work in Israel', *Journal of Palestine Studies*, 11, 1 (1981).

[27] See my 'Unholy struggle on holy ground: conflict and interpretation in Jerusalem', *Anthropology Today*, 2, 3 (1986); Loizos, *op cit*, 132.

[28] See Tamari, 'In league with Zion', 1983, on Israel's unsuccessful attempt to mobilize the rural/urban divide against the development of national identity.

[29] In *The Third Way*, movement – on foot, by car, by aeroplane – is a constant refrain. But unlike Said's 'Palestinian restlessness', the constant shifting of Shehadeh and those he describes is always goal-oriented and always impeded by an Other; the enemy. See especially 30-3 and 96-8.

[30] This population seems to exclude the larger part of those who are not taking part in the real struggle within the borders which constrain, and define, his existence: 'I don't go to Amman ... seeing Palestinians in the Jordanian capital, men who have grown rich and now pay only widly patriotic lip-service to our struggle, is more than my *summud* in my poor and beloved land could stomach' (p8).

[31] See Turki, *op cit*, 107, on the translation of 'Palestinian' into a term designating a universalist 'freedom fighter'.

[32] Edwin Ardener, 'Introductory essay: Social anthropology and language', in E. Ardener (ed), *Social Anthropology and Language*, Association of Social Anthropologists Monograph no 10 (London: Tavistock, 1971). Eric Hobsbawm, 'Introduction: inventing traditions', in E. Hobsbawm and Terence Ranger, *The Invention of Tradition* (Cambridge: Cambridge University Press, 1983).

[33] See Johnson, *op cit*, on earlier nationalist uses of the idea of Islam.

community

The photos in this section are by David Bate.

National Identity and Socialist Moral Majority

Renata Salecl

The present outbursts of nationalism in East European socialist countries are a reaction to the fact that long years of (Communist) Party rule, by destroying the traditional fabric of society, have dismantled most traditional points of social identification, so that when people now attempt to distance themselves from the official ideological universe, the only positive reference point at their disposal to their national identity. In the new struggles for ideological hegemony, national identification is used by the opposition as well as by the old Party forces. On the one hand, national identity serves as a support for the formation of a specific version of the 'moral majority' (in Poland, Slovenia and Croatia, etc.) which conceives Christian values as the ideological 'cement' holding together the Nation, demands the prohibition of abortion and other regressive measures; on the other hand, the Communist party in some countries (Serbia, for example) has assumed an authoritarian populist-nationalist discourse, this producing a specific mixture of orthodox Communist elements and elements usually associated with fascism (violent mass movements structured around a charismatic leader and directed towards an external-internal enemy, etc.).

The use of psychoanalysis to analyse these developments enables us to avoid simple condemnations of nationalism, as well as the false solution of its division into 'good' (progressive, anti-imperialist ...) versus 'bad' (chauvinist, colonizing ...) elements; it enables us to conceive the nation as something that 'always returns' as the traumatic element around which fantasies are interlaced[1], and thus to articulate the fantasy structure which serves as a support for ethnic hatred. Both nationalist movements – the opposition moral majorities and the authoritarian-populist Communist parties – have built their power by creating specific fantasies of a threat to the nation and so put themselves forward as the protector of 'what is in us more than ourselves' – our being a part of the nation.

It is first necessary to emphasize that with all nationalism, national identification with 'our kind' is based on the fantasy of an enemy, an alien who has insinuated himself into our society and constantly threatens us with habits, discourse and rituals which are not 'our kind'. No matter what this Other 'does', his very existence is perceived as threatening. The fantasy of how the Other lives on our account, is lazy, exploits us etc. is repeatedly recreated in accordance with our desire. For example, there is the criticism that immigrants are lazy, lacking in the work habit, etc. with the simultaneous accusation that they steal our jobs. The Other who works enthusiastically is especially dangerous – it is only his way of deceiving us and becoming incorporated into 'our' community. Similarly with their assimilation: they are usually accused of retaining their strange habits, of being uncivilized, etc. If however they adopt our customs, then we assume that they want to steal 'our thing' – the nation.

We are disturbed precisely by the fact that the Other *is* Other and that he has his own customs, by which we feel threatened. As Jacques Alain Miller says, hatred of the Other is hatred of the Other's enjoyment, of the particular way the Other enjoys. For example, when Germans are irritated by Turkish workers eating garlic, or when the English find unbeartable the way blacks enjoy themselves, what they are identifying is the threat of the Other not finding enjoyment in the same way as we do.

'I am willing to see my neighbour in the Other but only on condition that he is not my neighbour. I am prepared to love him as myself only if he is far away, if he is removed.... When the Other comes too near, when it mingles with you, as Lacan says, new fantasies emerge which concern above all the surplus of enjoyment with the Other.

What is at stake is of course the imputation of an excessive enjoyment. Something of that kind could consist, for example, in the fact that we ascribe to the Other an enjoyment in money exceeding every limit. The question of tolerance or intolerance is not at all concerned with the subject of science and its human rights. It is located on the level of tolerance or intolerance toward the enjoyment of the Other, the Other as he who essentially steals my own enjoyment.... When we are considering whether the Other will have to abandon his language, his convictions, his way of dressing and talking, we would actually like to know the extent to which he is willing to abandon or not abandon his Other enjoyment.[2]

The conservative English writer John Casey says of West Indians: 'they simply cannot form part of "our" group or belong to "our" kind, for their behaviour outrages "our" sense of what English life should be like and how the English should behave towards a duly constituted authority.'[3] The Other outrages our sense of the kind of nation ours should be in so far as s/he steals our enjoyment – to which we must add that this Other is always an Other in my interior, i.e. that my hatred of the Other is really the hatred of the part (the surplus) of *my own* enjoyment which I find unbearable and cannot acknowledge, and which I therefore transpose ('project') into the Other *via* a fantasy of the 'Other's enjoyment'.

Before the disintegration of really existing socialism, democracy was popularly conceived as a charge which would explode when the lid of Communist party terror was lifted. Today the countries of Eastern Europe are confronted with nationalist conflict, anti-semitism, anti-feminism and fascist populist movements. It appears that the present free nations of Eastern Europe in some way don't want to enjoy freedom: as if some kind of internal blockade obstructs their path to democracy, as if they are afraid to confront the fact that democracy (democratic freedom) is no more than a *form* and does not immediately procure positive material welfare. It is for this reason that they are forced – at the very moment of acquiring their long-desired freedom – to invent again and again a figure of an Enemy which prevents them enjoying 'effective freedom' (i.e. the welfare associated with the notion of 'western democracy'). Here, of course, we find a precise demonstration of hatred of one's own enjoyment. – the fact that the nations of Eastern Europe are seeking new enemies, obsessively reviving old national hatreds, demonstrates quite clearly that the Other is always the Other within us and that hatred of the Other is in the final analysis hatred of one's own enjoyment. Intolerance of Others' pleasure, whether Jews, immigrants or even members of the same nation, bureaucrats, for example, produces the fantasies by which members of particular nations organize their own enjoyment.

Serbian authoritarian populism, for example, has produced an entire mythology of the fight against internal and external enemies. The first enemies are Albanians who are perceived as threatening to cut off the Serbian autonomous province of Kosovo, and thus to steal Serbian land and culture. The second enemy is an alienated bureaucracy which threatens the power of the people: alienated from within. Both images of the enemy are based on specific fantasies. In Serbian mythology, the Albanians are understood as pure Evil, unimaginable, subjects who cannot be subjectivized – made people from – because they are so radically Other. The Albanian population is constantly presented as immigrant, although immigration took place in the Middle Ages and the Albanians are arguably the successors of much earlier Illyrian inhabitants of the region. The Serbs describe their conflict with the Albanians as a fight of 'people with non-people'. The only exception to the rule is the 'honest Albanian' who accepts the Serbian view and is held up as an example of one who had broken with his natural national environment – unlike the 'dishonest Albanian', who, in contrast with his 'honest' counterpart, appears all the more clearly 'Other'. Lacan says that jealousy as a pathological condition has nothing to do with real causes: my wife can deceive me, all my forebodings can be more than legitimate, but my jealousy is, nevertheless, no less pathological. We can thus say that the very real Albanian pressure on the Serbs in Kosovo does not legitimize the way that the Serbs react to it, the form in which they have made monsters of their opponents. The Serbs do not even begin to allow the Albanians a public voice – to appear as political subjects, thus making democratic dialogue possible.

The second enemy – the bureaucrat – is presented as a non-Serb, as a traitor to his own nation and as effeminate. The revolt against the bureaucracy doesn't take place because of its actual economic errors but because of its estrangement from tradition, its primarily spiritual, rather than material, betrayal of the people.

Both enemies are portrayed, importantly, as impotent. Just as English conservatives describe the danger to Britain from immigrants, especially blacks, as 'the rape of the English race' so the Serbs portray Albanians as rapists of the Serbian nation, as those who steal Serbian national identity, imposing their own culture. However, this figurative picture of rape is reinforced by the Serbs with stories of supposed actual attempts at the rape of Serbian girls by Albanians. What is important here is that it is always only attempted rape. A picture of the enemy is created, an Albanian who tries to rape Serbian girls but is actually unable to do so. This fantasy is based on portraying the enemy's impotence – the enemy tries to attack, to rape, but is confounded, is impotent, in absolute contrast to the heroic Serb.

The mythology of the new Serbian populism constantly stresses the difference between real men – workers, men of the people – and bureaucrats – effeminates. The bureaucrat in this mythology is portrayed as a middle-class feudal master, a kid-gloved capitalist with top hat and tie, 'clean outside and dirty within', in real contrast to the worker, the man of the nation, 'dirty on the outside but pure within'.[4] The essence of the argument is that the bureaucrat is not a real man – he is effeminate, slug-like, fat, drinking whiskey and eating pineapples – as opposed to the macho worker who eats traditional national food and dresses in worker's dungarees or national costume. Bureaucrats are not men because of their alienation from tradition and their betrayal of the heroic Serbian people.

To demonstrate its link to the nation, Serbian populism uses the dead bodies of national heroes. In the new Serbian populist mythology, those who are fighting today for Serbian sovereignty are constantly compared to the Serbian heroes who fought the Turks six hundred years ago.[5] Bones have a special role in this heroic identification with Serbian history. Serbian populism has rediscovered the old Orthodox custom by which the mortal remains of a ruler were carried through all the monasteries of the country before burial. The restoration of real Serbian identity was thus confirmed in 1989 by the transfer to Kosovo after more than six hundred years, of the bones of the famous Serbian hero King Lazar, who had been killed in battle with the Turks. The old Orthodox ritual of carrying the bones around the monasteries designated the new birth of the symbolic community. The bones can be seen here in Lacanian terms as the Real, that 'something more' which designates the symbolic community of the Serbian nation – the national thing comes out precisely in the bones. So Lazar's bones are the Real which has returned to its place – his return to Kosovo is symbolic confirmation that Kosovo has always been the cradle of 'that which is Serbian'.

As Lacan says, race is established in the way in which a particular discourse preserves the symbolic order. The same can also be said of national community – in the case of Serbia, the ridiculous ritual of transferring bones also functions in preserving the symbolic order. On the rational level, it involves only a pile of trivial bones, which may or may not be the king's, which may have some archaeological or anthropological value but which act in the symbolic community of society as a little piece of the Real. In the case of Serbia, the bones also represent what the enemy has always wanted to deprive us of, that which we must guard with special care. The national conflict between the Serbs and the Albanians, as well as that between Serbs and Macedonians has always used the symbolism of stealing bones from Serbian graves. A mythology has even been created by which Albanians are supposed to dig up the graves of Serbian children, and Macedonians are supposed to have used the bones of Serbian soldiers who fell in the First World War for anatomical studies in their medical faculties.

Intolerance of the Other's enjoyment, linked as it is to national identification, is also connected to the fantasies put into circulation by the newly created socialist moral majority in the countries of Eastern Europe. The socialist moral majority cannot be said to have the same significance as in the west. In view of its structural role, the moral majority in socialism is democratic and anti-totalitarian – its voice is an oppositional one. Moral revolt against a real socialist regime predominates in its criticism of the authorities. It thus articulates a distinction between civil society (in the name of which it speaks) and the totalitarian state, as a distinction between morality and corruption. A return to Christian values, the family, the 'right to life' etc. is presented as a rebellion against immoral real socialist authority which, in the name of the concept of communism, permits all sorts of state intervention into the privacy of the citizen.

Paradoxically, the moral majority in the east, in spite of its oppositional role, is comparatively more socialist than conservative in relation to its western counterpart. Where the latter is characterized by an anti-socialist market ideology in which each person answers first for himself and the state is not the guardian of his well-being, the new socialist moral majority, in the name of an organic national ideology, reforges a link with the socialist heritage. When it calls for the reinforcement of national affiliation and Christian values, it simultaneously stresses that we must not surrender to soulless capitalism, that we must create a state-supported national programme, etc.

The difference between western and socialist moral majorities can also be seen in their different perspectives on the problem of abortion.

First, we must point out that in Yugoslavia, as well as in the majority of other Eastern European countries (with the exception of countries practising extreme forms of nationalistic Communism, such as Ceaucescu's Romania), abortion is legalized and within easy reach of every woman; indeed often, it has been the only available form of contraception. It was the catholic-nationalist opposition that first raised the question of its restriction; but it did so in terms unfamiliar in western anti-abortion movements. The traditional 'moral majority', as known in western countries, does not oppose abortion on the grounds of the threat it poses to the nation, but in the name of the Christian values of santity of life, the sacred significance of conception, etc., from which it derives the thesis that abortion is murder. Objections to abortion from the moral majority in Slovenia and in Croatia are connected with their thesis of the threat it poses to the nation. The linkage of images of abortion as a crime against humanity to the image of a threat to the nation produces an ideology by which support for Slovenes or Croats becomes synonymous with opposition to abortion. When the Croatian opposition writes that 'a foetus is also a Croatian' it clearly demonstrates that any opinion about abortion will also be an opinion about the future of the nation. The production of these kinds of fantasies of a national threat must of course be seen in terms of the political struggle they engender. The strategy is to transfer the political threat of totalitarianism into a national menace which can only be averted by an increase in the birthrate – in other words, by limiting the right to abortion. This produces the hypothesis that to be a good Slovene or a good Croat means primarily to be a good Christian, since the national menace can only be averted by Christian morals.

In the ideology of national threat, women are simultaneously pronounced culprit and victim. The strongest opposition party in Croatia, the Croatian Democratic Community (which won the elections), has gone so far in this that it has publicly blamed the tragedy of the Croation nation on women, pornography and abortion. 'This trinity murders, or rather hinders, the birth of little Croats, that "sacred thing which God has given society and the homeland".'[6] The Croatian moral majority regards women who have not borne at least four children, not as women, but as 'female exhibitionists', since they have not fulfilled 'their unique sacred duty'. Women who, for whatever reason, decide on abortion have been proclaimed murderers and mortal enemies of the nation, while gynaecologists who have assisted them in this murderous act are pronounced butchers.

Women, then, are pronounced guilty; yet at the same time, they are depicted as victims of overly liberal abortion laws. Ideologists of the socialist moral majority take as their starting point the notion that a free decision about how many children a person will have is an inalienable human right, and that society is obliged to maintain population policies which enable them to have the desired number of children. They believe therefore that a state which prioritizes the right to abortion is refusing its citizens access to this second inalienable right – that of having the desired number of children. Here the real victims, in their opinion, are women.

> To insist only on free abortion ... means not only disregarding medical, ethical, religious, demographic, national and parent-human reasons, as well as the feelings of individuals, but also transforming women into victims, sacrificing their health, spiritual peace and material feelings, allowing them to be subjected to mortal danger in order to satisfy the instincts and demands of others. Essentially, it involves seeing women only as a resource which man can use and abuse, who is irresponsibly fertilized and then allowed to be subjected to bodily and spiritual maltreatment. The interruption of conception, the violent removal of a child from a woman's body and heart, amounts to a suppression of her ethical and religious beliefs and her maternal feelings, and a violation of her conscience.[7]

This fantasy of the woman victim is based on the hypothesis that the woman's wish and the desire of the nation are one – to give birth. If a woman is defined by maternity then abortion is an attack on her very essence; yet it is also an attack on the essence of the nation, since the national community, according to this ideology, is defined by the national maternal wish for expansion.

The arguments of ideologists of national threat have the same logic as Ceaucescu's answer to one journalist's question as to whether the ban on Romanians travelling abroad was not a violation of human rights. Ceaucescu's answer was: Since the most important human right is to be able to live in one's own country, the ban on travelling abroad simply guarantees this right. So, too, the ideologists of national threat represent their desire to limit the right to free abortion as simply reinforcing the human right to have the desired number of children. Just as Ceaucescu 'helped' people not to violate the right of living in their own country and not to suppress their deepest desire by banning them from travelling abroad, so the ideologists of the new moral majority protect human, national and maternal feelings. If for Communists, the capitalist and 'bourgeois' right are those who steal their enjoyment, then for the ideologists of national threat, these are women. For them, woman is an enemy in so far as her enjoyment threatens 'our kind'.

The meeting point of the two ideologies presented – official 'authoritarian populism' and the oppositional ideology of the national moral majority – can be located in their common offer of a collective fantasy whose message reads, between the lines, 'we are the sole defenders of the nation'. A real democratic transformation in the countries of socialism can only be expected when the driving force becomes the motto 'to each his/her fantasy'. This does not mean a refusal to admit national identity, only the removal of the Subject presented as the nation's only protector – as the only one who acts in the name of 'our kind'.

NOTES

[1] See Jacques Lacan, *The Four Fundamental Concepts of Psycho-Analysis* (Harmondsworth: Penguin Books 1979).

[2] Jacques-Alain Miller: Unpublished seminar 1985-86 – *Extimite*.

[3] Bhikhu Parekh: 'The "New Right" and the Politics of Nationhood', in *The New Right* (London: The Runnymede Trust 1986), 36.

[4] Ivo Zanic, 'Bukvar "antibirokratske revolucije" ', *Start*, 30.9.1989.

[5] The Battle of Kosovo, where in 1389 the Serbs lost a battle with the Turks has become the source of a whole series of associations in the contemporary struggle of the Serbian nation with the Albanians; the Serbian leader Milošević, for example, is compared to the former hero Obilič, the Albanian leader Vllasi with the hated Turkish sultan Murat. Symbolic identification with the place popular heroes have in Serbian mythology has given the new leadership a special position: not only have they been given an aura of sanctity as folk heroes, they have also been enabled to repair the historical damage which occurred with the loss of the battle of Kosovo. The discourse of the anti-bureaucratic revolution returned to the time of the Turkish struggle in so far as it wanted to stress that Milošević's warriors are the only ones who can end the six-hundred-year vasselage of the Serbian nation.

[6] *Dnevnik*, Ljubljana, 26.2.1990.
Ante Vukasovic: 'Zavaravanje zena', *Danas*, Zagreb, 27.3.1990.

Islands of Enchantment
Extracts from a Caribbean Travel Diary

Peter Hulme

What explains our constant literary evocation of Indian and indigenous themes? Is it just an echo of romanticism? No. In fact we are secretly moved by the sacrifice of those who were our last truly free countrymen. Our Indianist yearns show a nostalgia for freedom.
(Juan Antonio Corretjer, *Yerba bruja* (San Juan: 1970), pp10-11

I never find it easy to explain my fascination with the Caribbean, and in particular the arcane interest I have in its pre-Columbian history. Hardly an obvious research topic for a teacher of literature. My recent visit, between September 1986 and January 1987, had a reputable academic purpose – to research the background to the Caribbean Amerindian artefacts held in British museums, with a view to mounting an exhibition. But this wasn't enough to justify four months away from home. There had to be a different kind of journey involved, one which would aim to understand the pertinence of the Amerindian past to a Caribbean present in no need of antiquarianism; and would at the same time reveal something to me about my own motivations. I thought a diary might help. What follows is not a simple transcription of the journal I kept but a rearrangement, a construct, a fiction of a diary if you like; but one which I hope retains an openness so structurally absent from the kind of academic paper I'm more used to writing. Perhaps this will make it easier for people to respond to it.

I'm not sure that a diary did help me understand, it's probably too early to say. But when I first came across Corretjer's words in the library of the University of Puerto Rico I felt 'secretly moved' by them, felt they were telling me something, making a connection, although there was no way in which his 'our' could include me, a white English academic. I would like to think that, depite the differences, there is some kind of analogy at work, possibly one as banal, if vital, as that we are all struggling against the same imperialism.

*   *   *

KINGSTON, JAMAICA (5.ix.86)

In England 'research' usually involved London's Liverpool Street station and Holborn tube on the way to the British Library, so it's mildly ironic that my first stop in Jamaica should be the Indies Hotel in *Holborn* Road. Maps are often a good starting-point, at least for understanding official symbolization. In post-colonial Algiers it's difficult to follow the topography of Camus's novels and essays because most of the street-names were changed after the revolution. Here the imperial past is still present on the map: the name Kingston itself, of course, but, more evocatively still, the street-names: Piccadilly Road, Victoria Street, Vauxhall Avenue, Chelsea Close, Trafalgar Road. However, since independence there has obviously also been an official attempt to create a more 'authentically' Jamaican symbology. There is now a pantheon of national heroes, each with their statue in the National Heroes Park. Their faces are on the banknotes and their names added to the street-map: Marcus Garvey Drive, Bustamante Highway, Norman Manley Highway. But what interests me in particular is the resonance of the most central name of all – Jamaica itself. The word is the Hispanic form of the indigenous – Arawakan – name for the island, possibly meaning land of wood and water. For reasons I've never properly understood, Columbus's attempted redesignation of Jamaica as Santiago never took, and the island retained its native name. But does that native name have any symbolic import today? Is it a significant feature of Jamaica's contemporary image of itself ...?

*   *   *

The Jamaica National Heritage Trust has chosen Diego Pimienta as an appropriate symbol to denote guardianship of the nation's heritage. It is also one way to keep alive the bright glimpse of an early Jamaican of humble status, who fought courageously in defence of his country.
(Jamaica National Heritage Trust official booklet)

* * *

Jamaica's new national motto is 'Out of many, one people', stressing its heterogeneity of origin and of histories. The sentiment is impeccable. The official guardian of those histories, the National Heritage Trust (founded in 1958), chose for its coat-of-arms the figure of Diego Pimienta, an African who fought for his Spanish masters against the English invasion of the island in 1655. It's a subtle choice, evoking, if not an origin, then a relatively early moment in the island's recent history when the three cultures – Spanish, African, English – were brought together. Admittedly in hostile fashion, but three hundred years have passed and the national monument at the scene of the battle is pointedly dedicated to *all* who died there. (Nevertheless it is clearly a bonus, though not overplayed, that 'an early Jamaican' who was black was defending *his* territory against the invading English.) The dominant cultural note is one of reconciliation. The current heritage project focuses on those sites – New Seville, Port Royal, Spanish Town – where the component cultures overlap, either through historically documented contact, or archaeologically in the middens

Diego Pimienta – Guardian. Emblem
of the Jamaican National Heritage Trust.

and cemeteries that have been discovered in recent years. The mid-seventeenth century has become the focus for the construction of a national heritage.

Where though does this leave the Arawaks? Clearly on the margins of the national story. By the seventeenth century the Amerindian population of Jamaica had completely disappeared, exterminated by European weaponry and disease. Yet the archaeological excavations inevitably find Arawak remains, in part it seems because the Spanish built their settlements where the Arawak towns had stood. This is not exactly an embarrassment; the Arawak presence is given full due at the White Marl museum, the site of major Arawak finds. But there is some difficulty in knowing how to integrate an undeniable part of the Jamaican past – its first known inhabitants, after all, and the originators of its name – with the subsequent components, the two most important of which, African and English, had little known contact with the Jamaican Arawaks. The National Heritage booklet falls back, properly enough in the circumstances, on the importance to the Jamaican diet of foodstuffs – like cassava, pineapple, or guava – originally developed by the native cultures.

✳   ✳   ✳

KINGSTON (8.ix.86)

Meet with the director of the JNHT who tells me about the attempt a few years ago to change the old imperial coat-of-arms of Jamaica – which features two Arawaks.

✳   ✳   ✳

KINGSTON (9.ix.86)

Emerge from the library of the Institute of Jamaica badly in need of refreshment after reading through six months' editions of *The Daily Gleaner*. The native culture may not feature too prominently in Jamaican national life, but in the summer and autumn of 1983 it was at the heart of an extraordinary outburst of public fury over Prime Minister Edward Seaga's attempts to pension off the Arawaks – along with the alligator and the pineapple – as irrelevant. Tomorrow to the library at Government House to check out the parliamentary debate in the Jamaica Hansard.

✳   ✳   ✳

The coat-of-arms of Jamaica.

Can the crushed and extinct Arawaks represent the dauntless character of Jamaicans? Does the low-slung, near extinct crocodile, a cold-blooded reptile, symbolize the warm soaring spirit of Jamaicans? Where does the pineapple which was exported to Hawaii, appear prominently either in our history or in folklore?
(Edward Seaga, *Jamaica Hansard*, n.s., vol 9,
no 1 (1983-4), p363)

What would be relevant, Morris Cargill asked in the lead article of The Daily Gleaner *(5 August 1983): 'What about a design containing entwined marijuana plants against a background of US dollar bills, with Toyotas rampant and ladies couchant?'*

*　*　*

115

Seaga had announced in parliament, without a hint of irony, that he'd given the National Heritage Trust the task of organizing a competition to find a new coat-of-arms more 'relevant' to contemporary Jamaica. A creative use of the notion of 'heritage': to find a modern replacement for something which in all its essentials dates back to 1660. Obviously to his complete surprise the idea caused an extraordinary public outcry. There was a constant stream of letters to the newspapers, and the competition was eventually sabotaged by a well-organized campaign to send in the *existing* coat-of-arms with an extended justification for its importance. It was a strange and galling defeat for Seaga to suffer. He is, after all, a Harvard-trained anthropologist with a reputation for being able to manipulate popular culture to his political advantage, as with the recent returning of the body of Marcus Garvey to Jamaica. In the end, though, luck was on his side and he managed to drop the whole idea quietly when the murder of Maurice Bishop turned everyone's attention elsewhere. So Jamaica still has its two Arawaks.

✳ ✳ ✳

April 11, 1799. Isaac Alves Rebello, Esq.,
F.A.S., exhibited to the Society three figures,
supposed to be of Indian Deities, in wood, found
in June 1792, in a natural cave near the summit
of a mountain, called Spots, in Carpenter's
Mountains, in the parish of Vere, in the island of
Jamaica, by a surveyor measuring the land.
They were discovered placed with their faces (one
of which is that of a bird) towards the east.

(*Archaeologia*, vol 14 (1803), p269)

✳ ✳ ✳

PORT ROYAL, JAMAICA (22.ix.86)

The last three days have been hectic. I hired a car to travel round the island but didn't see much because of constant tropical storms. Then yesterday I went on the first real 'expedition' of the trip, in the savanna to the west of Kingston, with two new acquaintances from the Jamaican Archaeological Society. The aim was to locate the cave where

116

Arawakan wooden figure (Jamaica, c. 15th century).

several of the most spectacular pieces of Caribbean wood-carving were found in 1792, having presumably been hidden by their Amerindian owners in the early part of the seventeenth century. We drove as far as we could and then, in time-honoured manner, asked the oldest people we could see if they knew of Spots Mountain. Nobody did, but two men, one of them about seventy, offered to guide us to a series of caves. The trek through the bush was exhausting – and ultimately fruitless – but deeply exhilarating. Towards the end, all uphill, we had to rest frequently. The guides trotted off into the surrounding trees

117

and emerged with guineps and sweetsops to refresh us. I had this strange sensation of having been compelled by the circumstances to act out a whole series of pre-ordained moves, as if troped by the conventions of ethnography. Yet the atmosphere was relaxed. Perhaps the guides were acting out their roles too, just a little more effortlessly than I was. The last move – the payment – was the most difficult. I asked George, a long-time Jamaica resident, how much to pay the guides, and added 50 per cent to make sure. The traveller needs to be reassured by the smile of gratitude.

＊　＊　＊

Three weeks away from England now, and the strange rhythms of solitary travel are beginning to assert themselves. New friendships are intensely experienced, but the evenings can be lonely. I escape into the labyrinths of Conrad's *Chance*.

＊　＊　＊

SANTO DOMINGO, DOMINICAN REPUBLIC (27.ix.86)

The consciousness of an indigenous past is inscribed much more fully in the topography of Santo Domingo. The street-names again give an immediate impression: Guarionex, Caonabo, Anacaona, all the heroes of the Amerindian resistance are there. And a glance at the telephone directory shows that the names survive as names despite the usual Catholic resistance to anything other than saints' names. Here, too, there is a fine national museum – the Museo del Hombre Dominicano – more than half of which is given over to the indigenous Taino culture.

The higher Amerindian profile in the national consciousness clearly has historical roots. Dominican independence goes back to the nineteenth century and has a famous national novel, Galván's *Enriquillo*, which takes an Amerindian as symbol of the new nation. And from at least the early 1960s extensive professional archaeological work has revealed the island as a rich source of indigenous material, bringing into clearer focus a culture (the Taino) known from the early Spanish accounts as the most ceremonially and politically complex in the Caribbean.

As with Jamaica, though, the political thrust is towards synthesis. Outside the Museo del Hombre Dominicano the statues of Enriquillo and the African Lemba (leader of a slave revolt) stand on either side of

118

Statue of Enriquillo, Museo del Hombre Dominicano, Santo Domingo, Dominican Republic. Photograph: Peter Hulme.

Coat-of-arms of the Institute of Puerto Rican Culture.

– and slightly behind – the emblematic figure of Bartolomé de Las Casas, the 'good' Spaniard who can represent a supposed national synthesis between the different cultures. Behind this bland official history lies the recurrent problem of a divided island. It's difficult to avoid the suspicion that Dominicans welcome the sobriquet 'Indian' as a way of avoiding the term 'black': only Haitians are black.

*   *   *

RÌO PIEDRAS, PUERTO RICO (15.x.86)

First impressions of Puerto Rico suggest a surprising similarity with Jamaica. There is an *official* tripartite synthesis: the stamp of the Institute of Puerto Rican culture shows a black and an Amerindian flanking a Spaniard holding a copy of Nebrija's grammar. But unlike the use of Diego Pimienta in Jamaica there is no suggestion of conflict here – it's just as if the three had combined quite happily over the centuries to produce '*cultura puertorriqueña*'. But the official picture is under critique. As in Jamaica the early period of colonization (here the late fifteenth and the sixteenth centuries) is the subject of intensive historical investigation and, as in the Jamaican case, the topic is fraught with political reverberations. There is, to be sure, an older and more polite interest in Amerindians – part of that *indigenismo* which has always sat comfortably with a deeply conservative *hispanismo*; but the contemporary wave of interest is very different. In a country that has never, since 1493, been independent – but which has a large portion of its intelligentsia sympathetic to the *idea* of independence – the return

120

Poster for archaeological exhibition about Vieques, held at the museum of the University of Puerto Rico, March-April 1983.

to the *origins* of colonization is a return to the roots of conflict and ethnocide, which cannot help but disturb the equanimity both of the conservatives with their official, basically Hispanic, culture, and of the modernizers who want accommodation with the colonial successors from the north. Then again there are hints that the conventional picture of the development of Amerindian culture before 1492, which owes much to the work of US archaeologists and anthropologists, is on the point of radical revision, one of the grounds being the implicitly neo-colonialist bases of that conventional map, its diffusionism serving to suggest that the Caribbean always *receives* culture, never produces it.

※　※　※

RÍO PIEDRAS (24.xi.86)

I spend the weekend on Vieques, the small and spectacularly beautiful island of the eastern coast of Puerto Rico. Several thousand *viequenses* were displaced overnight in the 1940s to allow Vieques to become part of the massive naval facility that would accommodate the British fleet and the royal family should Hitler successfully invade England. The Atlantic Fleet Weapons Training Facility, as it is now called, offers strategic protection for the shipping lanes to and from the deep-water harbours on the south coast of the USA; and is a military training environment of unparalleled importance. Vieques was the place where the marines trained for the invasion of Grenada during Ocean Venture 81, the largest naval manoeuvres conducted by western forces during peacetime since the Second World War. This involves a totally hypothetical invasion of a Caribbean country called Amber and the Amberines, which of course bore no necessary relation to Grenada and the Grenadines. The US navy owns 70 per cent of the island and uses much of it for target practice, thereby provoking a good deal of local protest, both from the fishermen whose livelihood is destroyed, and from the *independentista* parties who can use Vieques as a symbol round which to gather support for their anti-imperialist policies. The navy admits that it's only able to get away with using Vieques in this way because local protests will have no repercussions in Congress, where Puerto Rico has no representation. So – whatever their positive attitude to the USA in other matters – all Puerto Ricans are outraged that the navy treats them, who are citizens of the USA, in a way that it wouldn't dream of treating citizens of the mainland.

122

However, Puerto Rican archaeological work carried out on the island of Vieques has been at the forefront of the possible revision of pre-Columbian Caribbean archaeology, and has provided, in the form of one of its most fascinating finds, a series of beautiful jade and serpentine birds, which have become a potent symbol of *viequense* indentity to set against the island's only other claim to anyone's notice. symbolically, this condor has come to represent a heritage which is literally covered by the buildings and weaponry of an occupying force. A centuries-old pendant, often proudly inscribed on the T-shirts made by local artisans, shows the continuing power of Caribbean Amerindian artefacts in the changed circumstances of political struggle.

※　　※　　※

A cinema advert opens with a young white couple completing a tracing of a pre-Columbian rock carving at the extraordinarily atmospheric ceremonial centre near Utuado in the central cordillera of Puerto Rico. A romantic voice begins to sing:
'Andando por nuestra tierra, buscando por lo que somos'
('Travelling through our land, trying to find out who we are').
They visit some older friends, possibly parents, have lunch, and head off home. The key word of the advert is 'nuestro'. *They enjoy* our *things: the native heritage, the countryside, the food, the rum, the coffee. They are joined by the last element in the partnership (as the couple stand, smoking, on the deck of the Vieques ferry) – ('Winston and Puerto Rico, nothing but the best').*

※　　※　　※

BRIDGETOWN, BARBADOS (5.xii.86)

An exhausting day. Having spent much of the previous three months *reading* archaeology I'm finally roped in to doing some digging. Living in Colchester I've become used to pre-construction archaeology: a site is cleared preparatory to some new shopping complex being built, and the archaeologists move in, sometimes for several months. In Puerto Rico there was a good deal of unease about this. Under federal law any construction even partly funded by federal finance has to employ an archaeologist, but it is suspected that 'private' arachaeologists can be paid to find nothing, thereby facilitating rapid construction. In the

Waitukubuli Karifuna Development Centre, Salybia, Dominica.
Photograph: Peter Hulme.

smaller islands there are no professional archaeologists to interfere with building programmes. Occasionally enthusiastic amateurs follow the bulldozers, finding masses of material, mostly pre-Columbian, but obviously outside any stratigraphic context. Here in Barbados a Peace Corps workers, trained in archaeology, was digging in an old suburban garden, soon to become a supermarket warehouse, and had found a pre-Columbian burial. This had stirred considered public interest and the removal of the bones had been filmed by the local television station. Teams of volunteers were now digging and sifting the surrounding areas in the hope of further finds.

※   ※   ※

The Caribs were a restless and migratory race,
often moving from island to island, and when
evicted by Europeans prone to return with their
friends in unexpected force. This mobility,
coupled with their secret and treacherous
mentality, rendered them a formidable obstacle to

the early settlers, and the ultimate solution of the
problem was provided only by a war of extermination.
(James Williamson, *The Caribbee Islands under*
the Proprietary Patents (Oxford: 1926), p4)

ROSEAU, DOMINICA (4.i.87)

Although most history books blithely assert that the native societies of
the Caribbean were utterly destroyed at the very beginning of the
European incursion, the Carib Territory in north-eastern Dominica
continues to survive and, relatively speaking, to prosper. The Caribs in
fact fought a long and bitter series of wars against the European
invaders, principally the English. Their final military defeat came only
in 1797 in St Vincent, from where several thousand of the so-called
Black Caribs were forcibly removed to Central America. The
Dominica Caribs, protected by their mountainous terrain from the
land-hungry sugar-planters, survived in relatively small numbers,
though gradually lost their language. A cultural revival now seems well
under way. A community centre has been built in the form of the

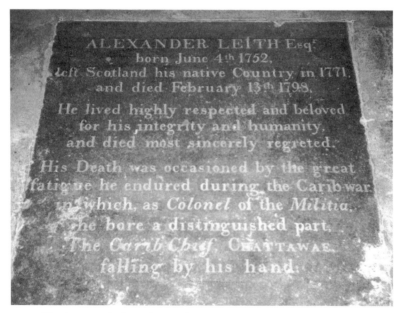

Tombstone of Alexander Leith, Kingstown Cathedral, St Vincent.
Photograph: Peter Hulme.

traditional carbet or long-house. A dance company flourishes (it visited London last year). And attempts are being made to relearn the language, at least for symbolic use in ceremonial and cultural events. Politically, too, the community seems active, trying to resolve a long-standing dispute with the Dominica government over the exact boundaries of its territory (within which all land is owned *by the community:* there is no private property), and – momentous news, this – organizing a conference with their confrères in St Vincent and Belize, the first time in two hundred years that the three surviving Carib communities of the Caribbean will have met.

A courtesy visit to the chief turns into an extended discussion of the boundary question. I promise to try to look out some of the old maps in the Public Record Office. The rest of my time on the territory is taken up with visits to two of the extended families who keep alive the tradition of basket-making which, as far as can be judged, has not altered significantly over the last five hundred years. The Horniman Museum in south London has asked me to collect West Indian material, so I buy a good number of the baskets.

※　※　※

KINGSTOWN, ST VINCENT (9.i.87)

A journey that began in Kingston ends in Kingstown. (The poverty of official toponymy must have led to constant confusion during the colonial period.) St Vincent is almost a microcosm of the cultural complexity of the Caribbean: African, English, Scottish, East Indian, Portuguese, Syrian – and, with their main communities tucked away in the north-east of the island at the end of an atrocious road, Caribs; the remnants of the indigenous population which, after more than two centuries of deculturation, is beginning to rediscover its cultural heritage and its place in Vincentian (and British imperial) history. A recent campaign has been pushing for St Vincent to emulate Jamaica by instituting a series of national heroes, the first one of whom would be Chatoyer, the Black Carib chief killed leading his people in the final indigenous war fought in the Caribbean, a war won by the British only after a prodigious outlay of money and lives. One of the key factors in the last Carib war has always been said to be the hand-to-hand combat between Chatoyer and a British officer, Alexander Leith. Leith's tombstone in Kingstown cathedral tells the official story; but on the two-hundredth anniversary of his death the Vincentians unveiled a

126

Fort Charlotte, Kingstown, St Vincent. Photograph: Peter Hulme.

monument to Chatoyer, with a plaque which reads 'Joseph Chatoyer, Black Carib Chief, For Freedom, Died Here, 14th March 1795'. Some of the money for the monument was provided by the Venezuelan government, to the reported displeasure of the British High Commissioner. I spend my last afternoon at Fort Charlotte, an impressive military bastion commanding Kingstown harbour, but whose guns still point *inland* in commemoration of the Carib threat.

NOTE

The title of this article is meant to allude to *The Tempest* but also, less familiarly, to *Yerba bruja* ('Enchanted grass'), a book of indigenist poems by the Puerto Rican writer and socialist Juan Antonio Corretjer (1900-85). Corretjer's preface to *Yerba bruja* begins with a quotation from a botanical treatise explaining that yerba bruja 'survives almost all attempts at eradication.... Its common name refers to its capacity to resist the harshest treatments.'

My trip to the Caribbean was financed with the help of grants from the British Academy and the University of Essex Research Endowment Fund. Many people helped me during those four months. I'd like to mention Roderick Ebanks, Rosalie Smith McCrea, Petrine Archer, Gordon K. Lewis, Jalil Sued Badillo, Lowell Fiet, Luis Chanlatte Baik, Yvonne Narganes Storde, Ricardo Alegría, Shelley Smith, Steve Hackenberger, Alissandra Cummings, Raymond Lawrence, Lennox Honychurch, Garnette Joseph, Diana Loxley, Mitch Stuart, Desmond Nicholson, Earle Kirby. And especially Lesley Theophilus, who shared the last month.

Vectors of Memory ...
Seeds of Fire
The Western Media
and the Beijing Demonstrations

McKenzie Wark

The People have lost the confidence of the Government. The Government has decided to dissolve the People and appoint another one.

(Bertold Brecht)

Our basic goal, to build socialism, is correct, but we are still trying to figure out what socialism is and how to build it.

(Deng Xiaoping)

1 AT PRESENT TENSE

Dateline: Beijing, 27 May 1989. Things at present are tense: this is more than a demonstration by workers and students – it is a carnival. For a few intense, electric seconds, Beijing has become the only city on earth, oscillating in a thrall of political furies, a teeming slo-mo dance relayed via satellite around the globe. Beijing is 'on' and the whole world is watching. I write of these things in the present tense, for now that the spectacle of the Beijing demonstrations is recorded and relayed around the world, it will always take place in the present tense of media memory. Taut images from this wild scenario will now always be present, ready and waiting to be replayed, over and over. I try to capture some of the densely pixilated images that are present here and now, reeling between the lines.

Beijing student demonstrations sometimes take on the appearance of a global positive feedback loop: a few thousand students demonstrate at Tiananmen; foreign journalists report it; Voice of America radio relays that report and amplifies it, saying that hundreds of thousands of students demonstrated; students pick up the broadcast, and while many of them are suspicious of the American version of the event, it rings truer than the Chinese press reports, so it becomes a self-fulfilling prophecy. That, in a stylized form at least, is pretty much what happened in 1987, when the anniversary of the death of Zhou Enlai became the pretext for students to lay wreaths at the Monument to the People's Heroes in Tiananmen Square, and demonstrations snowballed vainly and bravely until the police stepped in. 'Even if these disturbances had been more widespread,' Deng Xiaoping told Noboru Takeshita shortly afterwards, 'they would have no effect on the foundations of our state or on the policies we have established.'[1]

That may be so. The powers ranged against the students are enormous. Yet in spite of all that, they have managed to turn the monumental power of Tiananmen Square and the moral force of communist ideology against itself, and to plug the staging of their demonstrations into the global media at a level unprecedented for a popular movement in the Chinese socialist state. This is a politics of 'détournement', of turning a space and an ideology against itself. It belongs to what Greil Marcus calls a secret history of modern times, enacted as what official history sublimates or excludes: the possibility of its own negation.[2]

2   THE PERSISTENCE OF MEMORY

Tiananmen Square is a sacred space, a holy space of mythic proportions, and to understand why it is the focus for so many demonstrations is to delve into the many layers of monumentality that are Beijing, one of the world's most ancient capitals. Despite movements towards reconstruction and deconstruction, despite all of the attempts by the Communist Party of China (CPC) to change their symbolic and quotidian functions, the basic grid of the city and the major sites of historical memory, in Aldo Rossi's term, 'persist'.[3]

The only way to describe Beijing for someone who has never seen it is to say that it looks like Brazilia, Washington, or Canberra – not as they appear now, but as they will look in one thousand years' time. The central axis of Beijing passes through the 'Forbidden City', formerly the palace of the emperor. To the north is an artificial hill, the only hill in this otherwise completely flat city. To the south of the walled Forbidden City lies Tiananmen Gate, and further south again Qianmen Gate, both of which formerly had a symbolic and processional function. Only the emperor entered the Forbidden City through these gates. There were other gates for other visitors: the northern gate, for example, was for military officers, as the north was the direction the barbarians came from. The Forbidden City is now a museum. The exterior of the palaces and temples has been 'restored'. Yet while the palace is no longer forbidden and has been opened to the public, the space immediately to the west of it, Zhongshan Park, has been closed and forms a new Forbidden City for the new rulers of the old empire. The CPC did not abandon the site of symbolic power, it moved in next door.

The space in front of Tiananmen Gate had become cluttered with shops and stalls, and these were all cleared away. A vast square was created between Tiananmen and Qianmen gates. On the east side of the square the Great Hall of the People was built, and on the west side a museum. Thus if one mounts the hill to the north of Forbidden City and looks to the south, one can see a symmetrical arrangement of the old imperial palace and the gates, with Zhongshan Park and the Great Hall just to the east of the axis, and the Workers' Cultural Palace and the museum to the west.

Simon Leys (also known as Pierre Ryckmans) wrote some devastating criticism of the CPC's architectural appropriation of Beijing.

> In Beijing stands one monument that more than any other is a dramatic symbol of the Maoist rape of the ancient capital: the Monument to the People's Heroes. This obelisk, more than a hundred feet high, the base of which is adorned with margarine bas-reliefs, would by itself be of no particular note if it were not for the privileged place it has, exactly in the centre of the vista from Qianmen Gate to Tiananmen Gate. A good sneeze, however resonant, is not remarked upon in the bustle of a busy railway station, but things are somewhat different if the same explosion occurs in a concert hall at just the most exquisite and magical point of a musical phrase. In the same way, this insignificant granitic phallus receives all its enormous significance from the blasphemous stupidity of its location. In erecting this monument in the centre of the sublime axis that reaches from Qianmen to Tiananmen, the designers' idea was, of course, to use to advantage the ancient imperial planning of that space, to take over to the monument's advantage that mystical current, which,

carried along rhythmically from city gate to city gate, goes from the outside world to the Forbidden City, the ideal centre of the universe.[4]

Leys's brilliant description misses two points: first, besides being an emotional energy field, this monumental space is also a transmitter, a transmitter of information, information coded in the massive redundancy of the symmetrical arrangement and repetition of massive forms.[5] It is a transmitter tuned to the frequencies of monumental time, to the long duration. It is built to last. Secondly, while the CPC may have intended this symmetry as a massive affirmation of its power and culture, it has also created a powerful transmitter for quite other kinds of messages. Its original design tuned it to the frequency of monumental time, but as such it has already been turned into an image of all that it stands for, an image which can be broadcast on the quite different frequency of the media spectacle. It is this double transmitter that the demonstrators have learned to appropriate as a channel for their own messages. Messages that will be transmitted down the long duration of monumental time, the time of martyrdom and memory; but messages that will also be transmitted over the extensive, momentary network of saturation presence.[6] They are playing a double game with the signs and signifying practices of the revolutionary tradition and of a regime that has appropriated that tradition, reinterpreting those signs, turning them over upon themselves, sending them out into other space and forward into the future.

Their demonstration against the policies and practices of the regime is taking place on exactly the same site as the demonstrations the regime used to organize in its own honour, such as the giant Cultural Revolution era rallies, drilled and organized for days in advance.[7] But where serried ranks of Red Guards would line up in front of the reviewing stands built on top of Tiananmen Gate, for quasi-religious ceremonies presided over by Mao and Lin Biao, the demonstrators of today sit or stand with their backs to the old reviewing stand, facing in the exact opposite direction. Rather than facing the reviewing stand outside of their mass, the demonstrators focus inwards, facing the Monument to the People's Heroes in the centre of the square. The leadership of the movement and the hunger strikers cluster around the two-tiered podium of the monument, self-consciously presenting themselves as martyrs in the making. The whole composes itself as a televisual image, and, given the degree of support, sympathy, and advice some members of the Chinese media gave to some of the students, this is no accident. The regime's own expertise in organizing spectacles is here on display, for quite other purposes.

3 THE OPEN DOOR AND THE OPEN CHANNEL

There have been demonstrations like this before. In 1976, the funeral of Zhou Enlai unleashed a demonstration of popular sentiment against the Gang of Four. In 1979 the democracy wall movement gathered here and the prodemocracy slogans were publicly aired. Often written by disillusioned Red Guards from the Cultural Revolution era before the Gang of Four were toppled by Deng Xiaoping, many now famous tracts were written and pasted to a bus shelter wall near Tiananmen Square.

Some of that generation of rebels were co-opted into Deng's government. Some, including Wei Jingsheng, author of the famous tract 'The fifth modernization', and Chen Erjin, author of *China: Crossroads Socialism*, are now in jail.[8] One has to be careful with the gap that can appear between justice and the sign of justice; modernity and the sign of modernity; democracy and the sign of democracy. To flourish the sign of each on one's own brings the wrath of might down upon the hand that held the pen. This time, the act of flourishing the sign of democracy itself flourished, became democratic; it played itself out as a modern sign for the modern media, and was modern; it was self-contradictory and reached no consensus, and in a certain sense too it was just.[9] Not only what is signified, but signification itself must be modern, democratic, just, if it is to outmanoeuvre the regime in the narrow space between the sign and its material and discursive supports in the realm of power, and this signification must be enacted, over and over; it has no other register but the performative, no other arsenal but memory.

The demonstrators are well aware of all this. In fact, the demonstrations are like relays, public signals of a continuous, hidden process of resistance and affirmation. Just as in 1976 people used the funeral of Zhou Enlai as the moment or relay, so in 1989 the funeral of Hu Yaobang becomes a similar focus. The students seize upon every opportunity to recognize every moment of historical hope and wrest it away from conformism, and they know that if they do not continue to do so, then, in Benjamin's words, *not even the dead will be safe*.[10] The demonstrators mostly take sides within the regime rather than frontally opposing it, and in this sense they are not student radicals in the tradition of the new left, nor are they dissidents of the eastern European type. There is a long tradition of advice and dissent from within in Chinese intellectual history, not least under the post-Liberation regime, which has always been both dependent on intellectuals as a source of legitimation and contemptuous of them as a class.[11]

This historical memory of the students goes right back to 4 May 1919, to the demonstrations against the Treaty of Versailles, which handed Germany's Chinese colonial outposts over to the Japanese. The 4 May demonstration combined nationalist, liberal, and revolutionary sentiments, and is commemorated by the CPC. The most famous writer from that period, Lu Xun, has been deified, and his Beijing house is now a shrine. Yet the students of today know that not all of the passions of 4 May can be contained and appropriated by the CPC. The periodic demonstrations relay quite another set of memories in their enactment: 4 May this year produced quite a sizeable demonstration, despite government disapproval, and the 4 May slogan 'Hallo Mr Democracy' has been popularly revived, and not without a sense of irony.

Far from being a revival of the universal values which the western enlightenment once aspired to, much of the propaganda of the demonstrators reveals ironic and cynical impulses. Some factions seem to address their democratic rhetoric – written and sung in English – at an American television audience. Some of these people are not without sophisticated media skills. Others prefer to double back the regime's rhetoric at itself, by taking the signifiers of martyrdom, socialism, sacrifice, and enacting them, dwelling in the abyss between sign and referent. Others prefer to make the signs of socialism resonate, to make their inner cavities sing, their hollowness manifest.

While 4 May and Hu Yaobang's funeral provided pretexts for small demonstrations, it was the Deng-Gorbachev summit and the massive presence of the world's media to cover it that really provided the conjuncture for this most massive outburst. For one thing, Gorbachev is also a hero to some of the students. When Gorbachev says, 'Reason and conscience are beginning to win back ground from the passiveness and indifference that were eroding hearts. Naturally, it is not enough to know and to tell the truth. Acting on the knowledge of the truth and of understanding it is the main thing',[12] he speaks of the kind of process some students want for their own country. A process in which the intellectuals can ally themselves with the reformist elements of the party.

There are other foreign sources being appropriated by the students. The visual style of the new left, with its long hair and flowers, is one. The revolutionary tradition of American democracy is another: in Shanghai students built a 3-metre-high model of the Statue of Liberty out of styrofoam and paraded it before the party offices. The Beijing version, the Goddess of Democracy, was an even larger and more potent symbol. Replicas of it now spring up everywhere, copied from newsreel footage and press pictures. The headbands with slogans appear to come from Korean student demonstrations, televised on the government network. In short, native traditions and symbols of dissent are being retriggered and mixed with foreign signs and practices that the students find useful.

The open door policy initiated two years ago has brought in foreign investment, technology, and tourism, but has also brought with it a trickle of foreign culture and information. The campaigns against Spiritual Pollution and Bourgeois Liberalization in the late 1980s were feeble attempts to keep the cultural and political doors closed and the economic and technical doors open. In any case, China has long been a permeable membrane for foreign ideas coming from short-wave radio broadcasts. BBC World Service, Voice of America, and Radio Australia are all popular sources of news and information about the outside world and about China itself. In part at least the democracy movement is a politics created by people who no longer have roots but aerials.

While the party circulates its *Digest of Foreign News* – one of the biggest-circulation newspapers in the world – only within the party, it cannot control the information available on radio. During the crisis, accurate reports of demonstrations have been allowed in Chinese papers and broadcasts, not least because not to report such events would seriously compromise the credibility of the press, when foreign sources are readily available. The openness to the flow of foreign information weakens the central control over the flow of domestic information.

In saying this, one does not have to subscribe to the myth that the western press is open and free and reports the fact while the Chinese press is monolithically totalitarian and false. The difference is palpable but may not be quite so simple. It is perhaps more accurate to say that they are quite different systems of disinformation; quite differently constructed *circuits* within which information flows. The significant thing about these events in China is the exposure of these two different systems of disinformation to each other. It is not the veracity or the accuracy of the western press that matter, but its presence and its difference. Even if one were to assert that the western reporting on China was entirely false and misleading, it is nevertheless true that an alternative channel of false information can be just as powerful a weapon. The power of the media in an event such as this lies in its connectivity between points in an information loop, not in the ultimate foundation of that loop in a referent event and space outside of the circuit. The *occupation of time on the information network* becomes the first principle of this aspect of struggle, and the *occupation of space in the symbolic landscape* is merely a means to that end. One occupies the latter space with bodies and the former with disembodied signs. The referents of those signs can matter as little as the motivations of those bodies. In the politics of the information network, like any other politics, it is the effect which counts, not the intentional objective or the referential object.

The Deng-Gorbachev summit provided a fabulous window of opportunity. The world press had turned its attention to Beijing. Two American broadcasters, CBS and CNN, had even set up their own satellite uplinks for live broadcasts of the summit, under contractual arrangements with the government.[13] So with the city full of senior correspondents and camera crews, the students set out to steal this pre-prepared set from the government. The potential for Tiananmen Square to become a giant information transmitter has been appropriated on a massive scale, and the networks are here to broadcast it live to the world. The government had intended Gorbachev to lay a wreath at the Monument to the People's Heroes in Tiananmen Square – symbolizing the rapprochement of the two communist parties, on equal terms. This would indeed be a major symbolic event, a sign marking a turning--point in Sino-Soviet history.[14] The students just stole the show. The vector of information from Tiananmen Square to the world carries as its signal, not Gorbachev and his wreath, but hunger strikers and slogans. They stole the spectacle and made it their own. The CPC opened this information circuit for its own purposes. The students just discovered how to appropriate it; how to piggyback their messsage out with the other signals.

This vector of information from Tiananmen Square to the world is

136

relayed straight back again on short-wave radio services, contributing to other demonstrations elsewhere in the country. Meanwhile, in Beijing, foreign journalists become heroes, constantly asked for news updates from their wire service machines in the foreigners' compound on the outskirts of the city. Suddenly, Beijing is as plugged in to the international information network as it is possible to be. No longer could repression be carried out behind a screen of silence. This is what the students count on ...

4 DEMOCRACY AND 'DROMOCRACY'

Dateline: Beijing, 3 June. It is significant that just before declaring material law, the authorities cut the satellite links. This is an ominous sign of what they have in mind as the troops are trucked in from the provinces. Dan Rather of CBS argued live on air with bureaucrats armed with pliers. The networks had contracts to broadcast via satellite several more days, yet here were officials shutting them down – a clear sign of the flimsiness of the rule of law upon which the open door policy and the joint venture agreements rest. The Hong Kong stockmarket took a deep dive, and everyone prepared for the moment of repression.

Previous student demonstrations have exposed the differences between the demands the students make and the needs and wants of the workers. The students have ideological demands: democracy, accountability, a greater role for the intellectual class in political life, and a bigger share of the state's resources. Anyone who has seen the abysmal state of Beijing University will know the very real basis of these demands.[15] However, it is not exactly what the workers want. Many workers want less reform, not more. Their incomes have been hit by market-driven inflation and the security of their lives under the old system has been threatened.

Nevertheless, the workers and citizens of Beijing were not going to sit back and watch troops from the border regions being trucked into Beijing to crack heads. They blockaded the streets and encircled the railway stations. The issue shifted from the students' demands for democracy to the struggle in the streets for what Virilio calls 'dromocracy': a battle over who controlled the movement and the disposition of force in the city. As Virilio has argued, there has long been a strong dromocratic element to the CPC regime. The Long March was the ultimate war of movement, and the party applied the lessons learned then to a disciplinary regime based on the regimentation and control of movement, on pack drills and transmigrations. During the Cultural Revolution, the struggle between Mao and his cohorts and the party machine took the form of Mao counterposing the massive movements of Red Guards around the country in the Exchange of Revolutionary Experiences against the party's rigid controls of movement. Mao set loose the greatest transmigrations the world has known, and in the chaos that followed, the army stepped in, countering movement with force, and restoring order and a new political compromise. Variously labelled 'liberal' and 'conservative' by western news pundits, the CPC leadership all have one thing in common: they were victims of Mao's Cultural Revolution who hung on to power in those turbulent times or clawed their way back after Mao's death. As such the CPC leadership could look upon this fresh outbreak of disorder only with alarm, even though it was different in character to Mao's Red Guards.

This time, the people seized the symbolic heart of the country and blockaded the mobile force of the army out. The workers and the students had no clear unity of demands or slogans. Their collective opposition is one of gesture as much as of ideas, a postural crime. 'Bodies are guilty of being out of sync, they have to be put back in the party *line*.'[16] They have placed a brake on the circulation of force through the city. An unknown number of people, a multitude, perhaps a million, has kept 150,000 troops at bay. The troops were encamped at the railway station, a little to the east of Tiananmen. They were moved into position on the subway system and through the network of underground tunnels. Mao had built as fallout shelters. It is difficult to know how aware the people of Beijing are of the strategic layout and opportunities afforded by their city. There are no accurate, publicly available maps showing all of the possible routes the troops can move along. It is a case of troops from outside, using maps and logistical skills, vs the local knowledge of the people: a repetition of a very old historical conflict between military technique and popular defence.[17]

The *audio-visual enclosure* was also tightened. The radio and RV no longer referred to the students as 'patriotic' and began making ominous noises about 'counter-revolutionaries'. The 'conservative' faction, in favour of the economic open door and reform but opposed to political change, used the demonstrations as a pretext to declare its historic compromise with the political 'reformers' within the party null and void. Deng Xiaoping and Li Peng were firmly in control, with all but the Beijing military district behind them. Zhao Ziyang and his modernizing technocrats were by now clearly in jeopardy. To the demonstrators of Tiananmen it must at this point have been clear that short of martyrdom there wasn't much they could presently achieve. When Zhao Ziyang went to Tiananmen Square with a loudhailer and attempted to get them to go home, it was clear he feared a backlash against the 'liberal' faction. Now he may fear for his life.

So while the immediate outcome looks grim right now, this remarkable series of events will be recorded in a much longer, subterranean history. Zhao Ziyang may soon be airbrushed out of official history, but he had become a people's hero, alongside Zhou Enlai and Hu Yaobang. So too have the hunger strikers. They have joined Chen Erjin and Wei Jingsheng and many, many others in jail – or worse. Yet this event will relay into the future the whole hidden culture of the revolt and resistance that are the uncontrollable connotations of the revolutionary heritage the CPC claims as its legitimating moral force. A whole series of techniques has been learned: for manipulating historical signs and monuments, for co-opting the media, for using the pressure of foreign information vectors – and opinion will be relayed by this catastrophe into the future, piling up catastrophe upon catastrophe upon catastrophe in the contingent series of events that is history as it is lived. Watching the demonstrators again, replayed and relayed in the perpetual present tense of video tape, it appears as if to them every second is the historic gate through which democracy might enter.

Some day in the future, when Zhao Ziyang's funeral takes place, perhaps they will write poems for him as they wrote them for Zhou Enlai. Whether he deserves them or not is quite besides the point.[18] The people have to fashion their heroes out of available material, and thrust a simulated greatness upon them, if necessary. After Zhao's demise there may be trials, just as there were after Zhou's and after the democracy wall demonstrations. Perhaps the Bureau of Public Safety will once again offer as exhibits poems as marvellous as this:

> In our grief we hear the devils shrieking;
> We weep while wolves and jackals laugh.
> Shedding tears, we come to mourn our hero;
> Heads raised we unsheathe our swords.[19]

5   SEEDS OF FIRE

Dateline: Beijing, 4 July. It is customary to remember the dead one month after their passing, although in this case memory ought not to stop at that. It is extraordinary how moments in time can feel completely discontinous. Just over a month ago it seemed as if every second was the gate through which Mr Democracy might come. The troops and the slaughter came instead. Followed by the round-up. It probably all makes sense now. It didn't then, that's for sure. Beware of the smooth surface of history, looking backwards, making everything make sense. It made no sense at the time, like a random series of jump cuts. Indeed, like all insurrections, this one stood outside of time for a moment, hoping to catch hold of a different current, hoping to rise above the flux, hoping whoever or whatever edits history plumps for the right cut. You can still feel this other temporality, this futile hope in the video footage. At least video can now preserve history with all its jagged edges – if we choose to edit it that way for ourselves.

The media loop between China and the west was unprecedented. Some lessons were learned. The CPC used the western media loop as a surveillance system. Chinese embassies in the west taped the newsreels, perhaps the regime even intercepted the Visnews satellite feed from Hong Kong. Either way, they got access to news footage and used it as evidence for the round-up. Chinese TV rebroadcast American news footage of Chinese citizens explaining what happened. They then broadcast the phone number of the Bureau of Public Safety, so that anyone who recognized the counter-revolutionaries from the western news could drop a dime on them. The CPC managed to turn the positive feedback loop of the western media, while for a while encouraged and incited successive acts of civil disobedience, into a negative feedback loop, discouraging resistance and prompting complicity with the state. Just as the students seemed to be learning how to use the positive feedback aspect of this loop to their advantage prior to the 4 June massacre and round-up, the state appeared to be learning how to turn it around and use it to its advantage. The tyranny of distance that once separated events in China from the world has become a tyranny of difference – a proliferation of mediated messages from this event that can now be used against those who figure in the great gush of information generated by the demonstrations.

Meanwhile, in the west, the possibility of seeing, recording, remembering these events opened up by satellite broadcast has become more than that; it has become a duty. Already, the Goddess of Democracy statue has become an international emblem. In the big parade for the bicentenary of the French Revolution, the Chinese students took pride of place, and their image was broadcast again around the globe, as a melancholy echo of the fire of Tiananmen. Yet now this has a new dimension, that of the network, that of global recording. New vectors of memory have been opened up, and the neatly channelled information hierarchies that prevail in the CPC's China have, for a moment, been breached. New possibilities for constructing politics in the information landscape[20] have momentarily been glimpsed. Lu Xun once wrote that 'as long as there shall be stones; the seeds of fire shall not die', and one could not hope for a better expression of the spirit of resistance and the will to overcoming expressed in insurrection. Now, that fire is carried and captured in vectors traversing the information landscape in new and interesting ways; dangerous and fleeting, persistent and mercurial.

NOTES

[1] Deng Xiaoping, 'Clear away all obstacles and adhere to the policies of reform and of opening to the outside world', in *Fundamental Issues in Present Day China* (Beijing: Foreign Languages Press, 1987).

[2] Greil Marcus, *Lipstick Traces* ... (Cambridge, Mass.: Harvard University Press, 1989).

[3] Aldo Rossi, *The Architecture of the City* (Cambridge, Mass.: Opposition Books, MIT Press, 1986).

[4] Simon Leys, *Chinese Shadows* (Harmondsworth: Penguin, 1977), 53-4. Apologies to the author for altering the romanization of Chinese names.

[5] cf. 'Order and disorder: noise, trace and event in evolution and in history', in Anthony Wilden, *System & Structure: essays in communication and exchange*, 2nd edn (London: Tavistock, 1980).

[6] On the problem of the relation between contemporary media and the formation of collective memory, cf. McKenzie Wark, 'Just like a prayer', *Meanjin*, no 3 (Melbourne: 1989).

[7] Stanley Karnow, *Mao and China: inside China's Cultural Revolution* (New York: Penguin, 1984), 201ff.

[8] Chen Erjin, *China: Crossroads Socialism* (London: Verso, 1984); Wei Jingsheng, 'The fifth modernization: democracy', in Simon Leys, *The Burning Forest* (London: Paladin, 1988). Three excellent collections of contemporary dissident writings are: David Goodman, *Beijing Street Voices* (London: Marion Boyars, 1981); Gregor Benton, *Wild Lilies and Poisonous Weeds* (London: Pluto Press, 1982); and Geremie Barme and John Minford, *Seeds of Fire* (Hong Kong: Far Eastern Economic Review Ltd, 1986).

[9] Jean-François Lyotard and Jean-Loup Thebaud, *Just Gaming* (Minneapolis, Minn.: University of Minnesota Press, 1985).

[10] Walter Benjamin, 'Theses on the philosophy of history', in *Illuminations* (New York: Schocken Books, 1987).

[11] Merle Goldman, *China's Intellectuals: Advice and Dissent* (Cambridge, Mass.: Harvard University Press, 1981); Anne Thurston, *Enemies of the People* (Cambridge, Mass.: Harvard University Press, 1988). There are significant differences between the recent political events in eastern Europe and those that took place in China in May and June. The relative strengths of and relationships between the bureaucracy, the military, the intelligentsia, the working class, and the peasantry are quite a different matter in China.

[12] Mikhail Gorbachev, *Perestroika: a new thinking for our country and the world* (London: Collins, 1987), 76.

[13] Jonathan Alter, 'Karl Marx, meet Marshall McLuhan', in *The Bulletin/ Newsweek* (30 May 1989), 17.

[14] Robert Delfs, 'One stage, two plays' and Louise do Rossario, 'Safety in numbers', *Far Eastern Economic Review* (25 May 1989).

[15] cf. Gregor Benton, 'Beijing spring', *New Statesman* (26 May 1989).

[16] Paul Virilio, *Speed & politics* (New York: Semiotext(e) 1986), 33

[17] Paul Virilio, 'Popular defense and popular assault', in *Italy: Autonomia – Post-Political Politics* (New York: Semiotext(e) no 9, 1980).

[18] cf. Simon Leys, 'When the "dummies" talk back', *Far Eastern Economic Review* (15 June 1989); Robert Cottrell (ed), *The Rape of Peking* (London: The Independent in association with Doubleday, 1989).

[19] Quoted in Thurston, *op cit*, 15.

[20] I have developed this notion of the information landscape, the information vector, and the experimentation with modes of cultural politics appropriate to it, in more detail in McKenzie Wark, 'Spirit freed from flesh: cultural technologies and the information landscape', *Intervention*, no 21/2 (Sydney: 1988); McKenzie Wark, 'Homage to Catatonia', in *Meanjin*, no 2 (Melbourne: 1988); McKenzie Wark, 'On technological time: Virilio's overexposed city', in *Arena*, no 83 (Melbourne: 1989); McKenzie Wark, 'The news from Beijing', in *Arena*, no 88 (Melbourne: 1989). A critical response to it derived from a 'Frankfurt school' position can be found in Gerry Gill, 'The enchantment of openness', in *Arena*, no 89 (Melbourne: 1989).

B. Englishness and Imperialism

Narratives of Nationalism
Being 'British'

Iain Chambers

In her first public speech after the ending of hostilities at Port Stanley had closed the bloody adventure in the South Atlantic (not long afterwards marketed to the public as a video-cassette), Margaret Thatcher pronounced an ominous phrase: 'The lesson of the Falklands is that Britain has not changed.'

As always, the Prime Minister successfully put her finger on a contradictory but telling theme. She was personally intent on conjuring up a mystical vision from the past: that moment before the rot and decline had set in, when Britain was still 'great'. And the underlying steady-state condition to which her appeal was addressed that July afternoon in 1982 at the Cheltenham race-course before her cheering supporters was destined to strike deep into the British psyche. It was designed to draw out from the twilight world of the unconscious and parade on the surfaces of the everyday the seemingly indecipherable metaphysics of 'being British'.

THE OLDEST CLUB IN THE WORLD

> *Though modern constitutions typically locate the source of sovereignty in 'the people', in Britain, it is the Crown in Parliament that is sovereign. Nor is that merely a technical point. The political culture of democratic Britain assigns to ordinary people the role, not of citizens, but of subjects.*
> *(R. McKenzie and A. Silver)[1]*

In the often turbulent narratives of modern nationalism Britain

145

occipies a peculiar position. Although having witnessed lengthy struggles in its distant (and also in its more recent, not to say contemporary) history to absorb internal national units – Welsh, Scots, Irish – the British Isles have not experienced a serious invasion for a millennium. Partially dismantling the feudal state in the seventeenth century, the English state was also the first in the following centuries to experience the fracturing impacts and fruits of industrialization, urbanization, and empire. Such precedents have provided British political culture, and the particular English hegemony that lies at its heart, with a present-day mantle of benevolent overseer, as it looks down on more ragged procedures, more hurried and violent formations.

The 'suppressed superiority' (Tom Nairn) of this English ascendancy, hidden behind a self-deprecation that is usually unwilling to admit that nationalism exists at all, clearly has its roots in the quiet certainties of this stable and now deeply conservative tradition. The earlier connections between radical liberties and 'Englishness' that flared up in the seventeenth, eighteenth, and early nineteenth centuries have largely been extinguished and are now safely part of the native 'tradition'. Since the latter half of the last century such struggles over the different possibilities of patriotism have been publicly replaced by a tranquillizing image in which modern 'Britishness' invariably stands in for the quiet authority and organic continuity of an English conservatism; a conservatism that is not simply political but also, and quite significantly, cultural in its effect. Symbolically elaborated around consecrated relics, traditions, and shrines – Westminster, the monarchy, Oxbridge, the Royal Navy, the public school system, the syllabus of 'English' – it is as though, through an undisturbed continuity, the very spirit of 'History' has laid its blessing on the nation. More than this, it has also led to the successful establishment of an extensive *popular* cultural conservatism. For while, historically speaking, there exists an important popular dimension to British institutional politics, at least since the beginnings of the mass franchise in 1867, it has come largely to be represented in the timeless guise of a national mythology, where faithful subjects (rather than 'citizens') rally round the flag.[2] So, while today formally one of the least democratic of countries in the conduct of its political life, glaringly apparent in its unrepresentative electoral system, the maintenance of a non-elected House of Lords, and the powerful symbolism of its monarchy, the public image of Britain is still that of one of democracy's champions, one of its brightest jewels. On 3 April 1982, in the parliamentary debate the day after Argentinian forces had occupied the Falkland Islands, we can hear Michael Foot, then leader of the Labour Party, intoning this familiar litany, claiming Britain 'to be a defender of people's freedom throughout the world'.

The seemingly uninterrupted continuity and timeless rituals of these traditions and institutions have provided the comforting guarantees. The construction of an 'English' history in the nineteenth century, both in the world of academia, and, more effectively, in the literary milieu of the period, impregnated the whole debate on culture with this national mythology. In its neo-Gothic architecture, pre-Raphaelite paintings, chivalric poetry, fourteenth-century socialist utopias, and its insistence on the earlier harmonies of rural life and artisan production, Victorian intellectuals of the most varied political persuasions sealed a pact between a timeless and mythical vision of the nation and their selection and installation of an acceptable culture heritage. British 'culture', and its profound sense of 'Englishness' (the narrowing of the national nomenclature was not accidental), was found, in both the temporal and symbolic sense, to exist beyond the mechanical rhythms and commercial logic of industrial society and the modern world. It has subsequently bequeathed that deep-seated intellectual and moral ambiguity towards modernism, mass culture, mass democracy, commerce, and urban life, that has so frequently characterized English intellectual thought and official culture in the twentieth century. In its unending moral clarity and purpose it has 'given us the map of an upright and decent country'.[3]

Enoch Powell, a politician who rose to public prominence in the 1960s by denouncing the threat to the English 'race' by the waves of immigration and prophesying an imminent apocalypse of racial war and 'rivers of blood', used to give the impression in his public speeches that Britain possessed only two universities; elsewhere, figurative mummies – Queen Victoria, Disraeli, and Churchill – have been periodically unwrapped and dead metaphors (the 'Dunkirk spirt') resurrected. None of this appears ridiculous. The official political consensus on both sides of the House of Commons (and in Fleet Street and Wapping) is too deeply indebted to such appeals ever to take them into serious reconsideration. The isolated few that try are clearly vandals, obviously intent on desecrating the 'national heritage'.

This rhetoric has recently been supplemented and renovated by the vigorous language of Mrs Thatcher and her governments. The rather crusty world of yesterday's Britain has been harnessed to a more aggressive rhythm. Victorian values are still central, but these now reflect the business-like, utilitarian logic of that imagined epoch rather than its gloomy aesthetes and a cricket-playing, claret-drinking *noblesse oblige*. There has occurred a shift towards an *imaginary* modernity. Imaginary, because in all its talk of financial independence, profitability, and enterprise culture, the Thatcherite vision of the contemporary world is as significantly indebted to a backward-looking sense of the national heritage as the patronizing intellectual and aristocratic cultures it purports to be pragmatically reassessing.

Despite its sharp shifts and changes, and its undoubted success in translating the abstract structures of 'Britishness' into immediate and popular forms and lanaguages, Mrs Thatcher's project is also living on borrowed time. By appealing to the presumed continuity of a particular and highly selective thread in *our* national heritage this latest twist in the national saga is condemned to become an increasingly narrow and exclusive vision. Today's world is ultimately more extensive, complex, and interconnected than the inward view afforded from the garden of a mock Georgian mansion in Dulwich.[4]

NATIVE REASON

If there is a mode of thought that dominates both British intellectual life and its everyday culture it is empiricism. In asking ourselves why this is the case we can already begin to see that the foundations of what is called modernity were laid down many centuries ago, in the English case even before the rationalist explosion of the European Enlightenment. Crucial here was the massive process of secularization induced by the Reformation, when 'knowledge' was brought down to earth. Without going into the details of the sceptical rationalism of Bishop Berkeley and the Scottish philosopher David Hume, and their proposal to equate knowledge with the immediacy of sense data, it is perhaps sufficient to note that the seventeenth-century triumph of science in British intellectual life (Francis Bacon, Isaac Newton), that was to be extended in the eighteenth and nineteenth centuries (in particular in the figure of Charles Darwin), provided a fundamental endorsement to an empirical mode of knowledge. Knowledge was constituted by what could be reported, observed, measured, and classified. It was, of course, further supported by the very mechanics of the Industrial Revolution where what appeared to be the direct

148

application of scientific principles to nature was literally remaking the world. In this context an ideology to empirical pragmatism could be, and was, erected: the world was to be continually 'tested' and 'verified', not by a theory, but by an empirical intelligence. Knowledge is constructed in what you can touch, sense, feel, and physically transform.

Hume's position – that knowledge is completely dependent upon experience – was eventually refuted by the German philosopher Immanuel Kant in his *Critique of Pure Reason*; Kant's argument freed the field of knowledge from being limited to sense experience. He argued that although all knowledge begins with experience it does not follow that it all arises out of experience. This opened up the possibility of treating knowledge as a field in its own right, and offered the further attraction of the possibility of constructing a mental schema or structure for interpreting the world. This takes us to the continent, to Giambattista Vico, and then to Hegel, to Marx and Marxism, and to the whole continental tradition that is willing to think in terms of structures, totalities, and overt metaphysics. But all this developed elsewhere, initially in Germany, and obviously represents a quite different trajectory of thought and conceptualization of knowledge from that pursued in Britain. For this reason it does suggest an alternative, and, as verified in recent decades, an increasingly important presence in the debate on the realization of knowledge and culture in the contemporary world.

Now the development of a particular British cultural formation that was empirical and therefore deeply tied to a pragmatic view of things was, apart from the existence of the Industrial Revolution, greatly assisted by the particular insularity of the British national experience in the nineteenth century, cut off, as it was, from the rest of the world by the buffer and the barrier of its empire. In fact, it seemed, and many Britons in their 'splendid isolation' would have concurred, as though Britain was the 'world'. Everything else was simply 'foreign' and 'strange'.

What needs to be underlined here is that the successful and largely unchallenged establishment of an empirical mode of thought led away from any temptation to indulge in the construction of an intellectual or theoretical totality. If the world is composed of millions of empirical situations, it can be catalogued, but not understood, by a mental structure, by a single a-priori theory or overriding explanation, with the crucial exception of the mind of God. In this perspective, theories are just the accumulative frameworks of so many facts that make up an ultimately knowable world. It involves an implicit and unacknow-ledged metaphysics – the stable referent of an irrefutable and independently verifiable world – that was displaced into the apparently neutral language of 'science' and 'knowledge'. This drive to verify and possess the world comes to its conclusion on the Victorian high ground that sought 'to make the independent individual the ground of value'.[5] Here, religion was also based on the sovereign individual's experience of sense data. For Matthew Arnold there was no space for miracles and mysticism: 'Whatever is to stand must rest upon something which is verifiable, not unverifiable.'[6] While T.H. Huxley praised Hume's attack on metaphysics which, now supported by nineteenth-century physical sciences, was 'warranted to drive solid bolts of fact through the thickest skulls'.[7]

Such a prospect is not only empirical, it is also imperial. Everything falls within its domain and is susceptible to its immediate rule. This conception of knowledge, initially encouraged in the latter half of the nineteenth century by a positivist view of science, was extensively endorsed by the very real economic, political, and cultural sense of the national and the cultural projection of 'Britishness' that established itself at home and abroad at the same time. The native manner of looking at and understanding the world was the unique way. This native 'common sense', whose gendered and ethnic constructions were easily obscured beneath the neutrality of empirical data, has invariably suggested a secure native sense not only of what constitutes 'knowledge', but also of ethics, ethnicity, and nation. But, for all its bluff pragmatism and endorsement of the 'facts', the Victorian attempt continually to establish a moral ground does also suggest a deeper, underlying insecurity; the neurotic suspect that behind the rational *ratio* of its world there lay in its 'heart of darkness' perhaps altogether more disquieting realities: 'other', more dangerous, worlds.

The complex inheritance of empiricism and imperialism is deeply ingrained in the English 'structure of feeling'. Even without further analysis there is the contemporary intuition that quite clearly problems of race and racism – the 'empire strikes back' as a book title put it some years ago – together with a widespread disdain for intellectuals and theory in British public life share some common roots in this particular story.[8] The striking insularity and parochialism of much of British academia, pragmatically wedded to the 'facts' and observable realities, has tended to produce a 'naturalist' art and an empirical intelligentsia working with a naive theory of 'truth', which, in philosophical terms, has usually been limited to a pragmatically reductive sense of 'knowledge'.[9] For what is ultimately significant about the mythology of the transparent factuality of the world is what it hides, forbids, and represses. Behind its languages of 'neutral' representation lies a deeply ingrained and apprehensive moralism, itself a powerful legacy of a patrician culture accustomed to the quiet and pragmatic exercise of its authority in the belief that it can somehow fully 'explain' reality.

All this is not to suggest that we do away with empiricism; it is indispensable *within certain limits*. But it is to propose that we dilute its hold on our sense of knowledge, weaken its epistemological claims, and reduce it to a particular instance in the networks of sense. Why? Well, these words of Jane Gallop's, which I came across in Alice Jardine's *Gynesis*, admirably sum up the response:

> Belief in simple referentiality is not only unpoetic but also ultimately politically conservative, because it cannot recognize that the reality to which it appeals is a traditional ideological construction, whether one terms it phallomorphic, or metaphysical, or bourgeois, or something else. The politics of experience is inevitably a conservative politics for it cannot help but conserve traditional ideological constructs which are not recognized as such but taken for the 'real'.[10]

THE MAN IN THE WHITE SUIT

> *It is there, in the colonial margin, that the culture of the west reveals its 'différance', its limit-text, as its practice of authority displays an ambivalence that is one of the most significant discursive and psychical strategies of discriminatory power – whether racist or sexist, peripheral or metropolitan.*
>
> *(Homi K. Bhabha)[11]*

In his examination of the trial of Warren Hastings in 1788 for crimes and 'misdemeanours' committed while Governor-General of India between 1773 and 1784, David Musselwhite points to 'the confrontation of systems of thought and cultural codings and expectations which are completely impenetrable to each other and which encourage us, therefore, to try and imagine what it would be like to think the "unthinkable"'.[12] There is the crucial clash, as Musselwhite goes on to establish, between Hastings's principal

151

accuser, Philip Francis, 'imposing Enlightenment and European principles of political economy on India' and, on the other side, Hastings, 'concerned to manipulate as best he can the residual machinery of the Moghul Empire'.[13]

Although Hastings was formally acquitted, he was nevertheless morally condemned in the emerging daily press and popular opinion of the day. There, a native sense of values triumphed over the detailed knowledge and diplomacy that Hastings had exercised in dealing with Islamic law. As Homi Bhabha puts it:

> Colonial power produces the colonized as a fixed reality which is at once an 'other' and yet entirely knowable and visible. It resembles a form of narrative in which the productivity and circulation of subjects and signs are bound in a reformed and recognizable totality. It employs a system of representation, a regime of truth, that is structurally similar to realism.[14]

It was the constructed, and deeply 'English', view of 'India', rather than a respectful, local working knowledge, that was marshalled by Francis, Burke, and others seeking to have Hastings impeached. It was a myth, and one that clearly worked at home. It produced an 'India' that was both different but yet finally susceptible to domestication. What is being denied here 'is any knowledge of cultural otherness as a differential *sign*, implicated in specific historical and discursive conditions, requiring construction in different practices or reading'.[15] Such a religion would lead to the dispersal of the logic that fails to recognize 'otherness' in its fullness and for which 'otherness' is merely a corroboration, a point on the other side of the circle that completes the logo-centrism of the discourse (colonial, imperialist, male, hegemonic) in question. For racial and cultural 'otherness' does not complete the circle, it circulates and proliferates in the world in the 'spiral of différence'.[16] There it marks a difference and defers or postpones an obvious resolution.

This specific argument interestingly links up, and it is hardly accidental, to the important philosophical work on 'otherness' by the Jewish philosopher Emmanuel Levinas. In his book, *Totality and Infinity*, Levinas argues against traditional metaphysics for 'reducing the Other to the Same'. He points out that singular bodies appear merely as 'individuals' against a total background which renders them comprehensible only to the degree that they refer to that totality. The totality is what the knowing subject already knows prior to encountering such bodies, and such bodies being referred to the already noted or known are not recognized as such, but are immediately reduced to the same, to the knowing subject.[17]

In a similar vein, Bhabha points to how the colonial subject is constructed within 'an apparatus of power which *contains*, in both senses of the world, an "other" knowledge: a knowledge that is arrested and fetishistic and and circulates through colonial discourses as that limited form of otherness, that fixed form of difference, that I have called the stereotype'.[18] To conclude and to bring home this argument on Anglo-centric representation/realism: 'It is as if the very emergence of the "colonial" is dependent for its representation upon some strategic limitation or prohibition *within* the authoritative discourse itself ... in which to be Anglicised, is emphatically not to be English.'[19]

SOME NATIONAL MYTHOLOGIES

The discourses of nation and people are saturated with racial connotations.

(Paul Gilroy)[20]

To raise today the question of what it means to be 'British' means seeing how, in the forming of contemporary relations – cultural, ethical, sexual, and economic – ethnicity and racism can be identified as a structural element of the 'English', based, as it is, on a particular construction of history. Observing what is included and what is excluded, what remains hidden and passed over in silence, we can note how the idea of the nation is dependent upon an extensive appeal to ethnicity, frequently constructed against the threat of the 'alien', and his or her 'foreign' tastes, cultures, and habits. It has been precisely at this point, as Paul Gilroy has recently argued, that a populist politics of 'race' and nation has emerged in recent years in attempts to make sense of national decline.[21]

Here we face the possibility of two perspectives and two versions of 'Britishness'. One is Anglo-centric, frequently conservative, backward-looking, and increasingly located in a frozen and largely stereotyped idea of the national culture. The other is ex-centric, open-ended, and multi-ethnic. The first is based on a homogeneous 'unity' in which history, tradition, and individual biographies and roles, including ethnic and sexual ones, are fundamentally fixed and embalmed in the national epic, in the mere fact of being 'British'.[22] The other perspective suggests an overlapping network of histories and traditions, a heterogeneous complexity in which positions and identities, including that of the 'national', cannot be taken for granted, are not interminably fixed but are in flux.

In other words, in the construction of a sense of Britain and the 'British' there are ethnic implications of inclusion and exclusion. It can be noted, for example, that even radical critics and historians such as Raymond Williams, E. P. Thompson, and Eric Hobsbawm have, in their appeals to the continuities of *native* traditions and experiences, perhaps inadvertently conceded the ethical and racial pretensions of a national(ist) mythology. The questions and questioning of gender, race, and ethnicity are generally excluded from their account.[23] Richard Hoggart's 'traditional working class', as well as E. P. Thompson's, or Raymond Williams's almost Leavisite appeal to local tradition and the 'long revolution', tend to operate with ethnic assumptions concerned with native white males. In the same vein, recent appeals to popular culture or to the Gramscian concept of the 'national popular' can also drive into an even tighter fit the racial and nationalist connotations of a *particular* culture and 'people', thereby obscuring those other cultures and 'peoples' whose very presence is today forcing a critical redefinition of 'British culture *as a whole*'.[24]

In the construction of the nation as an 'imagined community', to use Benedict Anderson's term, we discover that 'race' is clearly a social and political construction; it is not simply something to do with the colour of our skin.[25] For while colour is a loaded signifier, an ethnic signal, it stands in for a range of meanings: linguistic, historical, and cultural. In the end we are dealing with cultural identity and with what is usually an attempt to hold at bay the disrupting and transgressive presence of the 'other'; we are dealing with a particular definition of 'Britishness', of being one of 'us', as opposed to one of 'them', rather than simply with the labelling of skin pigment on the colour spectrum.

So, for example, black people can become acceptable to Mrs Thatcher and much of the Conservative party if they respect a particular sense of 'Britishness'; that is, if they dress, talk, eat, and act as native-born Britons. It is this tradition that they are expected to enter and uphold, which correspondingly implies that they negate their own particular histories: imperial, colonial, racial, ethnic, cultural, and religious. They are expected to become the mirror of a homogeneous, white Britain; the invisible men and women of the black diaspora and the post-colonial world who are required to mimic their allotted roles in the interpretative circle to which they have been assigned.[26]

This Anglo-centric, and self-referring, position is based on a homogeneous 'unity' in which particular roles, including gender, are firmly established. In Mrs Thatcher's scheme of Victorian values it recalls not the liberal aristocrat but the sober virtues and rational order of a middle class whose personal capacities were realized in a moral relationship to the market and to domesticity.[27] Mrs Thatcher's own appeal is to a vague but potent symbol of national mythology. The details of her inspiration are even more revealing, however. In her research on the articulation of 'Britishness' through ethnicity and gender, Catherine Hall has charted an important shift in middle-class English male culture that emerges around the mid-nineteenth century.[28] The English 'gentleman' of the time was not tied initially to land but was associated with the early nineteenth-century European trinity of Romanticism, evangelicalism, and political economy. In his firm belief in Christian manliness and femininity, and the insistence on this gendered distinction through the division between public life and domesticity, this male figure represented a moral critique, organized around the dignity of labour and its independent realization in the market, of aristocratic degeneracy and effemininity.

But from its sturdy assurance in the market-place this Victorian gentleman gradually succumbed to a neo-Romantic, increasingly anti-market and anti-industrial ethos. Moral certitude, and an individual and pragmatic rationale, gave way to the collective mystique of the nation and its past – 'haunts of ancient peace' – in which questions of ethics were effectively translated into questions of ethnicity. To be 'British' was no longer to demonstrate Christian virtues and the pragmatic pursuits of *homo economicus*, but to pledge allegiance to the imagined state of grace which was the nation. As the wife of the protagonist in Alexander Korda's imperialist adventure film *The Four Feathers* (1939) neatly puts it: 'We are not free, we are born in a tradition, there is a code we must respect; we must obey in order to be proud of ourselves.' By the 1860s, liberalism, *laissez-faire* culture, and individual morality were giving way to life on the North-West frontier, the British Bulldog, and popular racism.[29] The nation is expressed in racially exclusive terms, and the connection between it and native 'manhood', formed in the zenith of imperialism, was to be extended even further by vulgar Darwinism and

155

metropolitan power. This has all been subsequently articulated through the long history of twentieth-century post-imperial decline, providing a repertoire of common sense and racial stereotyping capable of explaining Britain's position in the contemporary world. Talking of the provincial xenophobia revealed in present-day football riots and hooliganism, for example, John Williams has this to say:

> These trends, despite the indignant protestations of politicians, are not alien to or isolated from those more widely held in British society. They are apparent, for example, in our daily news coverage of local and foreign affairs and in the violent rantings of parliamentary spokespeople for 'revenge' on the terrace gangs. The Rambo-like xenophobia of such fans, their anti-intellectualism and racism and their Page Three sexism may be forged in mean streets and massaged by the popular rags, but such values also echo way beyond these dark passages.[30]

Of course, through the mists of time, both the earlier, dissenting, evangelical, romantic, liberal moment and its subsequent metamorphosis into Bulldog Drummond and blustering certitude, can be quietly telescoped into a common national heritage, distinguished not by challenge, change, and transformation, but by a continuity guaranteed through the undisturbed ethnicity of the nation.[31] Others are welcome to join, but on condition that they accept this narrow platform. Here, to be 'British', even though the empire has physically gone, is somehow still to be spiritually and morally at the 'centre' of the world.

THE TIES THAT BIND

> *Fiction seeps quietly and continuously into reality, creating that remarkable confidence of community in anonymity which is the hallmark of modern nations.*
>
> (Benedict Anderson)[32]

Still … many of the focuses, concerns, and individual biographies involved in 'being British' pass well beyond Mrs Thatcher's clear vision of Victoriana and the soft-focus retro words of television costume melodramas, along with all the other modes – from museums to stately homes – recently employed in popularizing the 'national' heritage and constructing the character of its 'people'.[33] And if, in all this, there is an ingrained cultural conservatism it is certainly not the sole property of a single social class, political party, charismatic figure, or narrative form ('history').

When during the 1970s the double knot of economic and political crises was drawn tighter, the dead appeal of much political, intellectual, and cultural leadership was increasingly revealed. For crises also involve the fragmentation of a particular historical bloc and the break-up of a particular temporal order that once arranged social matter according to certain criteria and directions. Only the renegades, those who step outside the previously ordained frame, offer the suggestion of real novelty and change. In Britain in recent years this possibility has been largely, although not completely, dominated by the 'Radical Right'. It has been 'Thatcherism' that has been the most radical politics to gain a wide consensus in recent times. Here the dreary predictability of previous politics has been brusquely challenged, yanked out of the narrow prospects of government and deposited in the rich humus of everyday experience. If only in name, but the symbolism is not empty, 'politics' has been returned to the 'people'.

Mrs Thatcher's insistence on the 'idea of the free market, with its stress on the sovereignty of the individual consumer, was diametrically opposed to all that Toryism stood for. To the Tory it was obvious that economic forces should be made to accommodate themselves to the established patterns of social relationships.'[34] However brutal and crude, the Thatcherite revival of the Hobbesian sense of 'possessive individualism' subject to the laws of the 'market' represents a real break with the previous Tory tradition.[35] In a paradoxical return to the native sources of liberal theory its contemporary radical edge derives from the fact that 'Toryism' as a cultural formation has come to represent the actual consensus across the political spectrum of much of Britain's political and cultural leadership throughout the twentieth century.[36] Part of the effect of Mrs Thatcher's 'revolution' is publicly to undo this established consensus.

We are clearly living through an epochal shift. The game has suddenly opened up. Particular narratives, that is the sequential linking of events that once sought publicly to legitimize power – whether in the modest tale of social democracy or the epic sweep of socialism – are no longer the privileged vehicles of sense. 'Politics' once again becomes a site of construction and potential popular interest, subject to new and more extensive definitions. The horizon of the

157

possible is enlarged. Much of this is, of course, symbolic; particularly as fresh initiatives from the under- and unrepresented are rapidly blocked in a mixture of eighteenth-century political machinery and nineteenth-century labour corporativism. But the sign play, the symbolism, in a mass media world in which the only representation that counts is increasingly a composite media image, becomes significant, if not crucial.

Still, the historical left in Britain, like Catholics caught up in the cursed winds of a Reformation, tends to cling to more traditional histories for its sense: the Trade Unions, the Parliamentary Labour Party, the Working Class, Marxism, Trotskyism (all written with authoritative capital letters).[37] Discussing democracy it finds difficulty in digesting the idea of proportional representation, the secret ballot, or black sections in the Labour Party; considering a politics of everyday life that breaks with the great prospects of 'British masochism' (Stuart Hall) and begins to recognize a politics of sexuality, style, and fashion (Britain's fourth industry) usually raises only a condescending smile.

Behind these official responses also lies the silent repression of the new politics and perspectives that have emerged in the last two decades – the embarrassing legacy of the 'permissive' '60s: the movement for women's liberation and the emergence of other forces organized around attention to the quality and textures of the particular, the specific, and the personal in terms of sexuality, race, pollution, nuclear energy, and war. The historical left's discomfort with these articulate 'intrusions' in the 'real' world of politics has usually been matched by an indifference or even outright hostility to the profane contributions that have emerged from an imaginative investment in popular culture that has transformed selected commodities – records, clothes, certain mass media icons, particular modes of transport – into loaded signs, and such signs into ways of life and a consequent reinvention of contemporary urban existence that suggests that 'out there' there exists another 'Britain'. It tends to leave us with a politics narrowed down to a politics of defence, even of despair. Further, it is a politics of defeat.[38]

The historical left also tends to look backwards for the authority and guidelines to justify its contemporary pragmatism. It is another sign of the numbing 'realism' of a 'native' culture tradition, in which the nation, as Patrick Wright observes, 'is portrayed as an already achieved and timeless historical identity which demands only appropriate reverence and protection in the present'.[39] The choice of period, although vaguer, is not too dissimilar from Mrs Thatcher's: the 'classic' period of nineteenth-century working-class struggle and the formation of organized political opposition. But in its romantic appeal to (industrial, white, and overwhelmingly male) traditions of rebellion and resistance, as opposed to the easily 'modernized' images of 'possessive individualism' and the 'market', it seems even less adapted than Mrs Thatcher's rhetoric in registering that present conditions are increasingly slipping beyond its ideological grasp.

In this historicism of politics, 'history in reverse' in Patrick Wright's phrase, there does emerge a rather telling distinction: with Mrs Thatcher the nostalgia is for success, with the historical left it seems to be largely about sacrifice.[40] Not surprisingly much left-wing politics finds itself playing to an increasingly empty house or else an irreducible and embittered audience that desires the religious security of cant rather than the open risks of the present. Until very recently firmly wedded to the prospects of a dwindling industrial working class it has tended to register wider structural changes in economic, political, and cultural life only obliquely. The response to the present has therefore been predictably defensive, and in a corporative spirit withdraws into an insistence upon the defence of the *status quo*, of the job, of the existing relations of production, of a way of life, of a tradition .... For those who have not got a job, or who do not participate in *that* particular tradition or way of life, the appeal is clearly excluding and, ultimately, senseless.

OUT OF TRADITION AND INTO HISTORY

The militant working-class confrontation of the 1984 miners' strike and the 'war of Wapping' over the introduction of microchip technology into British journalism are recent examples of traditionally endorsed logics of native resistance, articulated around the closed prospects of a single-economy working 'community' and the guarded secrets of a skilled trade, that are increasingly out of synchrony not only with the temporality of modern capital, but also with modern life and, in the second case, democracy. But if you are taught to believe that history is something that has *already happened* and is not actually *in act*, that the sense of the present (and hence of the future) ultimately lies somewhere back there, then you are clearly not in a position to engage fully with the only time you possess: your own present. 'Tradition' here functions not as a reservoir of hope, example, and experience, but as a prison, limiting not merely room for manoeuvre, but also the very sense of the possible.

No single tradition can function as a guarantee of the present, can save us. There are many traditions, constituted by gender, ethnicity, sexuality, race, class, that criss-cross the patterns of our lives. By bringing them into history, into recognition and representation, we appreciate the complexity that challenges the tyranny on the present of a single, official heritage: that of 'being British'. At this point, tradition, historical memory, 'roots', become important less for themselves, as though tokens of a vanished 'authenticity', and more as suggestive, active signs, stimulating a personal and collective confidence in assembling effective passages through the possibilities of the present.[41] In the subsequent cultural and ethnic commotion, the institutional sense of politics, of centre and margin, of economy and culture, of the 'nation' itself, is necessarily forced into movement and change.

There is ultimately the need to acknowledge the limits of the national framework, to recognize that local realities and details form part of different networks, that of black metropolitan cultures, of EEC legislation, or of the international division of labour and the transnational exigencies of capital, for example. It means to recognize that the 'nation' has a cultural and linguistic unit is not a closed history, something that has already been achieved, but is an open, malleable framework in the making.

The present does not automatically augur an info-tech paradise of reduced flexitime work, computer-integrated manufacturing, whirring discs, bleeping monitors, and computer print-outs (presented simultaneously as the new driving sector of the economy, of modern life, and of leisure), but it does usher in a new horizon of possibilities. It produces a space (in both the physical, temporal, and symbolic sense) in which previous social relations, economic organization, and established knowledges and expertise are thrown into question, crisis, and movement; in which work may become discontinuous; in which ecology will not be of peripheral concern to the economy but part of the same social budget; in which the gender of power and politics can no longer be assumed or ignored; in which the exhaustion of the post-war consensus and the hardening of ideological discourses may, paradoxically, encourage the creation of transversal connections over previous political divisions, as, for example, in the case of sexual rights and freedoms; in which native perspectives may be frequently interrupted and forced to accommodate transnational tendencies and realities; and in which consumption is not a by-product of industrial production but a self-generating economy and way of life no longer limited to the 'family unit' but now characterized by highly fluid and heterogeneous channels of consumption that, in turn, are symptoms of important changes in the very conception of 'production' and 'markets'.[42] The combination of such features is forcibly changing the context and nature of existing social and cultural powers and firmly 'puts on the agenda the emancipation of politics from its subordination to economics'.[43]

All of this, of course, also puts in question not merely the liberal and patrician sense of 'good government', but also the Marxist concept of the 'political' when it has remained fundamentally tied to the classical questions of production and the social redistribution of profit. Are those who do not participate in the production of that surplus, which involves a growing percentage of the metropolitan population in the overdeveloped countries, simply to be excluded from history and politics? The potential sense of all this – which most urgently requires a new sense of both 'politics' and 'democracy', if they are not to disappear for ever behind policed poverty, structural unemployment, the legal surveillance and public ostracization of minorities, and authoritarian government, and into dust-free data banks – has to be discovered and contested in the space of what is potentially and socially possible, and not in abstract hymns to an absolute 'emancipation', or dead appeals to a nostalgic past.

For ultimately it is only be testing our imagination on the possibilities of the present – 'the only times we've got', as the painter David Hockney recently put it – that we can hope to reconstruct both in the realization of a 'socialized individuality' (Henri Lefebvre), and enter another history.

NOTES

I would like to thank Catherine Hall for her comments and suggestions.

[1] Quoted in Tom Nairn, *The Break-up of Britain* (London: Verso, 1981), 40.
[2] In fact, it has been suggested that the Second Reform Act of 1867 'demonstrated that the liberal state was organized to counter mass democracy and universal suffrage'; Stuart Hall and Bill Schwarz, 'State and society, 1880-1930', in Mary Langlan and Bill Schwarz (eds), *Crises in the British State 1880-1930* (London: Hutchinson, 1985), 12. On the successful organization of

a popular Toryism around the images of the 'nation' and the 'people' in the late nineteenth and early twentieth centuries, see Bill Schwarz, 'Conservatism, nationalism and imperialism', in James Donald and Stuart Hall (eds), *Politics and Ideology* (Milton Keynes: Open University Press, 1986). Finally, the recent shift by both radical and conservative commentators to consider the concept of 'citizenship' – see Mrs Thatcher's speech to the Conservative Party Conference, Brighton, October 1988, and Chantal Mouffe's 'The civics lesson', *New Statesman & Society* (7 October 1988) – suggests that there is an important shift in Britain's political culture in act.

[3] Carolyn Steedman, *Landscape for a Good Woman* (London: Virago, 1986), 8.

[4] The neo-Georgian residence in Dulwich is, of course, the £400,000 home bought a few years ago by Mrs Thatcher. The apparent 'modernism' of Mrs Thatcher's policies is in fact deeply compromised by its own particular sense of native tradition. While anxious to anticipate the European 'free market' that attends us in 1992 not one inch of 'British sovereignty' is to be surrendered. However, the political and cultural consequences of 'free market' capitalism, increasingly oblivious to local and national 'traditions', together with the long-term consequences of inter-European legislation and government, threaten to extend their effects well beyond the local vision and power of Mrs Thatcher's administration.

[5] Michael H. Levenson, *A Genealogy of Modernism* (Cambridge: Cambridge University Press, 1986), 15.

[6] Quoted in Levenson, *ibid.*, 10.

[7] *ibid.*, 15.

[8] CCCS (eds), *The Empire Strikes Back* (London: Hutchinson, 1982).

[9] Naturally, there have always been exceptions. But, at a general level, fundamental changes in native intellectual practices in the social sciences occurred only after the invasion of 'foreign', largely French, theories in the late 1960s.

[10] Jane Gallop, quoted in Alice Jardine, *Gynesis* (Ithaca, NY and London: Cornell University Press, 1985), 155.

[11] Homi K. Bhabha, 'The Other question: difference, discrimination and the discourse of colonialism', in F. Baker, P. Hulme, M. Iversen, and D. Loxley, *Literature, Politics and Theory* (London and New York: Methuen, 1986), 148.

[12] David Musselwhite, 'The trial of Warren Hastings', in Barker *et al.*, *Literature, Politics and Theory*, 77.

[13] *ibid.*, 83.

[14] Homi K. Bhabha, in Barker *et al.*, *Literature, Politics and Theory*, 156.

[15] *ibid.*, 151.

[16] *ibid.*, 153.

[17] Emmanuel Levinas, *Totality and Infinity* (Pittsburgh, Penn.: Duquesne University Press, 1969).

[18] Bhabha, in Barker *et al.*, *Literature, Politics and Theory*, 165.

[19] Homi K. Bhabha, 'Of mimicry and man: the ambivalence of colonial discourse', in Donald and Hall (eds), *Politics and Ideology*, 198-200.

[20] Paul Gilroy, *There Ain't No Black in the Union Jack* (London: Hutchinson, 1987), 56.

[21] *ibid.*, 29.

[22] The central idea of nation, tradition, and culture was also deeply central to the particular critical and literary variant of modernism – 'to be as aware as possible of what is happening, and, if we can, to "keep open our communications with the future" ' (*Mass Civilization and Minority Culture*) – proposed by the Leavises in their project for 'English' in the 1930s. For although it was initially set up along oppositional lines, to contest the old order of academicism at Cambridge, it, too, was wedded to a unified sense of the past: 'The quality for which *Scrutiny* prized this vanished past was its social and cultural homogeneity': Francis Mulhern, *The Moment of 'Scrutiny'* (London: Verso, 1979), 63.

[23] For further criticism on 'the invisibility of "race" within the field' of contemporary historiography and cultural analysis, see Gilroy, *There Ain't No Black …*, especially chapter 2.

[24] See *ibid.*, 26, 153-7. It can also be noted that Gramsci developed the concept of a 'national popular' culture in the context of a recently established state seeking to establish its national identity, and not in a post-imperial country in decay that is officially choking on a rich diet of nationalist tit-bits.

[25] Benedict Anderson, *Imagined Communities* (London: Verso, 1983).

[26] See Homi K. Bhabha, 'The commitment to theory', *New Formations*, 5 (Summer 1988).

[27] For further details on how class and gender were articulated together in an emerging national formation in the first half of the nineteenth century, and of how this combination gave rise to a particular sense of 'Englishness' and its moral economy, see Leonore Davidoff and Catherine Hall, *Family Fortunes: men and women in the English middle class 1780-1850* (London: Hutchinson, 1987).

[28] Catherine Hall, 'England's manhood, England's glory: gender and ethnicity in the 1860s', a talk given at the University of Illinois, Champaign-Urbana, 15 April 1988.

[29] This shift was most symbolically marked in the long-drawn-out debate between John Stuart Mill and Thomas Carlyle over the Morant Bay insurrection in Jamaica in 1865 and its suppression by Governor Eyre. Once again, as in the Hastings case, the native, Anglo-centric view publicly triumphed over the liberal, pluralist, agnostic perspective.

[30] John Williams, 'White riots: the English football fan abroad', in A. Tomlinson and G. Whannel (eds), *Off The Ball* (London: Pluto, 1986), 17.

[31] A parallel reading of Dick Hebdige's *Cut'n'Mix* (London: Comedia/Routledge, 1987) and Gilroy's *There Ain't No Black in the Union Jack* forcibly underlines not only the necessity to rethink the nature of contemporary British culture but also the very concept of 'Englishness'.

[32] Anderson, *Imagined Communities*, 40.

[33] For more on the central theme of the 'national heritage' and its successful translation into a popular discourse, see Patrick Wright's *On Living in an Old Country* (London: Verso, 1985) and Robert Hewison's *The Heritage Industry* (London and New York: Methuen, 1987).

[34] T. F. Lindsay and Michael Harrington, *The Conservative Party, 1918-1970* (New York: 1974), quoted in M. J. Wiener, *English Culture and the Decline of the Industrial Spirit, 1850-1980* (Cambridge: Cambridge University Press,

1981), 98.

[35] The classic statement on the native roots of liberal-democratic theory in 'possessive individualism' and the 'market' is C. B. Macpherson's *The Political Theory of Possessive Individualism* (Oxford: Oxford University Press, 1962). The centrality of this deeply pragmatic philosophy to variants of 'Britishness' today, and hence its potential for popular appeal, hardly needs emphasizing. Its tradition includes not only Hobbes and Mrs Thatcher, but also the Levellers and Tony Benn.

[36] For evidence of the antipathy of much of classical Toryism to the 'market', see chapters 3 and 4 of Wiener, *English Culture ... 1850-1980*.

[37] There have been exceptions. There is the journal *Marxism Today* and the divisions its imaginative approach to politics have recently caused in the British Communist Party. But such details, whatever their long-term importance, do not, as yet, contradict the commanding tendencies.

[38] This is by no means purely a British phenomenon. Apart from the erosion of the French Communist Party, and the nostalgic imprint of the British Labour Party, the present difficulties of Italian trade unionism and the Italian Communist Party further underline the European and international dimension of the limits of a politics based on the struggle over the surplus value of labour and its crucial failure effectively to address the complex cultural reproduction, social mechanisms, and differentiated powers of existing society.

[39] Patrick Wright, 'Mis-guided tours', *New Socialist* (July/August 1986), 34.

[40] Wright, *On Living in an Old Country*, 175. According to Zygmunt Bauman, the source of this nostalgia lies in the left's historical adherence to the rationalist realization of the bourgeois ideas of liberty, equality and brotherhood. It added nothing to this agenda, but in taking these ideas seriously became the 'counter-culture of capitalism', criticizing the capitalist system precisely for failing to realize its promised goals. See Zygmunt Bauman, 'Fighting the wrong shadow', *New Statesman* (25 September 1987).

[41] On the constructed and 'artificial' character of 'roots' in contemporary metropolitan culture, see Kobena Mercer's 'Black hair/style politics', *New Formations*, 3 (1987).

[42] There are no 'cultural products, in an era when the economic has itself become cultural, and culture is an industry, that are not simultaneously items in the inventory of contemporary political economy': Clive Dilnot, 'Design, industry and the economy since 1945', quoted in Kathy Myers, *Understains: the sense and seduction of advertising* (London: Comedia, 1986), 149. At the heart of this shift lies the 'new anthropology of consumption' that characterizes the more flexible and dialogic sense of both modern production and the present-day ecologies of differential consumption. This has recently been designated as 'post-Fordism'; see Robin Murray, 'Life after Henry (Ford)', *Marxism Today* (October 1988).

[43] Zygmunt Bauman, *Memories of Class* (London: Routledge & Kegan Paul, 1982), 197.

How English Is It?
Popular Literature and National Culture

James Donald

If the body of objects we study – the corpus formed by works of literature – belongs to, gains coherence from, and in a sense emanates out of the concept of nation, nationality, and even of race, there is very little in contemporary critical discourse making these actualities possible as subjects of discussion.

– Edward Said

I have grown gradually more and more weary of having to deal with ... the forms of nationalism endorsed by a discipline which, in spite of itself, tends towards a morbid celebration of England and Englishness from which blacks are systematically excluded.

– Paul Gilroy[1]

In recent years, the peculiarities of English culture have become something of an obsession amongst historians and cultural theorists.[2] There is no great mystery about why this interest should coincide with the era of Thatcherism and Reaganism. In *There Ain't No Black in the Union Jack*, Paul Gilroy attributes the 'morbid celebration' of Englishness to the left's increasingly desperate search for an imagery in which to represent – even to think – political alternatives. I suspect that the repeated academic dissection of English nationalism also indicates an attempt to come to terms with the historical formation of English cultural criticism and exorcize (or disavow) its implication in the government of home and colonial populations. At the same time, Gilroy and other writers have been arguing that the way out of the impasse of the old politics may lie through different, less historically contaminated ethnicities – 'collective identities spoken through "race", community and locality' rather than through nationality and nationalism.[3]

Despite this ambivalence about the significance of ethnicity, both the critique of the old, terroristic ethnicity of Englishness and the endorsement of the new, heterogeneous ethnicities share at least one assumption: that *collective identities* are a necessary and inevitable feature of both politics and subjectivity. It is just a couple of the many questions provoked by that assumption that I want to raise here, with particular reference to the literature/nation/race nexus identified by Edward Said. The first concerns the *invention* of Englishness: what is the role of 'popular literature' in the institutional formation of the 'national culture'? The second concerns the *imagining* of Englishness: how might popular fictions shape our perception and experience of identity and difference?

NATIONAL CULTURE AND POPULAR LITERATURE

Culture, says Edward Said, refers to what is at stake in the phrases *belonging to* or *in* a place, being *at home in* a place. This emphasis on place may be a poignant index of Said's own displacement in the Palestinian diaspora, but it does underline the almost tautological nature of the concept 'national culture'. 'The nation' is itself, in Benedict Anderson's phrase, an 'imagined community' – in other words, the place or culture where we feel at home. As the Palestinian example shows, the bonds of national solidarity are not wholly dependent on the territorial existence of a nation state. What is essential is the representation of a mutually anonymous and potentially hostile population as 'the people', heirs to a common past and subjects of a shared destiny. This expansive version of nationalism became possible in post-medieval Europe as the result of the spread of vernacular languages, literacy, and forms of communication based on print technology. These put into circulation the characteristic symbolic systems of Western modernity, primarily the narrative conception of empty, homogeneous time embodied in the novel and the newspaper.[4]

Anderson sees nationalism as more comparable to 'kinship' and 'religion' than to 'liberalism' or 'fascism' – more a mentality than an ideology. I would suggest a slightly different, three-way distinction between, first, specific nationalist ideologies (whether imperialist, isolationist, or liberationist); second, a communality figured as a narrative of nationhood (Anderson's imagined community); and, third, the apparatus of discourses, technologies, and institutions (print capitalism, education, mass media, and so forth) which *produces* what is generally recognized as 'the national culture'. This third aspect implies that 'the nation' is an effect of these cultural technologies, not their origin. A nation does not express itself through its culture: it is culture that produces 'the nation'. What is produced is not an identity or a single consciousness – nor necessarily a representation at all – but hierarchically organized values, dispositions, and differences. This cultural and social heterogeneity is given a certain fixity by the articulating principle of 'the nation'. 'The nation' defines the culture's unity by differentiating it from other cultures, by marking its boundaries; a fictional unity, of course, because the 'us' on the inside is itself always differentiated.

Take as a small example of this internal differentiation and external drawing of boundaries the concluding remarks from a radio talk, on the Third Programme of course, which Lord Keynes gave in 1945 as chairman of the newly established Arts Council of Great Britain – a state institution designed to police hierarchies of cultural value within a national framework and protect them from the decline of private patronage and the hostility of the market-place.

> How satisfactory it would be if different parts of the country would again walk their several ways as they once did and learn to develop something different from their neighbours and characteristic of themselves. Nothing can be more damaging than the excessive prestige of metropolitan standards and fashions. Let every part of Merry England be merry in its own way. Death to Hollywood![5]

This is what a 'national-popular' culture looks like when seen from the chair at the head of the Arts Council table, rather than from Gramsci's fascist prison cell. Keynes acknowledges differences within the nation but, disavowing his own mandarin metropolitanism, domesticates them as diversity rather than antagonism. He draws them into a unity by contrasting his version of the organically popular (Merry England) to a different image of 'the popular' – the alien 'mass' culture of the old bogey 'Hollywood'.

In a case like Keynes's 'Merry England'/'Hollywood' binarism, the relationship between 'national' and 'popular' represents a high/low or positive/negative opposition. But, at the same time, he presents the two terms as synonymous – the national culture speaking to and for the English people. Underlying both usages, I think, is a tension between the fixity of 'the national' and the plurality or heterogeneity of 'the popular'. In Bakhtin's terms, culture can be seen as a field in which the forces of identity, standard speech, and the state exert a centripetal pull against the centrifugal forces of cultural difference, linguistic variation, and carnival. 'The popular' does not simply represent either the centripetal or the centrifugal pole; it reproduces the tension between them. Centripetal agencies (whether Keynes and the Arts Council or Gramsci and the Communist Party) attempt to impose their competing conceptions of a unified 'people-nation' on to a fragmentary and differentiated population.

How does literature – and particularly popular literature – fit into this model? Said claims that literature 'belongs to, gains coherence from, and in a sense emanates out of the concept of nation, nationality, and even of race'. By this, he probably means in part that literary writing formulates the characteristic chronotopes of a national mentality. He may also be making the historical point that the literary forms of the European languages provided the medium for the definition and diffusion of national vernaculars, in opposition to the trans-national jargon of Latin and subnational regional dialects. In this process, the imposition of a 'correct' or 'standard' national language established new patterns of linguistic dispositions and brought into being the new institution of 'Literature'. In the British context, for example, it has been argued that developments like the emergence of English as an academic discipline and the fixing of the national language in the *Oxford English Dictionary* ensured that, by the heyday of invented traditions in the latter part of the nineteenth century, Literature had been instituted as the point of reference around which relationships of difference and similarity within the field of writing were organized.[6] It became a centripetal force within the field of the national culture. This development can be related to a much broader reorganization of cultural life that occurred, very roughly, in the slipstream of the Disraelian political settlement and alongside the creation of the 'organic state' which extended new forms of governmentality throughout civil society.

The institutionalization of Literature in Britain can also be seen as one response to changing political perceptions of the potential dangers of popular literacy. In the period between Paine's *Rights of Man* and the rise of Chartism, these had been seen in terms of political radicalism. In the course of the nineteenth century, however, literacy lost its threatening aspect and became instead a means of 'educating our masters'. Increasingly, it was *illiteracy* and a taste for debased, sensational fiction that were identified as pathological symptoms. It provided a target and a justification for governmental intervention: hence the 'administered' forms in which the standard language and the national literature were taught in the elementary schools set up after Forster's Education Act in 1870. This shift, within the politics of literacy, from a rhetoric of power and confrontation to a rhetoric of cultural pathology was evident in changing strategies around publishing for the people. In 1819, for example, the Utilitarian publisher Charles Knight noted the influence of the radical press. 'There is a new *power* in society', he wrote, and warned that contemporary journals like Cobbett's *Political Register* and Wooler's *Black Dwarf* had 'combined to give that power a direction. The work must be taken out of their hands.' When the *Boy's Own Paper* was first published sixty years later by the Religious Tract Society, its aim was to provide '*healthy* boy literature to counteract the vastly increasing circulation of illustrated and other papers of a bad tendency'.[7]

From the start, the tensions inherent in the concepts of 'the nation', 'the people', and 'culture' were built into the institution Literature. It exists to give them form, to contain them. Retrospectively, it provides the criteria for selecting certain texts as 'the canon' of English literature, as the history of 'England' given imaginative expression. Programmatically, it calls for a vernacular national literature, characteristically in the form of the realist novel. So where does 'popular literature' fit in? Sometimes the term implies a residue left over after true Literature has been defined. Sometimes it refers to the writing that people actually choose to read – functional literature like 'railway fiction' to while away a journey, holiday reading for the beach, pornography for titillation, or Jeffrey Archer as a soporific. Occasionally, it means specifically working-class forms of writing or modes of reading.[8] But the idea of popular literature as failed Literature still seems to dominate, and limit, analysis. The pessimists treat it as a conduit for 'dominant ideologies'. Ignoring a book's formal or narrational properties, they will gut it for its ideological content – how sexist is it? how racist is it? how imperialist is it? The optimists, on the other hand, see popular literature as a carnivalesque subversion of literary pretensions – a centrifugal force ripe for political exploitation.

The trouble with both these (not terribly caricatured) approaches is that their Literature/popular fiction distinction remains within the terms of aesthetic and ethical evaluation set up by the category of Literature – authenticity, autonomy, and so forth.[9] What I am proposing instead is an historical understanding of the discursive and institutional relationships between 'national', 'popular', and 'Literature'. From this point of view, popular literature appears neither as ideological commodity nor as populist subversion. Instead, it can be understood as a concept with an important function in managing the diversity of fictional texts and modes of reading. It allows these to be incorporated within the hierarchy of values and differentiations that constitute both the institution Literature and the national culture.

This triangulating conception of national/popular/Literature calls into question not only the idea of Literature as the expression of 'the nation', but also the old binarisms of Literature/popular fiction and high culture/mass culture. That's not to say that these categorical oppositions have no cultural effects. Fredric Jameson is quite right to insist that they are 'objectively related and dialectically interdependent phenomena'. For him, though, the 'high' pole in literary culture is represented neither by a national canon (the Englishness of Quiller-Couch or its American equivalent) nor by realism, but by those forms of writing which resist the commodification of literature. And that, he says, means *modernism*. Laura Kipnis takes this further, suggesting that the high culture/mass culture binarism is a precondition for the existence of modernism: 'Dismantling the ideological scaffold of modernism allows the rereading of modernism as constituted solely within this split, and existing only so long as it could keep its Other – the popular, the low, the regional and the impure – at bay.' It is certainly true that, with the appearance of aestheticism, decadence, and symbolism in the last two decades of the nineteenth century, a recognizably modernist literary aesthetic of this type was set in place – around the same time, that is, as Literature was being 'pathologized'. But it is also true that the modernism/mass culture polarity is far less stable than Jameson and Kipnis imply – think only of Eisenstein's enthusiasm for Hollywood, the surrealists' championing of the tackiest forms of popular culture, the European intelligentsia's enduring love affair with jazz, or the recycling of popular imagery in Pop Art. Equally, many forms of modernism were, at least in the moment of their formation, profoundly hostile towards existing aesthetic and political institutions. The history of modernism in the visual arts is a cyclical one of anti-institutional moments of formation followed by consolidation into schools and traditions followed by breaks from the by now institutionalized forms. In literature, modernism has been identified as a 'source of opposition' to the pervasive ethos of Englishness around the turn of the century: it 'exposed the literary parochialism and ideological limits of dominant English liberal culture' and, at the same time, 'prompted ... a mutation in critical ideology'. The simple point is that modernism can be – has been – either 'pro' or 'anti' *both* high culture and popular culture. Equally, the history of how modernism has been taken up or rejected in the twentieth century is far too complex to assume that it can have a fixed political meaning. It has been equally championed and derided both on the right and on the left – where it has been seen as everything from the 'revolution of the word' to a CIA plot.[10]

This indeterminacy is by no means unique to modernism. In purely conceptual terms, there is nothing necessarily progressive about the popular, nor inherently reactionary about the national. Their history is another matter, of course. And that's the key point: 'Literature', 'nation', 'people', and the rest are never, in that sense, *purely* conceptual. They exist only as they are instituted through education, publishing, the press, the mass media, the Arts Council, and other such institutions. Measuring the 'progressiveness' or 'reactionariness' of a given text, genre, or movement takes for granted the categories and the relations between them as they are presented in this cultural apparatus. Worrying whether popular literature speaks for the 'real people' of England more faithfully than the canon is to treat Literature still as an evaluative category. What is really at issue is the management of the semantic field as one aspect of the policing of a population.[11] And, I would say, this is also what is involved in the production of a national culture: the definition and maintenance of publics, interpretive communities, the people-nation.

This approach undermines the possibility of the question 'How English is it?' Englishness cannot be a measure; it has neither substance nor stability. The concept of Literature is linked to nationality less through mechanisms of expression than through the discourses and the institutions that produce 'nation', 'literature', and 'people' – and so 'Englishness' – as effective social categories. This reorientation also suggests why 'cultural studies' have remained so national in outlook in this country. It is not, as Paul Gilroy suggests, that 'England's left intellectuals have become so many radical rabbits transfixed and immobile in the path of an onrushing populist nationalism'[12] – or not just that, anyway. The deeper problem is that the very terms available for thinking about 'identity' and 'community' derive from a post-Enlightenment cultural criticism which has been central to the creation of European national, or nation-producing, cultures.

The reconceptualization of 'national culture' in terms of the effects of cultural technologies seems to me a necessary corrective to many accounts of how ideology works. But, unlike Foucault and some of the new cultural technocrats, I don't think this means the concept of ideology should be junked, nor that questions of representation and subjectivity are superfluous. If the cultural technologies are going to work, must there not be some investment in the forms of subjection they produce by the people who have to live these terms of selfhood? I don't see how it is possible to understand the implications of Said's ascription of the currency of Literature to nationality and race – or to grasp 'race' as a cultural category more broadly – without confronting this other side of subjection.

FICTIONAL IDENTITIES

To put it another way, why are there so many grotesque foreign villains in popular fiction? 'Racism' is no doubt the short answer, but it does not in itself reveal much about the dynamics of identification and differentiation in fiction, about our subjective investment in cultural hierarchies and symbolic boundaries. What I am concerned with here are some of the processes investigated by Peter Stallybrass and Allon White in *The Politics and Poetics of Transgression* – especially the way that the cultural 'low-Others' I have already discussed become an eroticized constituent of fantasy life. In the 'inner dynamic of the boundary constructions necessary to collective identity', they suggest, these cannot simply be excluded. They remain a troublesome presence for an official culture, returning in the form of the *grotesque* – or rather in it two forms. The first is 'the grotesque as the "Other" of the defining group or self'. Distinct from this is 'the grotesque as a boundary phenomenon of hybridization of inmixing, in which self and other become enmeshed in an inclusive, heterogeneous, dangerously unstable zone':

> a fundamental mechanism of identity formation *produces* the second, hybrid grotesque at the level of the political unconscious *by the very*

172

struggle to exclude the first grotesque.... The point is that the *exclusion* necessary to the formation of social identity at [one] level is simultaneously a *production* at the level of the Imaginary, and a production, what is more, of a complex hybrid fantasy emerging out of the very attempt to demarcate boundaries, to unite and purify the social collectivity.[13]

Note that this can only ever be an *attempted* demarcation: the boundaries remain permeable, the 'inside' is always fragmented and differentiated rather than pure and united. This helps to explain the ambivalent 'repugnance and fascination' evident in representations of the low-Other. To illustrate the point, Stallybrass and White quote Edward Said's argument that the political discourse of Orientalism 'depends for its strategy on [a] flexible *positional* superiority, which puts the Westerner in a whole series of possible relationships with the Orient without ever losing the upper hand'. What is at stake in this play of 'identity' and 'otherness', then, is the establishing of boundaries as a condition of knowledge and of identity: 'European culture gained in strength and identity by setting itself off against the Orient as a sort of ... underground self.'[14]

I am almost embarrassed to admit what this account of the relationship between West and Orient made me think of – Sax Rohmer's *The Mystery of Dr Fu Manchu*. This is one of the most dementedly racist works in English popular literature: but doesn't Nayland Smith's description of Fu Manchu provide an uncannily apt example of the simultaneous revulsion and fascination provoked by the grotesque?

'Imagine a person, tall, lean and feline, high-shouldered, with a brow like Shakespeare, a close-shaven skull, and long, magnetic eyes of the true cat-green. Invest him with all the cruel cunning of an entire Eastern race, accumulated in one giant intellect, with all the resources of science past and present, with all the resources, if you will, of a wealthy government – which, however, already has denied all knowledge of his existence. Imagine that awful being, and you have a mental picture of Dr Fu Manchu, the yellow peril incarnate in one man.'[15]

Faced with this, literary realism or sociological veracity are clearly beside the point. More interesting, for me, is what fascination this characterization holds for the petit-bourgeois man riding in a railway carriage in 1913, who seems to be its implicit addressee, or for any of the book's actual readers. It is unlikely to be the plot, for the book hardly has one. It substitutes a sequence of short, magazine-like stories in which establishment figures come under ingenious attack from Fu Manchu (sometimes fatally, sometimes not). More intriguing is the topography it deploys. There is a certain play on the relation between the respectable parts of London, and the mysterious East End and the home counties suburbs. Overarching this, of course, is the symbolic opposition of West to East – across which the characters and the relationships between them are plotted. This is the key to the way difference is rendered in *Fu Manchu*. Rather than representing a self-contained identity (Englishness) which is then contrasted with other, equally coherent, identities (here Chineseness), it stages a crisis of identification. It enunciates the split in identity that is the ground of racial difference. Fu Manchu and Nayland Smith represent the poles of an opposition rather than pure difference. 'The head of the Yellow movement' provides a necessary horizon to the identity of 'the man who fought on behalf of the entire white race' (p104); no Fu Manchu, no Nayland Smith. Thus the potentially infinite plenitude of difference is reduced to a manageable polarization, and the anxiety difference produces is tamed by its theatrical representation as the binary England/Orient.

What are the conditions of possibility of *Fu Manchu's staging of difference? Why did it take this particular form? In part, this is an historical and generic question. Fu Manchu*, for example, repeats the familiar trope of the 'evil genius' masterminding the metropolitan underworld. Like Professor Moriarty or Fantômas, Fu Manchu seems to figure the social tensions and anxieties of city life. But he does so in archaic form. The modern fear of the irruption of the irrational within everyday normality (the monsters produced by Goya's 'sleep of reason', Baudelaire's 'savagery that lurks in the midst of civilization') is linked to a specifically post-imperialist paranoia about the 'return' of the alien. Within the discursive field of post-imperialism, which seems to appear around the South African War, this alien is *produced* as grotesque through its attempted *exclusion*.

> Ideal rural peace, and the music of an English summer evening; but to my eyes, every shadow holding fantastic terrors; to my ears, every sound a signal of dread. For the deathful hand of Fu Manchu was stretched over Redmoat, at any hour to loose strange, Oriental horrors

upon its inmates. (p53)

This logic of exclusion/invasion/production recalls both the ambivalence between censorship and figuration that underlies the excesses of fantastic fictions and also the idea of the abject: 'what disturbs identity, system, order. What does not respect borders, positions, rules.' In *Fu Manchu*, eugenic fears about the purity of the social collectivity (the white race) and perennial psychic anxieties about the irruption of the abject are condensed into a viral imagery – 'a menace to Europe and to America greater than the plague' (p108) – and also into an imagery of pervasive mists and aromas:

> A breeze whispered through the leaves; a great wave of exotic perfume swept from the open window towards the curtained doorway. It was a breath of the East – that stretched out a yellow hand to the West. It was symbolic of the subtle, intangible power manifested in Dr Fu Manchu, as Nayland Smith – lean, agile, bronzed with the suns of Burma – was symbolic of the clean British efficiency which sought to combat the insidious enemy.(p85)[16]

The forms taken by popular fictions are never *just* an historical matter, though. When they are effective, they also respond to the psychic dynamics of fantasy. The coincidence of revulsion and fascination noted by Stallybrass and White becomes especially marked in *Fu Manchu*, for example, when questions of racial difference are overlaid by questions of sexual difference. Dr Petrie, the narrator, has a hard time dealing with his feelings towards Kâramanèh, Fu Manchu's beautiful and mysterious slave-girl, a Circassian and therefore both white and not-white. He feels his identity undermined by desire.

> Her words struck a chord in my heart which sang with strange music, with music so barbaric that, frankly, I blushed to find it harmony. Have I said that she was beautiful? It can convey no faint conception of her. With her pure, fair skin, eyes like the velvet darkness of the East, and red lips so tremulously near to mine, she was the most seductively lovely creature I ever had looked upon. In that electric moment my heart went out in sympathy to every man who had bartered honour, country, all – for a woman's kiss.(p94)

> East and West may not intermingle. As a student of world-policies, as a physician, I admitted, could not deny, that truth. Again, if Kâramanèh were to be credited, she had come to Fu Manchu a slave; had fallen into

the hands of the raiders....At the mere thought of a girl so deliciously beautiful in the brutal power of slavers, I found myself grinding my teeth – closing my eyes in a futile attempt to blot out the pictures called up.(p146)

The 'complex hybrid fantasy' emerging out of poor old Petrie's 'attempt to demarcate boundaries' here recalls the logic of 'A child is being beaten'. In that essay, Freud stresses the extreme mobility of sexual identity at the level of primal fantasy, as the subject oscillates between various positions of identification within the scenario's *mise-en-scène* of desire. Indeed, the operations of desire seem to *require* the transgression of the positions defined as 'masculine' and 'feminine'. Laplanche and Pontalis make a similar point about the seduction fantasy. The mini-narrative 'A father seduces a daughter', they suggest, 'is a scenario with multiple entries, in which nothing shows whether the subject will be immediately located as *daughter*; it can as well be fixed as *father*, or even in the term *seduces*'. In the fantasy 'The yellow peril threatens the white man', the points of entry and identification are equally fragmented: hence the fascination of the villain and the racial ambivalence of the seductive woman.[17]

Freud, it seems, may have been right about what remains consistent in popular literature, however much their historical topics and occasions vary. At the centre of *Fu Manchu*'s tales of mysterious women and oriental villains stands 'His Majesty the Ego, the hero alike of every day-dream and every story'.[18] These lurid adventures turn out to be premissed on the same psychic economy of desire and transgression, fascination and revulsion, identification and rivalry, that others have identified in the play on sexual difference in more 'realistic' modes of popular fiction, like private eye stories and *film noir*. In a novel like Dashiell Hammett's *The Maltese Falcon* (1930), for example, the problem of identity is displaced from Sam Spade on to the female characters, especially the enigmatic *femme fatale* whose trust-worthiness and even identity are always in question – is she Miss Wonderly, Miss Leblanc, or Brigid O'Shaughnessey? What does she know? And above all, of course, what does she want?

That familiar but still scandalous question at the centre of psychoanalysis promises a way of connecting the form taken by narratives to the historical realities of sexual difference.

In the overall system of sexuality that is tightened to perfection in the nineteenth century, male sexuality is repetition, unquestioned; female sexuality is query, riddle, enigma. Or, to put it another way, increased awareness of and attention to matters of identity and sexual identity, including direct challenges to the fixed terms and assumptions of 'man' and 'woman' (by developing women's movements, for example), gives a problem of representation the working out of which is done by shifting the problem on to the woman. ('What does woman want?', to use Freud's famous question from within the perspective of this shift) and thus safeguarding the man (men are men and there is little else to say). Difference must be maintained and dealt with on *her*, not brought back onto him.[19]

That's why the *problem* of identity is so often played out by its projection on to dangerous women. But it does not mean that the differences between 'English' and 'foreign', 'white' and 'black', 'pure' and 'hybrid' are merely displacements of the same (heterosexual) difference – any more than the differences between 'live' and 'dead' in vampire or zombie films or between 'human' and 'replicant' in science fiction films. These systems of differentiation are eroticized, certainly, but they also draw contingent material – the historical, the social – into interaction with the primal or original fantasies to construct a psychic reality.

One implication of this is that it is less the gaudy images of dangerous women and foreign villains that are essential for popular fiction to work as the textual vehicles of fantasy scenarios than the system of identification/differentiation which produces them. In the article on Stevenson's *Strange Case of Dr Jekyll and Mr Hyde* from which I have just quoted, for example, Stephen Heath notes that here there are no women on to whom the problem of identity can be projected. As a result, instability cannot be displaced on to the figure of the woman: hence 'the fascination with the double, men as unstable, something else'. The split between the normal Jekyll and the beastly Hyde both represents and *contains* the question of male sexuality. 'The difficulty of representation', says Heath, 'is simply solved by pathology, turned into the strange case, Hyde.' The exclusion of women (and thus also of the sexual and of hysteria) brings to light 'the hidden male: the animal, the criminal, *perversion*'. Yet the symbolic poles of masculinity and femininity that constitute the system of sexual difference remain in place: 'perversion replaces and complements

Racializing Mr Hyde – Frederic March in Mamoulian's *Dr Jekyll and Mr Hyde* (1932) (*National Film Archive*)

hysteria, positive to negative, maintaining male and female, man and woman, at whatever cost, as the terms of identity'.[20]

The terms of identity, maintained at whatever cost ... These are the obsessive concern, in their different ways, of both *Fu Manchu* and *Jekyll and Hyde*. Each takes as its topic the abject and the schizophrenic: duality, transformations, the breaking of boundaries, the fragmentation of experience and identity. But their social function is aggressively centripetal. Conjuring up chaos, they drive towards unity, order, and wholeness. The textual rendering and widespread circulation of such fantasies, 'both stereotyped and infinitely variable',[21] gives at least some stability to the restlessness of desire, demarcating its familiar boundaries. Hence the *institution* of popular fiction.

But how does this institution impinge on its audiences? How are subjectivities formed within the collective fantasies and terms of identity organized in popular fiction – and at what cost? Quite simply, what do audiences do with popular fictions?

Again, I'm afraid, my response is anecdotal rather than theoretical. Such questions always make me think of watching Clint Eastwood as *Dirty Harry* in a West End cinema in the early 1970s. I felt uneasy about enjoying the film: its yield of 'fore-pleasure' (its generic familiarity, its urban iconography, the confident manipulation of image and music, the elegance of Eastwood's gestures) was only just winning out over the offensiveness of its Nixonite politics. At one point Harry, the policeman/hunter, shoots and tortures Scorpio, the psychopath he catches up with in a football stadium. What made me really edgy was not so much the image itself, as the spontaneous cheer of approval it provoked in the audience. At the time, I put this down to the then current populist rhetoric about law and order, spongers and muggers, the ungovernability of Britain and vigilante armies being raised in the shires. (Was this my first brush with a nascent Thatcherism?)

Ten years later, while researching Eastwood for some teaching on Hollywood stardom and sexuality, I found other people noting similar responses. In the States, these focused especially on the apparent identification with Harry by blacks and Puerto Ricans. Reviewing *Dirty Harry* in the *New Yorker* (15 January 1972), Pauline Kael condemned the 'fairy-tale appeal' of its 'fascist medievalism':

The movie was cheered and applauded by Puerto Ricans in the audience,

179

Dirty Harry and Abject Scorpio – Clint Eastwood and Andy Robinson in
Dirty Harry (1971) (*National Film Archive*)

and they jeered – as they were meant to – when the maniac whined and pleaded for his legal rights. Puerto Ricans could applaud Harry because, in the movie, laws protecting the rights of the accused are seen not as remedies for the mistreatment of the poor by the police and the courts, but as protection for evil abstracted from all social conditions – metaphysical evil, classless criminality.

In the *New York Review of Books* in 1982, Robert Mazzocco also tried to explain Eastwood's paradoxical appeal:

> It's no wonder that Eastwood has a big following among black audiences, even though the presentation of blacks in his films is not always flattering – as it's not always flattering to other ethnic minorities, among whom he's also popular. Each group may perceive in Eastwood a glamorized version of its own reveries of omnipotence, its own amorphous sense of distrust.

Despite all the protestations about the good-natured but deliberate credulity of the popular audience and its Manichaean desire to see rough justice meted out,[22] I don't think these worries should be dismissed as middle-class killjoys' uncomprehending contempt for popular 'false consciousness'. Nor are they just the squeamishness of white liberals confronted by the oppressed's embarrassing collusion with their oppression. By invoking fairy tales and reveries, both Kael and Mazzocco point towards the importance of fantasy in the audience's responses. But, by drawing back into familiar oppositions between fantasy and rationality (for Kael) or real collective interests (for Mazzocco), they miss the radical implication of the concept: the possibility of multiple points of entry into the scenario 'Harry kicks the shit out of Scorpio'. The point of fixity need not be either Harry or Scorpio. It can just as well be the shit-kicking.[23] And if, as I would argue, this figures the familiar doubling split between Harry as identity and Scorpio as non-identity (disorder, pathology, perversion), what it invites or demands is acceptance of the terms of identity; an identification with the polarity rather than with either pole.

This is where the emphasis on fantasy differs from a notion like interpellation. Identification becomes less an individual's self-recognition in a fictional 'hailing' than a phantasmatic disposition to a particular organization of terms of identity. So audiences' apparently perverse enjoyment of *Dirty Harry* perhaps suggests their engagement with the film's play on the terms of identity – and also on the *costs* of their maintenance. Scorpio's lack of identity indicates the cost of abjection: as the film, like *Jekyll and Hyde*, marginalizes women virtually to the point of exclusion, he might be read as Harry's monstrously feminized double-ganger. But what is the cost of Harry's identity? In the film's final scene, having killed Scorpio, Harry throws away his police badge. This anguished gesture certainly suggests a loss of faith in 'the law' in its contemporary institutional forms. The badge has lost its symbolic meaning; it becomes just a piece of tin. But there is more to the gesture than an amorphous resentment at being short-changed by history. The law had been the term of Harry's identity, but even *its* promise of perfection and completion turns out to be deceiving. Like Englishness, masculinity, or whatever, Harry's Law remains irreconcilably Other. It cannot satisfy his longing for the fulfilment of identity; it is not a position that anybody can *be*. Hence Harry's anguish. Hence too the instability of ordinary identity: neither pure abjection nor pure anguish, but the precarious course between.

This view of the Otherness of culture and identity recalls the arguments about the production of identity in the attempt to demarcate boundaries. But *this* Other is not alien, exotic, or grotesque. What we have here is the Otherness of what is known and familiar, of the culture where you are supposed to feel at home. This perception undermines the residual functionalism in much of the recent work on ideologies of nationalism and Englishness. It hints at the anguish that fuels anxieties about the permeability of boundaries (and so of collective identities, and of the personality) which is such a recurrent feature of fictions like *Fu Manchu, Jekyll and Hyde*, and *Dirty Harry*. It helps to make sense of what might be called the paranoid strand in popular culture, the clinging to familiar polarities and the horror of difference. Manifest in its racism, its violent misogyny, and its phobias about alien cultures, alien ideologies, and 'enemies within' is the terror that, without the known boundaries, everything will collapse into undifferentiated, miasmic chaos; that identity will disintegrate; that 'I' will be suffocated or swamped.[24] Returning for the last time to my epigraph from Said, could this be the sense in which certain traditions of popular fiction – and also populist politics – 'gain their coherence' from the concept of race?

THE 'ENGLISH GARDEN' EFFECT

I pinched the title of this article from Walter Abish's novel, *How German Is It?*, which examines how we render history livable. Abish's image of a Milton Keynes-like new town named after a Heidegger-like philosopher built on the site of a concentration camp suggests that sometimes we render it in concrete. This casts a chilling light on Edward Said's definition of culture as the place where we feel at home: however *heimlich* the culture may seem, its foundations are laid in violence. Before writing the novel, Abish trailed some of its themes and imagery in a short story called 'The English Garden'. This title he took from John Ashbery: 'Remnants of the old atrocity persist, but they are converted into ingenious shifts of scenery, a sort of "English Garden" effect to give the required air of naturalness, pathos and hope.'[25]

The domestication of atrocity, it seems to me, is not only the essence of a conservative 'Englishness' framed in a nostalgic rhetoric of landscape and heritage. It is evident in the recurrent bucolic imagery of Arts-Council-speak, from Keynes's 'pastures new' to *Glory of the Garden*, the current chairman's policy document. And doesn't it also return in the left's periodic attempts to rewrite England's atrocious history as a *Bildungsroman* in which the hero is 'the people'?[26]

I have stressed the *production* of 'the national culture' and the institution 'Literature' in an attempt to break the tenacious grip of such parochial images of Englishness. Treating them as an organized system of institutions securing both power and knowledge places them squarely within a history of policing and subjectification. But equally important for understanding either popular literature or the national culture, or the relationship between them, is a different history: the history of the subject. Here again John Ashbery's image seems apt. Aren't the origins of repression and desire and the pervasive sense of lost plenitude given their 'required air of naturalness, pathos and hope' through the 'ingenious shifts of scenery' achieved by the operations of *fantasy* in psychic life? In the history of the subject, is it not the overall structural *stability* of the fantasy scenarios discernible in (for example) popular fictions which regulates and organizes the otherwise formless displacements of desire?[27] The problem remains, of course, the apparent impossibility of establishing links between these two histories. The dual focus on both the institution Literature and the fantasies inscribed in popular fiction at least suggests the tension between them within which cultural criticism has to operate.

NOTES

This article is based on talks given at the Institute of Contemporary Arts, London (December 1986) and the conference of the London Association of Teachers of English (March 1987).

[1] Edward Said, *The World, the Text, and the Critic* (London: Faber, 1984), 169; Paul Gilroy, *There Ain't No Black in the Union Jack* (London: Hutchinson, 1987), 12.

[2] Among the more interesting examples are Tom Nairn, *The Break-up of Britain* (2nd edn) (London: Verso, 1981): Martin J. Wiener, *English Culture and the Decline of the Industrial Spirit*, 1850-1980 (Cambridge: Cambridge University Press, 1981); Eric Hobsbawm and Terence Ranger (eds), *The Invention of Tradition* (Cambridge: Cambridge University Press, 1983); Patrick Wright, *On Living in an Old Country: the national past in contemporary Britain* (London: Verso, 1985); Robert Colls and Philip Dodd (eds), *Englishness: politics and culture 1880-1920* (London: Croom Helm, 1986).

[3] Gilroy *op.cit.*, 247.

[4] Said, *op.cit.*, 8; Benedict Anderson, *Imagined Communities: reflections on the origin and spread of nationalism* (London: Verso, 1983).

[5] John Maynard Keynes, 'The Arts Council: its policy and hopes', *The Listener*, no. 34 (12 July 1945).

[6] Such work was pioneered in France by Renée Balibar and her colleagues. For examples of British work influenced by this approach, see Tony Davies, 'Education, ideology and literature', *Red Letters*, no. 7 (1978); Brian Doyle, 'The hidden history of English studies', in Peter Widdowson (ed.), *Re-Reading English* (London: Methuen, 1982), and 'The invention of English', in Colls and Dodd, *op.cit.*; Jacqueline Rose, *The Case of Peter Pan or the Impossibility of Children's Fiction* (London: Macmillan, 1984), ch. 5, 'Peter Pan, language and the State: Captain Hook goes to Eton'. On literature as an organizing principle, see Tony Bennett, 'Marxism and popular fiction', *Literature and History*, 7,2 (Autumn 1981), 7.

[7] See my 'How illiteracy became a problem (and literacy stopped being one)', *Journal of Education*, 165, 1 (Winter 1983); Jane Mackay and Pat Thane, 'The Englishwoman', in Colls and Dodd, *op.cit.*, 193.

[8] See, for example, Michael Denning, *Mechanic Accents; dime novels and working-class culture in America* (London: Verso, 1987), especially chs 3-5.

[9] Bennett, *op.cit.*, 152.

[10] 'Reification and Utopia in mass culture', *Social Text*, no. 1 (Winter 1979), 133; Laura Kipnis, ' "Refunctioning" reconsidered: towards a left popular culture', in Colin MacCabe (ed.), *High Theory/Low Taste: analysing popular television and film* (Manchester: Manchester University Press, 1986), 22; Peter Brooker and Peter Widdowson, 'A literature for England', in Colls and Dodd, *op.cit.*, 153. (Where the real *need* for the modernism/mass culture binarism lies is, I suspect, indicated by the quotation from Laura Kipnis. It is necessary

primarily for the argument that postmodernism explodes the polarity to make sense.)

[11] The best work from this perspective is exemplified in the articles by Ian Hunter, Colin Mercer, and Tony Bennett in *New Formations*, no. 4 (Spring 1988). See also Hunter's 'After representation: recent discussions of the relation between language and literature', *Economy and Society*, 13, 4 (November 1984), and Mercer's 'That's entertainment: the resilience of popular forms', in Tony Bennett, Colin Mercer, and Janet Woollacott (eds), *Popular Culture and Social Relations* (Milton Keynes: Open University Press, 1986).

[12] Gilroy, *op.cit.*, 54.

[13] Peter Stallybrass and Allon White, *The Politics and Poetics of Transgression* (London: Methuen, 1986), 5.

[14] Stallybrass and White, *op.cit.*, 193; Said, *op.cit.*, 3, 7.

[15] Sax Rohmer, *The Mystery of Dr Fu Manchu* (London: J. M. Dent & Sons, 1985 [1913]), 19. Further page references are given in the text.

[16] For an attempt to give a historical context for this sort of literature in the USA, see R. Valerie Lucas, 'Yellow peril in the promised land: the representation of the oriental and the question of American identity', in Francis Barker, Peter Hulme, Margaret Iversen, and Diana Loxley (eds), *Europe and its Others*, volume one (Colchester: University of Essex, 1985). On the change from the adventure story to the thriller: Michael Denning, *Cover Stories: narrative and ideology in the British spy thriller* (London: Routledge & Kegan Paul, 1987), 41. On the abject: Julia Kristeva, *Powers of Horror: an essay on abjection* (New York: Columbia University Press, 1982), 4.

[17] Sigmund Freud, 'A child is being beaten (A contribution to the study of the origins of sexual perversions)' (1919), in *On Psychopathology, Penguin Freud Library*, vol. 10 (Harmondsworth: Penguin, 1979). Jean Laplanche and J.-B. Pontalis, 'Fantasy and the origins of sexuality', in Victor Burgin, James Donald, and Cora Kaplan (eds), *Formations of Fantasy* (London: Methuen, 1986), 22-3.

[18] Freud, 'Creative writers and day-dreaming' (1908), in *Art and Literature*, Pelican Freud Library, vol 14 (Harmondsworth: Penguin, 1985), 138.

[19] Stephen Heath, 'Psychopathia sexualis: Stevenson's *Strange Case*', *Critical Quarterly*, 28, 1/2 (Spring/Summer 1986), 98.

[20] Heath, *op.cit.*, 100, 103, 104, 104-5.

[21] Laplanche and Pontalis, *op.cit.*, 22, referring to Freud's comments on the novelette form of reverie as the model fantasy.

[22] I am thinking of Pierre Bourdieu on the 'popoular aesthetic' (*Distinction: a social critique of the judgement of taste* [London: Routledge & Kegan Paul, 1984], 33) and Roland Barthes on the audience for wrestling in *Mythologies* (London: Cape, 1972), 21.

[23] See also Valerie Walkerdine's 'reading' of *Rocky IV*: 'Video replay: families, films and fantasy', in Burgin, Donald, and Kaplan, *op.cit.*

[24] A reference to Klaus Theweleit's formulation in *Male Fantasies* (Cambridge: Polity Press, 1987), 428.

[25] Walter Abish, *How German Is It?* (London: Faber, 1983); 'The English Garden', in *In the Future Perfect* (London: Faber, 1984), 1.

[26] This is the implication of both Gilroy's critique of cultural studies and Bill Schwarz's account of the communist historians in the 1940s and 1950s: ' "The

people" in history', in Richard Johnson *et al*, *Making Histories* (London: Hutchinson, 1982).

[27] Adapted from Victor Burgin, 'Diderot, Barthes, *Vertigo*', in Burgin, Donald, and Kaplan, *op.cit.*, 98.

His Stories?:
Narratives and Images
of Imperialism

Gail Ching-Liang Low

'Position', 'cultural difference' and 'pleasure' are all issues which must
be addressed in any critique of colonial representation. Yet they are
difficult to come to terms with, because they require an
acknowledgement of the ambivalences and complexities of political
address, and because they forestall any easy appeal to epistemological
certainty – 'the truth' – which authorizes critical transparency and
orthodoxy. Instead the poetics of writing, already informed and
inscribed by an agon of voices, involves, in Homi Bhabha's words, a
process of 'negotiation (rather than a negation) of oppositional and
antagonistic elements' and the opening of a space of 'translation' and
'hybridity'.[1]

Klaus Theweleit's psychoanalytic interpretation of history, *Male
Fantasies*, confronts just such a problem.[2] A suggestive and
provocative text, Theweleit's study of fascism begins with the
difficulties of conveying and translating sensibilities located outside
what is perceived as normal; he argues against theorists of fascism who
'never tire of finding fault with the "unreality" of fascists' fantasy
worlds, the "irrationality" of their behaviour, or the "subjectivity" that
gives rise to errors in their political theories.' Instead, an understanding
of fascism must be ' "lived through" … in such a way that our
understanding of history comes about *through the experience of our
unconscious*'.[3] *Male Fantasies* brings home the shock of fascist
experience precisely because it refuses the easy binarism of
fantasy/reality, them/us, myth/history and recognizes a hybrid space
of time and subjectivity. Also, by analysing fascist myth-making in

relation to sexuality and by returning authoritarian identities to their emotion and affective roots in the psychosexual traumas of childhood, Theweleit begins the process of explaining the grip that such mythologies achieve over ordinary people.

I begin this paper with Theweleit and Bhabha's 'fort/da of the symbolic process of political negotiation'[4] because these two theorists present a clear challenge to cultural historians to rethink – in a self-reflexive way – the whole politics and poetics of writing against the grain. In my own work on the literature of Empire, anger at the subjugation and exploitation of other worlds often *dismisses* these romances of imperialism as white patriarchal myths, justifying the conquest and occupation of non-western societies. They *are*, of course, all of the above; yet the easy negation of such writing does not address the power and hold of its mythologies, nor the trajectories of its desire.

In this paper, I want to focus on the writer Henry Rider Haggard and his contributions to a reading of imperialism as a culture of masculinity in the late Victorian period. I have set out to read Haggard's writings alongside Theweleit's work on fascism so as to provoke irruptions, contradictions and connections between the unstable authoritarian identities – imperial/fascistic – of these two very different historical formations of the right; such a juxtaposition will enable me to explore the dynamics of male identities which are located at – predicated on – national and institutional regimes. *Male Fantasies*, ostensibly an account of proto-fascism in the years 1918 to 1923, makes wider claims for the sexing of male identities towards a culture of warfare. Theweleit's theory, which has its ancestry in the work of William Reich, is an interpretive psychology centred on the *materiality* of the human body: the culture of warfare represents a polarization of sexual politics where the feminine is viewed as a radical threat to the wholeness and hardness of the 'soldier male'. The fascist warrior is a psychotic whose childhood did not pass through the stage of 'ego' formation and the establishment of bodily boundaries between self and other. As a result, the identities of these 'not-yet-fully-born' soldier males are extremely fragile and achieved only by proxy through militarism and a regime of discipline.

What I do not want to do within the confines of this paper is to write a systematic interrogation of Theweleit using Haggard's texts or vice versa. Neither do I want to interpret all authoritarian and imperial subjectivities as identical, nor read British imperial culture as essentially fascistic. That British politics and society did not take that direction despite the proliferation of paramilitary organizations, the crude appeals to Empire or the political activities of the radical right account perhaps for the vocal hysteria of the latter.[5] Yet the radical polarization of the sexes and obsession with a male militaristic culture which deliberately marginalizes women, are framed within the Haggardian adventure genre and are echoed in the culture of the right. My task is rather to examine a specific reproduction of the radical culture of the right in Britain at the turn of the century.

SEX, POLITICS AND SOCIETY

Contemporary historians have drawn attention to both centrifugal and centripetal tendencies in late Victorian and Edwardian politics and society in their attempts to mediate between previous polarities the 'crisis age' versus the 'golden age'.[6] In my attempt to read Haggard as part of the literature and mythology of the right, emphasis will be put on the former. For such a narration of history represents the paranoias and fears expressed by the forces of the pre-war right in their attempts to reverse what they saw as Britain's decline.[7] It also functions (ironically) as a way of centring a nation, of narrating its boundaries from precisely that difficult site of its external divisions – from what Homi Bhabha has called 'the heterogeneous and differentiated limits of its territory'.[8] On the one hand, fears for Britain's vulnerability in the face of economic competition from America and Germany were accentuated with the emergence of Italy and Germany as imperial powers.[9] On the other, a growing trade union and a more militant women's movement further fragmented the social consensus at home. The 'Condition of England' question also raised the spectre of racial and national deterioration; Haggard in *The Poor and the Land* speaks scathingly of 'puny pigmies growing from towns or town bred parents' in contrast to the 'blood and sinew of the race' – 'robust and intelligent' country-born English 'land dwellers' whose 'deeds are written large in history'.[10] Even a liberal like Charles Masterman remarked, 'the problem of the coming years is just the problem of this New Town type; upon their development and action depend the future progress of the Anglo-Saxon Race, and for the next half-century at least the policy of the British Empire in the World.'[11]

Eugenics located progress in the physical health of whole races; the body became a site where anxieties about urban poverty, degeneracy and national decline were represented. Britain's decline, it was feared, might follow that of the Roman Empire; over-cultivation, refinement, the love of luxury and ease were in Garnet Wolsley's words 'calculated to convert manliness into effeminacy', killing all the 'virile energy' that was vital to the 'greatness of the nation':

> It is the nature of the Anglo-Saxon race to love those manly sports which entail violent exercise, with more or less danger to limb if not life….This craving for the constant practice and employment of our muscles is in our blood, and the result is a development of bodily strength unknown in most nations and unsurpassed by any other breed of men.[12]

This *gendering* of decadence, 'indolence, love of ease, and clap trap sentimentality' as *feminine*, against a militaristic hardness of (British) male vitality is also reflected in the literary and generic divide of Romance/Adventure/Epic Narratives and Realism. Foreign 'Naturalistic' writers like Zola were criticized for subjects 'lewd, and bold, and bare, living for lust and lusting for this life and its good things': 'whatever there is that is carnal and filthy, is here brought into prominence, and thrust before the reader's eyes'. This wilful display, in Haggard's words, of 'Bacchanalian revellings' was unhealthy and detrimental to the moral fabric of the nation.[13]

While French and Russian Realism produced pessimism and morbidity, American writers like Henry James produced unmanly novels of 'silk and cambric' and emasculated heroes 'with culture on their lips'. In contrast to the swiftness, strength and directness of 'great English writers of the past', these works have an atmosphere 'like that of the boudoir of a luxurious woman, faint and delicate, suggesting the essence of white rose'.[14] Haggard's unease with what he saw as an unhealthy feminization of English culture, was supported by his friend, the influential critic Andrew Lang, in the very same year:

> If I were to draw up an indictment, I might add that some of them have an almost unholy knowledge of the nature of women. One would as lief explore a girl's room, and tumble about her little household treasures, as examine so curiously, the poor secrets of her heart and tremors of her frame….Such analysis makes one feel uncomfortable in the reading, makes one feel intrusive and unmanly.[15]

What was hailed as a relief to this enfeebled novel 'bred in and in'[16] was the appearance of a new romance of adventure. Extolling the invigorations of this new genre of fiction, George Saintsbury speculated: 'there is still too much healthy beefiness and beeriness (much of both as it has lost) in the English temperament to permit it to indulge in the sterile pessimism which seems to dominate Russian fiction.'[17] As Peter Keating notes, Saintsbury's rhetoric drew on the 'imagery of health and cleansing' which marked all these major manifestos for romance in 1887: 'the fresh wind of romance not only blows away morbidity and brings a return to health, it does this by liberating the imagination, thus making great art possible again.'[18] Yet Keating's remarks obscure the deliberate gendering of genres and it is to this complex of ideas in Haggard that I now want to turn.

Haggard's popularity in the last fifteen years of the nineteenth century was due chiefly to the success of his imperial romances; of the fifty-nine volumes of fiction to his credit, forty-seven are popular adventures set in countries ranging from South Africa, Mexico, Egypt to Scandinavia. Africa remained the favourite location. His first novel of adventure was published on 30 September 1885, after a massive publicity campaign mounted by Cassell. *King Solomon's Mines*, a best-seller by all accounts, was followed by a string of equally popular novels.[19] Haggard's success presents an interesting nodal point both in the literature of British Empire and my reading of a specific imperialist/male/authoritarian culture. Haggard's texts fed into and were sustained by a cultural map of epics, travel narratives, exploration and the 'boy's adventure', set within a contemporary history of new imperialism abroad and a growing pedagogic militarism in public schools at home.[20] The publication of Stevenson's *Treasure Island* in 1882 (with 12,000 copies sold by 1886) opened a mythic space for Haggard's address to 'all the big and little boys who read it'. Interwoven with the anxieties of 'Englishness', masculinity, militarism, patriotism and imperial ideologies, these romances attempted both to exploit and to answer all of these contemporary issues.[21]

THE DOMINION OF SONS: PASTORAL POLITICS, MEMORY AND ADVENTURE NARRATIVES

The desire of the hero of Haggard's adventure, *Allan Quartermain*, to escape the constraints of late nineteenth-century culture – defiled by the 'sinks of struggling, sweltering humanity' – into the arms of mother nature (a land 'whereof none know the history') initiates his quest and narrative of adventure.[22] Quartermain's version of the civilized life is drawn directly from that wider cultural feminization of decadence and decline, and is countered only by his *memory* of an empowering fantasy of male action. And yet, it is ironically a cultured and civilized life which colonialism offers to the native land.

Haggard, writing his autobiography in 1926, remembers Natal as one of 'the most beautiful' parts of the world by evoking the visual panorama of its landscape from veld to mountain:

> The great plains rising by the steps of the QuathLamba or Drakenburg Mountains, the sparkling torrential rivers, the sweeping thunderstorms, the grass-fires creeping over the veld at night like snakes of living flame, the glorious aspect of the heavens, now of a spotless hue, now charged with the splendid and many coloured lights of sunset, and now sparkling with a myriad stars; the wine-like taste of the air upon the plains, the beautiful flowers in the bush clad kloofs or on the black veld in spring.

All are indelibly marked in memory; 'were I to live a thousand years I never should forget them.'[23] Such a passage is noteworthy for the absence of native life and for its inscription of all human agency as natural. In this romance of wide, empty spaces, the adjectival and the verbal is made a predicate of the natural, so that unseen by human eyes, the rivers are sparkling, flowers beautiful and grass-fires creeping 'like snakes of living flame'. Metaphors appear in self-evident succession in inverse proportion to the deliberate effacement of the controlling human eye/I in the landscape.[24]

Significantly, Haggard's invocation of nature in the landscapes of his adventure is not that teeming primeval woman/nature of Conrad's womb of darkness, but an open pastoral idyll of masculinity. Such a vision deliberately marginalizes women both by constructing them as threats to male identities, and by feminizing all threats to this male self-containment. Akin to Theweleit's soldier male fantasies, nature as shaped by the desires of such men is the *cultural* dominion of men: 'In escaping to the forest, the fascist male does not flee from the frying pan of women to the fire of nature; for what he finds in the forest is ... male dominion made manifest in nature as the dominion of *sons* – his wishful dream.'[25] The sub-plot of the wolf-story in *Nada the Lily* presents just such a mythic scenario.[26] A curious story, it involves the bonding of two men who live a spartan existence in a forest and find themselves leaders over a pack of supernatural wolves. Women in this text of Haggard's are forces of instability and chaos. One character reproaches the other with the 'shame' of desiring women: 'From that source flow these ills, as a river from a spring ...' (*Nada*, p298). At the death of his friend, the other says mournfully, 'May we one day find a land where there are no women, but war only, for in that land we shall grow great' (*Nada*, p299).

The dedication in *Allan's Wife*, written in the style of a pastoral elegy, combines two differing moments of grief: a mourning for a lost youth – 'many a *boyish* enterprise and adventure' – and a mourning for a natural and wild land of 'misty charm' now lost to development, civilization and the scramble for diamonds.[27] That Haggard had never seen a Southern Africa without its diamond industry is irrelevant to the text's nostalgia; Northrop Frye, discussing the genre of romance, remarks, 'the elegiac presents heroism unspoilt by irony ... [and] is often accompanied by a diffused, resigned, melancholic sense of passing time, of the older order changing and yielding to a new one ...'.[28] The diurnal imagery which tracks that passage of time makes it evident that the lost innocence and freedom may never be regained, but in doing so, it reminds the reader that the *recall* from memory secures an imperial inheritance for future generations:

> [These further adventure of Quartermain] will ... perhaps ... bring back to you some of the long past romance of days that are lost to us....Where we shot and trekked and galloped, scarcely seeing the face of civilised man, there the gold-seeker builds his cities – the game is gone; the misty charm of the morning has become the glare of day. All is changed....Still we can remember many a boyish enterprise and adventure, lightly undertaken, which now would strike us as hazardous indeed....To you then ... in perpetual memory of those eventful years of youth which we passed together in the African towns and on the African veld, I dedicate these pages....(*Allan's Wife*, 5-7)

I have quoted from the dedication at length because the pastoral form, which suggests feelings of lost innocence and nostalgia (the elegy), seems to me to be one best suited to the poetics of empire. It achieves the twin tasks of disowning culpability for the destruction of indigenous cultures, and of producing a gendered and, as I shall make clear later, an *infantilised* notion of culture central to the imperialist mythopoetics of the boy's story.

William Empson writes that the pastoral form was 'felt to imply a beautiful relation between rich and poor',[29] while Kenneth Burke calls it a 'rhetoric of courtship between contrasted social classes ... a kind of expression which, while thoroughly conscious of class differences, aims rather at stylistic transcending of conflict'.[30] Yet this hymn to good relations between the colonized and the colonizer, significantly makes its entrance only when the former is under threat of extinction. As Mary Pratt points out of the Cape tribes, it is only after their virtual extinction towards the end of the eighteenth century that the so-called 'Bushmen' become textualized as objects of ethnographic study, and as objects of 'pathos and guilt'.[31]

While the histories of the Zulus and the Natal Ngunis are not identical with the 'Bushmen' and 'Hottentots' of the Cape region, a similar nostalgia applies to the tribes of Natal, Transvaal and Zululand which appear in Haggard's stories. As Abrams emphasizes, the pastoral is an 'elaborately conventionl poem expressing an urban poet's nostalgic image of peace and the simplicity of the life of shepherds and other rural folk in an idealised natural setting';[32] shepherds and rural folk do not in any ordinary sense write the poem. Transposed into our version of the pastoral, the elaborate courtesy of the first pair colonizer/city to the second, colonized native/country, is only made possible by the position of power held by the former, and by the exercise of that power towards a transformation of the latter. Another anthropologist accuses this nostalgia – 'imperialist nostalgia' – of being dishonest: 'a pose of innocent yearning both to capture peoples' imaginations and to conceal its complicity with often brutal domination'.[33]

Yet the colonizing subject is produced in that intersection between desire and power, for a double articulation is evident in every line of the pastoral vision. Annexation of the Transvaal brings the possibility of advancement and Haggard's letter home on 1 June, recording his appointment as English clerk to the Colonial Secretary in the new administration, testifies to a vision of a country and its settlers 'that must become rich and rising'.[34] This land 'whereof none knows the history' becomes a fantasized place 'of a kind that help *make a man*'; a place in which 'it was possible for a man of moderate means to start his children in some respectable career ... and have a fair chance of getting on in the world'.[35] Here the pastoral comes to represent not the open wilderness 'where we shot and trekked and galloped, scarcely seeing the face of civilised man' but the domesticated safe havens of managed locations and settlers' homes; the semantic slippage between various versions of the pastoral are crucial to the narratives of colonialism which are compelled to inscribe a text of development, civility and growth.

The second movement is a generated through an elision of the text of the boy-child and that of the adult man's inheritance. There is an enabling textual symmetry in this: the (recollected) innocence of the child is the (recollected) innocence of the land in a narrative where only the innocent may inherit the world, or find a new one. Discussing narrative closure in 'Afterthoughts on "Visual Pleasure and Narrative Cinema" ', Laura Mulvey argues that the two positions which bring pleasure for the male spectator of westerns are those associated with Oedipal drama: 'the symbolic' which represents social integration, marriage and inheritance of patriarchal power, and 'the phallic' whose 'rejection of marriage personifies a nostalgic celebration of phallic, narcissistic omnipotence'.[36] Mulvey asserts that such a narrative structure is predicated on 'an opposition between two irreconcilables':

> the two paths cannot cross. On the one side there is an encapsulation of power, and phallic attributes, in an individual who has to bow himself out of the way of history. On the other, an individual impotence rewarded by political and financial power, which, *in the long run*, in fact becomes history.[37]

Where Theweleit's findings come in useful is in the suggestion that his subjects, by virtue of their psychoses, do not have access to the Oedipal ego. What becomes apparent from my point of view is that Mulvey's irreconcilable differences are elided in a narrative of adventure *and* colonialism which depends on that narcissistic omnipotence of childhood, and on which is founded the imperial world.

Conrad, in *Geography and Some Explorers*, evokes a long established link between childhood, colonialism and geography. Conrad writes of his boyish fascination with maps based on the militant geographer's 'geography of open spaces and wide horizons built up on men's devoted work in the open air': 'My imagination could depict to itself there worthy, adventurous and devoted men, nibbling at the edges ... conquering a bit of truth here and a bit of truth there....' But if blank spaces were especially compelling, the 'boyish boast' was to sour in 'the distasteful knowledge of the vilest scramble for loot that ever disfigured the history of human conscience and geographical exploration.'[38]

Haggard's dedication, however, works towards reversing the movement in Conrad by privileging boyhood. As I have already suggested, because childhood presents a world of innocence unsullied by the corruption of age and civilization, the *boy* child is necessarily the only figure capable of inheriting or founding this blank new (colonial) world. The political implications of this conception of childhood innocence are all too clear. As Jacqueline Rose remarks,

> At this level, children's fiction has a set of long-established links with colonialism which identified the new world with the infantile state of man. Along the lines of what is almost a semantic slippage, the child is assumed to have some special relation to a world which – in our eyes at least – was only born when we found it.[39]

Furthermore, these boyhood experiences are never written by the *child* as such, but the adult man *remembering* himself as *a boy child*. The latter produces a (adult) dream text as a narrative of enchantment, which may be read forwards as inheritance, or backwards as memory and history. This turning backwards, which is simultaneously a turning forwards, produces a child and a dream which enables the boy/man and the man/boy to secure an inheritance of patriarchy and empire. Michel de Certeau reminds us that 'children are the repository of a culture that perpetuates itself on the fringes of adult culture, of which it represents an altered form.' In the 'mirror' of children's literature, it is 'adults who create an image of themselves, as they dream they are'[40] and the adults who *secure* for themselves that inheritance of continuity. As Rose argues, 'If children's fiction builds an image of the child inside the book, it does so in order to secure the child who is outside the book, the one who does not come so easily within its grasp.'[41] Haggard's dedication of 1887 expresses this fantasy of security and inheritance; he sincerely hopes that the tale may help 'all the big and little boys who read it' to reach what 'I hold to be the highest rank whereto we can attain – the state and dignity of English Gentlemen'.[42]

THESE FRAGMENTS I HAVE SHORED AGAINST MY RUINS

Yet in trying to secure the child that is outside the book, Haggard's writings give their strongest indication of the insecurity and instabilities which characterize the contradictory demands of imperial identities. This infantilizing of culture testifies to the desire for safety and control *more as an adult authoritarian fantasy*, than as a child's. The culture of the child, always reconstructed and already refashioned, provides the adult with a dream of its own origins. Such a fantasy of origins is ideally suited to the forms and conventions of the imperial romance; Northrop Frye's work on the genre may help unpick some major preoccupations.[43]

Frye writes that romances promoted the ascendancy of the aristocratic section of medieval society. They form a means of expressing the aristocracy's 'dreams of its own social function', and legitimizing their role through the ritualized and idealized portrayal of those social functions in the chivalric conventions.[44] Tracing the link between identity, alienation and wish-fulfilment, Frye also argues that of all literary forms, romance comes closest to functions of wish-fulfilment in dreams. But these dreams, rather than expressing the anarchic surfacing of unconscious desires, reflect a tightly controlled vision. For the die is cast from the very start; despite the trials which form the quest, identity and containment are always effected through the narrative's ending: 'Translated into dream terms, the quest-romance is the search of the libido or desiring self for fulfilment that will deliver it from the anxieties of reality but will still contain that reality.'[45] It is in this sense that Frye labels Haggard's adventures a 'kidnapped romance'; they represent the absorption and integration of the conventions of romance into the culture of imperialists abroad.

The landscape of difficulty central to the genre of romance is also integral to a discourse on masculinity. In *King Solomon's Mines*, this landscape is both African and consistently feminized: 'these mountains … are shaped after the fashion of a woman's breasts, and at times the mists and shadows beneath them take the form of a recumbent woman, veiled mysteriously in sleep.'[46] The mountains of Sheba's breast must be crossed in order that the treasure buried in the caverns of the African womb may be obtained. Acts of privation may also be read as heroic acts necessary to effect the submission of the native land reluctant to offer up its secrets; they are the signs of manliness which act to obliterate difference.

Acts of privation also narrate a story of the heroic performance of the male body under pressure. Associated with physical prowess, achievement, self-control and a regime of bodily discipline, physical pain becomes the means by which these ideals may be attained, and a ritual process by which an exclusively male community is created. Like Theweleit's soldiers ruled by the principle of pain, every exertion becomes a 'means of enhancing an already intoxicated consciousness, of adding strength to strength'.[47] The close of the day is invariably secured by 'yarns' – histories of travel and heroism – told around the campfire as (outdoor/male) substitute hearth: 'We ate our simple meal by the light of the moon … then began to smoke and yarn, and a curious picture we must have made squatting there round the fire' (*KSM*, 53).

Knowledge of the land, climates and peoples underscores narrative authority by reinforcing its privilege, possession and its science; like Conrad's geographical militant whose knowledge represents the reach of his power, maps enable the white adventurers to discover hidden treasure. These histories of anthropology, travel writing and adventure are intimately linked; detailed ethnographic description blends with adventure narrative to lock it within a 'realist' frame of reference. This 'manners and custom portraits', as Mary Pratt has pointed out, is part of an 'old and remarkably stable sub genre'.[48] In *Allan Quartermain*, the inventory of objects and precise measurements which form Haggard's description of the native warrior give an illusion of objectivity that belies the emotional investment that surfaces:

> To begin with the man was enormously tall … and quite beautifully though somewhat slightly shaped; but with the face of a devil. In his right hand he held a spear about five and a half feet long, the blade being two and a half feet in length, by nearly three inches in width, and having an iron spike at the end of a handle that measured more than a foot….Round the ankles he wore black fringes of hair, and projecting from the upper portion of the calves, to which they were attached, were long spurs like spikes, from which flowed down tufts of beautiful black and waving hair of the colobus monkey. Such was the elaborate array of the Masai Elmoran … only those who see it do not live to describe it. (*Allan Quartermain*, 33-4)

The overall effect of the passage is to credit the fear and negation of the cross-cultural encounter with the truth and measurement of science; difference is interpreted for the reader and made meaningful by the controlling figure of author as ethnographer. Difference becomes that same old story as the imperialist authoritarian identity fetishises his stereotype.[49] Yet even here the generality of the text bears witness to the ritual particularity of its fright: the Masai as exotic other carries a terrible spear, his shield is painted with 'strange heraldic-looking devices'; the ostrich feathers frame a 'diabolical countenance'; these descriptions climax in the hysterical statement which abandons all pretence of objectivity in a singularly shocking phrase: the Masai are 'bloodthirsty savages'. (p77)

THE ORIENTALIST GAZE: TOWARDS A FANTASY OF WHITE BODIES AND BLACK BODIES

While the Orientalist discourse of science provides knowledge as stability, this essentializing vision is always under threat from history and narrative as 'the site of dreams, images, fantasies, myths, obsessions and requirements'. As Bhabha points out, the fixity and fantasmatic oscillation which characterizes the stereotype belongs to the double articulation of the fetishist. The fetishist copes with the threat of difference by acknowledgement *and* by disavowal: 'the *same old stories* of the Negro's animality, the Coolie's inscrutability or the stupidity of the Irish *must* be told (compulsively) again and afresh, and are differently gratifying and terrifying each time.'[50]

But present in Haggard's detail of the Masai is an intense awareness of the *physicality* of his presence; the warrior is described as more 'ferocious or awe-inspiring' than any other figure seen in the past, 'enormously tall ... and beautifully, though some what slightly shaped; but with the face of a devil.' This qualifying clause, quickly uttered after the pause of the semi-colon, breaks the hypnotic effect of the Masai's presence on Quartermain, just as the horror of blood later jolts Quartermain out of another prolonged bout of fascination with the native subject: 'something warm spurted into my face. In an instant the spell was broken; I knew that it was no nightmare, but that we were attacked by swimming Masai' (*Allan Quartermain*, 38). The surreal description of the Masai attack contains all the tension of a sexually-charged encounter.

This narrative movement is not isolated, but belongs to the movement of the Orientalist gaze as both a disciplining and voyeuristic eye/I. As Kobena Mercer writes, this scopophilic look which lingers on the physicality – and parts and surfaces – of the black man's body is 'fundamentally predicated on a certain male narcissism ... a classical *mis-en-scène* of sexual fantasy in which [black men] are reduced to mirror images of what [white men] want-to-see'.[51] Marlow's difficulties with navigation when under attack record a similar moment of confrontation:

I had to lean right out to swing the heavy shutter, and I saw a face amongst the leaves on the level with my own, looking at me very fierce and steady; and then suddenly, as though a veil had been removed from my eyes, I made out, deep in the tangled gloom, naked breasts, arms, legs, glaring eyes – the bush was swarming with human limbs in movement, glistening, of bronze colour.[52]

The sudden encounter with the black face (which looks back at Marlow's own) operates on the level of metaphor *as* mirror; yet what is eventually seen, and which gestures towards the primitivity Marlow recognizes, are the *surfaces* and *severed parts* of the black body. In the striptease of the tangled gloom, these images of defiance are also sexual – 'glistening, of bronze colour', and naked breasts, swarming.

This semiotic of primitivity circulates a discourse which reads the black body as animal-like, sexually savage and regressive, and, within the conventions of romanticism and aestheticism, as noble savage.[53] Such a description can also be found in the writings of Haggard's contemporary, Baden-Powell, whose ideals of scouting were based in part on the contemporary cultural excitement of what was conceived as Zulu militarism. Baden-Powell describes a Matabele warrior as if he was part of the exotic and beautiful wildlife of the land; the image of such a warrior drinking parallels the spying of an animal at the waterhole:

Today, when out scouting by myself I lay for a quiet look-out among some rocks and grass overlooking a little stream.... Presently there was a slight rattle of trinkets, and a swish of the tall yellow grass, followed by the sudden apparition of a naked Matabele warrior standing glistening among the rocks within 30 yards of me. His white war ornaments ... contrasted strongly with his rich brown skin. His kilt of wild cat-skins and monkey's tails swayed round his loins ... he stood for almost a minute perfectly motionless, like a statue cast in bronze, his head turned from me, listening for any suspicious sound. Then, with a swift and canny movement, he laid his arms noiselessly upon the rocks, and, dropping on all fours beside a pool, he dipped his muzzle down and drank just like an animal. I could hear the thirsty sucking of his lips from where I lay.... He pulled his weapons up, and then stood again to listen. Having heard nothing he turned and sharply moved away.... I had been so taken with the spectacle that I felt no desire to shoot at him.[54]

Again *surfaces* are highlighted; the warrior's skin glistens, its 'rich brown colour' emphasized by his white war ornament. This appeal to surfaces is strategic to a discourse of racism; as Mercer argues for the case of the photographer Robert Mapplethorpe, the racial fetish of skin colour and texture is sexualised in the 'dilation of a libidinal way of looking that spreads itself across the surface of black *skin* ... its glossy allure suggest physical exertion ... intense sexual activity.'[55] Baden-Powell notices the kilt of *animal* skin which hides his loins from view and yet, paradoxically, also inscribes him as more – not less – naked through metonymic association with wildness. Yet both power and desire are muted and contained through a congruence with wildlife and sculptural form. The Matabele as animal becomes simply part of the landscape; his body framed by the conventions of high art. As Richard Dyer's study of Paul Robeson makes clear, this double articulation is needed to safeguard the heterosexual gaze – it is 'both a way of producing potentially erotic images while denying that this is what is being done, and also a way of constructing a mode of looking at the naked form ... "dispassionately", without arousal'.[56]

It seems to me that the problems of sexuality, race (nationality) and the body all *naturally* intersect in this late nineteenth-century text. Dyer highlights just such a discourse of nature when he writes that 'the ideology of the very notion of race invited these narratives; race is an idea in the discourse of biology, a way of grouping people according to perceptions of [skin colour and] bodily difference.'[57] Also, the perception of the black nude body sets in circulation a companion semiotic of otherness to that of the cross-cultural dress. This is what my work on the latter fantasy brushes against.[58] In the enactment of the fantasy of cultural cross-dressing, it is (more often than not) the white man who dresses up and the black man who reveals his body for consumption. If the black man presumes to the former as with Kipling's Eurasians and Bengali Babus, the narratives often work towards exposing him, revealing his blackness beneath the covering of clothes. This display of the black body, as indicated earlier, is caught up in the same movement of discrimination as the fetish of skin colour. The movement is linked to an atavistic trope of blackness, and marked against the white man's clothed and civilized body. Thus to claim his rightful inheritance, the black chief Umbopa (*KSM*) takes off his 'moocha' or girdle and stands naked before white men. John Laputa, the educated black missionary of John Buchan's *Prester John*, sheds his clerical garments to practise 'some strange magic'. The act of shedding his clothes uncovers evil by exposing it as merely a mask of whiteness, leading the boy hero to exclaim: 'I had no doubt it was the black art, for there was that in the air and the scene which spelt the unlawful.' The voyeurism and secrecy of this encounter is again unearthed when the minister strips for his coronation and effects a sexual and political 'black art': 'I had a mad desire to be of Laputa's party. Or rather, I longed for a leader who should master me and make my soul his own.'[59]

To return to Baden-Powell's text, the narrator as white English voyeur provides the organizing centre for the Matabele warrior's actions. His voyeurism, made all the more pleasurable by the warrior's seeming ignorance of his watching presence, transfixes him even where the curiosity of his gaze obsessively explores the detail of the warrior's body. Paradoxically, it is his *absence* that impels the diegesis; as perspectival vanishing point, his presence is only reconstituted through the black body of the warrior. Again Mercer's comments on Mapplethorpe are helpful:

> This emphasis on mastery is also evident in the imprint of a narcissistic, ego-centred staging of desire which imposes an isolation-effect whereby it is only ever *one* black man in the field of vision at any one time. This is a crucial component of the process of objectification ... [it] is the precondition for the fetishistic work of representation in which an absence is made present. Like the function of the solo-frame in pornography, this promotes the fantasy of an unmediated, unilateral, relation between seer and seen.[60]

But where Mapplethorpe's works freeze the body in black and white photography, the doubling of black/white is crucial to the heroic *narrative* of the white man writ large. In the battle of races, heroism on the side of the Zulu warriors (figure 1) only breeds more heroism. To be defeated by such men was to be their equals, to defeat such an enemy was to be more than their equals. On 6 September 1879 the *Illustrated London News* carried such a front-page spread of Lord Beresford's 'hand to hand single combat' with a native warrior (figure 2).

The image of the black body is necessary because it returns a physicality marginalized from the more conventional legacy of manliness which the Victorian Christian model idealizes. This dream of the black body results from tensions in the changing ideal of

Fig. 1   Fig. 2

manliness based on concepts such as 'character', honesty, earnestness, straightforwardness, chivalry, courage, fortitude and Christian values of paternalism. Manliness hovers on the one hand, in the older Christian model, around the privilege of rationality and reason (the soul) over the sensuous and the emotional (the body); as Magan and Walvin argue, 'it represented a concern with the successful transition from Christian immaturity to maturity, demonstrated by earnestness, selflessness and integrity....'[61] On the other, in the cult of Muscular Christianity which emerged at mid-century, the body finds centre stage when it becomes associated with self-control, discipline, physical perfection, achievement and patriotism. The athletic male body is a *disciplined* one, and as we shall see later, one which is crucial to a discourse of nationalism. Such reflection bespeaks desire; and as we shall see, it is in this dream of (sexual/racial) power that the white man (mis)recognizes his image/represents his mirror image in the physicality of the black body.

In Haggard's narratives, the spectacle of the male homosocial community is predicated on rituals of strength and comradeship that bind white men to their black counterparts; as Umbopa tells Henry Curtis in *King Solomon's Mines*, 'We are men, thou and I.' But this community is produced at the level of individuals, not races of peoples: '... ay I love thee, Macumazahn, for we have grown grey together, and there is that between us that cannot be seen, and yet is too strong for breaking.' (*Allan Quartermain*, 236)

Such singular – as opposed to communal – ties do not violate the *individual* identity of the male subject, which is predicated on boundaries. By narrating a relationship between individual men, these stories never have to negotiate the difficult problem of the relationship between whole races or nations. Significantly, these ties are also necessarily temporary relationships in the they terminate with the death of one of the pair near the close of the novel.[62] Umslopogaas is the *last* black warrior of his generation. As Zulu warrior, he also represents the mythical last of the 'military' nation destroyed in the Anglo-Zulu war. More importantly, Umslopogaas secures empowering narcissism in the white man; a story of boyhood romance away from women and the responsibility of the 'domestic':

> I [Umslopogaas] am weary of it, weary to death of eating and drinking, of sleeping and giving in marriage. I love not this soft life.... When we fought the Masai at the kraal yonder, ah, then life was worth the living ... (*Allan Quartermain*, 235)

The strong black man is necessary to a reproduction of the heroic male in contrast to his merely civilized counterpart; but by displacing women as the white man's object of affection, he narrates that impossible narcissistic romance of strong men predicated on the exclusion of women. In Kipling's words, this is the ballad of East and West:

> They have looked each other between the eyes, and there they found no fault.
> They have taken the Oath of the Brother-in-Blood on leavened bread and salt:
> They have taken the Oath of the Brother-in-Blood on fire and fresh-cut sod,

On the hilt and the haft of the Khyber knife, and the Wondrous Names
of God....

Oh, East is East, and West is West, and never the twain shall meet,
Till Earth and Sky stand presently at God's great Judgement Seat;
But there is neither East nor West, Border, nor Breed, nor Birth,
When two strong men stand face to face, though they come from the
ends of the earth!

THE BODY POLITIC: THE GLAMOUR AND TRAGEDY OF
THE ZULU WAR

These narratives and images of masculinity and warfare circulating in
the cultural currency of late Victorian Britain, while formed under
different historical and political conditions, are prominent in the
proto-fascist novels and autobiographies analysed by Theweleit. While
one must be wary of making simplistic correlations between Haggard's
narratives and those of the Freikorps', or British Imperialism with
Fascism, I want to use Theweleit's readings to tease out some
disturbing reverberations in the representation of Zulu culture. The
effect of such juxtapositions, as I see it, must be to provoke new
contradictions, interruptions, new connections and new meanings in
these differing male fantasies.

As I have indicated at the start of this paper, according to Theweleit,
the culture of warfare is a radical representation of sexual politics
where the feminine is viewed as a fundamental threat to the wholeness
and hardness of the soldier male as psychotic. The fragility of such
authoritarian/fascistic identities engenders a paranoia, a fear of the
softness, liquidity and flows of the feminine body, and leads the male
warrior to deny, expel and seal off what may be feminine in him. The
identity of the fascist warrior is achieved by proxy through militarism
and a regime of rules and punishment; 'the soldierly totality-body ...
made functional by drill' is obsessed with boundaries, hardness and
discipline:

> The most urgent task of the man of steel is to pursue, to dam in, and to
> subdue any force that threatens to transform him back into the horribly
> disorganized jumble of flesh, hair, skin, bones, intestines, and feelings
> that calls itself human.... This, I believe, is the ideal man of the
> conservative utopia: a man with machine-like periphery....[63]

War is the only permissible outlet for the fascist warrior to express his desires; sexualized, it holds 'the promise of massive velocities, explosions without number – the promise of consumate pleasure for the totality-component' without having to engage with the reality of another human being. Desire, continually dammed up and denied release, seeks relief in destruction and rage; 'explosion is likened to birth, the long-awaited birth of a fleshless body, a body that becomes the relished site of catastrophe'.[64] Descriptions of battle perform the same tasks; 'blood-ink is allowed to stream forth ecstatically':

> He incites his readers to be overwhelmed by the violence of his erupting self, to let his thoughts and feelings flow with him into the waterfalls of cascading words, to be penetrated until the blood rushes to their ears.... Blood appears repeatedly throughout fascist literature as a synonym for proper feeling.[65]

I want now briefly to address the reporting of the Zulu war in the popular metropolitan family weeklies, the *Graphic* and the *Illustrated London News*, as a frame for Haggard's romanticism of warfare. The Zulu War was started amidst paranoia about a black conspiracy in Southern Africa; as Schreuder remarks, the Zulu state 'stood as the symbol of African independency and challenge'. Described by Sir Bartle Frere as a 'man-slaying human military machine', it needed to be destroyed before the plan of confederation could be effected.[66] The war started on 11 January 1879.

The *Graphic* begins its recording of the war on 1 February, with ambivalent feelings towards the Zulu ruler. They describe Cetshwayo as a 'military despot, who has been for years training his Zulu warriors for the express purpose of trying conclusions with the English ...'; yet the paper also stresses the costly burden to tax payers of this war, and admits that the Zulu king's grievances are not totally misplaced. After the 15th, following news of the battle at Rourke's Drift and the defeat of Chelmsford at Isandlwana, the *Graphic* takes matters more seriously and ventures information on Zulu militarism: 'these men possess enough of the civilized instinct to submit to a stern military despotism, they are, after a primitive fashion, well-drilled and (as our loss has proved) well led....' (15 February, *Graphic*)

The *Illustrated London News* of 22 February shows a picture of the massive, naked half-body of the savage Zulu king on the front page (figure 3). Drawn for white audiences, it locates in Cetshwayo's body,

Fig. 3

Fig. 4 "ZULU METHOD OF ADVANCING ATTACK" *Illustrated London News* April 19th 1879

Fig. 5 "AT BAY – THE BATTLE OF ISLANDULA, JANUARY 22ND, 1879" *The Graphic* 15th March 1879

all the power and savagery of the black beast/nation. Again the nation is described as 'not, indeed, a very large kingdom, but its absolute despotic constitution and singular military organisation' renders in its peoples 'an innate love of fighting'. The *Illustrated London News* concludes that while this despotic nation ought to be destroyed and 'their tyrant deposed', adding that it is unworthy of 'English manliness' to practise 'indiscriminate slaughter of that brave peoples in the way of "revenge" '.

The Zulu method of open fighting, unlike the guerrilla tactics of 'other African tribes', was ineffectual against the superior firepower of the British, but came in for much praise. Their charging impis made sepctacular pictures (figure 4) of valour, again located in the national/collective body. Zulu (male) courage *exhibited* in this form(ation) of battle became a stereotype against which other African cultures were measured. And against this, Garnet Wolseley reminds his readers to beware this loss of the 'craving for constant practice and employment [of muscular activity] in [British] blood':

Fig. 6

Such is the difference ... between the Zulu and several of his neighbours in South-eastern Africa [is] ... cowardice. Over-cultivation is calculated to convert manliness into effeminacy ... which kill all virile energy, and when that dies, not only the greatness of the nation but its greatness of the nation but its independent existence are buried in the same grave.[67]

That the Zulu tactic would have been suicidal for the British army to emulate did not register in these portrayals of heroism; they became necessary to the glamour and the tragedy of war. But as J. J. Guy notes, questioning decades of misconception, the Zulus were not a standing army but 'merely an *armed* people' whose 'mobilization of the able bodies males must have disruptive effects on the society, [and]

Fig. 7

reduces the efficiency of the fighting force'.[68] Conventional accounts of the Anglo-Zulu war concentrate on the spectacle of war focusing intensely, as Guy notes, on 'pitched battles of Isandlwana, Rourke's Drift, the defeat of the Zulus at Kambula and Ulundi'; these 'accounts of the discipline Zulu regiments, armed primarily with shields and assegais, charging into the ranked volley-firing of the British coats, excited the British imagination at the time....'[69] (figure 5)

Haggard's representation of Zulu battle glory in *Nada the Lily*, *King Solomon's Mines* and to a lesser extent *Allan Quartermain*, both draw on and rework codes of masculinity and warfare centred on the self-contained world of men, and the glamour, grandeur and theatre of battle. The muscular contortions of the two illustrations (figures 6 and 7), drawn by Richard Woodville (the well-known illustrator of imperial warfare) for Haggard's serialization of *Nada the Lily*, offer the spectacle of masculinity as power and as narrative.[70] This is extended by Haggard to epic proportions in 'The Last Stand of the Greys' in *King Solomon's Mines*. Martin Green argues that the 'most impressive passages [in Haggard's works] are those describing battle, or mediating on it. Their stychomythic dialogues and rituals and rhythmic formulas are not original, but they have power.'[71] Such passages are evident in the heady days under Shakan (the legendary Zulu Napoleon) rule in *Nada the Lily*:

> Ah! the battle! – the battle! In those days we knew how to fight, my father! In those days the vultures would follows our impis by thousands … and none went away empty.... All night our fires shone out across the valley; all night the songs echoed down the hills. Then the grey dawning came … the regiments arose from their bed of spears – yes! they arose! the glad to die! the impi assumed its array regiment by regiment.... The morning breeze came up and fanned them, their plumes bent in the breeze; like a plain of seedling grass they bent, the plumes of the soldiers ripe for the assegai.... They knew it; they saw the omen of death, and, ah! they laughed in the joy of the waking of battle. What was death? Was it not well to die on the spear.... Was it not well to die for the king? Death was the arms of victory. Victory should be their bride that night, and oh! her breast is fair. (pp52-3)

Green calls this emphasis on the pride and glory of regimental training and organization, a 'lyrical or threnodic militarism'.[72] Yet what remains occluded in Green's commentary is the sexual politics that Theweleit brings to his analysis of warfare.

To return to Haggard's passage, what is apparent in the glorification of battle is the spectacle of supreme male power and bonding in death. The victory that is exhalted as *bride* to these warriors is death. The very act of battle is sexualized; the battleground is, in effect, a metaphor for the marriage bed. The laughter that the warriors fling in the face of violence and certain doom becomes, perversely, a sign of their power and their orgastic ecstasy. Such orgastic killing is punctuated by the Zulu war song, 'the music of which has power to drive men mad':

> The slaughter was truly awful … and from among the shouts of warriors and the groans of the dying, set to the music of clashing spears, came a

211

continous hissing undertone of 'S'gee, s'gee,' the note of triumph of each victor as he passed his assegai through and through the body of his fallen foe. (*King Solomon's Mines*, 244)

In the pulsing rhythms of the battle ground, *Nada the Lily*, also finds release for an explosion of death and destruction. Blood covers all and the field becomes a sea of red:

There was a roar, a thunder of feet, a flashing of spears, a bending of plumes, and, like a river that has burst its banks, like storm-clouds before a gale, we sweep down upon friend and foe. They form up to meet us; the stream is passed; our wounded rise upon their haunches and wave us on. We trample them down.... *Ou*! my father, I know no more. Everything grows red. That fight! that fight! We swept them away. When it was done there was nothing to be seen, but the hillside was black and red. (pp53, 55)

Haggard's battle scenes have none of the single-minded explosive release of Theweleit's proto-fascists' text; they hit a much more elegiac and tragic note, and present a much more romanticized notion of native warfare. Even so, the male fantasies evoked by Haggard share with Theweleit's *Freikorps*' narratives their evocation of the seduction of war and death, and their attempts to give expression to dreams of masculine power. This is sometimes expressed through the representation of a combination and fusion with other warriors to produce a disciplined military machine; 'the universal-service system of Germany[/Zululand] brought to an absolute perfection, obtained by subordinating all the ties and duties of civil life to military ends'.[73] It appears too in the obvious pleasure gained from the spectacle of the native army's response to command, as *one total male body*:

I looked down the long lines of waving black plumes and stern faces beneath them.... Never before had I seen such an absolute devotion to the idea of duty, and such a complete indifference to its bitter fruits.... 'Behold your King!' ... there was a moment's pause, then suddenly a murmur arose from the serried phalanxes before us, a sound like the distant whisper of the sea, caused by the gentle tapping of the handles of six thousand spears against their holders' shields. Slowly it swelled, till

212

Fig. 8

Fig. 9 "THE ZULU WAR: GENERAL LORD CHELMSFORD
REVIEWING THE NATIVE CONTINGENT ON THE BANKS OF THE
TUGELA; NATIVES SHOUTING 'H–H–OOO!' " *Illustrated London
News*, May 10th 1879

213

Fig. 10 "THE ZULU WAR –
THE GALLANT DEFENCE
OF ROURKE'S DRIFT" *The
Graphic*, March 15th 1879

its growing volume deepened and widened into a roar of rolling noise,
that echoed like the thunder against the mountains, filled the air with
heavy waves of sound. Then it decreased, and by faint degrees died away
into nothing, and suddenly out crashed the royal salute. (*KSM*, 238-40)

In a 'Zulu war-dance' he writes of another thrilling moment when the
chief is hailed: 'The next moment five hundred shields are tossed aloft,
five hundred spears flash in the sunshine, and with a sudden roar, forth
springs the royal salute, "Bayete".' Shaka's order (figure 8) to the
disciplined, glistening and erect bodies of the Zulu warriors 'there is
the foe. Go and return no more!', prompts instant obedience: 'We hear
you, father! they answered with one voice, and moved down the slope
like countless herd of game with horns of steel.' This is a grand illusion
of power; bio-power becomes a fantasy where representations of body

as state are inscribed. In Theweleit's words, 'the troop ... produces an expression: of determination, strength, precision; of strict order ... an expression of battle, and of a specific masculinity. Or to put it another way, the surplus value produced by the troop is a code that consolidates other totality formations between men, such as "the nation".'[74]

Haggard's texts have none of the frenetic energy of the *Freikorp's* novels; they also contain a variety of contradictory discourses, most of which are not sympathetic with the totalizing movement and paranoia of fascist literature. As indicated previously, colonialist narratives are impelled to inscribe a text of development, civility and growth even where they seek to erase native culture and civilization. It is significant that in *Nada* it is the Zulu nation that is praised; the fantasy there is precisely a fantasy of black men, and only by implication that of white men. Also, imperialism and colonialism at the level of state formation are deeply hierarchical and do not posit an equality between white and black races – even while the national image is both implicated *and* mirrored in a fantasy of black individual and collective heroism (figure 9). Fascism, on the other hand, is a demotic, 'utopic' and populist address pitched at the level of the 'masses'. But the dynamics of their specific authoritarian identity-formations and breakdowns are strikingly similar; their obsessive concern with military regimes and warfare express the inscription of male selves on wider institutional and national boundaries, while their differing sexualization of warfare and destruction express both the power and desire of a radical politics of race and gender reproductions (figure 10).

NOTES

Thanks to Erica Carter and Stuart MacFarlane for their very helpful comments and encouragement.

[1] Homi Bhabha, 'The Commitment to Theory', *New Formations* 5 (Summer 1988), 10-11.
[2] Klaus Theweleit, *Male Fantasies*, 2 vols (Oxford: Polity Press 1989).
[3] Theweleit vol 1, *op.cit.*, 218, 224-5.
[4] The phrase is Bhabha's; see Bhabha, *op.cit.*, 10.
[5] See Geoffrey Searle, 'The Revolt from the Right in Edwardian Britain' in Paul Kennedy and Anthony Nicholls (eds), *Nationalist and Racialist Movements in Britain and Germany before 1914* (London: Macmillan 1981).
[6] See Read's introduction, 'Crisis Age or Golden Age?' in Donald Read (ed.), *Edwardian England* (London: Croom Helm 1982).
[7] Paul Kennedy and Anthony Nicholls' collection of essays *Nationalist and*

Racialist Movements in Britain and Germany before 1914, (London: Macmillan 1981) provides a good history of the pre-war right; see also Geoffrey Searle, *The Quest for National Efficiency: A Study in British Politics and Political Thought 1899-1914* (Oxford: Basil Blackwell 1971) and Robert Colls and Philip Dodd (eds), *Englishness* (London: Croom Helm 1986).
8 Homi Bhabha, 'DissemiNation: Time, Narrative, and the Margins of the Modern Nation' in Homi Bhabha (ed.), *Nation and Narration* (London: Routledge 1990), 301. I am also drawing on Geoffrey Bennington's essay 'Postal politics and the Institution of the Nation' in the same volume. Bennington argues, 'In order to have a name, a boundary and a history to be told at the centre, the state must be constitutively imperfect. The closure of the state becomes the frontier of the nation, and, as we have seen, the frontier implies that there is more than one nation ... so national differentiation does not come along to trouble the state *after* its perfect constitution, but precedes the fiction of such a constitution as its condition of possibility' (p130).
9 Also see Robinson and Gallagher's argument on the 'official mind of imperialism' in their theory of the complex of motivations which led to the scramble for Africa. In their concluding summary of the motivations which impelled new imperialism, Robinson and Gallagher argue: 'The ambition of the late-Victorian ministers reached no higher than to uphold these mid-Victorian systems of security in Egypt and south Africa. They were distinguished from their predecessors only in this: that their security by influence was breaking down.' Ronald Robinson and John Gallagher with Alice Denny, *Africa and the Victorians: The Official Mind of Imperialism* (London: Macmillan 1961; second edition 1981).
10 H. Rider Haggard, *The Poor and the Land* (London: Longmans Green 1905), xix.
11 Charles Masterman, *The Heart of the Empire* (London: Unwin 1901), 7.
12 Garnet Wolsley, 'The negro as a soldier', *Fortnightly Review* vol XLIV (1 December 1888), 692.
13 H. Rider Haggard, 'About Fiction' *Contemporary Review*, vol 2 (February 1887).
14 *ibid.*
15 Andrew Lang, 'Realism and Romance' in *Contemporary Review* vol 52 (November 1887).
16 See George Saintsbury, 'The Present State of the Novel' in *Fortnightly Review*, vol 42 (September 1887).
17 *ibid.*
18 Peter Keating, *The Haunted Study* (London: Secker & Warburg 1989), 345.
19 A total of 31,000 copies were sold in the first year. *She* made even more spectacular figures; first serialized in the *Graphic* and then published by Longmans Green in January 1887 priced at 6s, Haggard was paid in the month of June, a sum of £1847.10 for the 30,792 copies sold. *Allan Quartermain*, the third of his more successful romances was serialized in the *Longman's Magazine* from January to June and was published in book form on 1 July, 1887. The reaction to *Allan Quartermain* from his publishers was not dissimilar; in June 1888, a year after *Allan Quartermain* was published, the Longmans ledgers show that a cheque of £1,470 (for 29,403 copies sold) was made out to Haggard.

While it is not possible to ascertain the exact number and nature of Haggard's readership, it is probable that a broad cross-section of the population did read his fiction. There is evidence that this readership even extended to the working classes, as may be glimpsed from Lady Florence Bell's study of an iron-works community in North Yorkshire (where the average household income per week is often below £4). Of the 200 families in her survey, 16 households had read seafaring stories, tales of adventure and travel, wide escapes and romances; 'Mrs Henry Wood seven times, Shakespeare twice, Dickens twice, Marie Corelli once, Miss Braddon once, Rider Haggard once.' (Lady Florence Bell, *At the Works: A Study of a Manufacturing Town* (London: Arnold 1907), 142-65. Also see Peter Keating, *The Haunted Study: A Social History of the English Novel 1875-1914* (London: Secker & Warburg 1989) for an analysis of the book-buying and book-borrowing public.)

[20] See John Mackenzie, *Propaganda and Empire* (Manchester: Manchester University Press 1984) and J. A. Mangan, *Athleticism in Victorian and Edwardian Public School* (Cambridge: Cambridge University Press 1981).

[21] For a survey of the culture of imperialism see John Mackenzie, *Propaganda and Empire: The Manipulation of British Public Opinion 1880-1960* (Manchester: Manchester University Press 1984), 6.

[23] H. Rider Haggard, *Days of My Life*, vol 1 (London: Longman 1926), 52.

[24]†2Descriptions centring on landscape – or on ethnographical 'manners and custom' portraits of natives – are not uncommon in travel writing where the effacement of the speaking subject (except in the passive sense) contributes to a production of the real within the intersections of geographical, biological, ecological, agricultural and anthropological discourses. Such knowledges were a part of the overall strategy of power as imperial and economic expansion produced new societies of exploitation. See Mary Pratt, 'Scratches on the Face of the Country; or, what Mr. Barrow Saw in the Land of the Bushmen' (*Critical Inquiry*, Autumn 1985) for an archaeology of the relationship between anthropology and travel writing within just such a moment.

[25] Theweleit, *Male Fantasies II*, p67.

[26] H. Rider Haggard, *Nada the Lily* (London: J. M. Dent & Sons (1892) 1933). All further references to *Nada* will only be paginated.

[27] H. Rider Haggard, *Allan's Wife* (London: Hodder & Stoughton (1889) 1950). All further references to *Allan's Wife* will only be paginated.

[28] Northrop Frye, *Anatomy of Criticism* (Princeton: Princeton University Press 1957), 36-7.

[29] William Empson, *Some Versions of Pastoral* (Norfolk, Conn.: New Directions 1950), 11.

[30] Kenneth Burke, *A Grammar of Motives and A Rhetoric of Motives* (Cleveland: Meridian Books 1962), 647, 648.

[31] See Mary Pratt, 'Fieldwork in Common Places' in James Clifford and George Marcus (eds), *Writing Culture: The Poetics and Politics of Ethnography* (Berkley and Los Angeles: University of California Press 1986).

[32] M. H. Abrams, *A Glossary of Literary Terms* (third edition) (New York: Holt, Rinehart & Winston 1971 (1957)), 120.

[33] See Renato Rosaldo, 'Imperialist Nostalgia', *Representations* 26 (Spring 1989), 108.

[34] 'So that whatever happens I think I shall always do pretty well here. However, my aim is of course to rise to the position of Colonial Governor, and to do that I must trust to good fortune my interest. I may, or may not, according to circumstances. At any rate I have now got my foot on the first rung of the Colonial ladder, and D.V. I intend to climb it.' Haggard (1926), 102.

[35] *ibid.*, 88.

[36] Laura Mulvey, 'Afterthoughts on Visual Pleasure' in *Framework* (Summer 1981).

[37] *ibid.*

[38] Joseph Conrad, *Last Essays* (London: Dent 1926).

[39] Jacqueline Rose, *Peter Pan and the Impossibility of Children's Fiction* (London: Macmillan 1984), 50.

[40] Michel de Certeau, *Heterologies: Discourse on the Other* (Minnesota: University of Minnesota Press 1986), 132.

[41] Rose (1984), 1-2.

[42] *Allan Quartermain*, Haggard (1887), dedication.

[43] Northrop Frye, *The Secular Scripture: A Study of the Structure of Romance* (Cambridge (Mass): Harvard University Press 1976); also see *Anatomy of Criticism* (Princeton: Princeton University Press 1957).

[44] Northrop Frye, *The Secular Scripture*, 57.

[45] Frye, *Anatomy of Criticism*, 193.

[46] H. Rider Haggard, *King Solomon's Mines* (London: Cassell & Co. (1885) 1940). All further references to the novel (*KSM*) will only be paginated.

[47] Theweleit, *Male Fantasies II*, 147.

[48] Pratt, *op.cit.*

[49] For a discussion of fetishism and stereotyping see Homi Bhabha, 'The Other Question' in *Screen* 24 (1983) and Steve Neale, 'The Same Old Story' in *Screen Education* (1979-80), 30-4.

[50] Bhabha, *op.cit.*

[51] Kobena Mercer, 'Imaging the Black Man's Sex' in *Male Order: Unwrapping Masculinity*, Rowena Chapman and Jonathan Rutherford (eds), (London: Lawrence & Wishart 1988) 144. See Laura Mulvey's classic, 'Visual Pleasure and Narrative Cinema' in *Screen* (Autumn 1975) for an analysis of the male gaze.

[52] Joseph Conrad, *Heart of Darkness* (Harmondsworth: Penguin (1902) 1963), 110.

[53] For the archaeology of 'the wild man' as primitive and as noble savage see Hadyn White, 'The Forms of Wildness: Archaeology of an Idea' in Edward Dudley and Max Novak (eds), *The Wild Man Within* (Pittsburg: University of Pittsburg Press 1972).

[54] Quoted in Tim Jeal, *Baden Powell* (London: Hutchinson 1989), 189-90.

[55] Mercer, *op.cit.*, p149.

[56] Richard Dyer, *Heavenly Bodies* (London & Basingstoke: Macmillan 1987), 121.

[57] *ibid.*, p138.

[58] See Gail Ching-Liang Low, 'White Skins/Black Masks' in *New Formations* 9 (Winter 1990).

[59] John Buchan, *Prester John* (London: Thomas Nelson & Sons 1947 (1938)), 18, 129.

[60] Mercer, *op.cit.*, 145.

[61] J. A. Magan and James Walvin, *Manliness and Morality: Middle class masculinity in Britain and America* (Manchester: Manchester University Press 1988).

[62] In Sedgwick's exploration of the political and psychological tensions between male homosocial desire and homphobia in *Edwin Drood*, she uncovers a 'de-individualizing, relatively universal Gothic critique of the organisation of male desire' and considers the question of narrative stability: 'If it collapses the rigid, vulnerable structures of Jasper's relations to the man and the woman he "loves," can it stop short of Crisparkle's deeply congruent ones?' Sedgwick's answer remains in the affirmative – the 'jagged edge of a racial faultline across the novel's plot and setting facilitates that coarse [visible *and* arbitrary] halving' of the good/bad bond. In my analysis of the male homosocial community of black and white men in the adventure narrative, Sedgwick's jagged line of race applies. Race, after all, refers to whole groups of people; in enacting the marginalization of women in these homosocial (not 'homosexual') bonds, Haggard's narratives are careful to insist on a *temporary* romance between individual peoples which deliberately obscures the wider politics of race and sexuality, nation and colonialism. See Eve Kosofsky Sedgwick, *Between Men: English Literature and Male Homosocial Desire* (New York: Columbia University Press 1985).

[63] Klaus Theweleit, *Male Fantasies II*, 159-60.

[64] Theweleit (1989), 178.

[65] *ibid.*, 184-5.

[66] Schreuder (1980), 75.

[67] Garnet Wolsley, 'The negro as a soldier', *Fortnightly Review*, vol. XLIV (1 December 1888).

[68] J. J. Guy, 'A Note on Firearms in the Zulu Kingdom with Special Reference to the Anglo-Zulu War, 1879', *Journal of African History 12(4) (1971), 503.*

[69] *ibid.*, 563.

[70] See Steven Neal for an analysis of 'Masculinity as Spectacle' in *Screen* 24 (1983).

[71] Martin Green, *Dreams of Adventure, Deeds of Empire* (London: Routledge & Kegan Paul 1980 (1979)), 232.

[72] *ibid.*

[73] Haggard (1882), 18.

[74] Theweleit, *Male Fantasies II*, 155.

The Content and Discontents of Kipling's Imperialism

Benita Parry

In 1939 when Auden wrote his wry lines, Time that 'Worships language and forgives / Everyone by whom it lives' had not yet 'Pardoned Kipling and his views',[1] nor was exoneration imminent. Despite the patriotic fervour of the ensuing war years, liberals continued to regret colonialism's excesses, the anti-colonialist struggle was a left-wing cause, and intellectuals were sceptical about the British Empire. T.S. Eliot's praise for Kipling's vision of imperial responsibility in a 1941 essay met with opposition from prominent writers and critics who considered Kipling's view of life to be incompatible with the principles of civility and were repelled by the bullying self-righteousness and racial vanity of his imperialism.[2] The reactions of Eliot's apologia secured Kipling's reputation as 'the prophet of British imperialism in its expansionist phase' (Orwell). During the following decades those who argued for his recognition as a major artist – although he had long since achieved popular acclaim as a 'classic', he had not been admitted to the canon – did so by pronouncing his social and political ideas irrelevant to evaluating his complex techniques and explorations of 'permanent human and moral themes'.[3]

By the mid-1960s, Western scholars whose discomfort at European aggression and conceit was receding in the aftermath of statutory decolonization, had compiled a balance-sheet of colonialism which provided critics with a permit for expressing sober satisfaction at empire's achievements. Contributors to the concerted reappraisal around Kipling's centenary year freely infused their 'disinterested literary assessments' with esteem for his idealistic commitment to empire and firm grasp of political realities.[4] Now that the ideological right is on the offensive in the West, an even more favourable climate exists for Kipling's rehabilitation, and the ending of copyright on his works in 1987 produced a plethora of paperback editions with new introductions and appreciations which are frequently buttressed with exculpations of his imperial vision. Such readings draw on and abet the anti-anti-imperialism fostered by Western ideologues eager to impugn post-colonial regimes, honour the colonialist legacy bequeathed by Europe, and justify the continuing asymmetry between the hemispheres.[5] At a time when politicians, journalists, and entertainers have joined in the 'refurbishment of the empire's tarnished image',[6] the vindication of Kipling's textual affirmations and denigrations has been completed. When the British Prime Minister announces that she is 'a faithful student of Rudyard Kipling', she is not deferring to his literary virtuosity. When critics proffer a gloss which underwrites Kipling's views on a patriotism enjoining obedience to an hierarchical status quo at home and bellicosity abroad, on the conservation of England's ancestral culture, and on Europe's title to global leadership, they are giving comfort to a domestic politics of social conformity and class deference, re-evoking an identity of race with nation, and sustaining the values of a white mythology.

Whether a revisionist criticism erases, commends, or reconstrues Kipling's imperialism, its various practices circumvent a critique of the texts' deliberated ideological enunciations and inadvertent registering of contradictory meanings. One devotee has summarily disposed of a body of historical utterances and their subsequent reinscriptions in critical discussion: 'Kipling the imperialist is dead and gone; it is Kipling the verbal prophet who commands attention now.'[7] From an opposite position, another champion embraces Kipling as the poet of empire, praising him for expressing that sense of imperial destiny which had formed a whole phase of national existence:

> That age is one about which many Britons – and to a lesser extent Americans and Europeans – now feel an exaggerated sense of guilt.... Whereas if we approach him more historically, less hysterically, we shall find in this very relation to his age a cultural phenomenon of absorbing interest.

Andrew Rutherford directs his commentary to a British audience perceived as an undifferentiated communality: for Britons 'of all social classes and cultural groups', the writings afford the gratification of identifying with 'our shared inheritance', the natives being rewarded with 'sensitive, sympathetic vignettes of Indian life and character'.[8] As a defence which so egregiously concurs with the writings' overt stance, this exposition lacks the ingenuity of that much-favoured reconstruction where an alternative set of meanings is substituted for Kipling's narratives of empire.

In this interpretation, Kipling is rediscovered as 'a student of alienation and the moral and spiritual predicament of industrial man'. To an historian of the British Empire who is comfortable with designating the colonial world as the raw and Europe as the cooked, Kipling's imperialism appears a means of curing modern anomie and restoring a balance to over-urbanized society 'by linking it in service with the underdeveloped world and renewing it spiritually by fresh contact there with Nature and "otherness" '.[9] For Western critics and the literary journalists who communicate their opinions, a reading which amplifies Kipling's address to the crisis of contemporary Western civilization, while muting the strident colonialist register of his thematic and rhetorical predications, has the advantage of allowing a renegotiation of his status as a serious thinker/artist. The foremost exponent of this view is Alan Sandison who argues that empire for Kipling was simply a 'Place des Signes', his real concern being with 'man's essential estrangement, illumined with such clarity in the imperial alien's relationship to his hostile environment'.[10] Because for Sandison, as for Kipling, India is 'a very powerful symbol of a nature intrinsically hostile to man', the figure of 'a world inimical to his physical and moral survival', a potent image 'of the forces of persecution ranged against the individual in his struggle to sustain his identity',[11] his commentary colludes with Kipling's specification of India as the negative pole in that ubiquitous structure of oppositions – mind/body, reason/passion, order/chaos, intelligibility/incoherence – deployed by dominant orders to legitimate relationships of power. On this basis, Sandison's exposition proceeds to reproduce the textual inscription of an imperialist discursive practice – the construction of an identity that is dependent on the conquest of another's self – as a description of 'the human condition'. Since, within this discourse, the places of subject and object are allotted to Europe and its others, and these others are denied agency, the colonized are by definition excluded from it. A gloss which recuperates Kipling's intended meanings in ontological terms could appear calculated to drain the writings of historical specificity; yet it also attests to the authenticity of his 'portraits', and it does so through extrapolating the 'historical realities' from the do-it-yourself hagiography of the Raj, among which Kipling's fabrications were pre-eminent. The outcome is a criticism which, by reiterating Kipling's ideological assumptions, naturalizes the principles of the master culture as universal forms of thought and projects its authorized representations as truths.

The terms of Kipling's rehabilitation have been virtually uncontested, with only a few of the new studies situating the writings within a discursive field and reading the texts as ambivalent enunciations of an imperialist world-outlook.[12] What has not yet emerged is a left critique of Kipling. It may be common knowledge on the left that, as Tom Nairn has written, Britain is the 'most profoundly and unalterably imperialist of societies', its state forms 'inwardly modelled and conditioned by prolonged external depredations', its national consciousness and culture subjectively marked by imperialist myths.[13] Yet this generalized awareness has not produced studies on the making and components of imperialism's discourse or on the imperialist determinants of the metropolitan culture, and the indifference to Kipling repeats the larger neglect of a project to which his work is indispensable. For in writings where the discursive aggression of the referential project is interrupted by utterances of uncertainty, desire, and fear, the precepts of imperialist ideology are reassembled and its deceptively unitary structure broken open. The recognition of such tensions and contradictions does not, however, remove the inherent restraints on reading fictions which are indelibly etched by thematic assertions and rhetorical coercions that make known and consolidate an imperialist triumphalism. Neither the influence of Kipling's demotic verse on Brecht nor his popularity in the Soviet Union, which are routinely cited as evidence of his universal appeal and ecumenical sympathies, can obliterate these inscriptions. What criticism can recover, through dismantling the plural discourses and reconstructing the displacements and erasures, is the effaced historical contest and unrehearsed enunciations of the anxieties in the conquering imagination, both necessarily repressed by the exigencies of ideological representation. Kipling did set out to be the bard of empire, and although the ambition was abundantly realized, this is not all that he became.

IMPERIALISM'S SCRIBE

Kipling's writings moved empire from the margins of English fiction to its centre without interrogating the official metropolitan culture. In cataloguing a lifelong devotion to dominant beliefs and values in *Something of Myself*, an autobiography written in old age, he had no occasion to repent youthful indiscretions of opinion. The Club, the Mess and the Freemasons Lodge are prized, while the 'perversions' and 'unclean microbes' infecting male communities are deplored; there is hostility to liberals, socialists, and the labour movement, xenophobia towards Jews and contempt for blacks. Such predilections would be a matter for biography, were it not that they are written into the authoritative discourses of the texts, put there by a writer who conceived his function as teacher, prophet, and public voice. Pointing out that both his grandfathers had been Wesleyan ministers, Kipling recalls an early ambition to tell the English 'something of the whole sweep and meaning of things and effort and origins throughout the Empire'. Later, when an established author and a pillar of the establishment, political conviction inspired him to write his Boer War verses and tributes to Joseph Chamberlain, Cecil John Rhodes, and Lord Milner. It was passion for the expansion of empire which moved him to offer his gift with language to Rhodes, the architect of a plan for territorial aggrandizement whose imagination of conquest encompassed annexing the planets to England: 'he said to me apropos of nothing in particular: "What's your dream?" I answered that he was part of it.... My use to him was mainly as a purveyor of words; for he was largely inarticulate.'[14] In the story 'On the city wall', Kipling has the narrator, himself a word-*wallah*, decry the uselessness of books and scorn the lying proverb which says that the pen is mightier than the sword.[15] This is the stratagem of a dissembling writer who, having committed his own books and pen to political causes, feigns disbelief in the power of writing and directs attention instead to 'the line of guns that could pound the City to powder'.

Kipling's writings were not confined to fictions 'about empire', but it was his fiction of empire which, aided by the enthusiasm of the popular periodical press, made him the uncrowned laureate.[16] To gauge his role in the invention of an imperialist English identity requires the study of how reader responses were catalysed over many decades as forms of consciousness, social conduct, and political behaviour. What is immediately available to critical attention is the address of instructional and inspirational writing delivered from the heartland of an imperialist culture. Directed at a readership positioned as a racially homogeneous and masculine community, unfissured by class allegiances, Kipling's imperialist writings articulate a new patriotism purged of the radicalism in its earlier forms, and fabricate a linear narrative of England's 'undefiled heritage' beginning with the inheritance of the imperial flame as it passed from their conquerors into English hands, and consummated in the British Empire. Through blandishment and prophecy the cautionary verses urge the English to curb the unruly in themselves (as in 'The children's song' and 'If') if they are to realize their natural aptitude for ruling others. In 'A song of the English' (1893), he wrote:

> Fair is our lot – o goodly is our heritage!
> (Humble ye, my people, and be fearful in your mirth!)
> For the Lord our God Most High
> He had made the deep as dry,
> He hath smote for us a pathway to the ends of all the Earth!
> …
> Hold ye the Faith – the Faith our Fathers sealèd us;
> Whoring not with visions – overwise and overstale.
> …
> Keep ye the Law – be swift in all obedience –
> Clear the land of evil, drive the road and bridge the ford.

Here the syntax of the sermon and the metre of the hymn regenerate the terms of imperialist propaganda into the notion of empire as a divinely appointed duty devolving on the English. Even as the mode shifts from the declamatory to the lyrical, and the stern call to imperial expansion and recall to ancestral belief is replaced by an indulgent longing to voyage beyond the constraints of metropolitan existence, Utopia is made instantly manifest in the colonial venture:

> We were dreamers, dreaming greatly, in the man-stifled town;
> We yearned beyond the sky-line where the strange roads go down.
> Came the Whisper, came the Vision, came the Power with the Need,
> Till the Soul that is not man's soul was lent us to lead.

Although Kipling has been hailed as a visionary, his mystique of empire more properly belongs to that worldly imperialist aspiration which imbued a predatory project with a revelational quality. In

226

Nostromo, Conrad identified this compound as 'the misty idealism of the Northerners who at the smallest encouragement dream of nothing less than the conquest of the earth'.

Where the address of the imperialist verse is solemn and portentous, that of the stories idolizing the British as colonial rulers joins the briskly exegetical with the gallantly sentimental. Since the language of European ascendency and Anglo-Indian conceit remains uncontradicted, the narrative structure of such tales is sealed against any interrogation of the Raj's self-presentation. On those occasions when the Indians do appear to speak, they are the mouthpieces of a ventriloquist who, using a facile idiom that alternates between the artless and the ornate, projects his own account of grateful native dependency. The monologism of these fictions is not Kipling's only mode, however. In those texts which call attention to their own fictional nature and stage the multivalencies of language, the pretence to authentic representation and the imparting of truths is caricatured. The playful posture towards words and writing of the narrator in 'On the city wall', who even as he presents himself in the process of composing his chronicle, distinguishes between 'living the story' and 'writing it', produces uncertainties in the proffered report of events. This ambiguity is sustained when the regulation reiteration of British discipline, fortitude, and devotion to duty, delivered in a diction which values social order and the exercise of stern political control, is undercut by the flamboyance of metaphor and the banter of puns:

> Lalun has not yet been described. She would need, so Wali Dad says, a thousand pens of gold and ink scented with musk. She has been variously compared to the Moon, the Dil Sagar Lake, a spotted quail, a gazelle, the Sun on the Desert of Kutch, the Dawn, the Stars, and the young bamboo.... One song ... says the beauty of Lalun was so great that it troubled the hearts of the British Government and caused them to lose their peace of mind. That is the way the song is sung in the streets; but, if you examine it carefully and know the key to the explanation, you will find that there are three puns in it – on 'beauty', 'heart', and 'peace of mind' – so that it runs 'By the subtlety of Lalun the administration was troubled and it lost such and such a man.' (326, 323)

When Kipling sports with the referential mode which he so ably used to prescribe codes of conduct and instil ways of seeing, he puts in question the very predications which elsewhere he so aggressively articulated. The absent subject of 'To be filed for reference' (*Plain Tales from the Hills*, 1890) is 'The Book' compiled by an educated English drunkard gone native, and reputed to contain the truths about the people of the country concealed from the British. Allusions to its substance suggest the sensational ethnography of an excited Western imagination – it is coyly referred to by the Anglo-Indian narrator as in need of expurgation, an opinion proudly shared by its author – and not the text of an alternative system of meanings. Nevertheless, 'The Book' does function to contest the colonialist claim of 'knowing the Real India', a boast made sometimes archly and sometimes not, in other stories. Here the reader is invited to believe that the official British version is indeed faulty, even though the potential counter-knowledge is strategically suppressed. In these self-reflexive tales, the univocal pronouncements of the polemical writings are undermined or countermanded, and these departures from the dominant mode are a reminder of just how firmly such doubts are elsewhere quelled. If 'To be filed for reference' both intimates and averts a challenge to British knowledge, then *Kim* (1901) confidently reaffirms its validity. It is the English curator of a museum, 'with his mound of books – French, and German, with photographs and reproductions' and his acquaintance with 'the labours of European scholars', who communicates new learning about his own heritage to the amazed lama. It is through collecting and collating information about India's roads, rivers, plants, stones, and customs that the Ethnological Survey makes available to the government that intelligence which is essential to the proper exercise of British power. And it is Kim, the sahib who can pass as any one of India's many peoples, who has access to the secrets of all India and puts these at the disposal of a benevolent Raj.

COERCION, DESIRE AND FEAR IN KIPLING'S INDIA

Kipling's India raises the problem posed by Edward Said in *Orientalism* as to 'how one can study other cultures and peoples from a libertarian, or a non-repressive and non-manipulative perspective'.[17] More specific questions are: can a writer immersed in and owing allegiance to a master culture, construe the radical difference of another and subordinated culture as yet another conceptual order within a multiverse of diverse meanings? Are Kipling's fabrications of India, as has been claimed, testimony to the possibility of such ideologically unfettered constructions? It is *Kim* which critics call upon to argue that in his representation of India's uniquely multiple being, Kipling did indeed transcend the boundaries of his own ethnocentric vision.[18] While this is not the position taken by Edward Said, who criticizes Kipling's fiction of an immutable and immobile India, he does in his generous essay on *Kim* credit Kipling with giving India a positive identity: 'We can watch a great artist blinded in a sense by his own insights about India, confusing the reality before him, which he saw with such colour and ingenuity, with the notion that these realities were permanent and essential.'[19] The implication is that despite a crucial flaw in its composition, this India is the product of a non-coercive perspective. It could be argued, however, that because Kipling's India is reified under Western eyes as a frieze or a pageant, and romanticized as an object of sensuous and voluptuous pleasure to be enjoyed by Europe, it is an invention which colonizes the space of India's own significations with Western fantasies. Moroever, this 'Orientalized India of the imagination ... an ideal India, unchanging and attractive, full of bustle and activity, but also restful ... even idyllic' is not Kipling's only India[20] and within this larger, heterogeneous configuration, India can signify nullity as well as plenty, and its difference can be variously constituted as deviant, menacing, or magnetic.

Kipling's journalism made a major contribution to the text of the Raj, working within and extending existing representations by vilifying the customs and manners of contemporary India and ridiculing its ancient literary heritages.[21] A glorious past was reconstructed by nineteenth-century European Indologists, who like their predecessors saw their role as making India's traditional learning known to the West and returning a noble legacy to peoples whose religious life had fallen into debased practices. This project was anathema to the architects of an absolute government in the metropolis and their agents in India. Their scorn was eagerly reiterated by an Anglo-Indian community outraged at Max Müller's postulate of an Indo-European family of languages and cultures – this was the source of the witticisms about 'our Aryan brothers', who so clearly were not. In 1886, Kipling wrote an article for the *Civil and Military Gazette* on *The Mahabharata*, then being translated into English by Pratap Chandra Roy, where his disparagement of the epic echoed the contempt for the Sanskrit classics earlier and famously expressed by Macaulay in his 1839 Minute on Education:

section after section – with its monstrous array of nightmare-like incidents, where armies are slain, and worlds swallowed with monotonous frequency, its records of impossible combats, its lengthy catalogues of female charms, and its nebulous digressions on points of morality – gives but the scantiest return for the labour expended on its production.... The fantastic creations of the Hindu mythology have as much reality in their composition and coherence in their action, as the wind-driven clouds of sunset. They are monstrous, painted in all the crude colours that a barbaric hand can apply; moved by machinery that would be colossal were it not absurd, and placed in all their doings beyond the remotest pale of human sympathy. The demi-god who is slain and disembowelled at dusk rises again whole and unharmed at dawn. As with the *Mahabharata*, so with the *Ramayana*.... Boars like purple mountains, maidens with lotus feet and the gait of she-elephants, giants with removable and renewable heads ... are scattered broadcast through its pages. ... The working world of today has no place for these ponderous records of nothingness.[22]

The utilitarian age of a relentless literalism that uses the vocabulary of commerce to castigate the extravagance of tropes could appear an aberration in one whose own trade was in literary language. Certainly in his capacity as licensed scribe of Anglo-India, Kipling is here reiterating an accredited means of insulting India's difference. But the derision that places articulations of the Indian imagination beyond human comprehension was not merely the expediency of a hack deferring to his readers' prejudices – this is clear in a letter he wrote at the same time mocking William Morris's high regard for 'that monstrous midden'.[23] Yet the fictions can tell another story: in 'The bridge-builders' (*The Day's Work*, 1898) a cosmology of becoming, dissolution, and re-emergence is juxtaposed to the Western notion of linear time.

Enunciations of India's otherness are never absent, but in those writings which project India as the incarnation of what a European self is constrained to exclude, alienation is intercepted by identification. A regret at the necessary ending of intimacy is registered in 'The native born' where India is characterized as the lost object of desire that must be relinquished for entry into the patriarchal law:

To our dear dark foster mothers,
to the heathen songs they sung –

To the heathen speech we babbled,
Ere we came to the white man's tongue.

A different specification of lack is inscribed in those fictions which, reproducing colonialist fantasy, transfigure India as the provider of libidinal excitation. The embrace of that which the European self denies becomes enmeshed with the colonialist appetite for possession and control. Such multiple exigencies are dramatized in the love stories 'Beyond the pale' (*Plain Tales*) and 'Without benefit of clergy' (*Life's Handicap*, 1891), where native subordination and Oriental passion, those staples of colonial discourse, come together in the ecstatic and ceremonial yielding of the native as female to the dominating presence of a masculine West. In the battle between creative man and castrating woman fought on English ground in *The Light That Failed* (1890), the figure of a hybrid alien is invoked to represent a notion of woman's Manichaean nature: 'she was a sort of Negroid-Jewess-Cuban – with morals to match [serving] as a model for the devils and the angels both' (155). In the tales of the white man's sexual encounters with the native woman, however, the Indian female, who must enact a double subjugation, is all innocence and ardent acquiescence. Ameera's obeisance to her English lover in 'Without benefit of clergy' stages the total abjection of India as colonized and female, the abasement of her address to the white man, 'My king, for all they sweet words, well I know that I am thy servant and thy slave and the dust under thy feet' (163) culminating in a deathbed blasphemy of her Islamic faith: 'I bear witness – I bear witness ... that there is no God – but – thee – beloved' (178).

Michael O'Pray has argued in *New Formations* for recovering Kipling as a key figure in a marginalized English tradition 'where romanticism merges with nostalgia ... and an exoticism and quasi-mysticism that have a complex relationship to the British Empire'.[24] But because, as O'Pray recognizes, the fantastical is condensed with the colonizing spirit, the effect is to invest domination with libidinal intensities – Conrad's 'insatiable imagination of conquest'. A central trope of Kipling's other Indian novel, *The Naulahka* (1892), is an erotically charged urge for colonialist acquisition. The necklace of the title joins a sign of the East's fabled wealth with a symbol of woman's body, and the narration of the quest for the priceless and sacred jewel mimicks a bellicose act that is both an imperialist invasion and a sexual assault. A desolate landscape is

231

transformed into a meaningless social space, giving the West a moral right to usurp its wasted resources: 'miles of profitless, rolling ground ... studded with unthrifty trees ... this abyss of oblivion.... The silence of the place and the insolent nakedness of its empty ways ... the vast, sleeping land' (59, 78, 164). But an overweening white confidence enunciated in disdain for India – 'Standing there, he recognized ... how entirely the life, habits and traditions of this strange people alienated them from all that seemed good and right to him' (212) – is undermined by articulations of the panic afflicting the conquering imagination. The holy well where the jewel is secreted has an intolerable smell of musk and is 'fringed to the lips with rank vegetation'; the surrounding rock is 'rotten with moisture'; from the stagnant waters rears 'the head of a sunken stone pillar, carved with monstrous and obscene gods'; the pool, overhung by a fig tree buttressing the rock 'with snake-like roots', is inhabited by an alligator, 'a long welt of filth and slime' (155-6, 165-6). From these signs of a rank and corrupting sexuality and of original sin, the white assailant flees in horror.

Sometimes a source of guilty lust, India elsewhere is constructed as the negation of reason, order, and coherence so that the anxiety induced by difference is dispelled by moral censure. At its crudest, as in 'The enlightenments of Pagett M.P.',[25] this is articulated as an uninterrupted calumniation of Indian social existence: 'the foundations of their life are rotten – utterly and bestially rotten....In effect, native habits and beliefs are an organized conspiracy against the laws of healthy and happy life.' Contempt for custom can be conflated with anger at India's climate, both standing in the way of implementing British purpose: 'storm, sudden freshets, death in every manner and shape ... drought, sanitation ... birth, wedding, burial, and riot in the village of twenty warring castes' ('The bridge-builders',5). Where disquiet at India's otherness is not allayed by reproof, its particularities are perceived as a hostile presence threatening to overwhelm the white community:

> There was neither sky, sun, nor horizon – nothing but a brown purple haze of heat. It was as though the earth was dying of apoplexy.... The atmosphere within was only 104° ... and heavy with the foul smell of badly-trimmed kerosene lamps; and this stench, combined with that of native tobacco, baked brick, and dried earth, sends the heart of many a strong man down to his boots, for it is the smell of the Great Indian

Empire when it turns itself for six months into a house of torment ... a tom-tom in the coolie-lines began to beat with the steady throb of a swollen artery inside some brain-fevered skull. ('At the end of the passage', *Life's Handicap*, 183, 198)

India's incomprehensible menace serves also to displace the colonialist nightmare of native vengeance, itself the verso of that fantasy where the country and its people are willingly held in the Raj's embrace. 'The mark of the beast' (*Life's Handicap*) uses the conventions of the horror story to narrate an act of native retribution that is 'beyond any human and rational experience' (251): the lurid circumstances effectively screening the import of colonial resentment. 'The strange ride of Morrowbie Jukes' (*The Phantom Rickshaw*, 1892), Kipling's most potent tale of European dread, veils this secular fright in the incertitude of hallucination. In detailing the ride of a delirious engineer with a head for plans but without imagination, 'over what seemed a limitless expanse of moonlit sands', the narration transforms the physical terrain into a metaphysical landscape. Accidently plunged by his horse into a crater, Jukes finds himself trapped in a grotesque community of pariah Indians who, having recovered from trance or catalepsy after being presumed dead, have been confined to conditions of appalling deprivation and degradation. Here Jukes, who no longer commands the deference due to a sahib, suffers the 'nervous terror' of being immured amongst hostile Indians. His rescue by a loyal servant both mimicks the relief of awakening from a bad dream, and acts therapeutically to restore British confidence in the invulnerability of a position undermined by the central narrative event.

STRATEGIC BOUNDARIES, NATIVE MARGINALIZATION

Within the specification of India as other, the figures of the alluring exotic and the minatory alien stand out, on the one hand, as the signs of the sensual temptations impeding the exercise of British rule and, on the other, of an unintelligible danger to its hegemony. Notably absent is India incarnate as political opponent to the Raj. Edward Said has proposed that Kipling studiously avoided giving us two worlds in conflict because for him '*there was no conflict* ... it was India's best destiny to be ruled by England'. This confidence Said attributes to the defining context in which he wrote: 'There *were* no appreciable deterrents to the imperialist world-view held by Kipling. Hence he remained untroubled.'[26] But potent counters *did* exist both in India's traditional system of knowledge and in emergent nationalist discourses and if Kipling was serenely unaware that these transgressed imperialist principles, then his writings were not, as attention to those strategies which silence voices able to interrogate the British Empire as cultural text and political concept will show.

Parataxis is a favoured procedure for organizing incommensurable discourses in ways that conceal an antagonism of ideas. The road, the river, and the wheel in *Kim* serve dual and opposing functions within the narrative. While Kim 'flung himself whole-heartedly upon the next turn of the wheel', the lama strives to free himself 'from the Wheel of Things' (210; 13). Whereas for Kim the Grand Trunk Road is a river of life, to the lama it is a hard path to be trodden in his search for a mythic river that will cleanse him from the sin of material being. Between Kim's pursuit of action, the life of the senses, and personal identity, and the lama's quest for quietism, asceticism, and the annihilation of self, there is no dialogue. Hence disjunctive goals, the one valued and the other denounced by imperialism's tenets, easily cohere as the mutual venture defined by the lama who in his studied indifference to the temporal, accepts Kim's recruitment into the Secret Service as yet another insignificant action: 'he aided me in my Search. I aided him in his....Let him be a teacher, let him be a scribe – what matter? He will have attained Freedom at the end. The rest is illusion' (407). This happy end, which allows Kim to have his nirvana and eat it, prompts another agent, the pragmatic Mahbub Ali, to say, 'Now I understand that the boy, sure of Paradise, can yet enter Government Service, my mind is easier' (407). There is a reprise of this expedient ending in the ceremonial healing of the crisis precipitated by the irreconcilable roles Kim must play as apprentice spy and *chela* to a holy man; his recovery is effected without any engagement with the competing commitments and it acts to abolish conflict.

The contradictory ideological imperatives of etching the division between imperialist self and native other at the same time as re-presenting colonialist/colonized hostility as British/Indian colla-boration, engenders the invention of boundary situations inscribing both exigencies. In a territory signalled in the titles – 'Beyond the pale', 'Without benefit of clergy', 'On the city wall' – and which is literally out of bounds to the English in colonial conditions, the frontiers drawn up by the imperial power can be crossed without endangering the relationship dependent on the policing of borders. This liminal space thus neither constitutes a zone liberated from the Raj, nor is the positioning of master/native displaced. Instead it is construed as a peripheral district licensed by the centre for the episodic transgression of colonialist interdicts. The movement between the languages of Law and Desire, the one enunciating the light of Anglo-India, the other the dark of India, reinstalls the chasm even as the protagonists from across the divide meet in intimacy. 'By day Holden did his work....At nightfall he returned to Ameera' ('Without benefit of clergy', 165). 'In the daytime Trejago drove through his routine of office work ... At night when all the City was still came the ... walk [to] Bisesa' ('Beyond the pale', 175). When Holden has performed 'the birth-sacrifice' to protect the son born to Ameera, by slaughtering goats and 'muttering the Mahomedan prayer', he is 'eager to get to the light of the company of his fellows' (157); and if Trejago's passion is an endless delight, it is also a folly and a madness.

The exclusions of the colonialist code are thus ambivalently displayed as necessary deprivation. The ecstasy which Englishmen find in Bisesa's room and Ameera's house, or the pleasures afforded by Lalun's salon on the city wall, none of which is available in the bungalow or the Club, are articulated in rhapsodic vein. But if the lucid world of Anglo-India inhibits sensual gratification, it also preserves reason and order. This demands that the poesy of the illicit crossings is disrupted by the prose of censure: in one case disobedience is punished by disease and death, in another by mutilation. After Ameera and her son have died, the house which Holden had taken for her is torn down 'so that no man may say where [it] stood', presaging her mother's prophecy that 'He will go back to his own people in time' (182; 137). 'Beyond the pale' opens with an ironic admonition:

> A man should, whatever happens, keep to his own caste, race and breed. Let the White go to the White, and the Black to the Black. Then, whatever trouble falls is in the ordinary course of things – neither sudden, alien, nor unexpected. (171)

Although this is contradicted by the 'Hindu Proverb' which serves as the story's epigram ('Love heeds not caste nor sleep a broken bed. I went in search of love and lost myself' [171]), its wisdom is confirmed by the ending. If the love stories are both eulogistic and censorious about the transgression of frontiers, the allegorical 'The bridge-builders' whole-heartedly applauds that passage through which the British donate and the Indians receive technological progress, for there is no encroachment on colonialist divisions. The gulf between the British doctrine on the conquest of nature and a deferential Indian stance towards the integrity of the physical environment is momentarily traversed by the British engineer's opium-induced vision of the gods in conclave. On awakening, however, he banishes all memory of what he has seen: 'in that clear light there was no room for a man to think dreams of the dark' (41). An alien perspective on the universe and time is made known and dispelled; once again the status quo is entrenched.

Representations which neutralize or elide the challenge to the British world-view, and which ensure that the positioning of master and native is not disturbed, close the space for a counter-discourse authored by the colonized as historical subject and agent. Yet in the act of muting these utterances, the texts reveal a knowledge of their existence and their danger. If we follow Fredric Jameson's proposition that the hegemonic discourse implies a dialogue with a dissenting voice even when this is disarticulated,[27] then Kipling's imperialist writings can be read as a pre-emptive reply to Indian opposition. What is heard instead is the idiom of grateful dependence from villagers and servants, of proud compliance from sepoys and war-like tribesmen, and of insolent malcontent from Western-educated 'babus'. When the language of legend or religion is spoken, this is not permitted to contest imperialist teaching; nor does it confront European ascendency on the political ground staked out by the text of the British Empire.

It is such suppressions which make the interlocution of voices in 'On the city wall' noteworthy, for in this fiction the Indians *are* autonomous and oppositional speaking subjects. Characteristically, the story moves between disjunctive modes. The Indian scene is represented in a vocabulary of parodic romanticism, its ironic effusions alternating with the pompous diction of British rule:

Year by year England sends out fresh drafts for the first fighting-line, which is officially called the Indian Civil Service. These die, or kill themselves by overwork, or are worried to death, or broken in health and hope in order that the land may be protected from death and sickness, famine and war, and may eventually become capable of standing alone. It will never stand alone, but the idea is a pretty one, and men are willing to die for it, and yearly the work of pushing and coaxing and scolding and petting the country into good living goes forward. (324)

But there is another and uncharacteristic arrangement of discourses. As always the might of the Raj is proclaimed loud and clear:

> Hugonin, the Assistant District Superintendent of Police, a boy of twenty, had got together thirty constables and was forcing the crowd through the streets.... The dog-whip cracked across the writhing backs, and the constables smote afresh with baton and gun-butt. (343-4)

Now, however, Britain's right to rule, whether projected as benevolent tutelage or brute force, is contested. Indian refusal is here spoken both in English, which was commonly used in the emergent nationalist writings and speeches, and also in the vernaculars, for once transcribed without coy and cloying archaisms. Opposition to colonialist claims thus joins Hindu, Muslim, and Sikh in a chorus of dissident voices. The Western-educated Wali Dad, exceptionally speaking an impeccable 'standard' English, recounts the consistent anti-British record of the unrepentant old Sikh warrior, Khem Singh, and also spurns on his own account the rewards offered by the Raj to the subaltern Indian:

> I might wear an English coat and trouser. I might be a leading Muhammadan pleader. I might be received even at the Commissioner's tennis parties where the English stand on one side and the natives on the other, in order to promote social intercourse throughout the Empire. (338)

In a quite different style, Lalun, the courtesan from whose house a rebellion is being planned, voices her disaffection in a song which joins the memory of war against the Moghul invaders with the hope of a present struggle against the British. This is intended for, and heard by, the imprisoned Khem Singh; he in turn speaks of his old hatred against the government and his wish to engage in further battle. Such utterances of enmity against the Raj are ironically compounded by the reversion of the agnostic Wali Dad to his ancestral religion during the Mohurran festival. Represented by the English narrator as proof of Indian fanaticism, communalism, and traditionalism, his action can also be read as a gesture of cultural resistance. This story imposes no formal rapprochement of opposites. The seditious plot is of course foiled, but without the instigators becoming reconciled to their subjugated condition – at the end Khem Singh is to be heard suggesting plans for the escape of other fighters jailed by the British administration. Still inchoate as an insurgent discourse, the speech of Indians confronting and rejecting British authority points up what Kipling's writings elsewhere effaced.

Kipling is an exemplary artist of imperialism. The fabrications of England's mysterious imperialist identity and destiny, reiterated in the Indian writings and carried over into the later English fictions; homilies on the development of character in the metropolitan population, hymned in one of the verses as adherence to a code of Law, Order, Duty and Restraint, Obedience, Discipline; the celebrations of a triumphalism extending from the conquest of the physical environment to autocratic relationships within the domestic society and between Britain and the colonies; the projection of the white race as the natural rulers of a global space created and divided by imperialism; the positioning of the other hemisphere as peripheral to a Western centre – these inscriptions of an outlook constructed in an historical moment continue to offer rich pickings to a militant conservatism seeking sanctions for authoritarianism, social conformity, patriotism, and Britain's commanding world role by references back to a splendid imperial past. To a criticism concerned with mapping the exclusions and affirmations of an imperialist culture whose legacy has still not been spent, these same texts can be made to reveal both imperialism's grandiloquent self-presentation and those inadmissible desires, misgivings, and perceptions concealed in its discourses.

NOTES

[1] 'In memory of W. B. Yeats', *The English Auden*, ed. Edward Mendelson, (London: Faber, 1977), 241-3. The verses on Kipling are omitted from the revised version in *Collected Poems*, ed. Edward Mendelson (London: Faber, 1976), 197-8.

[2] T. S. Eliot, 'Introduction' to *A Choice of Kipling's Verse* (London: Faber, 1941). Among the responses were George Orwell, 'Rudyard Kipling' (1942) and Lionel Trilling, 'Kipling' (1943), both reprinted in Andrew Rutherford (ed.), *Kipling's Mind and Art* (Edinburgh and London: Oliver & Boyd, 1964). Boris Ford's essay, 'A case for Kipling?', first appeared in *Scrutiny* (1942); see Elliot L. Gilbert (ed.), *Kipling and the Critics* (New York: New York University Press, 1965). See also E. M. Forster's earlier recoil from Kipling's outlook in 'The boy who never grew up', *Daily Herald* (9 June 1921), 7, and 'That job's done', *The Listener*, Supplement III (March 1937).

[3] See Gilbert, *op.cit.*, and Roger Lancelyn Green (ed.), *Kipling: The Critical Heritage* (London: Routledge & Kegan Paul, 1971).

[4] Among the studies which appeared in the mid-1960s were Andrew

Rutherford (ed.), *Kipling's Mind and Art* (1964), J. I. M. Stewart, *Rudyard Kipling* (London: Gollancz, 1966), C. A. Bodelsen, *Aspects of Kipling's Art* (Manchester: Manchester University Press, 1964), Alan Sandison, *The Wheel of Empire* (London: Macmillan, 1967), Louis L. Cornell, *Kipling in India* (London: Macmillan, 1966), Bonamy Dobrée, *Rudyard Kipling: realist and fabulist* (Oxford: Oxford University Press, 1967), T. R. Henn, *Kipling* (Edinburgh: Oliver & Boyd, 1967). J. M. S. Tompkins's *The Art of Rudyard Kipling* (London: Methuen, 1959) was reissued in 1965, and a few years later Elliot L. Gilbert's *The Good Kipling* was published (Ohio: Ohio University Press, 1970). Between 1960 and 1965 *English Literature in Transition* produced *An Annotated Bibliography of Writings about Kipling*, III, 3, 4, 5 (1960) and VIII, 3, 4 (1965).

[5] For citations of this tendency see 'Scrapbook: post-anti-imperialism?', *Inscriptions* 2 (1986), 45-51 (Occasional Bulletin published by the Group for the Critical Study of Colonial Discourse, University of California, Santa Cruz).

[6] The phrase is Salman Rushdie's; see 'Outside the whale', *Granta*, 11 (1984), 125-38.

[7] Paul Driver, Introduction to *A Diversity of Creatures* (Harmondsworth: Penguin, 1987), 23.

[8] Andrew Rutherford, general preface to the World's Classics new edition of Kipling (Oxford and New York: Oxford University Press, 1987), vii, viii.

[9] Eric Stokes, 'Kipling's imperialism' in John Gross (ed.), *Rudyard Kipling: the man, his work and his world* (London: Weidenfeld & Nicolson, 1972), 90.

[10] *The Wheel of Empire*, 112. For a variation of this thesis, see Gilbert, *The Good Kipling*.

[11] Introduction to *Kim*, World's Classics, xii, xv; *Wheel of Empire*, 78.

[12] See David Trotter, introduction to *Plain Tales from the Hills* and Edward Said, introduction to *Kim* (Harmondsworth: Penguin, 1987). See also Robert MacDonald, 'Discourse and ideology in Kipling's "Beyond the pale" ', *Studies in Short Fiction*, 23, 4 (1986), 413-18.

[13] Tom Nairn, *The Break-Up of Britain* (London: Verso, 1981 [1977]), 69, 267. The absence of a left critique of imperialist culture has been discussed by Edward Said, 'Reflections on American "left" literary criticism', *The World, the Text and the Critic* (London: Faber, 1984) and by Prebon Kaarsholm in a review article, 'British and European imperialism', *History Workshop* 16 (Autumn 1983).

[14] Rudyard Kipling, *Something of Myself* (London: Macmillan, 1937), 90-1, 173-4.

[15] 'In black and white', from a volume including *Soldiers Three, The Story of the Gadsbys and In Black and White* (London: Macmillan, 1895). Page references to the uniform Macmillan edition are given in the text.

[16] See Ann Parry, 'Reading formations in the Victorian press: the reception of Kipling 1888-1891', *Literature and History*, 11, 2 (Autumn 1985), 254-63.

[17] Edward Said, *Orientalism* (London: Routledge & Kegan Paul, 1978), 24.

[18] See, for example, Mark Kinkead-Weekes, 'Vision in Kipling's novels', in Rutherford, *Kipling's Mind and Art*, and Nirad Chaudhuri, 'The Finest story about India – in English', in Gross, *Rudyard Kipling: The Man, His Work and*

His World.

[19] Said, introduction to *Kim*, 45.

[20] *ibid.*, 28, 24, 40-1.

[21] See *From Sea to Sea*, vols. I and II (London: Macmillan, 1899).

[22] Thomas Pinney (ed.) *Kipling's India: Uncollected Sketches 1884–88* (London: Macmillan, 1986), 1728.

[23] *Ibid.*, 175.

[24] Michael O'Pray, 'Radical visionaries: Powell and Pressberger' (a review of Ian Christie's *Arrows of Desire*), *New Formations*, I (Spring 1987), 155-9.

[25] *Contemporary Review*, LVIII (September 1890).

[26] Said, introduction to *Kim*, 24.

[27] *The Political Unconscious* (London: Methuen, 1981), 85.

White Skins/Black Masks: The Pleasures and Politics of Imperialism

Gail Ching-Liang Low

The colonised is elevated above his jungle status in proportion to his adoption of the mother country's cultural standards. He becomes whiter as he renounces his blackness, his jungle.

(Frantz Fanon)

He [Strickland] held the extraordinary theory that a Policeman in India should try to know as much about the natives as the natives themselves. Now, in the whole of Upper India, there is only one man who can pass for Hindu or Mahommedan, hide-dresser or priest, as he pleases. He is feared and respected by the natives from the Ghor Kathri to the Jamma Musjid: and he is supposed to have the gift of invisibility and executive control over many Devils.

(Rudyard Kipling, 'Miss Youghal's sais')

The title of my article, which is an inversion of Fanon's *Black Skins/White Masks*, aims to draw attention to one of the more visible – but less noticed – aspects of the nineteenth-century imperial legacy. By this I refer to the phenomenon of cultural cross-dressing – the fantasy of the white man disguised as 'native'. From Sir Richard Burton to John Buchan, from the 'Lawrence of Arabia' legend to the recent screening of the Masters novel, *The Deceivers*, the visual and imaginative pleasure of stepping into another's clothes forms one of the central legacies of orientalism. Needless to say, much of the fantasy of native costume is reserved for the dominant White Man; as one of my colleagues puts it, it is the white man who dresses up and the native who reveals his body for consumption by dressing down.[1] Hence, unlike the theorization of cross-dressing which sees a deliberate reversal of gendered costume as calling into question the artificiality of such stereotyping,[2] the act of donning another's clothing, I would argue, is seldom indicative of the disruption of power hierarchies. Instead, it works – however problematically – towards reinforcing them.

This article will concentrate on the late Victorian and Edwardian literary manifestations of that cultural myth, and in particular on Rudyard Kipling. The Kipling stories which centre on the characters of Strickland and Kim draw on discourses which define the native urban underworld as dark, alien, polluted, diseased, and chaotic, even as they document a fascination with the romance of incursion into that forbidden territory. But to assess the implications of that 'transgression' of social boundaries, we must first address the history of the mapping of these territories in the development of the colonial city.

THE COLONIAL CITY

Anthony King's book, *Colonial Urban Development*, argues that the Anglo-Indian city presents a problem for the colonizing power, which is fundamentally one of contact between two different ideological systems. The problem is partly surmounted through the imposition of one culture's ideals on another; material and social space is 'structured and utilised according to the value system of the colonising structure, and regulated through its notions of purity and pollution'.[3] The colonial city is composed of two coherent blocks: the civil station, where administrative, political, and bureaucratic functions predominate, and the cantonment, where military presence ensures the perpetuation of the existing power hierarchy. Set against the Anglo-Indian city is the indigenous settlement, also called the native city, the native quarter, the City, or referred to by the anglicized version of its usual name.

Native, far from being taken to mean 'autochthonous' or indigenous to the region, was (re)constituted in the Anglo-Indian city to refer to something unnatural or foreign. Pains were taken to erase all trace of the native presence from the face of civilian and military life as the Anglo-Indian community struggled to attain a self-contained sufficiency. Civil stations, which included residential space of the European community, were established within a disciplinary regime of order and cleanliness. They figured in Anglo-Indian literature within a topos of linearity and geometry. W. H. Russell, special correspondent to *The Times*, describes the English part of the station in *My Diary in the Years 1858-9*, as 'laid out in large rectangles, formed by wide roads'; each house is detached, with walls 'enclosing large gardens, lawns and out-offices'.[4] Kate Platt's guide to the tropical colonies, *The Home and Health in India*, also characterizes the civil and military *lines* as being 'well laid out with wide shady roads'.[5] G. W. Steevens, writing in 1899, uses the same terms; there are 'broad straight roads', 'arcaded with trees', broad houses with 'pillared fronts', 'large, walled or hedged enclosure[s], part garden, part mews, part village'.[6]

These geometric lines are not only literal descriptions of the physical settlement patterns of the European community, but also vivid testimonies to the culture's obsession with naming, with demarcation, and with segregation. The obsession with walls, spaces-in-between, and detachment, signals a fear of an imagined pressure from the native quarters, whose metaphoric productivity runs riot, spilling and intermixing. Lines of demarcation were important to the Anglo-Indian residences as magical defences; the compound functioned both as picturesque frame, and as visual bulwark against undesirable outsiders. Dress, language, behaviour, the collection of objects in the house, and the cultivation of the garden presented the occupant with a set of references which helped secure the community's links to its cultural origins:

> Great efforts were made to grow English flowers, which generally looked rather sickly in the Indian climate. We could have had the marvellous gardens with orchids and all sorts of things, but no, they must be English flowers.[7]

English gardens became powerful totems transporting one back to English soil; they were fetishized for their ability to counter the polluting influences of what was reinscribed as *foreign*:

> The early mornings especially are as pleasant as anything I can imagine: they have all the sweetness and freshness of an English summer. The air smells of hay and flowers, instead of ditches, dust, fried oil, curry and

onions, which are the best of Madras smells .... I saw a real staring full-blown hollyhock, which was like meeting an old friend from England, instead of tuberoses, pomegranates.[8]

Regulations abounded when dealing with military residences; western medical knowledge reinforced prejudices to do with modes of habitation and structured concern about the nature of 'zymotic' and water-borne infections. Responses to these threats included the provision of adequate ventilation, an efficient system of drainage, waste disposal, and, of course, a supply of clean water. (Significantly, such standards did not apply when dealing with the native sepoys.) Elevated ground was considered most appropriate, while residences on the plains – where military control was really most strategic – became an undesirable but necessary evil. Careful attention was paid to prevailing winds; a site was ideally placed if there was 'plenty of cool and dry air', if vegetation was less dense, and if one could avoid 'ravines full of dead animals and the ordure of many thousands of natives'.[9] If the chosen site did not have these natural advantages, or was located in an already inhabited area, the new settlement had to be protected by high walls and wide spaces. The sanitation of the native city was an obsession; stations kept to the windward side of the offending area, erected barriers, and lived in fear of their lives. Such nervousness was apparent in an interview conducted by the Royal Commission of 1863:

> Did you not state that the neighbourhood was crowded by low native houses? – At a short distance it is so, in the Colinga, Durumotollah, and the Bow Bazaar neighbourhoods for example. The influence in certain winds of these places is quite perceptible ... although there is a very good esplanade between the fort and these bazaars. Is there not considerable space of open ground surrounding the fort? – Yes, it may be called considerable space; but on ascending to a height, Ouchterlony's monument, for example, a person at once perceives how trying this space is when compared with the vast densely covered area by which it is immediately surrounded.[10]

As the interview makes explicit, 'there is no doubt there would be much more mortality among the troops were they not to some extent separated from those [native] influences by the open space surrounding the fort'.[11]

Where relations with the native population were deemed inevitable, potential sources of danger were regulated through a variety of institutional supports. Lal bazaars (regimental brothels) and lock hospitals were set up to provide the Indian counterpart to provisions under the Contagious Diseases Act at home.[12] Furthermore, the Cantonment Acts managed the spatial area of the military encampment within; behaviour seen as breaking established codes of conduct (usually that associated with the indigenous culture) was subject to severe punishment.[13]

In much Anglo-Indian literature, a Manichaean allegory operates in the polarization of the vile native city versus the good, clean Anglo-Indian one.[14] The language of disciplinary and regulatory discourses produces an Other city which is always sinister, mysterious, and dark, and whose shadow always falls on areas of light. This Other always threatens to spill over geometric divisions, oozing its contaminated bodily wastes, disgusting odours, and noxious smells; it thrives under the sign of the ubiquitous native ever invading hallowed territory. Even W. H. Russell's liberal sympathies do not exempt him from this collective nightmare; his binary vision of the European versus the Indian station sets linearity and detachment against a contrasting 'aggregate of houses perforated by tortuous paths ... resembling a section of worm-eaten wood'. The east 'grumbles, propagates, squabbles, sits in its decaying temples, haunts its rotting shrines ... drinks its semi-putrid water'.[15] The Indian city of graveyards and ancient civilizations, of newly-sprung-up bazaars and tenements, is also the out-of-bounds city where the living and the dead intermingle. This hybrid fantasy is the carnivalesque world of the bazaar city where nothing is delineated but everything exists in a chaotic state of intermingling: a carnival of night and a landscape of darkness, noise, offensive smells and obscenities.

Disintegration also haunts Kipling's writing, where an inquiry into the milk supply of the European community becomes a journey into the City of Dreadful Night.[16] Guided by a policeman into a by-way leading from the main street of Lahore, the journalist-narrator tropes his anxiety. Lahore city, marked by the presence of overflowing sewage, is a dark, feminized native body. *Her* narrow high-walled passages become more and more claustrophobic as the male reporter hurries through 'still narrowing' gullies:

> past closed and shuttered windows; past small doors in blank walls,

245

giving access to the dark courtyards even more uncleanly than the region through which he was making his way; beyond the reach of sunlight, into high clefts (it is impossible to call them lanes) where it seemed that last summer's sultry breath still lingered; and eventually halted in a *cul-de-sac*.[17]

Closed doors, blank walls, and *culs-de-sac* deny the reporter's documentation and masculinized right of entry; Kipling's text reads like a journey back to the womb. This feminized grotesque body oozes with disgusting lower bodily fluids and 'unutterable aroma[s]' which spill into public places. Her pitiless dead walls, 'barred and grated windows ... were throbbing and humming with human voices' – all of which are hidden from the disciplinary gaze, as the scene turns on the vulnerability of colonial identity:

> Voices of children singing their lessons at school; sounds of feet on stone steps, or wooden balconies overhead; voices raised in argument, or conversation, sounded dead and muffled as though they came through wool; and it seemed as if at any moment, the tide of unclean humanity might burst through its dam of rotten brickwork and filth-smeared wood, blockading the passages below.

Private and public spaces are not delineated; *charpoys* (beds) are laid in streets and courtyards; men and women sit openly on beds and children crawl beneath them. And always, there is the ubiquitous Indian, ready to touch and to pollute. The text strains under its own paranoia of contamination 'by unclean corners of walls; on each step of ruinous staircases; on roofs of low out-houses; by window, housetop, or stretched amid garbage unutterable', and by its inability to control the encounter.

Homi Bhabha argues that the language of difference which enables the colonial authority both to survey and discriminate against its subjects also renders them elusive: 'if discriminatory effects enable the authorities to keep an eye on them, their proliferating difference evades that eye, escapes that surveillance.'[18] The labelling of the ubiquitous Indian by the discriminating discourse as *native*, also forces a re-enactment of the power struggle between the colonial authority and

246

its subjects; for it foregrounds the contradictory movement whereby authority is simultaneously recognized (assented to, agreed) *and* turned away from. Deformation and difference undermine the base of agreement on which authority is generated. The result is an evasion of the disciplinary eye; speech is afflicted by a 'repeated hesitancy ... when it contemplates its discriminated subjects':

> the *inscrutability* of the Chinese, the *unspeakable* rites of the Indians, the *indescribable* habits of the Hottentots. It is not that the voice of authority is at a loss for words. It is, rather, that the colonial discourse has reached that point when, faced with the hybridity of its objects, the *presence* of power is revealed as something other than what its rules of recognition assert.[19]

In the words of Kipling's reporter, the feminized body of Lahore is 'inconceivably foul', filled with 'nameless abominations'. Milk supplies sold to the *sahib logues* are subject to the most filthy contamination; cows are accommodated in 'stall, stable, or cesspit'; brass *lotahs* (vessels) bear traces of 'greasy fingers and daubs of cow-dung', and milkmen are scarred with smallpox. The narrative, weighed down by its Manichaean rhetoric, teeters on the edge of instability; metonymic associations, and metaphoric identifications of an underworld run amok, threaten the very structure of the piece through that underworld's excesses. A very particular inversion is also made possible through the text's subject – an inquiry into milk supply. Surely the feminized Indian body producing milk points towards a relationship of dependency between the Anglo-Indian community and its host nation? The usual parent-child relationship of colonial rhetoric is subverted by the child-mother relation which also inhabits Anglo-India: it is the feminine native body which produces life-giving milk for the alien community. The Anglo-Indian ideal of separation and independence disintegrates as the ambivalence of the prose is also reflected in the title: 'Typhoid at home'. As metropolitan alter-ego, Lahore looks towards England (Britain?) as home. But Lahore is also where the Anglo-Indian community resides: typhoid at home? – home is also India? Such contradictions exist at the very centre of the Anglo-Indian identity; British military and civilian establishments are still, despite all their efforts to the contrary, located in and dependent on their host nation. Here, the colonizing culture comes face to face with an indication of its own hybridity as Anglo-Indian; in the accents of the *gowalla*'s (cowherd's) innocent declaration: 'Protector of the Poor', 'the cows here gave good milk which went to the *sahib logue* ... if anything went wrong, the *Sircar* [government] would shut up the yard.'

A cultural identity based on the metropolitan ideal of post-Enlightenment civility – which is rearticulated in a colonial context – is unstable precisely because its universalist narrative always runs up against processes of hybridization. The ideal of the civil discourse *authorizes* a universalist narrative of English liberty; yet it continually encounters those of difference which have to be disavowed, if it is to achieve legitimation. The lie this involves is constantly foregrounded; as Benita Parry, writing on Bhabha, makes clear:

> In the slippage between the enunciation of the western sign and its colonial significance, the strategies of colonialist knowledge are undermined. As the civil discourse of a culturally cohesive community is mutated into the text of a civilising mission, its enunciatory assumptions are revealed to be in conflict with its means of social control, so that the incompatibility of the ideals of English liberty and the idea of British imperialism is exposed.[20]

Kipling's early work inhabits this area of ambivalences and dual accents: voices ever mournful of loss and of alienation exist alongside strident voices idolizing the master race.

THE FANTASY OF CROSS-CULTURAL DRESSING

If such pains were taken to erase the presence of the native and impose a culturally approved version of the metropolitan ideal, why then was a deliberate 'transgression' cultivated in the fantasy of cross-cultural dressing? In my view, this paradox results from the very processes of creation of the colonial identity. Much is risked in the exploration of lines of cultural demarcation; it foregrounds an instability which, as James Donald argues, is built into the system: 'boundaries remain permeable, the "inside" is always fragmented and differentiated rather than pure and united.'[21] But where there is much to be risked, there may also be much that may be gained in this play of identity and otherness. And it is here that we must turn to Kipling's *Kim* for answers.

Kim is a novel about a young Irish orphan[22] who grows up in India;

his boyish passion for tricks and disguises and his devotion to his Buddhist lama companion have endeared him to generations of Kipling readers. The opening sequence sets the scene for an exploration of the native underworld. Kim is a street-wise orphan who keeps company with natives of the lowest caste. He avoids white men of 'serious aspect'; living 'hand in glove with men who led lives stranger than anything Haroun al Raschid dreamed of; and he lived in a life wild as that of the Arabian Nights'.[23] The association of Kim's lifestyle with exotic tales of the east points to a colonialist fantasy which, as Benita Parry has pointed out, 'transfigures India as the provider of libidinal excitation'.[24]

In *Kim*, clothes act as signifiers within the locus of desire and pleasure. Eastern clothes, which possess the power to transform, also bring with them the pleasures of that other world. Thus, Kim prefers Hindu/'Mohammedan' (and the easy passage from one to the other is its hallmark) garb to carry out his exploits; 'a complete suit of Hindu kit, the costume of a low-caste street boy' which, 'when there was business or frolic afoot', gave him access to forbidden and desirable territory. His 'stealthy prowl through dark gullies' conjures up the 'sights and sounds of the women's world', and 'the headlong flight from housetop to housetop under the cover of the hot dark' evokes the mystery of dangerous assignments.

Clothes trap the essence of the east; they objectify it. Like souvenir curios which represent fetishized totems, they present the oriental world for consumption. It should come as no surprise then that their later circulation as signs in a capitalist economy ensured their commodification as luxury, opulence, consumption and spectacle.[25] The description of Kim's Afghan outfit testifies to this: the gold-fringed and embroidered cap signalling all the wealth and luxury promised by the oriental world; the ornamental design on the turban-cap and cloth pointing to alien artistry and mystique – a culture which is 'ample and flowing' and full of sensuousness (the touch of silk and heavenly smells of Russia-leather slippers 'with arrogantly curled tips'). Colour too forms part of the dress and is there to aid Kim's transformation – 'A little dye-stuff and three yards of cloth to help out a little jest'. A courtesan no less, 'dabbing a twist of cloth into a little saucer of brown dye' and twisting a turban around Kim's head, transforms him into a 'low-caste Hindu boy, perfect in every detail'.[26]

In Lurgan Sahib's curiosity shop, which overflows with emblematic totems of the east, there are ghost-daggers, Tibetan prayer-wheels, precious stones and jewellery, gilt Buddhas, ivory, friezes of fantastic details, and lacquer altars reeking of incense. This is the other house of wonders: a mystical and eroticized counterpart of the more static, sanitized presentation of knowledge as power found in the Lahore Museum.[27] Interestingly – and we shall return to this point – the shop is presented as the magical world of a child's playroom. But it is also a school for spies; significantly, it is here that Lurgan Sahib as the Keeper of Images teaches Kim the secret of 'dressing-up':

> He [Lurgan Sahib] could paint faces to a marvel; with a brush-dab here and a line there changing them past recognition. The shop was full of all manner of dresses and turbans, and Kim was apparelled variously as a young Mohammedan of good family, an oilman, and once – which was a joyous evening – as the son of an Oudh landholder in the fullest of full dress.

Kim's transformation is intense:

> a demon in Kim woke up and sang with joy as he put on the changing dresses, and changed speech and gesture therewith.[28]

The change effected by the clothes is (unsurprisingly) characterized by a release of libidinal energy; it leaves Kim with a freedom far beyond drummer boys, De Castros, and any of his peers at the St Xavier school. The sense of being totally familiar, totally at ease in an alien world, produces more than pleasure; the awareness of 'being'/'tasting' the other in its fullness gives orgasmic release:

> Kim sat up and yawned, shook himself, and thrilled with delight. This was seeing the world in real truth; this was life as he would have it – bustling and shouting, the buckling of belts, and beating of bullocks and creaking of wheels, lighting of fires and cooking of food, and new sights at every turn of the approving eye .... India was awake, and Kim was in the middle of it ... for he borrowed right- and left-handedly from all the customs of the country he knew and loved.[29]

A comparison with Sir Richard Burton's memoirs in India highlights a similar movement; the attention to oriental detail, the playful appreciation of costume, produces a parallel excitement to that of Kipling's text:

With hair falling upon his shoulders, a long beard, face and hands, arms and feet, stained with a thin coat of henna, Mirza Abdullah of Bushire – your humble servant – set out upon many and many a trip. He was a Bazzaz, a vendor of the fine line, calicoes, and muslins; – such chapmen are sometimes admitted to display their wares, even in the sacred harem, by 'fast' and fashionable dames – and he had a little pack of *bijouterie* and *virtu* reserved for emergencies .... What scenes he saw! what adventures he went through! But who would believe, even if he ventured to detail them?[30]

Both texts are as much about knowledge/power as they are about pleasure. Burton's awareness of his position as European in the orient is never blurred by any sense of an affinity with the native world. Edward Said reminds us that this reflects a strategy of 'flexible positional superiority': 'what is never far from the surface of Burton's prose is another sense it radiates, a sense of assertion and domination over all the complexities of Oriental life.'[31] Kim, by contrast, is but a child; what is more, he inhabits a world in which military control of native affairs is softened by an ideological sleight of hand. Colonel Creighton, for example, is home-grown unlike *foreign* sahibs; as the Sahiba rationalizes, 'these be the sort to oversee justice. They know the land and the customs of the land. The others, all new from Europe, suckled by white women and learning our tongues from books, are worse than pestilence.'[32] Thus a *syncretism* is offered in *Kim* which writes out conflict in an all-encompassing vision; black and white work for the same ends: 'We be all on one lead-rope, then ... the Colonel, Mahbub Ali, and I.' Kim is the Little Friend of all the World; and as one critic points out, he 'moves through India's range of caste, race and creed all condemning and judging one another ... offering universal friendship with no apparent awareness that anything is unusual'.[33]

Mark Kinkead-Weekes has described Kipling's vision as one that is mature, 'humane and affectionate', encapsulating a 'whole kaleidoscope of race, custom and creed'. Yet that critical position is also part of an orientalist violation which sees, structures, orders, and offers up India for pleasurable consumption.[34] Creighton's role as ethnographer, soldier, and scholar renders him privy to both material and discursive power:[35] the imperial spy-master finds no contradictions in his aspirations for recognition from the Royal Geographical Society.[36] More importantly, Kim is never allowed to forget who he is. The lesson Kim remembers, despite all his 'negative capability', is that he *is* white: 'One must never forget that one is a Sahib, and that some day, when the examinations are passed, one will command natives.' And Kim, we are explicitly told, took note of this, 'for he began to understand where the examinations led'.[37]

That the release from official identity is also intimately bound up with its development is evident in another, very different text – the Jack London exploration of urban poverty in the city of London at the turn of the century.[38] Strategies of demarcation which define the high and low, the civilized and the grotesque body in Anglo-India, have structural similarities with their Victorian counterparts in Britain. The 'Into Unknown England' tradition of writing produced a similar literature of documentary, discovery, exploration, and adventure; George Godwin writing in 1854 makes explicit connections: 'to brave the risks of fever and other injustices to health, and the contact of men and women as lawless as the Arab or Kaffir'.[39] While cross-class dressing cannot be taken to be identical to cross-cultural dressing, since the element of race/colour signifies an immutable difference, the dynamics of the two fantasies are very similar.

In the late nineteenth century, 'slumming' expeditions with police protection were not uncommon[40] and sociological and philanthropic literature was prolific; titles such as Henry Mayhew's *London Life and London Labour*, Andrew Mearns's *The Bitter Cry of Outcast London*, William Booth's *Into Darkest England* (echoing Stanley), and Charles Booth's multi-volumed *Life and Labour*, made visible the underside of London life. Yet what remains distinctive about London's *The People of the Abyss* is the very *drama* of his investigative reporting. London's position as the active, questing participant may be read as the romantic counterpart of the anthropologist as (participant) observer. Both present forms of knowledge and power; London's adoption of disguise as a poor working man enables his narrative to convey both a sense of *active* mastery and release. To adopt a Kiplingesque phrase, London, like Kim, is a player of the Game. He himself makes the allusion: 'Shades of Old Sleuth and Sherlock Holmes!' Dressed in a pair of 'well-worn trousers, a frayed jacket with one remaining button, a pair of brogans which had plainly seen service where coal was shovelled', London magics an instant transformation, which enables him to meet the lower classes 'face to face, and [know] them for what they [are]':

No sooner was I out on the streets than I was impressed by the difference in status effected by my clothes. All servility vanished from the demeanour of the common people with whom I came into contact. Presto! in the twinkling of an eye, so to say, I had become one of them. My frayed and out-at-elbows jacket was the badge and advertisement of my class, which was their class.[41]

London's account parallels Kipling's and Burton's for the importance he attaches to the magical power of his costume to turn him into one of 'their class'. For all three writers, the fantasy of cross-cultural dressing centres on their identification of clothes as 'badge and advertisement' of their ability to cross the class and cultural gap. Clothes become the signifer *par excellence*, both of the romance and danger of that Other world, and of a release from their own.

That this familiar orientalist trope is reproduced in more contemporary cultural forms is evidenced by Peter Brooks's recent comments on Balinese masks, which he describes as producing 'the most extraordinary sense of liberation. This [putting on the mask] is one of those great exercises that whoever does it for the first time counts as a great moment: suddenly to find oneself immediately for a certain time liberated from one's own subjectivity.'[42] Yet the fact that he, like the Victorian writers cited above, may choose to take off his mask at any moment, makes a crucial difference. Clothes as surface, visual, and imaginative signs are integral to the rhetoric of disguise; as in *Kim*, it is there very *superficial* quality – the fact that you can put them on or take them off – that renders them ideal in a fantasy which plays on identity and difference. That such a fantasy is unavailable to the orientalist Other is proved by the educated Indian of Bengal, whose fluent English, clothes, and mannerisms only serve to indicate the distance between the mother – or should I say father – culture and its bastards. This subject of disavowal – that 'subject of difference that is an almost the same but not quite'[43] – is continually betrayed in his attempts to pass as the real article, by subtle signs of something not-quite-right. Deception by a Eurasian (a real Anglo-Indian?) may always be uncovered by a practised eye:

> Pyramus carries a walking stick with imitation silver straps upon it, and there are cloth tops to his boots; but his collar has been two days worn. Thisbe crowns her dark head with a blue velvet Tam-o'-Shanter; but one of her boots lacks a button, and there is a tear in the left-hand glove .... Do you ever kiss Thisbe when Mamma is not by? – Garlic – yea, lusson of the bazaar. Mamma is generous in her views on garlic.[44]

At the end of their escapades, both London and Kim are able to cast off their costumes to return to their original identities. Kim's identity as a spy is marked by a silver amulet containing one small turquoise. London's descent into the abyss is cushioned by nothing less than a gold coin sewn into his outfit. His lodgings in the East End provide a refuge from the tide of *in*humanity in the city of London: 'not too far distant, into which I could run now and again to assure myself that good clothes and cleanliness still existed.'[45] In those sane surroundings, London could compile his notes or 'sail forth occasionally in changed garb to civilization'.

The primary attraction of the cross-cultural dress is, then, the promise of 'transgressive' pleasure without the penalties of actual change. Such metamorphosis does little to subvert existing power hierarchies, since the cross-dresser may always reveal or revert to the white identity underneath the native clothes. Kinkead-Weekes has remarked on Kipling's Keatsean attribute of projecting 'negative capability'. But perhaps there is a different form of 'projection' in Kipling's writing. Projection, after all, is a phallic attribute of the master. What makes Kim's cross-cultural dressing possible is the fact that he is white – with all its colonialist ramifications. As Michel Foucault has noted, transgression also traces 'the flashing line that cause the limit the arise'; it 'prescribes not only the sole manner of discovering the sacred in its unmediated substance, but also a way of recomposing its empty form, its absence through which it becomes all the more scintillating'.[47] Or, as Stallybrass and White have pointed out, the play of identity and difference in the act of demarcation also fuels a contradictory movement enmeshed in desire and lack. The release of libidinal energy which accompanies cross-dressing, despite its potentially 'exhilarating sense of freedom', may also be constitutive of the dominant:

> Often it is a powerful ritual or symbolic practice whereby the dominant squanders its symbolic capital so as to get in touch with the fields of desire which it denied itself as the price to pay for its political power ... it is counter-sublimation, a delirious experience of the symbolic capital accrued ... in the struggle of bourgeois hegemony.[48]

Kipling's fascination with the native underlife writes an alternative version of cross-cultural dressing. His letter to Margaret Burne-Jones shows a will to power:

Underneath our excellent administrative system; under the piles of reports and statistics; the thousands of troops: the doctors: and the civilian runs wholly untouched and unaffected the life of the peoples of the land – a life full of impossibilities and wonders as the Arabian Nights. I don't want to gush over it but I do want you to understand Wop dear that immediately outside of our English life is the dark and crooked and fantastic; and wicked: and awe-inspiring life of the 'native' ... I have done my best to penetrate into it.[49]

The native life, so full of the adjectival, is not only contrasted with the arid bureaucratic 'piles of reports and statistics'. It is also described as the 'underneath', that subterranean passage below English civil and military life which *seduces*. In the textualization of this fantasy – the Arabian Nights, which promises a magical world of 'impossibilities and wonders' – Kipling's other world, though demonic – 'dark and crooked and fantastic' – paradoxically also forms the source and inspiration of his artistry. Kipling's colonial appropriation of the romantic metaphor of the imagination reverses the sequence of rape; this is an alien world which invites his penetration. His letter goes on to allude to the 'queer jumble of opium dens, night houses, night strolls with natives' and the 'long yarns that my native friends spin me'. The contact, if not taboo, is illicit. Significantly, it is also textual (the stories he hears) and it is out of these associations that Kipling's artistry emerges.

Yet Kipling also speaks of how 'little an Englishman can hope to understand [these natives]': 'I would that you see some of the chapters in Mother Maturin [his unfinished lost novel] and you will follow more closely what I mean.' Here then is the contradictory movement at the centre of Kipling's project. His task is to make people 'see'; to become the authoritative voice on native affairs – the interpreter that would seek to translate native terms into English ones.[50] At this point, the full significance of Kipling's fantasy of cross-cultural dress emerges; the very words of his text take on native clothes and, by active appropriation, become signifiers of his authority. Gayatri Spivak, quoting Benjamin, makes a crucial point in this connection: Kipling's pidgin Hindustani, she suggests, should not be taken as translation, done 'lovingly and in detail, in its own language, form ... according to the manner of meaning in the original', but as violation where the 'violence of imperialism straddles a subject-language'.[51]

255

SURVEILLANCE AS DISGUISE

Where *Kim* presents a relatively gentle version of imperial authority, the Strickland stories more immediately document the thrill of imperial penetration. Strickland is a policeman-detective unlike any other character in Kipling mythology. He appears in stories like 'Miss Youghal's Sais', a tale of romance and disguises, 'The return of Imray' and 'The mark of the beast', two gothic tales of crime and detection, and 'The Bronckhorst Divorce-Case'.[52] Strickland is 'extraordinary' in Kipling mythology in the sense that he knows as much about native culture, customs, and dress as it is possible for a white man to know. He is able to pass undetected amongst 'the native riff-raff' of British India and, like Haroun al Raschid of the *Arabian Nights*, 'is supposed to have the gift of invisibility and executive control over many Devils'. He has even been 'initiated into the *Sat Bhai* at Allahabad ... knew the Lizzard-Song of the Sansis, and the *Halli-Hukk* dance', all of which prove, the narrative tells us, that 'he has gone deeper than the skin'.[53]

Strickland, like the journalist-narrator of his tale, has access to what otherwise would be classified as forbidden and taboo to the white inhabitants of British India.[54] A character with legitimate access to both worlds on account of his policing functions, Strickland's degree of familiarity with native life is proportional to his control over them: 'Strickland hates being mystified by natives, because his business in life is to overmatch them with their own weapons.' Even the educated Bengali is exposed in his attempt to appear what he is not; 'Strickland on Native Progress as he had seen it was worth hearing. Natives hated Strickland; but they were afraid of him. He knew too much.'[55] His affinity for 'native patter' and his talent for disguises help him solve the Nasiban murder case; his mere presence is enough to upset the lying Muslim into telling the truth in the 'Bronckhorst Divorce-Case'.

The figure of Strickland is very similar to the character of Sherlock Holmes in the Conan Doyle stories, for both revel in the cut and thrust of detection. Holmes also has contact with the urban underworld; from seedy visitors 'looking like ... Jew pedlar[s]' to 'slip-shod' elderly women to 'shallow, rat-faced, dark-eyed' fellows. Holmes's street urchins 'can go anywhere, see everything, overhear everyone'.[56] Holmes's disguises encompass various classes and are often invaluable in the solving of his cases. Once, dressed as an old man with wig, whiskers, eyebrows, weak legs, and a 'proper workhouse cough', Holmes confides:

You see, a good many of the criminal classes begin to know me – especially since our friend here took to publishing some of my cases: so I can only go on the warpath under some disguises like this.[57]

THE FANTASY DYNAMICS OF CROSS-DRESSING

What is achieved through these cross-cultural (and cross-class) incursions is a dream of surveillance. This is articulated through the fantasy of invisibility which gives Strickland, Holmes, and Kim omnipotence and omnipresence. Unlike the ideal of the panoptic eye which fixes its disciplinary subject,[58] the dream of cross-cultural dressing has to do with the pleasures of an active display of power. Peter Wollen, in an article on fashion and orientalism, writes that the nineteenth century witnessed the eroticization of the orient as well as its political domination.[59] The two are not incompatible; the Orient becomes, through western imagination, a site of excess sexuality and deviant behaviour that must be penetrated and controlled. The violation of a subject-culture may also be read as a sexualized text. Strickland's, Kim's, and Holmes's elaborate disguises allow them to pry voyeuristically into native affairs, just as the authors' narratives allow them to order and display the Other world.

An insight into the mechanics of cross-cultural dressing can be gained from a psychoanalytic reading, which makes apparent the dynamics of the fantasy, as well as the terms on which it is effected. The myth of the white man in Native Dress, I would argue, is based on the fetishization of clothes which enable the wearer to fantasize about mastery. In Freudian terms, a fetish is an object endowed with more power than it actually has; clothes as fetishes also render unto the White Man a wholeness which reinforces the difference on which his power is based. The fetish, by standing in for the woman's lack of a phallus, allows the (almost always male) fetishist simultaneously to acknowledge and disavow castration. The male child, refusing on one level to recognize the threat of the woman's lack, accepts it on another;[60] the fetish-as-substitute contains the castrating difference even as it disseminates its discriminatory effects. This double-take allows the male child to hold on to the power of sexual difference, for it is the possession of the phallus which instigates the discriminatory codings of sexual difference. Through the substitution of the fetish, the male child is able to sidestep the threat of castration, albeit at the cost of splitting his own identity.

In the context of my discussion of fantasy, Robert Stoller's treatment of transvestism and cross(gender)-dressing is particularly interesting.[61] While one may not agree with his notion of core identity (masculine, feminine),[62] Stoller's treatment of cross(gender)-dressing gives important insights into the psychoanalysis of cross-cultural dressing. In Stoller's terms, fetishistic cross-dressing is characterized by sexual excitement in the donning of garments of the opposite sex. This behaviour is almost 'non-existent' in women and is indulged primarily by heterosexual men who, when not cross-dressing, identify strongly with what may conventionally be labelled as 'masculine' forms of behaviour. Thus maleness and masculinity are an integral part of the disguise: 'The fetishistic cross-dresser believes his [phallus], his maleness, and his masculinity to be valuable, endangered and preservable only by means of his [cross-dressing] (more or less).' His double-take is frozen in a single moment; he is the woman with the phallus.

According to Stoller these men not only derive their greatest erotic pleasure from their genitals; their sexual excitement is also expressed through the active possession of the penis. More importantly, its hidden 'presence sensed beneath the women's garments' gives an added excitement: 'They never quite forget the trick: the hidden penis. The thought that they are fooling the world is surpassed in enjoyment only by the moment when they can reveal the secret.'[63]

Stoller's account of the problematic is important because it allows us to see the fantasy of the Strickland figure in the light of another fantasy, that of power as displayed in fetishistic disguise. That pleasure is exclusively reserved for colonial powers; as John Buchan writes in *Greenmantle* of British heroes, 'the truth is that we are the only race on earth that can produce men capable of getting inside the skin of remote peoples.'[64] Excitement and pleasure are expressed through the knowledge that the narrator is the white-man-in-native-garb, the powerful male with the phallus. To paraphrase Stoller, his greatest pleasure is in seeing his whiteness hidden beneath. Strickland's role of surveillance – his 'outlandish custom of prying into native life' – fits hand in glove with this elaborate fantasy whereby the European becomes the native-white. Constantly aware of the whiteness underneath the disguise, he derives great pleasure from his warding off of the native threat (the fear of castration); his clothes as fetish permit both the acknowledgement of difference (on which his identity as master is based) and the simultaneous disavowal of that castrating difference.

Is fetishistic cross-cultural dressing sexual at root? It is here that I must pause to acknowledge a hiatus in my own thinking. I have indicated that one may go a considerable way to reading the sexual as political. But perhaps one may also speculate – albeit wildly – on the reverse dynamic. The answer I shall hazard applies primarily to the native-born. The argument which Stoller presents may also be read as describing a fantasy of subjugated alterity, which identifies cross-cultural dressing as a violent expropriation or castration; the white man as native tearing the body of native from his self. Spivak speaks of a species of translation which should properly be termed violation rather than reproduction, when 'the violence of imperialism straddles a subject-language'.[65] May one read the dynamics of imperialist rape as similar to those of castration?

Kipling's position as native-born Anglo-Indian inscribes his relation with India as one not unlike that of son and mother. And as Parry, quoting Kipling, points out, the 'dear dark foster mother' of heathen song and speech is that 'lost object of desire that must be relinquished for entry into the patriarchal law'.[66] The primal link is one which must be broken in the interest of a colonialist identity. The connection between desire and law, forged at a crucial early stage in the child's development, renders encounters between the Anglo-Indian and Indian culture an oscillation between pain (suffocation, disintegration) and pleasure (release, dissolution). Fetishistic cross-cultural dressing *contains* both the threat of disintegration and the excitement of crossing official boundaries. But such dressing, as I have suggested, is also about *violation as castration*: the fetishistic cross-cultural dresser masters the threat of woman/native through penetration, possession, and exhibition – his rape – of her essential enigma; but in doing so, he also enacts and re-enacts castration by *placing* her as woman/native/ subjugated Other. The child (identifying with the patriarch) rapes his native-mother to maintain his colonialist identity. This *rape* secures patriarchal law because it repeats the terror (safely directed at the Other) and privilege of *castration*. By reinstating the Father/male heir as Law-giver and Law-provider, a whole sexual and political semiotic is set in circulation.[67] This movement, in a sense, generates the other side of the fetish as disavowal; acknowledgement, achieved *through* the presence of the fetish, allows the male child to fantasize about the *power* of castration. The white man disguised as native, dreams of his power to rip the body of the native from his (native) self. He glows with the satisfaction of having his cake and eating it.

At the end of these complicated manoeuvres, the white man stands alone. Freud's treatment of megalomania as narcissism invokes a magical *male* childhood world where everything functions to will. It reads curiously akin to the world of Lugan Sahib's curiosity shop:

> characteristics ... might be put down to megalomania: the over-estimation of the power of wishes, and mental processes, the 'omnipotence of thoughts', a belief in the magical virtue of words, and a method of dealing with the outer world – the art of 'magic' – which appears to be a logical application of these grandiose premises. In the child of our own day ... we expect a perfectly analogous attitude towards the external world.[68]

Ironically, Freud was to pin these characteristics firmly on the primitive. Perhaps the white man in native costume, like Narcissus, mirrors only his own image as that of another. Rape as a gendered act of violence is real; but is castration (of the kind the male child would like to secure) effected through the act of rape? I do not know the full answer to the question: but the native threat remains and the fetishistic cross-cultural dresser is repetitious in his secret pleasure and terror.

Said, in closing his discussion of *Kim*, speaks of the profoundly embarrassing truth which emerges from the overlap between the political control wielded by imperialism on the one hand, and the aesthetic and psychological pleasure it supplies on the other.[69] This is precisely what I have tried to argue; the fantasy of donning native costume, in the context of imperialism, is not mere play or liberation into another world. For me, on the outside of that mythology, that fantasy expresses another attempt at control of subaltern peoples, another attempt at laying the burden of representation on them.[70]

NOTES

Thanks to Robert Clark, Sylvan Bentley, and Stuart MacFarlane for their helpful comments, and to the National Trust for permission to quote from Kipling's letters.
[1] I am indebted to Diana Smith for this expression.
[2] Sandra Gilbert, 'Costumes of the mind', in Elizabeth Abel (ed.), *Writing and Sexual Difference* (Brighton: Harvester, 1982). Also see Mark Finch, 'Sex and address in *Dynasty*' in *Screen*, 27, 6, (1986), 24-42, on camp, and Jonathan Dollimore, 'Different desires', in *Textual Practice*, 1, 1 (1987), especially 54-8, and 'The dominant and the deviant: a violent dialectic', in *Critical Quarterly*, 23, 1 & 2 (1986), 179-92, for a discussion on transgression.
[3] Anthony King, *Colonial Urban Development* (London: Routledge & Kegan Paul, 1976).

[4] William H. Russell, *My Diary in the Years 1858-9*, Vol 1 (London: Routledge, Warne & Routledge, 1860), 180.

[5] Kate Platt, *The Home and Health in India* (London: Baillière, Tindall & Cox, 1923), 26.

[6] Quoted in King (1976), 125.

[7] Quoted in Charles Allen, *Plain Tales from the Raj* (London: Deutsch/BBC, 1978 (1975)), 125.

[8] Quoted in King (1976), 143.

[9] *ibid.*, 108.

[10] *Royal Commission on the Sanitary Conditions of the Army in India, 1863.*

[11] *ibid.*

[12] See Kenneth Ballhatchet, *Race, Sex and Class Under the Raj* (London: Weidenfeld & Nicolson, 1980).

[13] 'Whenever it shall appear necessary for the protection of troops ... it shall be lawful for the Governor General in India to extend the limits of any military cantonment ... and to define the limits around such within which such rules ... shall be in force.' Examples of prohibited behaviour included carrying 'exposed meat', letting fall 'nightsoil', carrying an 'indecently covered corpse'; failing to bury a corpse within twenty-four hours. Storing any substance emitting an offensive smell, and torturing or abusing animals were all offences punishable by law. Cited in King (1976), 119-20.

[14] See Abul JanMohamed, 'The economy of the Manichean allegory: the function of racial difference in colonialist literature', *Critical Inquiry*, 12, 1 (1985), 59-87. JanMohamed writes: 'The dominant model of power- and interest-relations in all colonial societies is the manichean opposition between the putative superiority of the European and the supposed inferiority of the native ... the manichean allegory – a field of diverse yet interchangeable oppositions between white and black, good and evil, superiority and inferiority, civilization and savagery, intelligence and emotion, rationality and sensuality, self and other, subject and object' (63).

[15] Russell (1860), 180.

[16] This is a phrase taken from the title of two of Kipling's prose pieces, on Lahore and Calcutta respectively. Kipling, of course, adopted it from James Thomson's long poem of the same name.

[17] Rudyard Kipling, 'Typhoid at home', in Thomas Pinney (ed.), *Kipling's India* (London: Macmillan, 1986), 70.

[18] Homi Bhabha, 'Signs taken for wonders', *Critical Inquiry*, 12, 1 (1985), 154.

[19] *ibid.*

[20] Benita Parry, 'Problems in current theories of colonial discourse', *Oxford Literary Review*, 9 (1987), 41.

[21] James Donald, 'How English is it? Popular literature and national culture', *New Formations*, 6 (Winter, 1988), 37.

[22] Kipling seems to show as much obsession with marginal figures as with more central ones. His stories are peopled with loafers and down-and-outs as well as district officers and imperial engineers.

[23] Rudyard Kipling, *Kim* (London: Macmillan, 1912 (1901)), 3.

[24] Benita Parry, 'The contents and discontents of Kipling's imperialism', *New Formations*, 6 (Winter, 1988), 56.

25 Peter Wollen in his article on 'Fashion/orientalism/the body' (*New Formations*, 1 (Spring, 1987), 5-33) maps the revival of the decorative, the 'extravagant' and ornamental trend in art and fashion, on to the revival of the orientalist vogue. This Wollen argues is 'symptomatic of the decline of modernism'; its history is articulated through a series of 'antinomies': 'functional/decorative, useful/wasteful, natural/artificial ... machine/body, masculine/feminine, west/east'. The French translation of *The Thousand and One Nights* in 1899 was to give orientalism in French visual culture a new impetus. Inscribed as a site for the erotic and political projects of the west, the Orient – embodied in *The Thousand and One Nights* – unfolds as a 'secular, licentious narrative, with almost no trace of moralism (or even Islam), but full of tales of deviant, transgressive and fantastic sexuality'. The 'oriental' look in fashion design – for example, the 'harem-pantaloons' in Wollen's article – may be read as an example of what I mean by the fetishism and commodification of the Orient in a capitalist economy. The periodic revival of 'ethnic' fashion may be taken as another. Such fashions function as *signifiers* of the Orient and circulate within a capitalist economy in a synecdochical form.

26 Kipling (1912), 179-80.

27 For an account of the pleasures of anthropology as imperialism in *Kim*, see Edward Said, 'Kipling, pleasures of imperialism', *Raritan*, 7, 2 (Fall, 1987), 27-64.

28 Kipling (1912), 226.

29 *ibid.*, 103.

30 Sir Richard Burton, *Selected Papers on Anthropology, Travel and Exploration* (London: A. M. Philpot, 1924).

31 Edward Said, *Orientalism* (London: Routledge & Kegan Paul, 1980 (1987)), 7, 196.

32 Kipling (1912), 107.

33 Mark Kinkead-Weekes, 'Vision in Kipling's novels', in Andrew Rutherford, *Kipling's Mind and Art* (Edinburgh/London: Oliver & Boyd, 1965 (1964)).

34 Also see Said (1987).

35 By this, following Chandra Talpade Mohanty writing on a different subject, I refer to the relation between ideologies and their 'effects'. Mohanty writes: 'The definition of colonization I invoke is a predominantly *discursive* one, focussing on a certain mode of appropriation and codification of "scholarship" and "knowledge" ... particular analytic categories employed in writing on the subject which take as their primary point of reference ... interests as they have been articulated in the [west] ... [which may be] neither singular nor homogeneous in its goals, interests or analysis. However, it is possible to have a coherence of *effects* resulting from the implicit assumptions of "the west" (in all its complexities and contradictions) as the primary referent in theory and praxis.' I acknowledge that there is, in John Tagg's words, no 'ontologically prior unity of being to which discourse may be referred', nor can material reality be imagined as a 'universal, common or necessary referent' existing autonomously from the discursive. The point I wish to emphasize in using the terms 'material' and 'discursive', is a simple one: a specific historical and social space must also be foregrounded on which the *effects* (in all its contradictions and complexities) of a politics of colonialism are inscribed. Benita Parry calls

for the restoration of the 'historical density and effectivity' of a colonial text: one must read 'literature as a cultural text and rhetorical practice produced and performed within determinate historical, social and political conditions which enable and constrain the construction of meaning'. See Chandra Talpade Mohanty, 'Under western eyes', *Feminist Review*, 3 (Autumn, 1988), 61-88, and John Tagg, *The Burden of Representation* (London: Macmillan, 1988), 24, and Benita Parry (1987), respectively.

[36] The connection between geography and politics is more literal than it may seem at first glance. The Great Game referred to in the novel was a phrase historically coined by an officer, Arthur Conolly, to refer to the North-Western Frontier skirmishes and the suspected Russian intrigue. The formulation of an adequate defence strategy needed an adequate geographical knowledge of the lands beyond British rule in the North-West. This was initially neglected by the East India Company, which had decided that trade on this front was minimal. But from the 1800s onwards, the possibility of invasion, by Europe, through the Persian Gulf or the Caspian Sea initiated a new phase in rethinking these issues; the importance of an accurate knowledge of the geographical spread of the land gained acute importance, and agents took on surveying work. As H. W. C Davis in his British Academy Raleigh Lecture on History of 1926 says, 'Part of their business was to make the exact scientific observations of latitudes, heights, and distances on which every map had to be founded ... the best Indian maps of this period consist of routes meticulously described, and measured with the help of instruments called "perambulators" in which towns, roads, and natural features are inserted on the strength of information obtained from native maps or from the descriptions of travellers .... Such was the surveyor's primary task. But in his travels, the surveyor was expected to bear in mind the interests of Indian commerce, of the Indian army, and of political departments .... Surveyors visiting more accessible and populous regions were also expected to describe, from the soldier's point of view, every route which had been or might be used for military purposes. Men who were habitually thus employed often became valuable as political agents.' Knowledge of native language was paramount and to be able to 'pass muster in an Asiatic disguise when that was expedient' was a matter of life or death. Not only were famous British agents used (Henry Pottinger, Charles Christie), but even native agents were used to good effect. Ingenious devices such as hollowed-out prayer-wheels and decimated rosary beads were used to help measure distances. Some cases of this trans-border secret reconnaissance work were so well known to have taken place that a native proverb was coined in their honour: 'First comes a Sahib, and then two who make a map; after that comes an army and takes over our country.' Furthermore, they conclude, 'the Sirkar [Government] is nowhere without a map, but directly the map is made it is invincible; therefore, if we catch a man making a map we kill him.' See Capt. G. J. Younghusband, *Frays and Forays* (London: Percival, 1890).

[37] Kipling (1912), 177.

[38] Jack London, *The People of the Abyss* (London: Macmillan, 1903).

[39] Quoted in Peter Keating, *The Working Class in Victorian Fiction* (London: Routledge & Kegan Paul, 1971). London's antecedent may be found in James

Greenwood (*A Night in the Workhouse* (1866); *The Seven Curses of London* (1869); *The Wilds of London* (1874)). Of Greenwood Keating writes: '[his] name alone was sufficient to gain him entrance to lower London, and to reach those places where his name meant nothing he travelled in disguise. From these journeys he sent back detailed reports on various aspects of working-class and criminal life, ranging from hop-picking to a "knock-out auction", from thieves' kitchens to slum missions, always carefully noting peculiarities of dress, behaviour and speech.' Also see Peter Stallybrass and Allon White, *The Politics and Poetics of Transgression* (London: Methuen, 1986) and Robert Colls and Philip Dodd (eds), *Englishness* (London: Croom Helm, 1986).

[40] Sheila Smith, *The Other Nation* (Oxford: Oxford University Press, 1980). Dickens, for example, writes about just such an expedition in 'On duty with Inspector Fields' (Charles Dickens, *Reprinted Pieces* (London: Chapman & Hall, 1899), 174-89). Dickens's text also provides the inspiration behind Kipling's 'City of dreadful night'.

[41] London (1903), 13-14.

[42] Peter Brooks, 'Coming out of our shell', in *The Shifting Point* (London: Methuen, 1988). I am indebted to Franc Chamberlain for directing my attention to this passage. I am also, of course, deliberately misreading Brooks and his quest for a spirituality (*predicated*, precisely, on the Orient) which he sees as missing from the West. Hence Brooks talks about mask as a 'soul-portrait' and of 'good' masks (which are true masks or really 'anti-masks') and 'horrible' masks (the lying, sentimental, and distorted kind of the West's subconscious, and interestingly, also of Africa). Balinese masks are good masks and completely 'naturalistic': 'an outer casing that is a complete and sensitive reflection of the inner life'. Yet what remains absolutely crucial for a Balinese mask to work – and this insight, as Franc Chamberlain points out, is absent from Brooks's theory – is the sheer amount of physical training and learned performance skill that goes into making the Balinese mask signify. It is not, as Brooks writes, merely a matter of putting a mask on.

[43] Homi Bhabha, 'Of mimicry and man', *October*, 28 (Spring, 1984), 126, 127.

[44] Rudyard Kipling, 'The city of dreadful night', *From Sea to Sea*, Vol 2 (New York: Doubleday and McClure, 1899), 242.

[45] London (1903), 13.

[46] Kinkead-Weekes (1965).

[47] Michel Foucault, *Language, Counter-Memory, Practice* (Oxford, Blackwell, 1977).

[48] Stallybrass and White (1986), 201.

[49] Letter to Margaret Burne-Jones dated 13 February 1886; *The Kipling Papers* (11/6-7), University of Sussex Manuscripts.

[50] The myth of the authorial voice which is all-knowing of native life is one which clings on to a culturally sanctioned (western) view of Kipling's status. Kay Robinson, his contemporary journalist and editor, writes of Kipling precisely within this *construct*. Robinson speaks of Kipling's wonderful insight into the 'strangely mixed manners of life and thought of the natives in India' in the following way: 'He knew them all through their horizontal divisions of rank and their vertical sections of caste; their ramifications of race and blood; their antagonisms and blendings of creed; and their hereditary streaks of

calling or handicraft. Show him a native, and he would tell you his rank, caste, race, origin, habitat, creek and calling. He would speak to the man in his own fashion, using familiar, homely figures which brightened the other's surprised eyes with the recognition of brotherhood and opened a straight way into his confidence.' In an earlier article in *McClure's Magazine* (1896), Robinson writes: 'No half-note in the wide gamut of native ideas and custom was unfamiliar to him: just as he had left no phase of white life in India unexplained.' Harold Orel (ed.), *Interviews and Recollections*, Vol 1 (London: Macmillan, 1983), 82, 72.

[51] Gayatri Spivak, 'Imperialism and sexual difference', *Oxford Literary Review*, 8, 1 & 2 (1986), 234. While one might argue that there can be *no* translation (i.e. translations are marked precisely by what is *left out* of the 'translation'), there is a sense in which the *easy parade* of knowledge assumes a transparency which translation does not possess – as if it was not a matter of translation but transparency. As Eric Cheyfitz writes, this is an act of dispossession; 'the activity of colonization as translation, both in the meaning of the word as conversion from one language into another and as use in a metaphorical or transferred sense. In this case, however, the sense of translation is precisely not to understand the other that is the original inhabitants, or to understand that other all too easily, that is, as if there were no question of translation, solely in terms of one's own language, where the other becomes a usable fiction.' Eric Cheyfitz, 'Literally white, figuratively red: the frontier of translation in *The Pioneers*', in *James Fenimore Cooper: New Critical Essays*, edited by Robert Clark (London: Vision Press, 1985), 74.

[52] See Rudyard Kipling, *Plain Tales from the Hills* (London: Macmillan, 1898 (1890)): *Life's Handicap* (London: Macmillan, 1897 (1891)).

[53] Kipling (1898), 26.

[54] 'The first order that appeared when you got a new station usually stated that all Indian villages, Indian shops, Indian bazaars and the civil lines were out of bounds to all troops.' Quoted in Charles Allen (1978). Also see King (1976) and Russell (1860).

[55] Kipling (1898), 27.

[56] Arthur Conan Doyle, *The Complete Illustrated Sherlock Holmes* (Ware, Hampshire: Omega Books, 1986), 17. The tradition of disguise is much in evidence in the detective, police and 'spy' fiction of the same period; Holmes has antecedents in Godwin's *Caleb Williams* and Vidocq's *Memoires*.

[57] Conan Doyle (1986), 79.

[58] Michel Foucault, 'The eye of power', in *Power/Knowledge* (Brighton: Harvester, 1980). Also see *Discipline and Punish* (London: Allen Lane, 1977).

[59] See note 25.

[60] Sigmund Freud, *On Sexuality* (Harmondsworth: Penguin, 1981 (1977)), 352-3.

[61] Robert Stoller, *Sex and Gender*, Vol 2 (London: Hogarth/Institute of Psychoanalysis, 1975).

[62] See, for example, Mary Jacobus, *Reading Woman* (New York: Columbia University Press, 1986), 7-8.

[63] Stoller (1975), 144, 154.

[64] John Buchan, *Greenmantle* (London: Nelson, 1946 (1917)), 32.

[65] Spivak (1986).

[66] Parry (1988), 56.

[67] 'Along with the demolition of the Oedipus complex, the boy's object-cathexis of his mother must be given up. Its place may be filled by one of two things: either an identification with his mother or an intensification of his identification with his father. We are accustomed to regard the latter outcome as the more normal .... In this way the dissolution of the Oedipus complex would consolidate [also define?] the masculinity in a boy's character.' Sigmund Freud, *The Ego and the Id* (London: Hogarth/Institute of Psychoanalysis, 1974), 22.

[68] Sigmund Freud, 'On Narcissism', in *Collected Papers*, Vol IV (London: Hogarth, 1925 (1914)), 32.

[69] Said (1987).

[70] Tagg (1988).

C. CITY SPACE

Chance Encounters

Flâneur and Détraquée
in Breton's Nadja

Victor Burgin

nous sommes tous plus ou moins des psychotiques guéris
(Octave Mannoni, 'La part de jeu')

About two-thirds of the way through his book *Nadja*, Breton describes meeting Nadja in a restaurant. The clumsy behaviour of a waiter prompts her to tell an anecdote about an exchange she had, earlier in the day, with a ticket collector in a Métro station. Clutching a new 10-franc piece in her hand, Nadja asks the man who punches her ticket: 'Heads or tails?' To which the man replies 'Tails' and adds, indicating perhaps a vocation as a psychoanalyst: 'You were wondering, Mademoiselle, if you would be seeing your friend just now'. No one would suppose that Nadja is going down the Métro for nothing, but, as the ticket collector discerned, she is not necessarily aware of what she hopes to find there. There is more to our wanderings in the city than urban planners take account of.

Freud said that when he put on his hat and went into the street he stopped being a psychoanalyst. On at least one occasion he demonstrated that analysts may be no better than the rest of us knowing their own motives while out in the city. He writes:

> As I was walking, one hot summer afternoon, through the deserted streets of a provincial town in Italy which was unknown to me, I found myself in a quarter of whose character I could not remain long in doubt. Nothing but painted women were to be seen at the windows of the small houses, and I hastened to leave the narrow street at the next turning. But after having wandered about for a time without enquiring my way, I suddenly found myself back in the same street, where my presence was

269

now beginning to excite attention. I hurried away once more, only to arrive by another *détour* at the same place yet a third time. Now, however, a feeling overcame me which I can only describe as uncanny, and I was glad enough to find myself back at the piazza I had left a short while before, without any further voyages of discovery.[1]

By his own account Freud's ignorance of his most apparent motives for returning to that street, motives which for him were 'blindingly obvious', was not shared by the street's inhabitants. Freud fails to see what is 'under his nose' because his nose is buried in his *plan*, his conscious goal and the diagram which will lead him there. He has temporarily forgotten what he himself taught us: there is always another side to this map, 'another place' in this topography.

In his book *The Practice of Everyday Life*, in the chapter entitled 'Walking in the city', Michel de Certeau inaugurates a dual mapping of urban space. There is first what he calls the 'Concept city', 'founded by utopian and urbanistic discourse', whose first operation must be: 'The production of its *own* space (*un espace propre*)'. Certeau comments: 'rational organisation must thus repress all the physical, mental and political pollutions that would compromise it'.[2] However: 'Beneath the discourses that ideologise the city, the ruses and combinations of powers that have no readable identity proliferate; without points where one can take hold of them, without rational transparency, they are impossible to administer.' 'No readable identity', writes Certeau, but he nevertheless goes on to inaugurate a reading of walking in the city; moreover, one conducted in terms of linguistics. After a discussion of pedestrian displacements in terms of classical rhetoric, Certeau remarks – agreement with such writers as Benveniste and Lacan – that such tropes characterize a 'symbolic order of the unconscious'. He observes: 'From this point of view, after having compared pedestrian processes to linguistic formations, we can bring them back down in the direction of oneiric figuration'.[3] Certeau goes on to identify

> three distinct (but connected) functions of the relations between spatial and signifying practices ... the *believable*, the *memorable*, and the *primitive*. They designate what 'authorizes' (or makes possible or credible) spatial appropriations, what is repeated in them (or is recalled in them) from a silent and withdrawn memory, and what is structured in them and continues to be signed by an in-fantile (*in-fans*) origin.[4]

270

I understand the word 'believable' here to designate those material-factual conditions which furnish the occasion, pretext, alibi or disguise for what would otherwise be illegitimate, 'merely subjective', constructions of reality. As for the 'memorable', Freud's discussion of the uncanny is only a special case of his more general observation that what appears to come to us from the outside is often the return of that which we ourselves have placed there – something drawn from a repository of suppressed or repressed memories or fantasies. All this is familiar enough. It is the final term in Certeau's trilogy of 'relations between spatial and signifying practices' – the 'primitive', that which is 'signed by an in-fantile (*in-fans*) origin' – which calls for a clarification which Certeau does not provide. Certeau concludes his essay on 'walking in the city' with these words:

> The childhood experience that determines spatial practices later develops its effects, proliferates, floods private and public spaces, undoes their readable surfaces, and creates within the planned city a 'metaphorical' or mobile city, like the one Kandinsky dreamed of: 'a great city built according to all the rules of architecture and then suddenly shaken by a force that defies all calculation'.[5]

He says no more on the subject, but what *are* these 'infantile determinants' of our experiences and practices in and of the city?

Writing of certain instances of the experience of the uncanny, Freud remarks: 'They are a harking-back to particular phases in the evolution of the self-regarding feeling, a regression to a time when the ego had not yet marked itself off sharply from the external world and from other people'.[6] The space of this time, 'primitive' to us all, was later mapped in some detail by Melanie Klein, of whom Lacan has written:

> Through her we know the function of the imaginary primordial enclosure formed by the *imago* of the mother's body; through her we have the cartography, drawn by the children's own hands, of the mother's internal empire, the historical atlas of the intestinal divisions in which the *imagos* of the father and brothers (real or virtual), in which the voracious aggression of the subject himself, dispute their deleterious dominance over her sacred regions.[7]

It is often observed that much as Freud discovered the child in the adult, so Klein found the infant in the child; as is well-known, her 'royal road' to this discovery was the analysis of play. Klein wrote that she approached the play of the child 'in a way similar to Freud's interpretation of dreams'. In her therapeutic technique the child's play takes on the function served by the verbal associations of the adult patient; consistently with Freud she cautions that, 'we have to consider each child's use of symbols ... in relation to the whole situation which is presented in the analysis; mere generalized translations of symbols are meaningless'.[8] Klein's interpretations were not based simply on the child's manipulations of its toys, they concerned the totality of the field of the child's play – the consulting room, and its furniture, within which the child displaced its body just as it deployed its toys. Klein came to view the spatialization of this theatre of play as the exteriorization, 'projection', of an internal world, a world of relations between 'objects'. Much of Klein's work is concerned with the description of internal objects, bound up with the somatic origins of fantasy.[9] We are familiar with such expressions as 'a lump in the throat', or 'butterflies in the stomach'; we are also accustomed to hear that hunger 'gnaws' at the stomach, or fear 'grips' the heart. In these examples from ordinary language, bodily sensations are identified with actual entities, endowed with an agency of their own, either benevolent or malevolent. There may also be times when we feel 'empty inside'. As adults we employ such metaphors without abandoning our knowledge of actual physiology. The infant has no such knowledge. The infant's, primitive understanding of its own bodily feeling is its only reality. What we call 'milk' the infant (what we call 'the' infant) may experience, after feeding, as a benevolent object which emanates bliss. This object is destined to fade. Hunger will take its place – a malevolent agency, bringing destruction of the 'good object', and pain. At this primitive level, the 'object' is the fantasmatic representation of the phenomenological form of the infant's earliest experience. In the Kleinian description, the infant's reality is a battleground of and for such objects.

The subsequent formation of a bounding body-ego, to which the much-discussed 'mirror stage' contributes, does not put an end to the movements of projection, introjection and identification described by Klein; they are rather transposed into different registers and extensively subjected to repression. Upon a world understood in terms of the fantasmatic mother's body there is imposed a world whose salient features are projected from the corporeal envelope of the newly formed subject. Sándor Ferenczi observed:

The derisive remark was once made against psycho-analysis that, according to this doctrine, the unconscious sees a penis in every convex object and a vagina or anus in every concave one. I find that this sentence well characterises the facts. The child's mind (and the tendency of the unconscious in adults that survives from it) is at first concerned exclusively with its own body, and later on chiefly with the satisfying of his instincts, with the pleasurable satisfactions that sucking, eating, contact with the genital regions, and the functions of excretion procure for him; what wonder, then, if also his attention is arrested above all by those objects and processes of the outer world that on the ground of ever so distant a resemblance remind him of his dearest experiences.... Thus arise those intimate connections, which remain throughout life, between the human body and the objective world that we call *symbolic*. On the one hand the child in this stage sees in the world nothing but images of his corporeality, on the other he learns to represent by means of his body the whole multifariousness of the outer world.[10]

For example, when 'Little Hans' saw some water being let out of a railway engine he responded with, 'Oh look, the engine's widdling. Where's it got its widdler?' Freud completes the anecdote: 'After a little while he added in reflective tones: "A dog and a horse have widdlers; a table and a chair haven't." He had thus got hold of an essential characteristic for differentiating between animate and inanimate objects.[11] Such distinctions, founding the real world – the 'normal' – are learned, which is to say they may fail to be learned, or may be learned badly. Prior to such distinctions, spacing, there are only identifications, fusion. Spatial metaphors necessarily accompany the 'object' metaphors which abound in everyday language: for example, we may feel 'one' with someone, be 'on the side' in a dispute, and worry when, even though physically close to us, they appear 'distant'. Paul Schilder has given a schematic description of the continuum between normal and pathological space:

> There is the space as a phylogenetic inheritance which is comparatively stabilized, which is the basis of our actions and orientations. It is the space of the perception ego. We live our personal lives in relation to love objects, in our personal conflicts, and this is the space which is less systematized, in which the relations change, in which the emotions pull objects nearer and push them further away. When the emotional life regresses very far the perception ego-space loses more and more of its

importance. In this regressive space identifications and projections change the space and its value continually. This is the Id space which finds a very far-going expression in schizophrenic experiences. It is the space of magic.[12]

The space of magic: it is supposed that in the infant's early experience it is as if it summons the breast into being; unconscious survivals of this state into adult life may contribute to obsessional neurosis. Freud writes:

I have adopted the term 'omnipotence of thoughts' from a highly intelligent man who suffered from obsessional ideas ... He had coined the phrase as an explanation of all the strange and uncanny events by which he, like others afflicted with the same illness, seemed to be pursued. If he thought of someone, he would be sure to meet that very person immediately afterwards, as though by magic.[13]

Obsessively, a distraught Breton is tormented by thoughts of Nadja. He desperately feels the need to see her, but has no rendezvous with her until the following day. He goes out in a taxi:

Suddenly, while I am paying no attention whatever to the people on the street, some sudden vividness on the left-hand sidewalk, at the corner of Saint-Georges, makes me almost mechanically knock on the window. It is as if Nadja had just passed by. I run, completely at random, in one of the three directions she might have taken. And as a matter of fact it is Nadja.... This is the second consecutive day that I have met her: it is apparent that she is at my mercy.[14]

The normal infantile space of magic recedes ('once upon a time, long ago and far away ...') as the ego forms out of the nucleus of early object relations – a precarious process. In her paper of 1946, 'Notes on some schizoid mechanisms', Klein remarks, 'the early ego largely lacks cohesion, and a tendency towards integration alternates with a tendency towards disintegration, a falling to bits'.[15] The 'cracks in the structure' which may result may lead to subsequent crises of delimitation of ego/object boundaries, to 'psychosis'. Early object identifications are, as Edith Jacobson expresses it:

founded on primitive mechanisms of introjection or projection corresponding to fusions of self and object images which disregard the realistic differences between the self and the object. They will find expression in illusory fantasies of the child that he is part of the object or can become the object by pretending to be or behaving as if he were it. Temporary and reversible in small children, such ideas in psychotics may turn into fixated, delusional convictions.[16]

Laplanche and Pontalis write: 'Fundamentally, psychoanalysis sees the common denominator of the psychoses as lying in a primary disturbance of the libidinal relation to reality; the majority of manifest symptoms, and particularly delusional constructions, are accordingly treated as secondary attempts to restore links with objects.'[17] In psychosis, the internal and external world are poorly differentiated, or not differentiated at all; for example, whereas, in 'normal' life we may encounter a person *A* who 'reminds us of' another person *B*, the schizophrenic patient may simply substitute the latter for the former; or, again, he or she may experience the internal representations of 'fantasy' as actual representations of external reality.[18] We should remember that psychoanalysis systematically insists that there are no fixed boundaries between 'normal' and pathological realities. The precondition of the pathological is in early 'normal' experience; it is in this sense that we may understand Mannoni's remark that, 'we are all more or less healed psychotics'[19] – to which we may add that there is never anything more than this 'more or less'.

To the 'psychoses' belong those forms of mental disturbance which everyday language names 'madness'. Towards the end of *Nadja*, Breton writes: 'I was told, several months ago, that Nadja was mad … she had had to be committed to the Vaucluse sanitarium'.[20] The first published fragment from Breton's *Nadja* appeared in the penultimate issue of *La Révolution Surréaliste*. In this same issue, in an article illustrated with Régnard's photographs of 'Augustine' from the *Iconographie photographique de la Salpêtrière*,[21] Breton and Aragon celebrate 'The Fiftieth Anniversary of Hysteria', which they find to be 'the greatest poetic discovery of the end of the nineteenth century', and, 'in every respect … a supreme means of expression'.[22] The intentionally ironic indifference of these two psychiatrically trained poets to the diagnostic niceties of their former profession is evident. Nevertheless they might more consistently have reserved their approbation for the psychoses rather than the neuroses.[23] According

275

to Lacan, writing in another surrealist journal, *Minotaure*, paranoic deliriums 'need no interpretation whatsoever to express by their themes alone, and marvellously well, these instinctive and social complexes which psychoanalysis has the greatest difficulty in bringing to light in neurotics. It is no less remarkable that the murderous reactions of these patients very frequently emerge at a neuralgic point of the social tensions with which they are historically contemporary.'[24] History was very shortly to provide Lacan with an exemplary case of such violence; his subsequent study of paranoia to appear in *Minotaure* was dedicated to 'The crime of the Papin sisters'. Léa and Christine Papin were domestic servants who for six years, in the words of Paul Eluard and Benjamin Péret, 'endured, with the most perfect submission, commands, demands, insults', until the day they 'literally massacred their employers, tearing out their eyes and crushing their heads'.[25] About the same time that the awed comments of Eluard and Péret appeared in *Le Surréalisme au Service de la Révolution* the surrealists had published a pamphlet in support of the patricide Violette Nozière. Much earlier, the inaugural issue of *La Révolution Surréaliste* had featured a 'mug shot' photograph of the anarchist Germaine Berton surrounded by portrait photographs of all the surrealist group (a guard of honour to which a picture of Freud has, for the occasion, been conscripted). Berton had assassinated the royalist Marius Plateau, editor of the extreme rightwing journal *L'Action Française*. The assembled photographs are accompanied by a fragment from Baudelaire: 'Women is the being who throws the greatest shadow or the greatest light on our dreams.' The dream is of violent revolution. Eluard and Péret had spoken of the Papin sisters' hatred, 'this very sweet alcohol which consoles in secret for it promises, sooner or later, to add physical force to its violence'.[26] These particular women – clinically paranoiac or not – were seen as exemplifying the production of legitimate violence at three key 'neuralgic points' of social tension: in the case of Nozière, the family; in the case of the Papin sisters, the workplace; and in the case of Berton, politics.

Breton's description of his first, pedestrian, encounter with Nadja indicates precisely what he was looking out for:

> Last October fourth, toward the end of one of those idle, gloomy afternoons I know so well how to spend, I happened to be in the Rue Lafayette: after stopping a few minutes at the stall outside the *Humanité* bookstore and buying Trotsky's latest work, I continued aimlessly in

the direction of the Opéra. The offices and workshops were beginning to empty out from top to bottom of the buildings, doors were closing, people on the sidewalk were shaking hands, and already there were more people in the street now. I unconsciously watched their faces, their clothes, their way of walking. No, it was not yet these who would be ready to create the Revolution. I had just crossed an intersection whose name I don't know, in front of a church. Suddenly, perhaps still ten feet away, I saw a young, poorly dressed woman walking toward me.[27]

Nadja, for Breton – for a time – is to be the locus of the transformation of everyday life, as if the social revolution absent from the France of 1928 could be acted out on the stage of sexuality. Breton is out looking for an explosive, Nadja is looking for a container. Breton celebrates the affirmative 'being in the world' of the Nadja who 'enjoyed being nowhere but in the streets, the only region of valid experience for her'.[28] But Nadja seems to have little sense of her own independent existence *without* the streets, and the encounters they offered. Breton writes: 'She uses a new image to make me understand how she lives: it's like the morning when she bathes and her body withdraws while she stares at the surface of the bath water. "I am the thought on the bath in the room without mirrors." '[29] Schilder reports some of the utterances of his patients: 'I am not sure whether this room is one or more'; 'You can't go out of this house, there is no other world'; 'I do not know where I am. I feel that I am in the space between. That frightens me'.[30] It is as if Nadja is in the street to find those scattered objects she cannot contain when alone – an anxious search. Breton writes: 'Here on the right, is a low window that overlooks the moat, and she cannot take her eyes off it. It is in front of this window which looks so forlorn that we must wait, she knows that much. It is from here that everything can come. It is here that everything begins. She holds onto the railing with both hands so that I will not pull her away';[31] or again: 'Nadja cannot endure the sight of a mosaic strip extending from the counter across the floor, and we must leave the bar only a moment after we have come in.'[32] Lacan observes, 'the perceptual field [of the paranoid subject] is imprinted with an immanent and imminent "personal signification".'[33] Breton muses: 'Perhaps life needs to be deciphered like a cryptogram.' Aragon, in his own book about the city streets, *Le Paysan de Paris*, writes:

Where the most ambiguous activities of the living are pursued, the inanimate may sometimes catch a reflection of their most secret motives: our cities are thus peopled with unrecognised sphinxes, which will not stop the musing passer-by and ask him mortal questions. But if in his wisdom he can guess them, then let him question them, and it will still be his own depths which, thanks to these faceless monsters, he will once again plumb.[34]

What is most familiar in that to which Aragon alludes is discussed by Freud in such papers as 'The uncanny', or his paper on *'fausse reconnaissance'*. Fundamentally, 'What is involved is an actual repression of some content of thought and a return to this repressed content',[35] which may additionally involve 'the identity being displaced from the really common element on to the locality'.[36] Breton misrecognizes Nadja's illness because it is centred perfectly upon that which surrealism was in the process of celebrating – the encounter with the enigmatic in the everyday. However, the accompanying affect in Nadja's encounter with the enigmatic is qualitatively and quantitatively different from that in the encounter with the 'uncanny' (which the French equivalent of 'uncanny' spells out as *'l'inquiétante étrangeté'*). Nadja's experience is of a world in which the two terms of Breton's simile are collapsed into an identity – for her, life *is* a cryptogram. It is precisely in *this* that her relation to the streets is 'infantile'.

Jean Laplanche has identified the early and inescapable encounter of the subject with 'primal seduction', the term he gives to 'that fundamental situation where the adult presents the infant with signifiers, non-verbal as well as verbal, and even behavioural, impregnated with unconscious sexual significations.'[37] It is these that Laplanche calls 'enigmatic signifiers': the child senses that such signifiers are addressed to it, and yet has no means of understanding their meaning; its attempts at mastery of the enigma, at symbolization, provoke anxiety and leave unconscious residues. Such estrangement in the libidinal relation with the object is an inescapable condition of entry into the adult world, and we may expect to find its trace in any subsequent relation with the object, even the most 'normal'. About a quarter of the way into *Nadja* Breton devotes some ten pages, and four photographs, to a description of his desultory visits to the theatre: to the Théâtre Moderne, with its bar like 'a living room at the bottom of a lake'; and to the Théâtre des Deux Masques, where he witnesses a 'Grand Guignol' drama, *Les Détraquées*, 'which remains ... the only dramatic work that I choose to recall'. The plot of *Les Détraquées*, in Breton's four-page summary, seems to turn on the encounter of a child with perverse (here, female) adult sexuality. I say 'seems to concern' as we are made to share Breton's own uncertainty: 'The lack of adequate indications as to what happens after the balloon falls and the ambiguity about precisely what Solange and her partner are a prey to ... is still what puzzles me *par excellence*.'[38] Breton immediately follows his account of *Les Détraquées* with a partial description of a dream which 'includes a reference to certain episodes of *Les Détraquées*', and which Breton found 'remarkable' in that it 'emphasized only the painful, repugnant, not to say cruel aspect of the considerations I had embarked upon' (included in the dream is an insect-like creature which attempts to choke Breton, who experiences 'an inexpressible disgust'). It is also within the space of these pages about his visits to the theatre that Breton confesses: 'I have always, beyond belief, hoped to meet, at night and in a wood, a beautiful naked woman or rather, since such a wish once expressed means nothing, I regret, beyond belief, not having met her.' He then recalls the occasion when, 'in the side aisles of the "Electric Palace", a naked woman ... strolled, dead white, from row to row' – an occurrence he admits was unextraordinary, 'since this section of the "Electric" was the most commonplace sort of illicit sexual rendez-vous'.[39] I suspect that these scenes refigure, transcribe, symbolize each other, contain each other – just as the Théâtre Moderne is contained as a scene within the theatrical space of *Nadja*, which is a maze of façades. For *Nadja*, Breton commissioned photographers to take pictures of that which he might otherwise have felt obliged to describe. Images of places and things, including the drawings which Nadja made for Breton, are deployed throughout the book like so many decorated curtains, rising and falling between scenes with the turn of a page – or like so many theatrical 'flats'. We may recall that one of the origins of perspective is in the art of scenography. Breton's city is a stage for the encounter with the marvellous in the everyday. Breton is actor-director and general manager. Brilliant illusions are conjured on this stage, but they are imposed on a space whose co-ordinates are fundamentally Cartesian, whose geometries are Euclidean. In this, Breton's space is different from that of Nadja's, and there is a sense in which, throughout the book, they are never in the same place, and never meet.

Accompanying the celebration of the 'anniversary of hysteria', and the fragment of *Nadja*, in the penultimate issue of *La Révolution*

Surréaliste is the transcript of an extended discussion (amongst the surrealists themselves) of sexuality. Intervening in the exchange, in response to his own question 'Does love necessarily have to be reciprocal?', Breton states: 'It is necessarily reciprocal. For a long time I thought the contrary, but I have recently changed my mind.' Breton was elsewhere to voice his regret that he had not been able to love Nadja as she had loved him, which is to say that he was not fully able to participate in a world which the surrealists had so far eulogized only from a safe distance – that of the *détraquée*. Towards the close of the book Breton reflects that Nadja was 'born to serve human emancipation ... in its simplest revolutionary form', which includes 'thrusting one's head, then an arm, out of the jail – thus shattered – of logic, that is, out of the most hateful of prisons'. He concedes that this is 'dangerous', adding: 'It is from this last enterprise, perhaps, that I should have restrained her'.[40] Breton did however exercise *self*-restraint, placing his own boundaries on *l'amour fou* and hence, implicitly, on surrealist revolution.[41] To speak more accurately, Nadja *introduced* Breton to his own limits and limitations. Breton reports that while speeding back from Versailles by car, at night, Nadja had 'pressed her foot down on mine on the accelerator, tried to cover my eyes with her hands in the oblivion of an interminable kiss, desiring to extinguish us, doubtless forever, save to each other, so that we should collide at full speed with the splendid trees along the road. What a test of life indeed! Unnecessary to add that I did not yield to this desire.'[42] Speaking of the Papin sisters, Lacan remarks: 'One has heard in the course of the debates the astonishing affirmation that it was impossible that two beings should both be struck, together, by the same madness.... This is a completely false affirmation. Joint deliriums (les *délires à deux*) are amongst the most ancient of known forms of psychosis.'[43] Breton regrets, 'Whatever desire or even illusion I may have had to the contrary, perhaps I have not been adequate to what she offered me'. But what was offered was that dark side of the drive whose only objects are fragments, and whose aims are destructive.

Laplanche observes that pride of place amongst the 'enigmatic signifiers' is reserved for what Freud called the 'primal scene', where (the scene now dramatically lit by Klein): 'the parents are united in an eternal coitus which combines *jouissance* with death, excluding the baby from all capacity to participate, and therefore to symbolize'.[44] Breton returns from his walk only to pose the question of the city again in its most unanswerable terms:

280

It is not for me to ponder what is happening to the 'shape of a city', even of the true city distracted and abstracted from the one I live in by the force of an element which is to my mind what air is supposed to be to life. Without regret, at this moment I see it change and even disappear. It slides, it burns, it sinks into the shudder of weeds alongs its barricades, into the dream of curtains in its bedrooms, where a man and woman indifferently continue making love.[45]

NOTES

[1] Sigmund Freud, 'The "uncanny" ', *The Standard Edition of the Complete Psychological Works of Sigmund Freud* (SE) (London: 1951), vol 17, 237.
[2] Michel de Certeau, *The Practice of Everyday Life*, (Berkeley, Calif.: 1988), 94. The term *'propre'*, to which the translator alerts us here, means not only 'own' but 'clean', and 'that which is proper'. The term 'pollution' which closely follows confirms that Certeau may be alluding to Julia Kristeva's *Pouvoirs de l'horreur: Essai sur l'abjection* (trans. *Powers of Horror; An essay on abjection*, New York: 1982) and/or to the book which so substantially contributes to Kristeva's argument, Mary Douglas's *Purity and Danger* (London: 1966). For a discussion of 'abjection' in relation to space and vision, see my 'Geometry and abjection', *AA Files*, 15 (summer 1987), and in J. Donald (ed.), *Thresholds: Psychoanalysis and Culture* (London: 1990).
[3] de Certeau, *Practice of Everyday Life*, 103.
[4] *Ibid*, 105.
[5] *Ibid*, 110.
[6] Freud, SE 17, 236.
[7] Jacques Lacan, 'Aggressivity in psychoanalysis', in *Ecrits: A selection* (New York: 1977), 20-1.
[8] Melanie Klein, 'Notes on some schizoid mechanisms', in Juliet Mitchell (ed), *The Selected Melanie Klein*, 51.
[9] See Jean Laplanche and Jean-Bertrand Pontalis, 'Fantasy and the origins of sexuality', in Victor Burgin, James Donald and Cora Kaplan (eds), *Formations of Fantasy* (London: 1986).
[10] Sándor Ferenczi, 'Stages in the development of the sense of reality' (1913), in *First Contributions to Psycho-Analysis* (Brunner/Mazel: 1980), 227-8.
[11] Sigmund Freud, 'Analysis of a phobia in a five-year-old boy' (1909), SE 10, 9.
[12] Paul Schilder, 'Psycho-analysis of space', *International Journal of Psycho-Analysis*, 16 (1935), 278.
[13] Sigmund Freud, *Totem and Taboo*, SE 13, 85-6; the man to whom Freud refers is the 'Rat Man' (see SE 10, 233ff).
[14] André Breton, *Nadja* (London: 1960), 91.
[15] Klein, 'Notes on some schizoid mechanisms', 179.
[16] Edith Jacobson, *The Self and the Object World* (International Universities Press: 1964), 47.
[17] J. Laplanche and J.-B. Pontalis, *The Language of Psycho-Analysis* (London: 1973), 370.

[18] See Harold F. Searles, 'The sources of the anxiety in paranoid schizophrenia' (1961), in *Collected Papers on Schizophrenia and Related Subjects* (New York: 1965).

[19] Octave Mannoni, 'La part du jeu', *L'Arc*, 69 (special issue on D. W. Winnicott).

[20] Breton, *Nadja*, 136.

[21] See Georges Didi-Huberman, *Invention de L'Hystérie: Charcot et l'iconographie photographique de la salpetriere* (Macula: 1982).

[22] *La Révolution Surréaliste*, 11 (15 March 1928), 22.

[23] Laplanche and Pontalis point out that Freud, at an early stage in his work, did entertain the idea of a hysterical *psychosis*. See Laplanche and Pontalis, *Language of Psycho-analysis*, 105.

[24] Jacques Lacan, 'Le problem du style et la conception psychiatrique des formes paranoïques de l'expérience', *Minotaure*, 1 (June 1933), 69.,

[25] *Le Surréalisme au Service de la Révolution*, 5 (1933), 28.

[26] *Ibid.*

[27] Breton, *Nadja*, 63-4.

[28] *Ibid*, 113.

[29] *Ibid*, 101.

[30] Schilder, 'Psycho-analysis of space', 292. Harold Searles speaks of 'the draining off into the outer world, through projection, of much affect and ideation which belong to [the schizophrenic's] self' ('Sources of the anxiety in paranoid schizophrenia', 467).

[31] Breton, *Nadja*, 85.

[32] *Ibid*, 89.

[33] Lacan, 'Le problem du style', 69.

[34] Louis Aragon, *Le Paysan de Paris* (Paris: 1978); quoted in Peter Collier, 'Surrealist city narrative: Breton and Aragon', in E. Timms and D. Kelley, *Unreal City* (Manchester: 1985), 221.

[35] Freud, 'The "uncanny" ', 249.

[36] Sigmund Freud, 'Fausse reconnaissance (déja raconté) in psycho-analytic treatment', SE 13, 204.

[37] Jean Laplanche, *Nouveaux fondements pour la psychanalyse* (Paris: 1987), 125. Trans. *New Foundations for Psychoanalysis* (Oxford: 1989), 126 (my translation differs).

[38] Breton, *Nadja*, 50.

[39] *Ibid*, 39.

[40] *Ibid*, 143.

[41] Laclau and Mouffe have imported Lacan's notion of *points de capiton*, 'buttoning down' the otherwise endless sliding of meaning in discourse, into a discussion of the social order. They remark that 'a discourse incapable of generating any fixity of meaning is the discourse of the psychotic'; by implication, a society that would be totally 'free' would be a psychotic society. (See Ernesto Laclau and Chantal Mouffe, *Hegemony and Socialist Strategy* (London: 1985), 113.) Lacan similarly admits the necessity of the law as 'anchorage' in his article on the Papin sisters, where he remarks, 'the adage "to understand is to forgive" is subordinate to the limits of each human community ... beyond these limits, to understand (or to believe that one understands) is to condemn'

(Jacques Lacan, 'Motifs du crime paranoïaque (le crime des soeurs Papin)',
Minotaure, 3 (15 December 1933), 27.)
[42] Breton, *Nadja*, 152 n.
[43] Lacan, 'Motifs du crime paranoïaque', 27.
[44] Laplanche, *Nouveaux fondements*, 126 (trans., 127).
[45] Breton, *Nadja*, 154.

The City and the Imaginary
Translated by John Koumantarakis

Donatella Mazzoleni

Why 'the city and the imaginary'? Why these two words together? Why ask about the meaning and non-meaning of architecture and the city? Why approach a subject which touches not only on levels of cultural consciousness but also on those of the collective unconscious? Why not, instead, concentrate on those aspects of architecture and town planning which have always been considered an integral part of this discipline, and have always been so urgently invoked: Function (*utilitas*), Form (*venustas*) and static Solidity (*firmitas*)?

May we be forgiven, in proposing this topos of encounter, for not sharing the same opinion as Vitruvius? The habitat (city, metropolis, post-metropolis) does not seem to be representable merely as a physical phenomenon, a material extension of constructed things.

Buildings, streets, squares are just part of the habitat; the tip of an iceberg: the visible and tangible part. Behind and within this tangibility and visibility, there is something else which is difficult to represent with concepts and words because it belongs to a pre-logical field of experience, to non-verbal communication; it has more to do with what Minkowski calls the spaciousness of existence. The question of habitat thus becomes the question of the concretization of the great oneiric structures of our collective body (the communal body, if it has a monocentric structure, or the social body, if it has a polycentric structure). It is constituted in each case by the mass of our bodies living in space. We must note, at this point, a different urgency (diverse, oriented in a different way but also deeply rooted in the here and now, which regards the continual emergency situations which fill our lives and affect our work as architects): the urgency of confronting collective living right where its most radical possibility of crisis exists: that is, in its imaginative roots. The destruction which comes from outside (even from earthquakes) seems to us less serious than the destruction which comes from within if we cannot learn to live in our post-metropolitan condition, to live beyond the uprooting of the affinity between the I and the world by positing a possibility of a new imaginary.

Work on 'the city and the imaginary' cannot take place within the traditional limits of the disciplines. We must compare differing disciplinary perspectives. But we must also move on interdisciplinary levels and be open to the re-examination of the disciplines themselves. Thus, in considering architecture and urban studies we must propose that the culture of the habitat be deconstructed, dehistoricized, and returned to a primary experience by means of an epistemological inquiry which questions its foundations and shows its deeply psychic roots.

Structuralism and historicism have been even in recent years powerful means for dramatizing the criteria that have ordered those ideas which have been obstinately (one could say heroically) employed to interpret a physical reality which has become ever more distant and heterogeneous. They are, in fact, more limited to the culture of the city than to the ultra-urban culture found in the contemporary habitat – where the phenomena of metropolis, post-metropolis and hyper-metropolis have emerged.

Structuralism has allowed us to reorder the materials of the culture of space on the axis of synchronicity, in the 'present'. It has allowed us to recognize in the discontinuous body of the urban habitat cells, textures, organs, organic systems, and systems of systems (the importance of working with such biological and body metaphors will be seen below). It has enabled us to describe and represent urban phenomena as elements and relationships, and totalities with different levels of complexity (and we will also see below the importance of using such mirrors of reason).

The architecture of habitat has become, in the structuralist imaginary, 'language': signs, parataxis and syntax, codes and keys to interpretation, invariables (typologies), and variables (morphologies). That aspect of architecture (which is a means of self-expression through the body) is thus represented in an ordered way and put into words (which is a means of self-expression through a part of the body, the tongue).

Historicism, on the other hand, has allowed us to reorder the same materials on the axis of diachrony: as 'through time', 'past', 'present', 'future'. The phenomena of constructing and living have been linked in a linear imaginary of time (from before us to after us). From it has been 'reconstructed' (from behind) the sum total of the precedents and (forwards) also the follow-up (history as 'active and selective memory of the past, consciousness of the present and projection of the future' in Argan's words).

The architecture of habitat has become, in the historicist imaginary, story, in the 'strong', 'binding' sense: story that recognizes within itself processes and laws of transformation, connections of cause and effect, and genealogies. In the weak sense, story contains lists of rules on which it is possible to make free choices, equal among themselves, or which dissolve the 'objects' into their interpretations, declaring itself *Unendliche Analyse*, admitting that the ordering power of the narrator is nothing but his legitimate delirium.

But the lived experience of non-verbal, pre-logical space is only partly translatable into language or narratable in story. In it we find the spatialization of primary pulsations – Eros and Thanatos – that cannot be contained by the web of any structure or story. The articulation of these pulsations is always twofold: there is a need to return to a space which is a container of life, which can metabolize death itself (living) – then there is the need to symbolize, to deflect outwards the death instinct (constructing). We could perhaps say that constructing, in so far as it is a symbolizing activity, arises from the dwelling of the instincts because of that 'primary paranoia' which attempts to redeem the overwhelming relationship with one's own overshadowing mother figure. The uncontainable quality of these elementary pulsations (both in their aspects of sorrow and exaltation) emerges violently in our contemporary consciousness in post-industrial cultures because the habitat here has clearly lost its ancient organic characteristics, its similarity to the body (as in the ancient cities) and has come to be seen, as we shall see below, in profoundly different modalities. The modality of continuity between body and space has been replaced by the modality of 'difference'. Structuralism and historicism are still offered today as instruments for an analysis of the problem in 'reasonable' terms, but are instruments which, perhaps, are more adapted for the removal rather than the interpretation of the tragic intimacy of this difference.[1]

If, by habitat, we mean the concretization of the great oneiric structures of our collective body, semiology is not sufficient for our interpretation. What is needed is a 'geotica' and an 'anthropanalysis' of the psychic structures deeply rooted in our cultures: thus, an architypology of the imaginary. Above all, it is necessary to return to lived experience, to an awareness of questions of space and its origins: that is, in our bodies. We must abandon, then, the thread of discourse, and – if we are brave enough – work by free association.

We have spoken of the need to return to lived experience; the question of habitat brings us back to the issue of the body. But at this interpretative level (which is much deeper than the 'superficial' points of Vitruvius, three levels constituted by function-form-technique) the objective is lost. We find ourselves trying to speak about something which is both much less, and much more, than verbal: the body. A difficult paradox: language stops at the 'mystery' of the body.

Like certain primitive notions which seem to belong to all codes (for example, the notion of 'mana'), the body, as opposed to language, is a fluctuating signifier, a zone of semantic disorder, something which situated itself 'beneath' language; the supporter (of exchanges of codes) and therefore the transmitter of signs in this signifying function and in symbolism; the crucible of the mutations of energy, in trances, in shamanism and in certain psychoanalytic relationships. In a word: infralanguage.[2]

It is the body which makes metaphor possible, and which is at the centre of symbolic thought. We can see this clearly in so-called 'primitive' cultures. Reviewing Leenhardt's studies of the way Melanesians 'live' their bodies by identifying themselves with trees,[3] José Gil goes on to describe the transmitting function of the body: 'When a Melanesian says, "Look at these arms, they are water", to show that his child's arms are like the buds of a tree, "At first watery, then in time wooden and hard", he uses a metaphor in which the signifiers are interchangeable and the signified, though remaining the same, moves on so that a new meaning can arise.'

According to structural linguistics there is a semiotic intersection here. Yet the very possibility of substituting one signifier for another is contingent upon there being an operator capable of making a substitution that is simultaneously a superimposition and a differentiation between the two terms of exchange. The arms do not identify themselves with the buds to the point of becoming one with them. Difference is preserved by means of the body and the perceptions of the body: the Melanesian sees arms, yet *says* that they are water. The body maintains a space between the codes even while allowing the exchange, thus permitting a semiotic encounter.

Thus, in a shamanistic sermon, the shaman gives the sick person a language in which he can immediately express certain non-formulated states which otherwise would be inexpressible.

> Disease – exactly like any other event which provokes the eruption of casual or unforeseen significations brimming with danger or chance – gives rise to many signifiers without objects, too many signs ('symptoms', we might say in psychoanalytic language) to which it is impossible to attribute things. The shamanistic session offers a point of application to those signs.

In shamanism and exorcism this point of application is a 'god', a 'spirit', a 'monster', a 'devil': in psychoanalysis it is a displaced ghost. The transition to symbolization stimulates the unblocking of the physiological process of the disease: the disappearance of the symptom. This transition is able to take place precisely because this symbolic language is lived, by the patient, *in the body*.[4]

We wanted to return the problems of habitat to the body, and we realize that the body is in some way indescribable, something that *sustains the signified* of language, but which in itself is not expressible in language. Let us turn again to architecture, but this time with the awareness that architecture is nothing if not: (1) *an extention of the body*, a modality that the body expresses to try to satisfy the need for totality; (2) *a metaphor of the body*, a modality that the body expresses to symbolize itself. A replica – and a double.

In this way we come to understand architecture in a very broad sense, not as an array of more or less monumental works, made by technicians, artists, or 'masters' etc., and above all not as a complex of finished objects (the products of the art of construction, but rather as an array of continuously open processes, in which construction is simply a phase in a complicated life which continues without limits infinitely to manipulate the habitat.

We understand architecture as the totality of the integuments and exoskeletons of our individual and collective body; this totality includes those vast groups of objects which are known in everyday language as clothes, furniture and architecture in the more restricted meaning of the word.

The awareness that this very broad sense of architecture, implying as it does the recognition of its profound link with the body, is present in very few of the 'historic' exponents of this discipline, should induce all architects to serious reflection in the dramatic preconceptions that hegemonic cultures continue to build upon, through a specific type of historiography, criticism and teaching.

There are few but significant examples. In 1923 the 'master', Ludwig Mies van der Rohe, drily formulated the theory which was to become the supporting principle of rational-functionalism, in words which carry a deep contempt for the possibilities of body expansion: 'structures in concrete are, in essence, skeletal structures'. 'Thus, buildings, skin and bones'.[5] In opposition to this, his contemporary Hermann Finsterlin – who remains today a visionary – called passionately for an architecture lived as an extension of the body: 'Do not content yourself with the outline and the surface, you who are aware of the corporeal.... Forget your existence, construct huge vessels worthy of the gods, and when in an hour of repose your soul sheds its leaves and hardens, then you can consecrate this monument to the permanent matrix of your body or to your peers. Human space is no longer an impression of hollowness in elementary and stereometric bodies, but a system of giant kettles of the soul ... the unmoving substitutes for those ancient pieces of furniture which are physically alien to us.' And further: 'The covering of the most divine animal with a fabulous body profile, which, being of a soft nature, disappeared as the material wore out, would live again and leave behind as an inheritance only the intimate image, perfectly consolidated, as testimony.[6]

Here architecture begins by rituals of appropriation, manipulation, transformation of the first space perceived as 'external' space; that is, external to the body: the surface of the skin. I refer here to the various forms of cosmetics and to tattoos. It is not by accident that Adolf Loos, 'master' of that proto-rationalism which is behind the reductive and geometric styling to which we referred earlier in Mies' work, in scandalously associating 'ornament' with 'crime', felt the need to express his contempt for tattoos, for decorations of the body, and for every type of artistic dabbling – that is, for every action that reveals (as he himself says) the 'erotic origin' of art – affirming that these despised things are suitable only for children and savages, and indignantly comparing them with the soiling of toilets.[7]

It seems to me extremely important for anyone who wants to make architecture a complex and not a reductive experience to recognize the chromatic and plastic treatment of skin as an act of creativity and spatial communication. We are in fact in space, in the proxemic space of zero radius: the sphere that is the limit which both guarantees separation and continuity between the inside and the outside of the body; that is to day, the topology of the body. Skin is simultaneously the limit of space (*Raumgrenze*) of the body experienced as an internal cavity (a breathing cavity, a digestive cavity, a pregnancy cavity) and the limit of the mass (*Massengrenze*) of the body experienced as a dense and full entity situated in the void of the environment.[8]

Immediately following on from this, in the closer proxemic spheres, spatial communication makes use of the construction of artificial skins of the body: what we call clothing. Clothes are not simply a covering or a disguise, they are also a profound investment of the body; they can modify not only its surface aspect but sometimes even bone structure and the layout of internal organs. Think of the dystrophy of the bust and the pelvis in female bodies caused by corsets in the eighteenth century, or of the anamorphosis of the feet (also female) produced by the Chinese binding system, or of contemporary pointed high-heeled shoes.[9] Here we begin to see how certain clothes and shoes are the reinforcing support which, even in the body's absence, repeats and amplifies the message of the body.

Distancing ourselves further: in the proxemic sphere of hand movements we find that the making and design of equipment multiplies and amplifies non-verbal communication. Open accessories duplicate and empower the openness of the hands: the gesture of gathering; cutting tools, our nails: the gesture of dividing; the equivalent for reading and writing, the joints of our fingers: the gesture of bringing together. In the proxemic spheres of body movements we have larger tools: those of rest and love (the bed), those of nutrition (the kitchen), those of living together (the table with chairs around it).

Finally, we have actual architecture itself: which is to say essentially the house, since the various buildings of our modern cities, differentiated according to their function (factory, school, hospital, market and so on) are in effect no more than separated and greatly enlarged organs of a primordial house. At this level of existential space, architectural space concretizes the body in its totality. It then becomes, to all intents and purposes, its Replica, the Double of the body which can substitute for the body, in the sense that it can function as infra-language at times when the body cannot assume its trans-semiotic role. I am thinking here of the body's 'catastrophes', in the sense of the term as used by Thom:[10] those moments in which a balance of factors cancels itself out: birth (catastrophe of the symbiotic body, the pregnant woman/foetus couple, that takes form as two new individualities; intercourse (catastrophe of the sexualized body, in the moment when male and female take on non-dual form); death (the catastrophe of the individual's return to the state of being indistinct). At these moments of topological discontinuity of the body, which imply an instant of disappearance or nothingness, the house surrogates for the body by ensuring the material continuity of support, in a symbolic exchange. The primordial house (in Joseph Rykwert's words, 'Adam's house in paradise')[11] has the specific function of containing – physically and symbolically – these catastrophes. There is only one body transformation comparable in intensity and total regeneration to those mentioned above, and it takes place outside the house: the fourth catastrophe of the body, initiation. This, though it always happens in space (for example, the forest in some primitive societies, or the metropolis in some advanced industrial societies) which is defined as 'elsewhere', begins and ends within the walls of a house. Here it becomes clear how the walls of a house carry out the same function as *Raumgrenze/Massengrenze* (limits of space/limits of mass) that we experience in the skins of our own bodies.

'Adam's house in paradise', the primitive house, can (at least in its mythological function) fulfil this function as container of the body, precisely because in a sense it imitates the body and its catastrophes, becoming, as we have said, its double. Among the underground foundations of the house there is the basement, storeroom of memory, of the dead, and of food. In the ancient hut, and in the church, the dead were buried in the crypt. In the palace of Knossos, oil and grain were stored in the underground cellar. It is 'the identity of memory and storeroom, of the dead whose resurrection is hoped for, of grain whose rebirth is a necessity, that is one of the most ancient reasons for human religious belief'.[12]

In the opposite direction, though on the same vertical axis, the house's windows mime the opening of the eyes to light, and the structural area of the roof mimes the achievement of an erect posture, the domination of the world through sight and the exercise of constructive rationality.

Between the basement and the roof, liveable space offers a mimesis of intercourse. It is well known that certain people, such as the Dogon, see the house not only as the scene, but also as the representation of this act: the base of the house is the supine woman, the roof structure is the man's chest, the four pillars which usually support it are his legs and arms. The same image is present, though turned upside-down sexually, in the embrace between Nut, sky goddess, and Geb, earth god, in ancient Egyptian mythology: 'The goddess was on top of him, supporting herself on her hands and feet, while the god held up her chest, and her starry body extended over him like a canopy. At night the sun would pass through him, entering his mouth and being born the next morning through his genitals.'[13]

Beyond the proxemic sphere defined by the house, architecture reaches its maximum extent in the city. The city (that is to say, the organism of collective life produced by the pre-industrial culture of the habitat) is still a *part*, the extroverted part, the *outside*, of the body. Urban construction is a solidification of space experienced in wideranging social relationships: relationships activated concretely by the body, because the dynamics of urban exchanges operate completely on the scale of the movements of individual bodies in locomotion. One walks around the city in a time-span measured in units of hours or days: units of daily lived time. The city is used and touched entirely by those who live in it in their various phases of being.

But the city is also the body's Double. Like the house, it is also, in some way, a lived space, anthropomorphic. We can speak of a city as long as the totality of those who produce and live a collective construction constitute a collective anthropoid body, which maintains in some way an identity as a 'subject'. The city is therefore a site of an *identification*. The image of the city can be grasped in its totality as a 'figure' in a differential relationship with a 'surrounding'. (Up until the Industrial Revolution, the relationship between 'city' and 'country' was clear, as was its belonging to and situating itself within a 'countryside'.) Thus the city has a somatic individuality and a membrane, which may be palpable (in the case for example of city walls), or impalpable, and which both surrounds and *limits* its somatic individuality. It guarantees, therefore, the city's concentration of energy, its topological separateness, and, at the same time, the osmotic exchange between internal and external. On the other hand, precisely because it is limited by its membrane, and thus relatively *closed*, the body of the city lives and grows in an *organized* way: within it an order and a mutual structural dependence between the parts is created, in both a functional and a symbolic sense. The body of the city is at once deeply penetrable (you can touch its 'heart') and, equally, easy to leave.

293

Finally, the city has a face, recognizable in its physiognomy, and inimitable. Its topological identification is thus specified within a formal and a dimensional limit. The city takes shape as a body which is much bigger than that of the individual living person, yet similar in its metabolic functions (of production, of assimilation, of self-control), in its organization, and also, more or less covertly, in its form – with which latter it is possible to establish a two-way relationship, of mutual belonging and of mutual independence.

The city, finally, is the largest of the body's possible Doubles. The city is the container that supports, surrounds and metabolizes the catastrophe of family and small social groups, ensuring the continuity of symbolic exchanges at the level of collective life. 'My city' is a phrase than can refer to emotions as deep as those concerning 'my home', and can in fact be a substitute, in a metonymic sense, for the latter. But we are now in a limited dimension. The internal dynamics of the city take place on the scale of the movement by natural locomotion of individual bodies. But, from this point on, the proxemic spheres of spatial communication become abstract.

In a lifetime one can make very few 'journeys' accomplished by body movements of natural locomotion. Even by empowering the body through the use of a prosthesis, whether it be animal (horses, camels, elephants, llamas), or mechanical (automobiles, trains, ships, planes), the amount of travelling one can actually do in a lifetime is always far less than the number of imagined trips through which we can claim to know how our world is made. At territorial, geographical, planetary and astronomical levels, the appropriation of space is above all a cognitive action (in the sense defined by Piaget: virtually a mode of action that takes place in mental space, which reproduces in our minds a real route without our needing to take it). But here, at the level of enormous space, cosmological space reflects its analogy with and response to the body, to the furthest limit of imaginable size around us. The centrality of the individual is reflected, in structural similarity, in the centrality of images of the world.

The most ancient cosmologies of our western world – which are really cosmogonies, and virtually theogonies – could they not be understood in practice as projected representations of the origin of the self? Birth: the earth of Hesiod 'gives birth' to mountains; the earth of Euripides originates in a 'separation' from the sky, from the catastrophe of an original non-duality. Breath: Anassimanes explains that the function of air in the world is similar to man's breathing.

294

Individuation: it is no coincidence that, although geocentric images (Ptolemy) were initially present in Greek thought alongside heliocentric (Aristarchus), acentric (the 'innumerable worlds' of Democritus), and the central invisible fire of Pythagoric Philolaus, in the long run it was the geocentric figurations which prevailed, with all their ambiguous symbolism of omnipotents/impotence (one thinks of *Somnium Scipionis* ...). Just as it is no coincidence that the spheric image of the earth, present throughout antiquity and the Middle Ages, was so forcibly denied by Catholic authoritarianism, so also the denial of the existence of the Antipodes (man upside down, the alarming Double of Adam's descendant, erect man), if nothing else, appears as a violently 'superegoistic' art.

Finally the limited parallel between the cosmological and the astrological cannot be coincidental: that is, the continual attempt 'scientifically' to gather not only the resemblance, but also the continuosly active *link* between body and world. (This calls to mind the astrological relations between the seven planets, the seven metals, the seven bodily orifices ...). 'Spheric' or 'natural' astrology – what we currently regard as astrology *tout court* – was, for many centuries, merely an instrument of 'judicial' astrology – the interpretation of life through the recognition of that Double of the body that is the starry sky. Cosmological thought died not only with Copernicus, Tycho Brahe, Kepler, Galileo and Newton. It also died with Linnaeus, who in the first half of the eighteenth century *classified* man as one being among many – and with Darwin's 'epistemological error'.[14]

We see, then, not only that the body-architecture relationship is both metaphoric and metonymic, but that the same is equally true of the body-world relationship.

So far, we have spoken of the classical culture of space and the classical-bourgeois cycle of architecture. It seems interesting here to point out that classical culture reveals its deep ambivalence in producing, alongside and in opposition to the image of the *cosmological* body (which generates, as we have seen, its own possibility of producing architecture), the *other* image, that of the *grotesque body*. Think of the imaginary of Rabelais: the exclusive materialization of Gargantua and Pantagruel's bodies, created with hyperbolic and grotesque realism:

> The orifices open unnaturally wide, protrusions swell, and the entire body is bent, contorted, disfigured with joy under the assault of stormy,

organic life. The waves of food, drink, sperm, excrement and urine meet and mix inside the carnivalesque receptacle that the body has become, and then it explodes, scattering its contents to the end of the Universe.[15]

The grotesque body, because it is without shame, is a body which is open in all directions. It chooses incessantly to enjoy its own performance, and, confronted with the excessive, miraculous – stupid and stupendous – fertility of its organs, and of the magical transformations of everything that goes through it, it quakes with irrepressible laughter. It is a body without measure, a body without limits in all senses of the word, even spatially.

Here the corporeal and the cosmic emerge as confused together, indissolubly linked to the point of being coincidental; there is no passage between them, nor any possibility that they may mirror each other. The immeasurable empowerment enables the grotesque body to avoid (as it cannot contain, and so cannot metabolize) every type of catastrophe – death, perhaps, above all – no longer by producing a substitute for itself (the Double), but through gigantic organic manifestations occupying *the whole of* space. Within the 'culture of cities', the grotesque body appears somehow as the opposite of architecture; that is, essentially (as we have seen) something born out of the representation of the communicative relationship between an inside and an outside, in the body and beyond the body, and as a production of Doubles of and separate from the body.

We could therefore say that at the extreme opposite end of architecture (which remains, as before 'cosmo', both container and *composer* of chaos), in the field of spatial communication, there are acts in which the body disintegrates and expands chaotically, vortex-like in space: these acts are those of dance and laughter.

In this possibility of symmetrical opposition between cosmic and grotesque, one sees how, in 'the culture of cities', the Apollonian and Dionysiac are poles of a dialectic, of a game which is therefore *dramatic*, and which can be re-composed at a superior level, while the culture of metropolises seems instead to be asymmetric, non-dialectic, *tragic*.

If the city is macro-anthropic, the metropolis is a beast.[16] The technological instruments available today are much more than extensions of the hand, the arms, the legs, the body: they have become extensions and infinite multiplications of the mind. This boundless and immeasurable projection has modified the ecology and the topology of the mind.

Like the computer, the metropolitan habitat is now experienced as something which is not only *outside* our body, but also *beyond* the body, and therefore *other* than the body: it seems to have assumed an alien subjectivity, to have become something with which one has a dialogue, as one would with a stranger.

For Bateson, there is an element in the house of the crab, and in the city something of the lobster (let us recognize their bodies as living bodies, because we perceive them as similar to our own bodies at a level underlying the diversity of the species: we perceive that the parts of the crab can be compared to the parts of the lobster – that the comparison between crab and lobster can be likened to the comparison between man and, for example, horse. Thus the parts of the house are comparable to each other – the house is comparable to the city – the comparison between the house and the city is itself comparable to the comparison between the man and the communal grouping). Symmetries and homologies reveal that there is a *metastructure* that connects the body of the house, and the body of the city, to the body of man.[17]

In the metropolis there is something rather more similar to a shell: the spiral *pattern*. Absence of symmetries and segmentations, because there are no (for the moment, or for ever?) *results, conclusions* of the growth processes. The metropolis reactivates modalities of organization vital at a level deeper than what we call 'life': it is a structure of structures – but this even at the limits between organic and inorganic: it resembles, in its spiral nature, features such as gorges, galaxies and whirlwinds.

Metropolises are no longer 'places', because their dimensions exceed by far the dimensions of the perceptive apparatus of their inhabitants. The widest sensory aperture, that of sight, is shattered. It was the visual field, in some respect, which defined the city dimensionally: in the metropolis there is no longer pan-orama (the vision of all), because its body overflows beyond the horizon. In the metropolitan aesthetic the eye fails in its role as an instrument of total control at a distance; once more the ears, and then the nose and skin, acquire an equal importance. The sensory field of the metropolis is ultra- and infra-visual: it is the field of a *total aesthetic*.

The mutation does not only concern perceptive behaviour, but also deeply involves the modalities of appropriation and symbolization of space – since it reaches the horizon, the metropolis is a habitat without a 'somewhere else'. It is, therefore, a *total interior*.

But the metaphor here is no longer solely ultra-corporeal, it is also infra-corporeal. These are two experiences of the lived body with which it can be compared: the 'memory' of the mother's womb, and the 'projection' of the mind.

To immerse oneself. To be swallowed up. The space around us becomes gigantic, the body shrinks. To lose one's identity in the 'ant-heap' of the crowd. These are metropolitan experiences, in which are intertwined and reactivated memories, inextricably knotted into symbiosis at deep, pre-individual levels of life – those which precede birth. In a phylogenetic sense, those experiences precede the origin of our species. They are what links us unconsciously, for example, with insects and, even further back, to the vegetable world, the pre-locomotive, pre-separated, pre-mental world. The archetypal image of this return to an 'ancient' state of pre-separation, of prevarication, but also of the increasing nutrition of the I, and so of the loss of the I's borders in a vital mass without surroundings, is the fantasy of the mother's womb and of the primordial *thalassa*. This demonstrates that in metropolitan life there is a 'knot' of spatial experience, a point at which the most elementary distinction of space – the distinction between 'inside' and 'outside', which is the very distinction between 'I' and 'the world' – grows weaker.

Laing recites liltingly:[18]

> One is inside
> then outside what one has been inside
> One feels empty
> because there is nothing inside oneself
> One tries to get inside oneself
>   that inside of the outside
>   that one was once inside
>   once one tries to get oneself inside what
>   one is outside:
>   to eat and to be eaten
> to have the outside inside and to be
>   inside the outside
>
> But this is not enough. One is trying to get
> the inside of what one is outside inside, and to
> get the inside outside. But one does not get

inside the outside by getting the outside inside for;
although one is full inside of the inside of the outside
and by getting inside the outside
one remains empty because
while one is on the inside
even the inside of the outside is outside
and inside oneself there is still nothing
There has never been anything else
and there never will be

Thus the 'western' culture of habitat rediscovers the 'void', and in some way this culture is once more forced to deal with its own 'negative': 'the other half of the sky' – and of the world – that is to say, 'the Orient' (from which the west detached itself, around the year 1000, at the time it had begun to generate the city).

Oriental culture and its meditative practices offer an ulterior metaphor for the representation of the experience of metropolitan space. The metaphor is that of the imaginary space of the mind.

Infinite webbed connections. Cellular ramifications and interstices. Plurality and miniaturization. Aggregations, desegregations, reaggregations. Co-existence of microstructures and systems of centralized control. Co-existence of the infinitely big and the infinitely small. These are other modalities of the metropolitan experience, which in some respects resemble the experience of self-representation of the mind, the 'figure' that the mind imagines to represent itself. One thinks of the figurative similarity of the extremes of the biggest and the smallest of human products, so that the shape of Los Angeles (1,200 km²) becomes related to that of a monolithic electronic circuit (25 mm²). Consider the powers of *Anima* and *Mahima* (of becoming as small as you want, and of seeing the tiniest objects such as the internal structure of atoms; of becoming immensely big, able to see the solar system and the universe), powers obtainable through the practice of yoga.

Laing again:

All in all
Each man in all men
all men in each man

All being in each being

Each being in all being

All in each
Each in all

All distinctions are mind, by mind, in mind, of mind
No distinctions no mind to distinguish

Laing's 'knots' represent thought 'going fugitive' in the metropolitan condition: the loss of logical linearity, the soldering of deductive reasoning into an obsessive circle – madness. But also the epistemological post-metropolitan breakage; the catastrophe of obsession where an increasingly whirlwind-like motion, obsessive in its excessive speed, finally becomes elusive, and the circle forms a *mandala* – ecstasy.

'THIS REMINDS ME OF A STORY'[19]

If all cities have always been somehow anthropomorphic, the ultra-cities (metropolises and after) reveal other more archaic and threatening mutual similarities of which we are only now becoming aware. In the post-metropolis, thought once again reveals its repetitive mythopoeic nature. The plots of *Maya* appear (the cosmic illusion, the totality of illusions that form the world).

This is why it is necessary to think in terms of multiple and heterogeneous fragments, organized *around* the city experience: because the discourse on the post-metropolis, a *metastructural* discourse (that which connects, beneath the specific differences; that which represents and examines the structure of structures, and the 'beauty' of the *connecting structure*, 'the glue which holds together the stars and the sea-anemones, the redwood forests and the committees and councils of humanity', as Gregory Bateson put it) – such a discourse can only be a careful, ordered and patient collection, of rejects and clues (landscapes with ruins, utopias and realities, the other side, the Gianni Versace collection, Babel, mute desires, discipline, the moral of the fable, chinoiserie, polyanthropy, lived cities, tourist guides, great Atlantises, sirens and *lazzeroni*, the division of time, the antechamber of the temple, the cult of the dead, the outmoded present, Hermes and Hestia, closed images, cartographies, city balance-sheets, mythopoeic values, consumer utopias, private scenes, post-seriality, schizoparanoid metropolises, islands ...) all around an empty epicentre.

NOTES

[1] For a deeper reflection on the use and the limitations of structuralist and historicist methodology in architecture, see the first part of 'Habitat as a discontinuous body', in D. Mazzoleni and P. Belfiore, *Metapolis* (Rome: 1983).
[2] Cf. C. Levi-Strauss, 'Introduction to the work of Marcel Mauss', in M. Mauss, *Sociology and Anthropology* (Paris: 1950); R. Jacobson, *Essai de Linguistique generale* (Paris: 1963); José Gil, 'Corpo', in A.A.V.V., *Enciclopedia* (Turin: 1978).
[3] M. Leenhardt, *Do Kamo. La personne et le mythe dans le monde melanesien* (Paris: 1947).
[4] Cf. C. Levi-Strauss, 'Le sorcier et sa magie', in *Les Temps Modernes*, vol 4, 41, and 'L'efficacite symbolique', *Revue d'histoire des religions*, 135, 1; both republished in *Anthropologie Structurale* (Paris: 1958).
[5] Ludwig Mies van der Rohe, work manifesto in 'G' (1923), republished in U. Conrads, *Programme und Manifeste zur Architekur des 20 Jahrhunderts* (Frankfurt/Berlin: 1964).
[6] H. Finsterlin, 'Casa Nova'. Zukunftsarchitekur', *Wendingen*, March 1924.
[7] A. Loos, *Trotzdem, 1900-1930* (Innsbruck: 1931).
[8] For the terminology, cf. C. Norberg-Schulz, *Intentions in Architecture* (1963).
[9] A notable study of the intimate relationship that exists between the culture of clothing and the culture of the body can be found in B. Rudofsky, *The Unfashionable Human Body* (1975).
[10] R. Thom, *Stabilité structurelle et Morphogenese – Essai d'une theorie generale des modeles* (Paris: 1972).
[11] J. Rykwert, *On Adam's House in Paradise* (Rykwert: 1972).
[12] J. Rykwert, 'Un modo di concepire la casa, "Lotus" ', 8 (September 1974).
[13] *Ibid.*
[14] Cf. C. Blacker and M. Loewe (eds), *Ancient Cosmologies* (London: 1975), in particular G. E. R. Lloyd, 'Greek cosmology', and P. Grierson, 'The European heritage', Cf. AA.VV., *Cartes et Figures de la Terre* (Paris: 1980). Gregory Bateson speaks of the 'epistemological error' of Darwin, in *Mind and Nature: a necessary unity* (London: 1979).
[15] Cf. M. Bakhtin, *L'oeuvre de Francois Rabelais et la Culture populaire au Moyen Age et à la Renaissance* (Paris: 1970); N. Chatelet, *Le corps á corps culinaire* (Paris: 1977).
[16] On the mutation of the city into metropolises, I refer the reader to what I have written in *Metapolis*.
[17] For the use of crabs, lobsters and shells, and for the idea of *metastructure* (patterns of patterns) cf. G. Bateson, *op. cit.*
[18] R. D. Laing, *Knots* (London: 1970).
[19] Cf. G. Bateson, *op cit.*

Prisoners of the City:
Whatever Could a Postmodern City Be?

Kevin Robins

Europeans tiptoe through their cities as museums *because they are museums*.

Agnes Heller

RECOVERING URBANITY?

In this essay, I want to look at the wider framework within which urban regeneration and property development are evolving, and to explore some of the broader dynamics that are now shaping urban structure and form. My central concern is with the culture of cities and with that obscure object of desire that is called urbanity. For this, it seems, is now the order of the day. Not only among cultural critics, but also in the fraternities of planners and property developers, there is a renewed interest in the quality of urban life. In various development schemes now underway in Britain – in Leeds, Birmingham, Edinburgh, and Spitalfields and Paddington in London – there is a new consensual 'belief in "public space", the idea that a city should create some sort of communal vessel for shared activity'.[1] The piazza and the galleria are the physical containers for this new spirit of urban public life and community.

This they are calling 'postmodern'. The postmodern city is projected as the antithesis of modernist abstraction and anomie: it is about the renaissance of urban culture and sensibilities. In this city, architecture and planning are informed by a new respect for place and tradition. If modernism was driven by universalizing forces, then postmodernism is about a return to difference and particularity. The historical development of capitalist societies and cities is seen in terms of a kind

303

of duel between the universal and the particular. Robert Stack gives one variant:

> A place is often thought of as a unique set of attributes at a unique location. This is especially so before a place becomes 'commercialised'. Therefore we can expect that when a place 'enters the market', so to speak, it must advertise itself as having generic qualities such as being accessible and having this type of service or that. As places become 'consumed', they lose much of their former uniqueness. Commercialisation makes them appear more like other places. At this point they (like other generic mass-produced products) must differentiate themselves from competing places.[2]

Universalism and uniformity are associated with a crisis of urbanity. The postmodern city is then about an attempt to re-imagine urbanity: about recovering a lost sense of territorial identity, urban community and public space. It is a kind of return to (mythical) origins.

Of course, this is not an unproblematical agenda. How is this act of re-imagination to be achieved? Strategies of postmodern re-enchantment assume a number of forms. One strategy, a kind of neo-romanticism, straightforwardly aims to rekindle a pre-modern sense of place and tradition. Writing at the end of the twenties, Lewis Mumford argued that already the Age of Enlightenment had

> turned people's minds away from the essential relations of geography and history; for it broke the established ties of tradition and place ... Enlightenment and progress meant the spreading of London and Paris, Berlin, and St. Petersburg, over wider and wider areas.[3]

Nineteenth-century Romanticism was a response to this process, involving the preservation of history and tradition, and also the revaluation of regional (and rural) cultures and ways of life. The resurgence of regionalist sentiments in the 1920s represented another such attempt to reassess the importance of 'a differentiated way of life' against 'the dream of uniform and complete standardisation'.[4] Certain kinds of postmodernizing strategy should be seen in this long-term context. In terms of *historical* revival, much has been written about the heritage boom during the 1980s, with its nostalgic theme parks and its marketing of 'soft' and pastoralized popular memories. These 'memory places' represent 'moments of history torn away from the movement of history, then returned; no longer quite life, not yet death, like shells on the shore when the sea of living memory had receded'.[5] The return to geography is apparent in the new enthusiasm for locality and regionalism, as in certain developments within architectural practice for example. 'Regionalism', as one of its advocates says, 'attempts to put back into architecture what Modernism conspicuously took out, namely continuity in a given place between past and present forms of building'.[6] Recognizing the 'fragility of local culture', Kenneth Frampton invokes a 'self-consciously cultivated regionalism' that will link place-form and cultural identity.[7]

A different approach, a kind of hi-tech neo-romanticism, seeks to revitalize urban life courtesy of new communications technologies. It is, in fact, reviving a long tradition of what we might call techno-organicism in urban planning, a tradition that has sought to mobilize electrical, and then electronic, technologies to promote decentralization and community. At the beginning of the century, Patrick Geddes contrasted the 'palaeotechnic' of the steam engine, which he argued had made for centralization and the growth of the metropolis, with the 'neotechnic' of electricity and electrical communications which would promote 'democratic location' and a return to smaller settlement sizes and the best of pre-industrial values.[8] Theodore Roszak describes how, back in the 1960s, a 'reversionary technophiliac vision' imagined a global culture of electronic villages, a culture associated with 'community memory' in which the computer would help to keep things decentralized and humanly scaled.[9] Recently Geoff Mulgan has rekindled this kind of soft technological urbanism. Mulgan argues that the new 'soft infrastructures' of information and communications technologies can support the local and different, that they can encourage conviviality and promote a sense of community and citizenship. He suggests that they can be used 'to recreate communities disrupted by the fragmentation of the modern city, bringing "neighbourhood without propinquity" '. They could 'sustain new kinds of social relationship: health training and distant education projects on cable television, tele-shopping for the old and disabled, on-line access to councils and assemblies'.[10] What we have in this idea of enchanted networks, with their remote and virtual conviviality, is in fact a markedly anti-urban vision, a kind of postmodern, electronic garden city.

Yet another postmodernizing strategy has involved the development of city image campaigns. If city cultures cannot be re-imagined, then perhaps they can be re-imaged. Modern cities have always, of course, advertised their civic grandeur to the outside world, and, recognizing that the identities of cities are constituted through a network of relationships, they have sought to secure their positions within the urban hierarchy. Now, in a world in which inter-urban competitiveness operates on a global scale, cities are propelled into a race to attract increasingly mobile investors (multinational corporations), consumers (tourists), and spectacles (sports and media events). As cities have become ever more equivalent and urban identities increasingly 'thin', however, it has become necessary to employ advertising and marketing agencies to manufacture such distinctions.[11] It is a question of distinction in a world beyond difference. What this also reflects, however, is a significant shift in the nature of the city. Whereas for the early modernists architecture was the medium for expressing a vision of the city, for the postmodern marketers the city exists through a range of other media. Kenneth Frampton even links the current triumph of television with the general demise of architecture.[12] In this process, the signifier becomes dislocated from its referent, the image of the city floats free from the 'reality' of the built environment. Images become means, instruments for manipulating perceptions. And so images displace ideals:

> The image is made to order, tailored to us. An ideal, on the other hand, has a claim on us. It does not serve us; we serve it. If we have trouble striving towards it, we assume the matter is with us, and not with the ideal.[13]

The particularity and identity of cities is about product differentiation; their cultures and traditions are now sustained through the discourses of marketing and advertising.

This question of particularity is central to the idea of the postmodern city. There is a general feeling, Philip Cooke argues, that 'the local dimension has been for too long neglected by an overcentralised, dominating and exclusive modernist culture.' Postmodern architecture and planning therefore 'seeks to restore identity to local cultures swamped hitherto by the austere universalism of modernist aesthetics'.[14] If modernism was about abstraction and functionalism, then postmodernism is about the renaissance of tradition and re-enchantment of place.

According to the Arts Council, Britain is now experiencing an 'urban renaissance', with culture and the arts coming to play a new role in revitalizing and re-enchanting city life. The arts 'create a climate of optimism – the "can do" attitude essential to developing the "enterprise culture" this Government hopes to bring to deprived areas'; they 'provide focal points for community pride and identity'.[15] The positive significance of the arts in the 1980s and 1990s is defined against the negative reference point of the 1960s. For the Arts Council, the 1960s have come to symbolize the alienating force of modernism: at that time, urban renewal 'resulted in concrete tower blocks on a vast, inhuman scale, destroying established communities in the process'. Now, in the 1990s, we must learn the lessons of the past and 'get it right this time': 'To succeed, redevelopment must consist of more than bricks and mortar. It must rebuild communities'.[16] *An Urban Renaissance* is a superficial and opportunist document, reflecting the 'can do' attitude of the Arts Council in the face of the new enterprise logic. Its very conformism, however, also makes a good statement of what is now turning out to be a very broad consensus on the nature and course of urban regeneration. Its key terms – enterprise, renaissance, culture, image, community – reflect an optimism for our times.

It is the same kind of optimism and vision that characterizes Prince Charles's recent pronouncements on architecture and urban planning. In the Prince's discourse, there is the same emphasis on restoring the spirit of enterprise and rebuilding community, and the same belief that this might be the basis of a 'new renaissance for Britain'. And, again, there is the same starting point, based on the critique of modernism and particularly of its post-war manifestations. As Patrick Wright has argued, the Prince of Wales's ideas are centred around 'a highly schematic interpretation of the British nation and its history since the Second World War'. After the high point of British history in 1945, he believes, the country entered a bleak forty year decline, a period of bureaucratic planning and of 'destructive modernization'. The present period seems to offer a potential way beyond this inhumanity and alienation; it could be 'the miraculous moment of reawakening when the return to true values can begin'.[17] This might be the historical moment to move beyond modernization and beyond modernism. For the Prince, the way forward is through both the revival of traditional forms of building and the stimulation of neo-vernacular and community architecture.[18] A new era of postmodernism will be about a return to human scale and the re-creation of community. As the Prince argued in his Pittsburgh speech (March 1988), 'man [and he probably means "men"] seems to function best in small, recognisable units – hence the village – where he is part of a community of people to which he can relate'. The future beyond modernism is rooted in traditional and vernacular forms: in the ruralism, particularism and organicism that have long characterized British architectural and planning theory.[19] After forty years of devastation and devaluation, this is now seen as the key to reviving and re-enchanting cities and communities.

If this aristocratic, or more accurately pseudo-aristocratic, idea of urban renaissance offers a conservative vision of contemporary urban transformation, there are other, more radical and usually more complex, variants. In these approaches, too, there is the sense that cities are at a turning point, and that this turning point might offer the possibility of moving beyond 'the faceless abstraction of modernist urban development'.[20] Within this discourse, the key agenda is about the shift from the Fordist to the post-Fordist city.[21] Postmodernism is then seen as the cultural expression of that economic transformation. Thus, for John Montgomery, if British cities have been characterized by 'drabness, impoverished culture, monotony, and mono-functionalism', there is now the possibility of 'a paradigm shift in the way we think about cities and liveability'. He imagines an urban future characterized by a post-Fordist economy (flexible specialization, small firms); by a flourishing of the cultural industries ('culture is central to the way cities should develop'); and by 'a cultural sense of place' (including local history and traditions, cosmopolitanism, diversity and choice, vitality and flow, identity).[22] Franco Bianchini is far more nuanced and cautious in his approach, but he too identifies a shift from the modern to the postmodern city. For him, too, cities are now in a position to transform local economies and local democracy, to develop cultural industries, to revitalize public spaces and to sustain a politics of identity.[23]

An important point of reference and authority for this perspective has been the work of David Harvey.[24] Harvey argues that we have seen the shift from a 'managerial' approach to urban governance in the 1960s to contemporary forms of 'entrepreneurial' governance. This shift in urban politics is associated with 'a transition from locationally rather rigid Fordist production systems backed by Keynesian state welfarism to a much more geographically open and market-based form of [post-Fordist] flexible accumulation'.[25] It also crucially involves the shift from modernist to postmodernist kinds of design, cultural forms and lifestyle. For Harvey, postmodernism signifies

> a break with the idea that planning and development should focus on large scale, technologically rational, austere and functionally efficient 'international style' design and that vernacular traditions, local history, and specialized spatial designs ranging from functions of intimacy to grand spectacle should be approached with a much greater eclecticism of style.

Postmodernity, he argues, 'is nothing more than the cultural clothing of flexible accumulation'.[26] In contrast to more deterministic accounts of the postmodern city, Harvey suggests that the precise trajectory of change remains indeterminate and, ultimately, uncertain. If there are potentialities for resisting the demands of the new regime of accumulation, there is also the danger that postmodernism could simply conform to the new capitalist imperatives.

Harvey is cautious in presenting this account of recent changes in the economy, governance and culture of cities, and in stressing the complexity and uncertainty of change. Other commentators, appealing to Harvey's authority, have presented a more schematic and simplistic trajectory of change. There has been a tendency to conflate economic, political and cultural spheres, and then to assume a straightforward logic of development from Fordism/managerialism/modernism to post-Fordism/entrepreneurialism/postmodernism. The consequence of this has been to obscure the complex rhythms and periodicities of change, and also to overstate the contrast between what are (wrongly) seen as distinct historical phases. Indeed, in those less cautious than Harvey, the account converges surprisingly with that of conservative postmodernists. Their postmodernism, too, develops as a kind of simple (historical) inversion of modernism and modernity. For them, too, the logic of modernism was centred around efficiency, functionalism and impersonality; as it eroded the sense of place so it undermined the sense of identity, or, rather, severed the links between identity and place. Against this uniformity of the modern movements, David Ley, for example, has argued that we are now seeing a renewed interest in regional and historical styles of architecture and in the diversity of local cultures:

> In contrast to the isotropic space of modernism, post-modern space aims to be historically specific, rooted in cultural, often vernacular, style conventions, and often unpredictable in the relation of parts to the whole. In reaction to the large scale of the modern movement, it attempts to create smaller units, seeks to break down a corporate society to urban villages, and maintain historical associations through renovation and recycling.

'The postmodern project', Ley emphasizes, 'is the re-enchantment of the built environment'.[27]

Postmodernism is thought to be about the struggle for place in the face of modernist 'rationality' and abstraction. In one strand of thinking, the return to the particular is about revalorizing locality, community, and the vernacular. For Ley, it is about the 'attempt to restore meaning, rootedness and human proportions to place in an era dominated by depersonalising bulk and standardisation'.[28] For Michael Rustin, we must confront the limitations of abstract universalism and again acknowledge the boundedness of human lives in time and space: 'Even though mobility and choice of place has grown, territorial locations remain nodes of association and continuity, bounding cultures and communities'.[29] According to Geoff Mulgan, there is renewed interest in what he calls the 'soft architecture' of the city, that is 'its feel and atmosphere, its social networks and its sense of community and citizenship'.[30] From this perspective, reclaiming the city is about re-establishing personal and collective roots. The re-enchantment of the city is about the re-enchantment of identity and community.

An alternative postmodern response to the abstraction and rationalism of modernism has been a renewed concern with urban spectacle and imagery. This development is rooted in the new consumerism of post-Fordist times, with its culture of fashion, advertising, design and display. 'the relatively stable aesthetic of Fordist modernism', writes David Harvey, 'has given way to all the ferment, instability, and fleeting qualities of a postmodernist aesthetic that celebrates difference, ephemerality, spectacle, fashion and the commodification of cultural forms'.[31] It may, however, be the case that his mobilization of spectacle and display can, at the same time, function as a form of social control: 'The orchestrated production of an urban image can, if successful, create a sense of social solidarity, civic pride and loyalty to place and even allow the urban image to provide a mental refuge in a world that capital treats as more and more place-less'.[32] Through spectacle and image, it may be possible to create a spurious sense of togetherness and participation in urban life.

Once again, where Harvey is cautious, others have been more reckless. They have adopted a less critical stance towards this theatrical side of post-modernism. For Mike Featherstone, it is about identities in a 'no-place space' in which 'traditional senses of culture are decontextualised, stimulated, reduplicated and continually renewed and restyled'. This is the city of malls, museums, theme parks, shopping centres and tourist sites, the city 'in which cultural disorder and stylistic eclecticism become common features of spaces in which consumption and leisure are meant to be constructed as "experiences" '. In this city, 'the concern with fashion, presentation of self, "the look" on the part of the new wave of urban *flâneurs* points to the process of cultural differentiation which in many ways is the obverse of the stereotypical images of mass societies in which serried ranks of similarly dressed people are massed together'.[33] For Featherstone, this mobilization of spectacle and display could be a positive force in urban life, pointing to the deconstruction of existing symbolic hierarchies and the opening up of a playful, popular democratic impulse. Spectacle and theatricality might even be reconnected to territory and used for positive political ends to reconstruct civic identity and transform urban relations.

WHAT IS THE CRISIS OF URBANITY?

Of course, these various accounts contribute to our understanding of contemporary urban change. But in the end, I want to argue, the analysis is too easy and the solutions too anodyne. If cities are in crisis, their very real problems are not being adequately addressed by these 'new paradigm' urban regeneration scenarios. And if urbanity is in crisis, then it is doubtful that fashionable projects for urban refurbishment are meaningful responses. The new urban postmodernism is simply too partial and limited, and fails to confront – and often to even recognize – some of the more profound and refractory issues affecting urban futures.

What is at issue is the significance of urban modernism. There is the question of what it now is; there is the question of what its consequences have been; and there is the question of whether it is being replaced by something called postmodernism. For most of those we have been discussing the answers are straightforward. The urban postmodernists are moved by a sense of having been betrayed by post-war architects and planners. In one respect, this might be seen, as the more sensitive modernists themselves recognize, as a reflection of 'modernism's inability both to adapt itself to changing needs and more specifically to learn from its mistakes'.[34] Invariably, however, it tends to be seen in more dramatic terms, as a crisis of modernism and of modernity itself. The uniformity and inhumanity of contemporary planning are seen as manifestations of modernist abstraction and universalism. The hope is then that the present might perhaps be a turning point. If there is a crisis of the modern (or Fordist, or managerial) city, then there may, perhaps, be the prospect of creating the postmodern (post-Fordist, post-managerial) city. And postmodernism, it is felt, will be about the re-enchantment of cities and the return to particularity. Through the conservation of tradition and the recovery of place, or through theatricality, spectacle and style, we shall begin to fashion a new urbanity beyond modernism.

It is difficult not to see this kind of historical scheme as simplistic and reductionist. The binary opposition of modernism to postmodernism, or of universalism to particularism, may have a certain heuristic value, but there is the real danger that it will flatten the complexity and contradictoriness of social transformation. There is the danger that we will see change in terms of abrupt and decisive stages separated by historical divides. Such historical binarism invokes a teleological development in which modernism will (necessarily) give way to postmodernism, Fordism to post-Fordism, managerialism to entrepreneurialism. In this way, the 'disfunctions' of the modernist city can be safely consigned to the historical dustbin. Disenchantment is buried in the past, while the future can be unproblematically given over to the project of re-enchantment.

What this fails to address are the real complexities and contradictions thrown up by urban modernization. If there is now a revival of interest in community and sense of place, this can only be seen in the context of what is in fact the increasing fragmentation and segmentation of urban life. According to Manuel Castells, the dual city is 'the urban expression of the process of increasing differentiation of labour in two equally dynamic sectors within the growing economy: the information-based formal economy, and the downgraded labour-based informal economy'. The fundamental meaning of the dual city, he continues, 'refers to the process of spatial restructuring through which distinct segments of labour are included in and excluded from the making of new history'.[35] In the contemporary metropolis, the territories of the new postmodern *flâneurs* and consumers coexist with the ghettoes of ethnic minorities and the socially marginalized. Margit Mayer argues that 'it is not a "pluralism" of lifestyles and consumption patterns which reigns, but rather that the high income consumers' ideas and definitions of the "good life" have become the influential ones'. We are seeing the consolidation of the divided city, in which 'urban space, while it is functionally and economically shared, is socially segregated and culturally differen-tiated'.[36] And, if there is a renewed concern with public space and public life, this is in contradictory relation to an increased privatism. New communications and media technologies, particularly, encourage further privatism and isolation: 'households are plugged into the world, but not open to it' and 'in this sense, the city exists no more'.[37]

Changing urban governance is not about engineering the transition from the bad old times to the benign new times, but, rather, it must be about trying to find new ways to hold these increasingly explosive contradictions in tension. If there is an urban crisis, it will not be resolved in the straightforward way the postmodernists suggest. We should not, then, think of the present as a point of (evolutionary) transition from the modern to the postmodern city. It is not about settling accounts with modernity in order to make way for an urban renaissance; it is not about the possible shift beyond modernist disenchantment to the re-enchantment of cities. As Zygmunt Bauman reminds us, postmodernism is far from being an achieved state: it is perhaps no more than 'modernity taking a long and attentive look at itself, not liking what it sees and sensing the urge to change'.[38] What has been called the 'new urbanity' can scarcely be about resolving the crisis of cities, not yet at least. It is, rather, about a rupture that is now 'forcing us to re-think our understanding of cities and of good uses of the city'.[39] Just because we feel the need to re-think and the urge to change, however, we should not assume that history has obligingly come up with the answers. The new urban sensibility that is emerging may be more about not liking what it sees in the modern city than about really imagining an alternative vision.

This historical teleology of the postmodern perspective encourages soft optimism and voluntarism in the policy and political arenas. It seems but a short step from imagining the user-friendly city to its felicitous realization: it is simply a matter of soft social engineering, centred around refashioned cultural and consumption districts, and of cosmetic design and façades, whether they be hi-tech glitz or neo-historicist classicism. The crisis of urban modernization is a good deal more intractable. We must consider what is, in fact, a profound and long-term crisis of the city and of urbanity. At one level, this is a question of the very scale of physical and social problems in the modern city. Inequality, segmentation and alienation are inscribed in the physical and social landscape of cities (and this is a matter for urban politics, not urban cultural regeneration). But, at another level, there is a very real crisis of urbanity itself. What do we think cities are for? What are the values that should regulate urban life? What does civic identity mean (or not mean) now?

Thirty years ago, Lewis Mumford began *The City in History* with some thoughts on this question of urbanity, and on the imperative 'to find a new form for the city'. 'Can the needs and desires', he asks, 'that have impelled men to live in cities recover, at a still higher level, all that Jerusalem, Athens, or Florence once seemed to promise?' Or, alternatively, might 'post-historic man' no longer have any need for the city? Might 'what was once a city ... shrink to the dimensions of an underground control centre ... and all other attributes of life be forfeited'?[40] Since, then, other writers have highlighted the devaluation of older forms of urbanity and the crisis of the city as an imaginative focus. Michael Walzer, for example, has described the erosion of what he calls 'open-minded spaces' – ones that have in the past been the 'breeding ground for mutual respect, political respect, civil discourse' – and their replacement by intimate spaces and 'single-minded', that is instrumental and functional, spaces.[41] Richard Sennett has written of the growth of 'purified communities' which devalue the complexity, difference and otherness that have been so much at the heart of classic urban culture.[42] Suggesting that our relation to the city is marked by a 'crisis of language', by a 'loss of semiotic apprehensibility', William Sharpe and Leonard Wallock suggest that the 'waning sense of city as place is intimately linked to the inability to say what the city might mean'.[43] Johannes Birringer, too, points to 'the end of the city as an imaginative or emotional focus even of cultural alienation'.[44]

The very idea of the city itself is now thrown into doubt. 'The question that is brought to mind', Jürgen Habermas writes, 'is whether the actual *notion* of the city has not itself been superseded'. The problems of town planning, he argues, 'are not primarily problems of design, but problems of controlling and dealing with the anonymous system-imperatives that influence the spheres of city life and threaten to devastate the urban fabric'.[45] The new urban agglomerations and systems seem remote from traditional conceptions of city life and culture. Is it then possible to reconcile older notions of urbanity with the system-functional imperatives of contemporary society? Can we sustain 'mediating institutions that can nurture direct relationships in a world increasingly characterised by indirect ones?'[46]

These various observations raise the question of the city as an imaginary institution. The city as a physical structure and system embodies or incarnates particular social significations; these imaginary significations are realized or 'institutionalized' in and through this urban fabric. This imaginary institution of the city defines the scope – the possibilities and their limits – within which, at any particular time, we can imagine, think and experience city life; it defines the aesthetic and the intellectual field within which cities will be designed, planned and engineered. What we are addressing is the crisis of the city in this imaginary dimension. 'Like the computer', writes Donatella Mazzoleni the metropolitan habitat, 'seems to have assumed an alien subjectivity, to have become something with which one has dialogue, as one would with a stranger'.[47] For her, the question is whether we can learn to live in our 'post-metropolitan condition'; whether there is the possibility of a new imaginary.

COMPLEXITY AND BANALITY, AND THEIR DIS-CONTENTS

The meaning of the city is rooted in the *longue durée* of its historical development. In this process, of course, there have been significant points of reorientation and revaluation. Such a moment was that which, in reaction and revulsion against the nineteenth-century metropolis, gave birth to a distinctive new approach to planning in the urban visions and utopias of figures as different as Ebenezer Howard, Frank Lloyd Wright and Le Corbusier.[48] In contemporary urban regeneration strategies, it is these developments of the early twentieth century that remain the key reference points. It is precisely this continuity that explains the familiarity and predictability of so many supposedly innovative (and supposedly postmodern) schemes of the past decade. As Peter Hall argues, 'there are just a few key ideas in twentieth-century planning, which re-echo and recycle and recon-nect'.[49] At this end of the twentieth century, I want to suggest, these same few ideas are simply continuing to re-echo and recycle and reconnect. The present does not constitute a further point of reorientation in the urban imaginary, but rather the exhaustion and crisis of the modernist vision and programme.

The process that has brought the very idea of the city into question has also undermined the kind of promethean and utopian ambitions projected by the early modernist planners and architects. The old paradigms, now stretched to their limits, are unable to contain the *complexity* of urban systems on the eve of the twenty-first century. As the scale of urban systems has exploded, and as they have become increasingly networked into global systems, planning has become more fragmented and piecemeal. At the same time, there has been a kind of imaginative collapse: what was once driven by vision and energy is now drained of affect. The utopian has collapsed into the *banal*. We do not plan the ideal city, but come to terms with the 'good enough' city. Complexity and banality are significant consequences of urban modernization that now impede its further development or its supersession. These are critical issues with which urban policy must come to terms.

What, then, is the significance of complexity and banality for contemporary urbanity? And in what ways are these two phenomena interrelated? These are the questions I now want to pursue. My starting point is a fundamental dichotomy that has always been at the heart of urban life and culture. In Lewis Mumford's terms: 'Human life swings between two poles: movement and settlement'.[50] These two poles have always been at the heart of urban development – the city as container and the city as flow – and have been held in productive tension. Arguably, the vibrancy and excitement of modernist planning in the late nineteenth and early twentieth century was a consequence of this creative tension. It is well symbolized in *fin-de-siècle* Vienna through the contrasting figures of Camillo Sitte and Otto Wagner and their plans for the Ringstrasse. Carl Schorske captures the dyanmic:

> Sitte, out of the artisan tradition, embraced Ringstrasse historicism to further his project of restoring a communitarian city, with the enclosed square as his model for the future. Wagner, out of a bourgeois affirmation of modern technology, embraced as essence what Sitte most abhorred in the Ringstrasse: the primary dynamic of the street. The conservative Sitte, fearful of the workings of time, placed his hope for the city in contained space, in the human, socialising confines of the square. Wagner, even more than the Ringstrasse progressivists before

him, subjected the city to the ordinance of time. Hence street was king, the artery of men in motion; for him the square could serve best as goal of the street, giving direction and orientation to its users. Style, landscaping, all the elements through which Sitte sought variety and picturesqueness in the fight against modern anomie, Wagner employed essentially to reinforce the power of the street and its temporal trajectory.[51]

On the one hand, Sitte's romantic archaism, with its communitarian values and its idea of the city as settlement and enclosure; on the other, Wagner's functionalist and futuristic celebration of movement, circulation, speed. This was the distinctive culture of space and time[52] which informed urban sensibility in that early modernist period. The city as an imaginary institution was oriented around these conflicting tendencies; these constituted the parameters of debate, action and vision in the planning field.

This remains our fundamental reference point. At that historical moment the tension between settlement and movement, between community and mobility, was at its most heightened and intense. If, as Georg Simmel argued in his classic essay, 'The Metropolis and Mental Life', written at the turn of the century, the characteristic feature of the modern metropolis is that 'its inner life overflows by waves into a far flung national or international area', it was then still the case that this process had not become absolutely divorced from the 'self-contained and autarchic' values of the small town.[53] The city could still combine, and balance, a sense of the boundless and the bounded.

In the later nineteenth century, the dynamic forces that were irrupting into the urban community were those of transportation systems (trams, trains, and then the automobile). As one commentator on the Haussmannization of Paris put it, 'the straight lines to the railway stations were meant to express the fact that Paris was henceforth part of a national and international economy'.[54] In the 1920s, Le Corbusier would point to the changes in urban morphology that these developments occasioned:

> Right up to the twentieth century, towns were laid out with a view to military defence. The boundary of a town was a definite thing, a clear organisation of walls, gates with streets leading up to them, and from them to the centre.
>
> Moreover, up to the nineteenth century a town was entered from the outside. Today the city's gates are in its *centre*. For its real gates are the railway stations.[55]

The consequence was that public space increasingly became contingent upon motion, a derivative of movement.[56]

Now, sixty years further on, the whole process has accelerated dramatically, and the city has become integrated not only into more complex, international transportation systems, but also into global information and communications networks. We can now talk of a process of globalization or transnationalization in the transformation of urban space and form. Manuel Castells describes the advent of the 'informational city', and identifies 'the historical emergence of the space of flows, superseding the meaning of the space of places'.[57] Others have described this same process in similar ways. Suggesting that 'things are not defined by their physical boundaries any more', the architect Bernard Tschumi points to the advent of the 'exploded city'.[58] Paul Virilio calls it the 'overexposed city': 'In the place of a discrete boundary in space, demarcating distinct spaces, one sees spaces co-joined by semi-permeable membranes, exposed to flows of information in particular ways'.[59]

With these developments the holding tension between settlement and movement is broken apart. We have the 'disarticulation of place-based societies': 'The fundamental fact is that social meaning evaporates from places, and therefore from society, and becomes diluted and diffused in the reconstructed logic of a space of flows whose profile, origin, and ultimate purposes are unknown'.[60] With the triumph of flow, it becomes increasingly difficult for urban governors and planners to afford cohesion to the fragmented and dislocated urban system. New kinds of network – physical and virtual – subvert 'traditional' territorial formations, deconstructing and recomposing them in more complex ways. In the process, established forms of urban community, culture and sensibility are disrupted. The key issue, then, is whether it is possible to manage these new dynamics of deterritorialization. The question is whether speed and flow can now be contained within a coherent sense of urbanity.

If an excess of movement has brought about disorientating complexity and the disruption of settlement, it has also been at the heart of another disabling tendency. Already in the 1880s Camillo Sitte was confronting banality as a problem for urban planning and design. For Sitte, the essence of 'community life' was captured in the public square, for example the cathedral place at Pisa which was 'not depreciated by profane or banal surroundings of any kind'. In his own practice, Sitte advocated the development of such places as a challenge to 'the already proverbial banality of modern streets'.[61] Closer to our own time, Guy Debord has been concerned with this same predicament. Whilst the flow of tourism, for example, is apparently about the particularity and difference of cities, Debord suggests, in reality it reflects their increasing equivalence. It is 'fundamentally nothing more than the leisure of going to see what has become banal.... The same modernisation that removed time from the voyage also removed from it the reality of space.'[62]

In both observations, there is the same felt sense of particularity and difference being overcome by forces of homogenization. The predicament of banality is about the neutralization and the de-realization of space. Movement and flow appear to overwhelm the identity of place. Richard Sennett provides an interesting starting point for understanding this process. Sennett is concerned with the grid system as it developed in American cities, first in the horizontal form of nineteenth-century street networks, and then, in the twentieth century through the vertical grids of the skyscraper. The argument has more general implications, however, insofar as 'the American pattern is in many ways the extreme toward which other forms of new development tend'.[63] Sennett's prime concern is to explore the profoundly anti-urban spirit at the heart of this paradigm. Grid planning, he argues, is driven by a compulsion to deny difference and to neutralize the environment. This neutralization of the external world is then associated with a flight from urbanity, a withdrawal into the home. Sennett refers to the 'dualities of denial': 'to build you act as though you do not live in a city'.[64] Denial and withdrawal: 'The one acknowledges that complexity exists but tries to run from it. The other tries simply to abolish its existence. In our cities home are places of withdrawal, grids are places of denial.'[65] Such urban systems – ones that cohere, not around 'centres', but around 'nodes' – have become what Sennett calls 'bland developments': 'The very fuzziness of the word "node" indicates the loss of a language for naming environmental value: "centre" is charged with meanings both historical and visual, while node is resolutely bland'.[66]

Sennett's account can be pushed further. These horizontal and vertical grids are now being extended to a new dimension. The grid of the twenty-first century is the global reticulation of information and communications networks that I referred to earlier. This is the space of flows, the space of electronic nodes and of virtual reality. This abstract space also works to neutralize particularity and difference. Peter

Emberley suggests that this is the culmination of a long-term process that has brought about the increasing technologization of society. The 'global village' is

> a world of circuits and integral patterns of total environments and fused interdependencies [in which] the old order of prescriptive and exclusive places and meaning-endowed durations and sequences is dissolving ... the notions of space as enclosure and time as duration are unsettled and redesigned as a field of infinitely experimental configurations of space-time.[67]

In this depthless and decentred world, 'the possibility of space being invested with human meaning, such that it could be interpreted as "place", has evaporated'.[68] As electronic information and communications grids become more central to social processes, so does 'reality' cede to this 'hyper-reality. As electronic and urban spaces tend to fuse in this new hyper-reality, so does the public space of the city become overshadowed by a new image reality.[69] Here, the grid logic has been taken to a new order of magnitude. These new technological networks are associated with a significant acceleration in the processes of unification, homogenization and neutralization. Where once Le Corbusier imagined the city as machine, the postmodern metaphor invokes the city as cybernetic machine: 'The city is now an "open" city with amorphous public-space, open to an invasion which is turning the city into a field traversed by strategic command positions and lines of communications and movement'.[70] Tokyo is described as being 'like a computer program which ceaselessly keeps adding new subroutines', and as a city making 'the transformation from a hardware to a software city'.[71]

These developments we should take very seriously because they 'overload' our sense of urbanity, and because they can provoke feelings of dislocation and disorientation. For Le Corbusier, the modern city was about order – the geometrical order of straight lines and right angles – and 'the more this order is an exact one, the more happy [man] is, the more secure he feels'.[72] In the banality of hyper-reality, however, the city may no longer be legible, and urbanity may be more about feelings of insecurity. Of course, it is possible to become seduced by this loss of bearings. Jean Baudrillard describes a state of fascination and vertigo linked to what he calls the 'obscene delirium of communication'. In this world, 'we are no longer a part of the drama of alienation; we live in the ecstasy of communication'.[73] Baudrillard takes up where Debord left off. There is no 'reality' outside or beyond the banality of this hyper-reality: there can be no alienation because there is no longer any authentic ('real') place or position from which we can be alienated. More likely, however, is the conservative and defensive response of the 'postmodern' urban regeneration strategies. This is a regressive reaction, where 'postmodern' is really about a return to a pre-modern sense of urban life. 'How', it asks, 'especially in a world that names itself homeless, are we to create places for ourselves?'[74] How might we re-enchant the life of cities? The challenge, in this perspective, is to revitalize tradition and community and to revalidate the kinds of particularity and difference that have been lost.

POSTMODERN? WHAT FOR? WHO FOR?

Through urban regeneration strategies, the urban fabric is being patched up, and urban sensibility is being 're-imagined'. Perhaps we are succeeding in producing 'good enough' cities for some, and perhaps that will do. But let us not believe that this is about genuinely re-imagining the city. Let us not think that this is really something we can call 'postmodern'.

In spite of the rhetoric of renewal and renaissance, contemporary urban regeneration schemes are not the harbingers of a new urbanity. They are, rather, about recycled visions. They yearn for a concept of urban life which seems no longer sustainable, and they are characterized by a vocabulary of nostalgia and loss. This postmodern imagination is, in essence, a new form of Romanticism. Nineteenth-century Romanticism created an idealized image of rural life, as characterized by community and authenticity, to pit against the debased and alienated life of the great city. The new urban romanticism, too, seems to want a cosy and cleaned-up version of city life, one which avoids the real conflicts and stresses of urban life.

As with the earlier pastoral romanticism, the values and interests articulated in the new 'urban dream' seem to be above all those of the middle classes. With its emphasis on art, culture, consumption and a cappuccino lifestyle, the fashionable new urbanity seems to be shaped in the image of exactly the same social group that stands behind the wider political programme of post-Fordism. This group, as Michael Rustin has pointed out, is made up from elements of the new middle classes, 'products of education, modern communications and mental labour'. This is clear in the emphasis given to discriminating consumption. 'Even the liberated view that consumption and shopping are now really all right', Rustin argues, 'cannot but reflect the fact that the bearers and primary intended recipients of this message are not the poor but the active enfranchised participants in consumer and cultural markets'.[75] Against what it sees as the massification and homogenization of an earlier (Fordist) time, this group works, through strategies of cultural differentiation and distinction, to realize its own particularity. In the project for urban renaissance, we can see how this particular identity and lifestyle is now being mapped onto city space and landscape.

And what do these postmodern developments represent in terms of urban values and sensibilities? Clearly the idea of piazzas and squares, of spaces for lingering, for the promotion of cafe life and browsing and window shopping, has its attractions. Yet, we must recognize that this is a public space dedicated to the living out of a particular function and lifestyle. It precludes other functions and activities; and it excludes those without the appropriate entry visa, the urban poor and other 'deviants'. And if there is a search for difference and diversity, motivated by a reaction to the perceived homogeneity of the earlier surburban dream, this too falls well short of the ideal. What we have is the proliferation of gentrification kitsch with its patina of false antiquity. In new developments, such as the Central London Barratt estates, Neil Smith argues, cultural difference itself becomes mass produced and 'this infill gentrification is [ironically] accomplishing a visual suburbanisation of the city'.[76] In large-scale developments, those influenced by the stylistic glitz of American architects like Philip Johnson, the commodity status of buildings is advertised through brash facades. This kind of architecture

> treats the city as a colonial conquest. The existing city is shut out, replaced by a fantasy urbanism in a climate-controlled and secure mall.... Suburbanised malls and atriums minimise the shock of living within close proximity of different cultures and classes. For men and women fixated on the making of money, there is little interest in hassling the natural disorder of the street. The architecture eases the transition from work in a high-rise glass tower to play and consumption in a glassed-in mall. Order and control is the message as the city is exploited for its picturesque local colour.[77]

This architecture and this urbanism celebrate a society afraid of engagement.

This is the response of a particular group to the crisis of the modern city. It is about what urban culture and sensibility might continue to mean for that particular group. This postmodern vision is about the pleasures of consumption, about the enjoyment of public spaces, about sustaining elements of culture and tradition, and about stimulating diversity and difference. Because of its partiality, however, it is only about revitalizing fragments of the city. It is about insulating the consumption and living spaces of the postmodern *flâneur* from the 'have nots' in the abandoned zones of the city.

The question is whether the crisis of urban modernity can be confronted otherwise? And whether it can be for other groups too; whether it can be more democratic, less exclusionary? My concluding points are not intended to provide blueprints for an alternative postmodern vision. I think we should eschew this kind of urban utopianism. We should recognize that we are still part of urban modernity, and that we must still come to terms with the modernist city in all its contradictoriness and ambiguity. The modern metropolis has always evoked feelings of alienation and disorientation, but it has equally been associated with new possibilities for encounter and solidarity and there has always been a sense of the 'vitality, the variety, the liberating diversity and mobility of the city'.[78] These contrary tendencies have been closely, and necessarily, related – reflecting the tension between the dynamics of movement and settlement – and have been fundamental to the excitement of metropolitan life. The ideal has been to match community and security with the kind of openness that can stimulate a positive sense of challenge and contestation.

This balance has become destabilized. We must, therefore, acknowledge and confront those forces that work to deconstruct the coherence and cohesion of urban systems. We cannot disavow the unthinkable complexity, the segmentation and polarization, the dynamics of homogenization and banalization that have moulded the contemporary city. We cannot but recognize the new technologies of movement and flow that threaten further disruption. As our existence becomes increasingly mediated, so does our relation to place, and to place-bound identities and communities, become fundamentally changed. Individual experiences are differentially shaped according to their multiple inscriptions in a variety of information spaces: 'each of us operates in a universe of disparate, fragmented and discontinuous spatial references, between which there is no necessary coherence and unity'.[79] And if it was the case that the city was the 'site of an *identification*', that it could be grasped in a differential relationship with a 'surrounding', it would seem that such identification has been increasingly disabled as the metropolis has become a habitat without a 'somewhere else'.[80]

We can see how this has provoked a conservative postmodernism of nostalgia (in which urban identification is now achieved through a differential relationship between 'postmodern' islands of urbanity and a surrounding 'somewhere else' inhabited by an alien underclass of 'have nots'). In a world shaped by the universalizing forces of capitalism and modernity, this postmodernism asks, how is it possible to sustain the unique and the particular? How can place, identity and community be conserved in the face of those homogenizing forces that threaten to erode and dissolve them? 'Modernism decreed that architecture would signify the uniform utopian life of the new age', David Kolb argues, 'and it continued industrial society's march toward rationalised homogeneity'. This, he continues, gave rise to the tendency to pit modernity against tradition: 'We imagine the past as filled with intensely local places each with its own unique character: European villages, regional American small towns'.[81] The relationship between universal and particular is resolved by splitting them apart, and then projecting them onto successive historical periods. The disavowal of modernist universalism is then about regaining the pre-modern 'authenticity' of particularism and localism.

If such a fugitive strategy of response to urban crisis is comprehensible, it remains for that inadequate. If increasing mobility and flow have threatened the integrity of cities, there is no doubt that they are also the basis for new possibilities. The physical migrations of populations have always worked to sustain diversity and difference within the urban system. And the flows associated with new communications technologies have both allowed individual to 'escape' informationally from place-defined groups and permitted outsiders to 'invade' many groups' territories without ever entering them.[82] Within the territory of the city this has brought about the possibility of new encounters and new kinds of encounter. It may be that the whole relationship between movement and settlement is being transformed, and that this is creating new possibilities for urban life and urbanity. Doreen Massey emphasizes the potential for developing 'a global sense of place'. In a world where it is increasingly difficult to 'distinguish between an inside and an outside', perhaps we should try to look at cities now as meeting places: 'Instead, then, of thinking of places as areas with boundaries around, they can be imagined as articulated movements in networks of social relations and understandings'.[83]

It may be that the city no longer has a 'surrounding', that it can no longer define itself in relation to a 'somewhere else'. This is because that 'somewhere else' has now installed itself *within* the city. We can then speak, not of cities in the world, but rather of a world – a world of difference – within the city. And this means that the relation between universal and particular must be fundamentally reassessed. For the urban postmodernism we have been discussing, the totalizing dynamic of modernization has dissolved the particularity of pre-modern societies and cities. For them, urban regeneration is then about recovering the local and sustaining a place-rooted sense of continuity and identity. In this sense, however, universal and particular are never in conflict, and should be seen as accomplices of each other. As Naoki Sakai argues, 'they need each other and have to seek to form a symmetrical, mutually supporting relationship by every means in order to avoid a dialogic encounter which would necessarily jeopardise their reputedly secure and harmonised monologic worlds'.[84]

The universalizing forces of modernity have, indeed, been associated with processes of homogenization and have, indeed, undermined this locally-based particularism. This we cannot doubt. However, new kinds of particularism are now being created. These are particularisms which question universal values as they have been defined and imposed. That is to say, they call into question the idea of values which claim to transcend particularities, and they point to the particularity of all values. The logic of globalization has brought together diverse cultures, in new and multiple combinations, within urban spaces. New cultural configurations are more mobile and fluid in their attachments, more contingent in their relation to territories. Modernist universalism has compressed multi-cultural particularities within the metropolis.

Encounters are now more immediate:

> Uprooted juxtaposition is how people live: not only displaced peasants cast into the megalopolis, where decontextualised images proliferate, but also TV viewers confronted with the interruptus of American television as well as financial honchos shifting bits of information and blips of capital around the world at will and high speed.[85]

Such juxtapositions can be disorientating and disconcerting, and they can provoke defensive responses that look to old certainties, securities and familiarities. In the end, however, these new contestations cannot be evaded. 'Aliens appear inside the confines of the life world and refuse to go away', and this throws up a fundamental political and ethical challenge: 'how to live with those who are morally distant yet physically close'?[86] Perhaps this provocation might now force us to consider how cities have always managed and policed their 'aliens'. Perhaps, too, we might realize just how extensive that 'alien' population has been. As Doreen Massey says, 'the "universals" on which so much analysis is based are so often in fact quite particular: not universals at all, but white, male, western, heterosexual, what have you'.[87] The old certainties, securities and familiarities are simply predicated on the fact that some 'aliens' have developed a certain 'invisibility'.

The diverse and different populations of cities must be seen as active political entities constituted through these encounters and confrontations, and urbanity must be a consequence of the bargaining and negotiation this makes necessary. And for this we need 'tougher' notions of public space (rather than consumerist notions). As Marshall Berman argues, 'no doubt there would be all sorts of dissonance and conflict and trouble in this space, but that would be exactly what we would be after. In a genuinely open space, all of a city's loose ends could hang out, all of a city's inner contradictions can express and unfold themselves.'[88]

Complexities, contradictions and difficulties are shaping the transformation of cities. Contemporary developments are frequently disturbing, yet often exciting. The modern city is problematical, yet we do not know what a postmodern city might look like. For the urban postmodernists, the urban *flâneur* is the symbolic figure of the new urban dream.[89] A more meaningful reference point might derive from the sensibility of German Expressionist poetry, which evokes a figure who is caught up in the complexity – the dangers and the excitement – of the city. Unlike the *flâneur*, this figure 'is no longer a passive receiver of impressions. Her and his imagination galvanizes poetic discourse into a compressed collocation of images conveying an underlying sense of tension, menace and conflict.' This figure is not like the *flâneur* who finds refuge in aesthetic contemplation, but is 'inextricably caught up in the urban turmoil he [and she] portrays', bombarded by the city: 'The Expressionist poet is himself [and herself] the prisoner of the city'.[90] Are we not still prisoners of the city?

ACKNOWLEDGEMENTS

I would like to thank Asu Aksoy, James Cornford, Patsy Healey and Doreen Massey for comments and suggestions.

NOTES

[1] R. Moore, 'Open and shut', *New Statesman and Society* (12 October 1990), 27.

[2] R. Sack, 'The consumer's world: place as context', *Annals of the Association of American Geographers*, 78, 4 (1988), 661.

[3] L. Mumford, 'The theory and practice of regionalism', *Sociological Review*, 20, 2 (1928), 133-4.

[4] *ibid.*, 136.

[5] P. Nora, 'Between memory and history: *les lieux de memoire*', *Representations*, 26 (1989), 12.

[6] C. Abel, 'Regional transformations', *Architectural Review*, 180 (1986), 37. See also J. Pallasmaa, 'Tradition and modernity: the feasibility of regional architecture in postmodern society,' *Architectural Review*, 183 (1988).

[7] K. Frampton, 'Place-form and cultural identity', in J. Thackara (ed.), *Design After Modernism* (London: Thames & Hudson, 1988).

[8] J. Carey, *Communication as Culture; Essays on Media and Society* (Boston: Unwin Hyman, 1989), 127.

[9] T. Roszak, *The Cult of Information* (Cambridge: Lutterworth Press, 1986), 146-7.

[10] G. Mulgan, 'A tale of new cities', *Marxism Today* (March 1989), 21.

[11] See, for example, D. Haider, 'Marketing places: the state of the art', *Commentary* (Spring 1989); D. Haider, 'Making marketing choices', *Commentary* (Summer 1989). See also F. Bianchini, 'Alternative cities', *Marxism Today* (June 1991).

[12] Frampton, *op.cit.*, 62.

[13] D. Boorstin, *The Image* (Harmondsworth: Penguin, 1963), 202.

[14] P. Cooke, 'Modernity, postmodernity and the city', *Theory, Culture and Society*, 4, 2-3 (1988), 114-15.

[15] *An Urban Renaissance: The Role of the Arts in Urban Regeneration – The Case for Increased Public and Private Sector Co-operation* (London: Arts Council of Great Britain, 1987), n.p.

[16] *ibid.*

[17] P. Wright, 'Re-enchanting the nation: Prince Charles and architecture,' *Modern Painters*, 2, 3 (1989), 27.

[18] C. Jencks, *The Prince, The Architects and New Wave Monarchy* (London: Academy Editions, 1988).

[19] See M. Rustin, 'Postmodernism and antimodernism in contemporary British architecture', *Assemblage*, 8 (1989).

20 S. Lash, 'Bright lights, big city', *Times Higher Education Supplement* (16 February 1988).

21 See Cooke, 1988, *op.cit.*; Rustin, 1989, *op.cit.*; G. Stoker, 'Creating a local government for a post-Fordist society: the Thatcherite project,' in J. Stewart and G. Stoker (eds), *The Future of Local Government* (London: Macmillan, 1989).

22 J. Montgomery, 'Cities and the art of cultural planning', *Planning Practice and Research*, 5, 3 (Winter 1990), 17-23.

23 F. Bianchini, Urban Renaissance? The Arts and the Urban Regeneration Process in 1980s Britain, working paper no 7, Centre for Urban Studies, University of Liverpool (April 1989); F. Bianchini and H. Schwengel, 'Re-imagining the city', in J. Corner and S. Harvey (eds), *Enterprise and Heritage: Crosscurrents of National Culture* (London: Routledge, 1991).

24 D. Harvey, 'Flexible accumulation through urbanisation: reflections on "postmodernism" in the American city', *Antipode* 19 (1987); D. Harvey, 'From managerialism to entrepreneurialism: the transformation in urban governance in late capitalism', *Geografiska Annaler* 71B (1989a); D. Harvey, *The Condition of Postmodernity* (Oxford: Basil Blackwell, 1989b).

25 Harvey, 1989a, *op.cit.*, 12.

26 Harvey, 1989b, *op.cit.*, 262, 279.

27 D. Ley, 'Modernism, post-modernism and the struggle for place', in J. Agnew and J. Duncan (eds), *The Power of Place* (Boston: Unwin Hyman, 1989), 53.

28 *ibid.*

29 M. Rustin, 'Place and time in socialist theory', *Radical Philosophy*, 47 (1987), 33.

30 Mulgan, 1989, *op.cit.*, 19.

31 Harvey, 1989b, *op.cit.*, 156.

32 Harvey, 1989a, *op.cit.*, 14.

33 M. Featherstone, 'City cultures and postmodern lifestyles', paper presented to the 7th European Leisure and Recreational Association Congress, Cities for the Future (June 1989), 9, 17, 4-5.

34 R. Rogers, 'In praise of the modern', *Marxism Today* (March 1989), 27. See also R. Rogers, *Architecture: A Modern View* (London: Thames & Hudson, 1990), 11-16.

35 M. Castells, *The Informational City* (Oxford: Basil Blackwell, 1989), 225, 228.

36 M. Mayer, 'Local politics: from administration to management', paper presented to the symposium on Regulation, Innovation, and Spatial Development, Cardiff (September 1989), 10-11, 12. See also J. Esser and J. Hirsch, 'The crisis of fordism and the dimension of a (postfordist) regional and urban structure', *International Journal of Urban and Regional Research*, 13, 3 (1989).

37 H. Häussermann and W. Siebel, *Neue Urbanität* (Frankfurt: Suhrkamp, 1987), 227.

38 Z. Bauman, 'From pillars to post', *Marxism Today* (March 1990), 23.

39 Haussermann and Siebel, 1987, *op.cit.*, 7.

40 L. Mumford, *The City is History* (London: Secker & Warburg, 1961), 3-4.

41 M. Walzer, 'Pleasures and costs of urbanity', *Dissent* (Summer 1986).

42 R. Sennett, *The Uses of Disorder: Personal Identity and City Life* (Harmondsworth: Penguin, 1971).

[43] W. Sharpe and L. Wallock, 'From "great town" to "nonplace urban realm"': reading the modern city', in W. Sharpe and L. Wallock (eds), *Visions of the Modern City* (Baltimore: Johns Hopkins University Press, 1987), 28, 15, 26.

[44] J. Birringer, 'Invisible cities/transcultural images', *Performing Arts Journal*, 33/34 (1989), 122.

[45] J. Habermas, 'Modern and postmodern architecture', in J. Forester (ed.), *Critical Theory and Public Life* (Cambridge, Mass: MIT Press, 1985), 326.

[46] C. Calhoun, 'Computer technology, large-scale social integration and the local community', *Urban Affairs Quarterly*, 22, 2 (1986), 341.

[47] D. Mazzoleni, 'The city and the imaginary', *New Formations*, 11 (1990), 100.

[48] R. Fishman, *Urban Utopias in the Twentieth Century* (New York: Basic Books, 1977).

[49] Peter Hall.

[50] Mumford, 1961, *op.cit.*, 5.

[51] C. Schorske, *Fin-de-Siècle Vienna: Politics and Culture* (Cambridge: Cambridge University Press, 1961), 100-1.

[52] See S. Kern, *The Culture of Time and Space, 1880-1918* (London: Weidenfeld & Nicolson, 1983).

[53] K. H. Wolff (ed.), *The Sociology of Georg Simmel* (New York: Free Press, 1950), 419.

[54] T. J. Clark, *The Painting of Modern Life* (London: Thames & Hudson, 1984), 54.

[55] Le Corbusier, *The City of Tomorrow* (London: Architectural Press, 1929), 109.

[56] R. Sennett, *The Fall of Public Man* (Cambridge: Cambridge University Press, 1977).

[57] Castells, 1989, *op.cit.*, 348.

[58] R. Ravlich, 'City limits', *Meanjin*, 47, 3 (1989), 472, 476.

[59] M. Wark, 'On technological time: Virilio's overexposed city', *Arena*, 83 (1988), 84.

[60] Castells, 1989, *op.cit.*, 349.

[61] C. Sitte, *The Art of Building Cities* (New York: Rheinhold Publishing Corporation, 1945 [1889]), 9, 1.

[62] G. Debord, *The Society of the Spectacle* (Detroit: Black & Red, 1977), para. 168. See also P. Fussell, 'The quest for reality', *Guardian* (18 October 1990).

[63] R. Sennett, 'Americans cities: the grid plan and the Protestant ethic', *International Social Science Journal*, 125 (1990), 272. See also R. Sennett, *The Conscience of the Eye: The Design and Social Life of Cities* (New York: Alfred A Knopf, 1990), ch. 2 ('The Neutral City').

[64] *ibid.*, 274.

[65] *ibid.*, 278.

[66] *ibid.*, 272.

[67] P. Emberley, 'Places and stories: the challenge of technology', *Social Research*, 56, 3 (1989), 748, 756.

[68] *ibid.*, 754.

[69] See P. Virilio, *La Machine de Vision* (Paris: Editions Galilée, 1988).

[70] J. Knesl, 'The powers of architecture', *Environment and Planning D:*

Society and Space, 2, 1 (1984), 17.

[71] J. Thackara, 'Seeing is disbelieving', *The Listener* (23 March 1989), 36.

[72] Le Corbusier, 1929, *op.cit.*, 41.

[73] J. Baudrillard, 'The ecstasy of communication', in H. Foster (ed.), *Postmodern Culture* (London: Pluto Press, 1985), 129.

[74] D. Kolb,*Postmodern Sophistications: Philosophy, Architecture and Tradition* (Chicago: University of Chicago Press, 1990), 146.

[75] M. Rustin, 'The politics of post-fordism: or, the trouble with "New Times" ', *New Left Review*, 175 (1989), 64.

[76] N. Smith, 'Of yuppies and housing: gentrification, social restructuring, and the urban dreams', *Environment and Planning D: Society and Space*, 1987), 168.

[77] R. Miller, 'Putting on the glitz: architecture after postmodernism', *Dissent* (Winter 1990), 31.

[78] R. Williams, 'The metropolis and the emergence of modernism', in E. Timms and D. Kelley (eds), *Unreal City: Urban Experience in Modern European Literature and Art* (Manchester: Manchester University Press, 1985), 19.

[79] M. Bonetti, and J-P. Simon, 'Du municipal à l'urbain', *Annales de la Recherche Urbaine*, 34 (1987), 55.

[80] Mazzoleni, 1990, *op.cit.*, 97, 100.

[81] Kolb, 1990, *op.cit.*, 146.

[82] J. Meyrowitz, *No Sense of Place: The Impact of Electronic Media on Social Behaviour* (Oxford: Oxford University Press, 1985), 57.

[83] D. Massey, 'A global sense of place', *Marxism Today* (June 1991), 28. See also D. Massey, 'The political place of locality studies', *Environment and Planning A*, 23, 2 (1991).

[84] N. Sakai, 'Modernity and its critique: the problem of universalism and particularism', *South Atlantic Quarterly*, 87, 3 (Summer 1988), 487.

[85] T. Gitlin, 'Postmodernism – roots and politics', *Dissent* (Winter 1989), 104.

[86] Z. Bauman, 'Effacing the face: on the social management of moral proximity', *Theory, Culture and Society*, 7 (1990), 24-5.

[87] D. Massey, 'Flexible sexism', *Environment and Planning D: Society and Space*, 9 (1991), 53.

[88] M. Berman, 'Take it to the streets: conflict and community in public space', *Dissent* (Summer 1986), 484.

[89] And we should note the impossibility of the female *flâneur*. See J. Wolff, 'The invisible *flâneuse*: women and the literature of modernity', *Theory, Culture and Society*, 2, 3 (1985).

[90] E. Timms, 'Expressionists and Georgians: demonic city and enchanted village', in E. Timms and D. Kelley (eds), *Unreal City: Urban Experience in Modern European Literature and Art* (Manchester: Manchester University Press, 1985), 117, 118.

Milton Friedman's Smile
Travel Culture and the Poetics of a City

Peter D. Osborne

the ineluctability of fictionalising.

(Stephan A. Tyler)

Ladies and Gentlemen, the Describers are not working.

(London Underground announcement)

CITIZEN

Wandering and travelling appear driven by transgression and lack, that is, by fear and desire – fear and desire drawn by the attraction of cities.

In Latin the word *civitas* signifies a community of citizens, the body politic. Its antonym is *peregrinus* meaning alien, foreigner or wanderer. The word can also carry the connotation of vagrant or even fugitive; each outside or opposed to the order of the city.

The wanderings of Cain were ended when the 'sundering of one brotherhood' was redeemed by the founding of another, the first city.[1]

TREMBLING

I massaged my old mother's naked back. It was covered with dozens of tiny veins like so many red and purple worms as fine as thread – her buttocks spread out below the back, her innocent, needing shoulders leaned forwards – childish, waiting for my hands to settle on her. All bitterness melted – 'Oh, that's wonderful', she sighed, as my palms

331

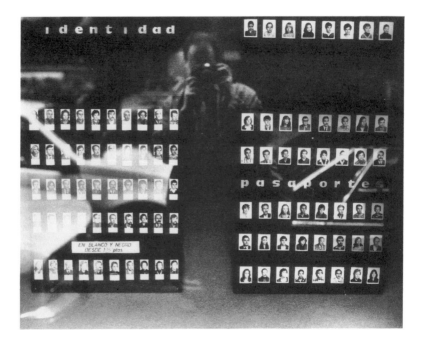

began their sweep across her lonely skin, 'I persuaded your brother to massage me but he's got no love in his hands – you seem to have the knack.'

Somewhere things were in conflict. I felt disturbed by tremblings of love, repulsion, pity – all angled up angrily inside each other but far away in an emotional distance.

The bitterness returned. She spoke of her brother's death, 'the blue-eyed, my first baby'. I felt she was talking about me, about my death, about this journey. And she spoke of the shame, the shame in Catholic families: 'Seán began his drinking after his marriage. Something happened, she turned out to be a dirty bitch. Her corset hadn't been washed for weeks. It almost got up and walked out the door on her wedding night.'

Something else to travel away from, I was thinking, another reason for getting out of earshot – one way or another.

BOGOTÁ IS NO WELTSTADT

Bogotà is no *weltstadt* – many middle-class Bogotanians are haunted by a sense of isolation. They conduct their lives convinced that nobody beyond the nation knows of their existence, that all global sensations are defined and transmitted from elsewhere. They will tell you it's no accident that the great national book is called *One Hundred Years of Solitude*.

Yet it is a modern city with all the necessary cruelties – a rationalist grid of numbered streets laid across a lumpy snooker table of savannah 2,500 m up in the northern Andes. A rim of grey mountains encircles it, looming close along its eastern edges. It has no seasons. Time hangs permanently between autumn and spring. Though it has weather. When it isn't raining the sky above the city fills with a rare bluish sunlight. At dawn its powerful Andean rays burn the upturned faces of sleeping drunks.

But it rains often in Bogotá. Clouds roll in across the plateau. White mist creeps down from the foothills, blinding the highest apartments, brushing through the tallest palms and throwing down brief squalls into the eyes of the crowds. They say it was raining the day the founder, Gonzalo Jiminez de Quesada, brought his party out of the mountains in the 1530s. Reaching the site of today's city he is supposed to have said to his men: 'We'll camp here until it stops raining.'

MALE

Male travellers in mythology and ancient literature were often the displaced persons of ancestral, patriarchal orders pushed to the road for disturbing their repressive and paranoid mysteries. Many were impelled by rumours of identity, passing through the shadows of dream-mothers, lost king-fathers. Some were cursed as bearers of cultural contradiction, as confusers of the categories of knowledge: heretics, matriphiles, bastards, androgynes, homosexuals, the insane, the incestuous.

THE JOURNEY OF 'O'

The journey of Oedipus tells a story about the impossibility of telling a story. It relates a series of detours, of blockings aimed against the wording of the protagonist's own foundation – fruitlessly, as the teller ends by being told.

The telling is feared not primarily because of the terror of incest but because it would reveal that the law and the social order, which claim natural or divine ordination, rest upon a fiction. The fiction which held that human beings and their traditional social hierarchies sprang complete from the soul untouched by the original sins of incest and dynastic murder.

The journey excludes, heroizes then exorcizes the polluter of the city. It becomes tamed – the exterior adventure that confirms the interior order. Yet, like the lessons of the days of carnival, the knowledge the journey has released – that if everything is fiction then everything could be written differently – may not be held forever within that imprisoning cycle of emigration and return.

MILTON FRIEDMAN'S SMILE

On the first day, the aircraft door opened, figures clustered towards the light. A signbearer stood waiting for the London plane –

God bless Father Roper and his remarkable devotion to the Virgin.

A dirty, competitive traffic filled the autopista from the airport, fighting for space. There were squads of old Dodge buses crammed with faces and salsa music – dusty, beaten Renaults and VWs – brutish trucks spuming soot. The time of Uneven Development turns back on itself. In these foldings moved Buicks of the 1940s with humped backs and the paranoid rear windows and jet-finned Cadillac saloons from the 1950s – as glossy as new film prints.

A sleek Mercedes slid past shooting off light and reflections, passing easily through the crowded lanes more spirit than substance like our poor dreams of wealth. An oily smoke plumed from almost every exhaust pipe and over it all stood a warm sluggish atmosphere hazy with fumes where Milton Friedman's smile seemed to hover.

But this was a sadder economy than those of his imaginings. At every traffic light and junction women and boys in cheap clothes pushed cigarettes and flowers through the window and small children ran dirty rags over the windscreen demanding payment with the tenacity of the poor.

HAPPINESS

Happy are those ages when the starry sky is the map of all possible paths.[2]

It is said that in traditional society the self was entirely at home in the world. This unity began to fail during the Renaissance. In *The Order of Things* Michel Foucault describes Don Quixote as wandering in the emptiness left between written words and the world of things which had 'dissolved their former alliance', an alliance to which the Don remained heroically loyal.

> His adventures will be a deciphering of the world: a diligent search over the entire surface of the earth for the forms that will prove that what the books say is true.... Don Quixote reads the world in order to prove his books.[3]

Don Quixote's scenes along the road are allegorical. He rides for the symbol against the arbitrary sign across a landscape of analogies in the same way that contemporary Quixotes travel out from the disenchanted secular worlds to discover cultures where they believe the sacred unity of thing and thought still persists in the spaces beyond the hotels and the leisure complexes.

A MARGINAL ZONE

The autopista ran between worn-out fields fenced with barbed wire. Business had planted huge billboards in them carrying an imagery in primary colours: the head of a gigantic supine blond – some muscular white surfers – a luxury hotel floating outside history – a man in evening dress forever motoring-home-at-dawn. A few cattle and an occasional horse tugged at the grass among half-built apartment blocks. It was a marginal zone of unclear ownership, neither country nor city. The sort of place where circuses pitch their tents and bodies are dumped.

FICTITIOUS

A remarkable event occurs when Don Quixote is diverted into Barcelona to investigate the goings-on in a printer's shop. There he discovers that he himself is being written, constructed out of words, manufactured. The city is shown as the conscious producer of fictions, a sceptical place, but also as one where it may be possible to reinvent the self. Carlos Fuentes believes this incident dramatizes one of the essential themes of western modernity: 'That the world is not consonant with the way we read or speak of it'.[4]

Don Quixote had been dragged from the old road of imaginary feudalism onto the urban highway of modern self-consciousness. But he decides to live up to the fiction that he is, to dissolve himself into his own representations. The medieval hero, adrift in the bourgeois world, thus becomes the lunatic, 'alienated in analogy'.[5]

> *Some were thought so strange by the Spanish that they believed that god had created them to serve the devil. For them the Indians were death – because they couldn't recognise themselves in them – it was as if they had come to the end of themselves and that's like death, when we lose who we are. They hated the Indians for that, for being like their deaths. When they killed the Indians perhaps they were killing their own deaths.*
>
> *And I think they hated the Indians because they did not suffer from Original Sin. They cut off their ears for that – La Envidia!*
>
> *For the Spanish, any of the Europeans I guess, coming here was like suddenly arriving in a world where the mirrors no longer worked. All of nature was strange. Nothing reflected them, especially not in the jungle. There was no familiar nature there. There was no echo of their human nature. Nothing cared. They had come to the end of themselves. And – they had to abolish everything that abolished them. Crazy!*

AND

And immersed in the Third World city, stripped off the carapace of imperialist certainties, contemporary western travellers feel their own otherness, grow conscious of their psychologies as being merely conventions peculiar to their own traditions. They learn that they too are fictions.

A MAN IN UNIFORM

In the centre of a field a man in uniform stood in a sentry box cradling a machine gun. I couldn't tell what he was guarding. My driver pointed to the other side of the road where a cluster of white modern apartments rose above some exquisite shops. She pointed back to the other side beyond the guard towards a large group of breezeblock shelters sprouting TV aerials and tattooed with political and pop graffiti. It was a poor *barrio*, the other face of a class relationship mediated by the armed man. As an image it had a harsh, free-market clarity to it.

ROAMANTICISM (*SIC*)

Like advertising and tourism, like so much else in European culture, modern travel descends most directly from Romanticism. After all it invented the secular pilgrimage, the uncommercial journey. It originated the essential objects of Travel: sublime and picturesque nature, exotic cultures and the sites and springs of truth and beauty.

Romanticism regarded itself as born into a world that had been paralysed. The Enlightenment had desacralized nature. The bourgeoisie were filling it with 'the miserable details of commerce' and Science was content to decode the starlight of dead suns. From out of its cultural unconscious, where the apocalyptic structure of Old Testament journeys jostled with the redemptive allegories of Bunyan, English Romanticism produced the archetype of the journey to image the escape from the overknown world* back into wild unconsciousness and authenticity. Romantic travel as ecstatic – *ex-stasis* – 'Roam-antic.'

SMEARED

Further on some ragged youths were gathered on a rubbish dump among dry eucalyptus trees. Streamers of litter hung from the branches above them. The place resembled the site of a plane crash. Everybody will tell you of the thieves in Bogotá, of places where gangs roam smeared by social misery and as merciless and impersonal as insects.

TODAY ONLY HIPPIES

Today only hippies and others marooned out of their time fancy themselves on those pre-industrial journeys. The multinational world is zoned for the market and the military classes. Its space is electronic, informational, spectacular. The round Renaissance planet is once again flat and nothing really moves – things are merely transmitted.

Yet there *are* outlaws and drifters on the electronic highways. The computer hackers – addicted to the labyrinth – or the makers of fiction as they call up more algorithms to construct another Odysseus, another Penelope – their endocrinal systems drinking in the green

---

* and even the noticing beasts are aware
    that we don't feel securely at home
      in this interpreted world.   (Rilke, First Duino Elegy)

computer light that masks their faces – the x-rays that are turning them all back into blind Homers reeling home, but by the longest and most fascinating roads – white grapes filling their eyesockets.

For the rest, travel is governed by arrangements for being seen under the gossipy eyes of the satellites. Everything in modern travel is known in advance, already storyboarded. To travel was once to reinvent oneself. To imagine oneself as Elsewhere was once to imagine oneself as Other. But now travellers are consumed conspicuously by what has already been consumed. In televised, commodified space there is pleonasm not heroism.

Besides, the metaphysics of Romantic travel had already been ruined as consumerism replaced the transforming vision with conservative daydream. Travel became one form of the forever-deferred Second Life, materialized as a living image by the tourism business. In Franco Moretti's words:

> Daydreams – even the most subversive ones – really have no interest in changing the world because their essence lies in running parallel to it, and since the world is merely an 'occasion' for their deployment, if may as well remain as it is.[6]

EVENTUALLY

Eventually we slipped away from the sound of traffic into a suburb of white and pink Hispanic-modernist villas set in abstract lawns. In the gardens security men moved silently among the fuchsias. The air was warm and smelled faintly of petrol fumes and flowers.

SPIRIT

Kierkegaard once ridiculed the grandness and abstraction of Hegel's system of mind and history by saying that it was as much use in clarifying lived experience as a map of the cosmos would be for finding one's way around Copenhagen. Possession of the metaphysical co-ordinates may not guide us across a city but a city map can be something more than a merely pragmatic index. Certain traditional cities were living diagrams of the cosmos in which the dispositions of the soul could be traced. Equally, within the apparent heterogeneity of the contemporary metropolis, lies the determining topography of the contemporary spirit.

CENTRE

I sat in the Plaza Bolivar, a grand square under a high, clear Andean sky. It is edged by churches, the law courts, government buildings and houses associated with Simon Bolivar and the Independence movement. I suppose it's the centre of the republic, a heart built of steak and emeralds and salt and gold and textiles and oil and cocaine. Most provincial capitals in Colombia will have a space which duplicates this one. Each is a dreaming of the national capital, all towns are elements in a dreaming of national unity and, before Independence, the whole empire was a dreaming of Spain, the Plaza Major in Madrid, the King and, of course, God. This was not uncommon in a Latin America haunted by interior and exterior distance and marked by the terror of social disintegration. For example, some provincial churches in Mexico are exact facsimiles of those in Mexico City. They are thus merely the subordinate clauses of a national sentence. Of course it's an Hispanic text but, as so often in Latin America, pre-Colombian mentalities are stirring within the European.

A few old people sat around watching clouds building up behind the twin towers of the cathedral. One old man scrutinized me for a while then spoke: 'Splendid plaza eh caballero? – the government over here, the lawyers on the other side, the Archbishop's place there, Bolivar's woman in her little house just here and the Holy Church opposite us. Splendid eh? And in the middle of all this, a great big wonderful empty space. 'That's for us "mano" ', he laughed, 'to get lost in!'

HOME

People in Bogotá don't have addresses, they live at map references. There are few street names, almost all numbers. From north to south run the Carreras rising from 1 to beyond 130. Crossing them from east to west are the Calles which are counted from the centre rising outwards in both directions with the southern numbers distinguished from their northern equivalents by the addition of the letter S. For example, a house reference might be Calle 105, 29-63. This means that the house stands on Calle 105 about 63 m from the intersection with Carrera 29, on the odd numbers side of the street – I think. It is a System, a Method – and it works. With a reference you can know precisely which part of the city the house will be at.

It reminds me of French notebooks with gridded pages and I imagine it descends from the same Enlightenment transported through the metrical visions of South American republicans and modernists resolved to invent the nation out of their heads, to impose the Idea onto the awesome nature and convulsive history that surrounded their beleaguered circle of Reason. In naming streets after saints, or battles, after half-forgotten politicians or other cities, the possibility of exhausting the supply of names is at least raised by the reliance on the limited world of events or persons or places. It is a humanist project. But number is infinite, transcendent. As the number One implies the number One Hundred and One or One Thousand and One so Calle 1 implies the appearance, one day, of Calle 101, or 1,001 or even 100,001. The system is programmed with the Idea of Progress. Development without end is assumed as mathematical necessity. And to lose one's way in Bogotá can be to misunderstand a whole system and a whole philosophy.

IMAGINARY

Yet cities also rise out of chance and coincidence. Idealist and authoritarian geometries are countered by the indeterminacy of the Colombian streets – by their energy and violence, by the refractions of popular belief. Like many Latin American cities Bogotá is, to borrow Adorno's phrase, a crossroads of magic and positivism. Among the average clerks who dream of fame and commodities, there are Shamans who pursue mental jaguars through spirit jungles. From among the faces of the bureaucratic crowd eyes look out from other, older worlds, still turning within the official order. Priests cast holy water over sick car engines and bury holy medallions in the foundations of new banking towers. A computer programmer mutters into a glass coffin where an agonized plaster Christ gasps for air. The marxists debate the existence of Evil. People pray to the patron saint of Television. Some believe that AIDS is spread by American soap operas – some that oil companies are organized armies of vampires. In the sky jets cross the flightpaths of spirits. More than once a South American pilot has saved his aircraft by shifting onto one of these ancient routes.

IN THE MODERN SHADOWS

In the modern shadows of the museum there was a deity with both cunt and prick about to copulate with itself. They keep the lights dimmed. They have statuettes of the mentally disturbed, the physically deformed, the imbecilic. There are skeletons in log coffins. Everything here comes from before the Conquest. Many of the forms bear the characteristics of reptiles, the features of birds. They rise out of a very different darkness from mine.

UNEQUALLY

Bogotá is layered by a racial and class geology. As you wander south the human landscape changes: in the rich northern suburbs light-skinned, even blond *mestizos* and Europeans are in the ascendency – all classes hustle unequally through the centre – and in the southern *barriadas* you see olive-green Romany faces and the short, Asiatic-featured people of ancient America. Beyond lie the *barrios de invasion*, vast peripheral *ad hoc* cities of tin and breezeblock, where the incoming waves of people from the country end up. Their mysterious and uncensused inhabitants are much feared by the rich. At night their lights burn on the hillsides like the campfires of a besieging army.

TWO MEN WERE FIGHTING

Two men were fighting near the National Museum – Cain and Abel watched by a lunchtime crowd. The eyes of one were full of acid. The other slid insults through a dirty mouth. Yet there was something missing. These bad brothers were merely automatic. The fight was a ritual without faith or passion – a necessary routine long emptied of interest. Even as they changed gear and the punching broke out, as a tooth cracked and petals of blood began to flutter from one man's nose, their movements continued to express a listless fatalism. After a few minutes a friend of one of the fighters sauntered up with a pickaxe handle and, like a mechanic passing a spanner, handed it to his pal. In seconds he clubbed his opponent to the ground.

'YOU ARE NOTHING!'

It's the traffic you recall most of Bogotá. And it's the wandering packs of buses that most embody something essential in its reality. In San Augustín, in southern Colombia, numbers of large stone heads have been found set into the ground. They are very old. Their creators are long vanished. The squat megalithic faces have wide, fanged mouths and eye sockets empty of detail yet filled with a ferocious, unseeing consciousness. Here is a very simple psychology, an unswervable, unquestioning, negating will which is saying: '*I am invincible – you are Nothing!*' The souls of these entities live on in the buses of the capital. Many are old Fords or Dodges whose lifetimes have been extended through an eternity of reservicings and organ transplants, like street dogs who've come through numberless fights. When they bear down on you, blaring their horns, belching carbon, their resemblance to the statues is complete: the same brutal, hunched bodies – the same provisional intellect – the same peremptory message: '*I am invincible – you are Nothing!*'

THE NINETEENTH CENTURY INDUCED

The nineteenth century induced the hallucinogenic spreading of cities governed by commercial or administrative necessity and embodied in functional architectures whose symbolism was tenative or arbitrary. Much of urban space was henceforth instrumental, pragmatic, speculative. This was the disenchanted city or, as the semiologists put it, the 'de-semanticized' urban space.[7] The age of Positivism and Realism brought forth cities which played mute, the degree-zero of planning and design.

Of course, whole reaches of the city were already silent, entirely mysterious. In the rookeries and slums the ruling order faced its Other, an anti-matter which refused to reflect back its features and, instead, haunted it with the possibility of its own disappearance.

PROGRESS – MELANCHOLY – FAILURE – FEAR OF THE POOR

Today, like amulets worn against this nothingness, the guides and postcards pronounce Bogotá a bright capital of Hispanic tradition and progressive middle-class modernity. Architecture is mobilized to establish this vision: the colonial mansions filled with flowers – the white sky-lining abstractions of American hotels and corporate centres – the exclusive housing projects with their satellite dishes like tethered moons and contented people at Sunday barbecues.

Made from a brightness that flattens everything, these images are disavowals. They deny, for example, the city's melancholy: the cheap grey office boxes and the tired light they exude – the underpaid men and women they contain, who wait for marriage, or for the end of marriage – the late-afternoon streets which fill with pools of cold shadow – the fatalism of the drunks.

They deny the residues of failure and isolation. In some neighbourhoods you can still see the nineteenth-century villas and guess at the insecure respectability which preceded today's exhausted rooves and scabby exteriors and the poor, massed streets with the bleak and driven life that goes on beneath the surface bustle. Some of these quarters press right up against the indifferent bourgeois-classical rears of the most important government buildings.

And they deny the poor. Before the Second World War the population stood at around half a million. Photographs of the time seem to picture the provincial silences and empty squares of a town without appointments. Now the population is bursting through 5 million and it can barely contain its implosive energies.

Riots wasted most of downtown Bogotá in the 1940s. A popular leftist mayor was assassinated. There followed a night of burning which left the centre a ruin full of wandering drunks. The young Fidel Castro was in town. He wondered why the crowds never took the radio stations.

So began the civil war they call *La Violencia*. In a way it has never really ended.

THIS STORY IS TOLD

A new and expensive Mercedes is parked outside a theatre where the rich owner is enjoying a play. A poor street kid walks up to the car and with close concentration begins to drag a coin along its side making a long, deep scar in the paintwork. At this point the owner leaves the theatre.

'You little son-of-a-whore', he shouts, 'what the fuck do you think you're doing!?'

The kid pulls himself up, looks the man in the face and replies: 'What I do with my own money, senor, is my own business.'

CHILD

A beggar woman thrust her small girl at me. Her eyes were liquid, they seemed to suck everything into them. I gave the woman some money.

A man along the street shouted: 'Why don't you buy the kid and take it home with you!?' his mates laughed. It felt bitter.

POTATOES AND MAIDS

There are jokes about the poor and powerless. Here's one: Q. 'What do potatoes and maids have in common?' A. 'Both are grown in Boyacá and eaten in Bogotá.' (Eaten can mean 'fucked/consumed'; Boyacá is a country region close to the city and long a source of cheap labour.)

POETRY

Often you will come across a nest of small boys asleep on the pavement beneath a cardboard duvet. These will be the Gamines – Bogotá's pale, sooty spawn, i.e. most are unwanted runaways, beaten, unacknowledged, unaffordable, lost, used or casually forgotten. On all the streets poor boys *and* girls sell gum and cigarettes and shoelaces. They beg, or shine shoes. Some pick pockets or sell the crudest form of cocaine, basuco. Others drag little wooden trolley behind them in which they transport dusty bottles, wire, piles of sad shoes, spent car batteries, exhausted typewriters – anything. I guess they sell the stuff to junk merchants. They carry other things. I once saw a kid hauling a statue of the fat Buddha with a porcelain smile and wrapped in folds of albescent porcelain flesh, floating through Bogotá like a mandarin in a rickshaw.

The Gamines decorate their trolleys with all the beautiful flotsam the city washes up: plastic flowers, pieces of wallpaper, playing cards from the Spanish deck, fragments from comic strips, portraits of footballers and other cheap saints. Bruce Lee and John Travolta, eternally in flared trousers, retain a faded currency – icons, in turn, of the Asiatic and the latin underclass on its feet – one fighting, the other dancing. Often the kids use more conventionally holy pictures in sharp acidic colours – the Virgin, or gentle Jesus or José Gregorio, a dead Venezuelan healer, still the object of popular devotion. Along the prow of their trolleys some install a family of small dolls' heads.

Verse grows from rubbish and this is an unconscious and forgiving poetry of objects. From forgetfulness they rescue the abandoned thing, the used up, orphaned thing – and return it to life.

MILTON FRIEDMAN'S SMILE

THE KINGDOM OF THE STREET

The crowd opened for him – he had that kind of presence – or menace: the short but powerful mesomorphic body – the rigid back, like that of a soldier – and the walk that expressed a self-assurance you sensed had been bought with violence.

This man was about 50 with a wide, indigenous face that recalled the high-boned features of a Plains Indian seen in the pages of the *National Geographic*; predatory calm – the expression of absolute remoteness. He wore a doublebreasted light-blue suit ola-fashioned. His skin was a bright orange tan and his black hair was shorn – almost to the crown.

Three young men flanked him protectively – a leather jacket, two modern dark suits. They didn't speak. All moved slowly, with proprietorial ease. People watched them. They knew who these men were – or what they were.

As he passed, the man turned his head towards me for a moment. His black eyes registered something poised between indifference and derision. Then, to my surprise, he smiled – and turned away. One of his escorts recorded me with a professional glance. And the crowd closed over their backs.

MICKEY MOUSE

The bus passed the American embassy, a heavy complex shrouded by trees and encircled by metal, like a huge strongbox. Under the eagle lines of supplicants were threading from the doors of the visa section. Lugubriously the man next to me nodded towards them: 'If necessary they'll tell the gringos they're related to Mickey Mouse.'

GOLD MUSEUM

The Indians said that the Spanish 'only smiled on gold'. One can understand why. Although this was a spiritual economy deliriously misunderstood by them, they knew that what they saw were the magical agents of their social transformation. A pig farmer from Andalucía was transformed into an American prince by simply looking on gold.

For the Indian, though, it represented nothing and everything but itself. Gold was sunlight and sunlight was spirit and the essence of God.

Space and Place: Theories of Identity and Location

The Conquest dragged spirit and matter apart, killing the unique and sacred things of gold, turning them into signs of exchange, tokens of something else. Yet, even as they liquidated these cultures some say the Spanish were becoming bewitched by a belief that gold was in itself magical; that even unused, hoarded treasure radiated wealth from its core. They were not mistaken. But the radiation brought on a sleeping sickness that withered the life of the Spanish economy and brought about its paralysis. As they submitted, the Indians had laid a curse on their oppressors.

The curse did not touch the icy capitalists of London and Amsterdam proceeding, undisturbed, with their bookkeeping – counting the empire of Spain down to zero.

TAIL OF STRAW

Near the railway station – bodies pressed closer – faces magnified towards me. An old laughing face at my right shoulder. I turned. In his hand a white handkerchief fluttering like a dove. Behind, somebody making bird whistles. Then came a light slap on my left arm. I turned again. A gentle push from behind and all of a sudden I knew – invaded, lightened, naked – the discovery of the empty pocket like a small death – robbed.

The old face smiling back at me as it sank into the crowd. The essential membrane between self and world gone. A giddiness. I swore in English: 'Fuck the lot of you!' A youth dragged a finger across his throat. I decided to return to the less desperate streets and hide among the museums and churches. As they say in Colombia: '*El que tiene rabo de paja al la candela no se acerca.*' ('Whoever has a tail of straw shouldn't walk near fire.')

STRANGER

Strangers like me are dunces with pointed heads condemned to stare into blind corners, incapable of tracking the codes which coil back through cities like spoor trails and circuits. They are the bad scouts in stories filled with the fear of gypsies who miss the patrins in the wood, the infants who get themselves lost.

People bare their souls to strangers. They feature them in their pornographies. They look through them, threaten them. Strangers are blamed for obscure wrongs in history.

Strangers are prone to infection, to fragility, to loneliness, given to panic and nostalgia.

Yet they are like illiterates enchanted by neon signs, freed by their innocence to see sacred events – involuntarily magicians who release things from their prison of instrumentality – pilgrims abandoned by God – detectives struck by amnesia.

CENTRELESS

The city consumes itself, history is dragging it northwards – and Bogotá grows centreless. The rich and the middle classes have abandoned the density of the old sectors to the crowds, have forsaken the old civic spaces for their northern white *barrios* among the gardens and the private police and the mythical orders of satellite television and the shopping mall, as far from the poor and as close to Florida as possible.

For my friend Don Augusto, a man in his early sixties who speaks a great deal in the imperfect tense, the process is an irrational affair, a curse on civilized living which has abolished those clear spaces in which he once strolled and conversed with masculine equals. He lives today's city as a blindness, a sector of misrecognition. The Tango-loving republican crowns of his youth have been replaced by the massed strangers glimpsed through the car windscreen, known through the crime statistics scanned in the press.

'They have lost the skill for city living', says Don Augusto, 'they treat Bogotá like a rented room.'

AND THE MIDDLE CLASSES

And the middle classes of Bogotá lead besieged and highly speculative lives which are devoted, at their core, to the getting of US dollars. Any deal will do – from the most prudent money exchange with a tourist up to trawling in the backwash of the cocaine business. Even bohemians who lack talent dream of release through magical solutions – a successful telenovella, a fast-food franchise, a launderette in a working-blass *barrio*, importing bullet-proof automobiles – whatever.

Any surplus dollars are transferred to the USA along unofficial capillaries. A friend insists I must have dreamed this, but I seem to recall ads offering to create in Miami a replica of your Bogotánian house, detail by detail, interior and exterior. So that if the economy should finally buckle and collapse or the three guerilla armies should one day probe the outskirts of the capital, the client can pass through the mirror and join the torturers and the failed mercenaries in an instant simulacrum of the Colombian home – in Florida.

BARRIO DE INVASION – 'YOUR TRAVEL WRITING'

Evening was coming on as we rose out of the centre. 'Something for your education', Roberto smiled.

In Bogotá they call these places *barrios de invasion*. They're created by people taking over land and throwing up shelters, forming the great ragamuffin cities. These are the houses that Jack built, the shoes in which the Old Women With Too Many Children live. Their instant architectures are the familiar bricolage of the poor, constructed from bits of wood or breezeblock and roofed over with corrugated iron. If there's electricity, a haze of TV aerials will soon appear above the rooves.

Without foundations they are prey to mudslides and tremors. Occasionally a house will mysteriously collapse – burying a whole family. This may be brought on by the slightest cause, such as the passing of a truck, or the trembling of the planet as it turns in space.

Militants of the M-19 Guerrilla group were said to be organizing in the *barrios*. According to the press one of their commandantes was an 'ex-teacher of the History of Culture'.

There was the smell of cooking and a road with a broken back. It passed through the heart of the *barrio*. Dirt lanes of dogs and hens branched off deep into the secret order of the place. One or two street lights glimmered weakly against the rising darkness attracting smoke and a few mosquitoes. We overtook men and women hauling themselves up through the violet light from the bus stops with that end-of-the-shift weariness. An old woman in a trilby was driving a small black pig before her.

A huddle of men opened up as we passed. Among them bottles stood on a box. One of the men rose drunkenly and, holding up a playing card, called out to us with a smile – 'Here, one of the pleasures of America!' – then sent it spinning into the flank of the car. I couldn't see which it was – Death, Work, Love or Riches?

A wall slogan announced – *Jesus Christ the Hope of the World!* Another – *Invasion 85*.

A large squad of conscripts appeared – their heads cropped. Heavy semi-automatics swung from their shoulders. Some were carrying enormous bullseye cards high upon long poles like the standards of a Roman legion. I raised my camera, but Maria stopped me. 'Never take pictures of the military', she warned, 'it is very dangerous.'

In a few minutes we were in the foothills at the top of the *barrio*. We stopped and looked back. Where there was no electric light the shelters formed eccentric shapes against the vast diagram of Bogotá's official lights down on the plain. People in the *barrio* called out to each other, moved around, sat by their doors. Dogs barked and the usual urgencies blared from a hundred televisions. Quite near us the door of a wooden shelter opened and a tongue of light leapt out onto the ground. A young woman appeared with a bowl in her hand. She noticed us immediately and paused. For a few moments she watched us watching her then turned and tossed a rag of dirty water out of the bowl and down the hillside. She remained in the doorway looking at us. Maria started the engine and we descended, passing the woman, the rear lights of our car fading from her life.

'Something for your travel writings', said Maria. I couldn't see the expression on her face.

> *Ya llego la calavera / de su viaje extraordinario.*
> *(See now the skeleton has returned / from his amazing journey.)*
> (Mexican popular verse)

Maria said to me: 'You know that when you get buried here they put you in a wall for a few years. A tomb in a wall. Then they take you out when you're nice and dry and clean you up. Then they break you up so you can be folded into a neat, little parcel. And they put you back in the tomb.'

'It looks like an oven', said Roberto.

'Yes', Maria continued, 'So they put you back in the oven. Once, when I was only about 7, my family took me to the cemetery to pray at the tomb of my Uncle Paulo. As we were kneeling there saying our prayers I could see out of the corner of my eye some people breaking up a body in this way. I think I could hear the cracking of the bones. I don't think that the body had been left for long enough. I don't think it was very dry. I was terrified. Me, a small girl with my hands over my eyes saying Hail Mary's and staring out at this dreadful operation going on just a few metres away. And the sounds they made, Mother of God!'

HAGAZUSSA

Richardo Hagazussa was obsessed. He was young, rich and handsome but a loner and forever on edge as though tantalized by some obscure addiction.

He was a fan of European high fashion, favouring the aristo-fascist look of the type found in Helmut Newton's photographs. There were rumours of odd sexual practices with immobile fashion models.

But his true obsession was Tango. At the age of 22 he'd become caught on a carousel of repeating visits to the sites of old Tango clubs and dance halls and, of course, to the tomb of Gardel, the master, killed in a Colombian aircrash in 1935. He was a sedulous collector of anything associated with Tango – from sheet music and gramophone records to the taylor's accounts of Tango dancers.

In one scene Hagazussa interviewed an old man who'd been a renowned dancer in prewar Buenos Aires. The old man told him something curious – that most of the male Tango dancers in the 1930s had used the same lotion to give their hair 'the dangerous blackness of moon-reflecting harbour water'.

What interested Hagazussa even more was the old man's almost casual revelation that the hair lotion had displayed powerful preservative qualities and how he imagined that all that was guaranteed to remain of the long dead dancers, whose souls were most certainly roasting in hell right down there under the Plaza de Mayo, were their hairstyles, preserved intact by the mummifying lotion. So many had died, you might say, at work, with hair and dancing shoes shining. Some had been stabbed in ridiculous disputes, others brought down in the crossfire between the police and their enemies. Several had been taken off when their hearts had collapsed in brothels or burst under the rush of blended stimulants.

Finally the old man supplied him with priceless information – the locations of the graves of several important dancers.

Hagazussa strangled him, leaving his body hanging from a window grill. Momentarily the camera abandoned the hero and moved in gently on the unconscious feet performing the steps of a Tango for the last time on a dance floor of thin hotel air.

Then we floated at Hagazussa's shoulder like ghosts as he hauled up the inelegant remains of the dancers. Especially memorable was his first expedition through the Recoleta cemetery in Buenos Aires, a necropolis drowning in the blue shadows of an American night. With effort he located the vault he was seeking and opened the tomb. The bones were dry. While their owner still lived on in the memory of others they had been cleaned and polished. But that had been decades back. Now they were yellow and scored by worm tracks. Rats had gnawed at them. The shreds of a black suit clung to them like feathers around the bones of a crow. But flopping cleanly from the back of the skull and glistening in the beam of Hagazussa's torch was the hair, or rather the hairstyle. It was longer than it would have been in life, having continued to grow for a time after the burial, but still recognizable: ruthlessly swept back, black and oily, almost living, the imperishable Platonic *Idea* of a Tango dancer's hairstyle. Hagazussa was exultant. His eyes shone in the mad close up. He grabbed the prize and vanished among the monuments like a starving animal that at last has found food.

Hagazussa, now hairdresser to the dead, began to cover the walls of his apartment with the hirsute trophies....

I left the cinema. The movie rolled on without me.

When the bleakness of travel comes over you, any novel, any film will do that offers shelter – a story is a kind of home.

POTHOS

The Romantic movement also invented a certain kind of traveller. He was (and remains) a wandering male figure, bound on a road of endless nostalgic desire, a force named as Pathos by the Greeks. Driven by loss and journeying towards what cannot be recovered, his way was filled with the absence of what he sought. For the Romantic traveller the whole world, all space, became a vast homeless home, through which the object was trailed: the love lost or never encountered, the absent child, the longing for sleep or for death, the yearning for the Mother. The Romantic traveller was drawn on helplessly by fantasies and idealizations – fictions which ensured the endlessness of his desire. The journey became, in a sense, the object itself, loved as much for deferring what was as equally feared as desired. As Fassbinder said: 'Nothing so terrifying as a dream come true.'

Pothos arose as an attribute of the great power of Eros. And doesn't everybody travel so as to fall in love? – whether it be with a woman or a man or with a whole people – with their cities, their landscapes, their music, their cooking, their children, their hunger for justice – or even with their hunger. And the traveller hopes and fears that the journey will end 'there' – in Victor Turner's phrase 'at the centre out there',[8] perhaps in a unity with the Other which will destroy Otherness, in an infatuation that will abolish the need for the return and ensure the escape from the traveller's own time and history.

Or perhaps it's death the traveller dreams of, for other conditions were signified by Pothos: the process of Dissolution – it found further emblems in flowers customarily placed on graves – and Intoxication, a condition holding a special and tragic allure for the Pothos-governed – makers of interior Utopias, architects of dream cities. Calvino's city of Zobeide must have been filled with them – a labyrinth of streets out of the memories of 10,000 men who'd all dreamed of the same naked woman running through a city and imagined that by re-creating it they would find her again running through its streets. But the 10,000 dreamers had each dreamed of different streets and the city of Zobeide became a confusion of all their desires into which the woman was decomposed and lost.[9]

POTOSÍ, BOLOVIA

Letter to Henderson: *'Once this place was the centre of the world, now it's more or less forgotten ...'.*

I've been here a month, perhaps longer. There's only the German and myself in the hotel.

A plane ticket awaits me in the capital. If I don't pick it up soon I'll lose 500 dollars. But I hesitate. I hang on. If I wait much longer I'll be caught up in the strikes. Political graffiti is covering everything. The miners will block the roads, the transport workers will hold up petrol supplies and everything will stop moving. Then the military will come ...

Sometimes there's no bread or fresh food in the shops. Sometimes there's just a lack of shampoo. Every so often they refuse to open at all until the latest devaluation is announced and prices can be adjusted. At night it is very cold and very quiet. People say the town is dying. Maybe that's what I'm waiting to see.

GALLERY OF RELIGIOUS ART

St Gertrude is writing in a notebook – in the palm of her free hand lies a red egg which has opened to reveal inside a red heart ... a group of holy people are pointing at the rain – it is full of pink and white roses.

St Augustine is being called from his arrogant preoccupation with the intellect by the eye of God which beams purple light from a floating pyramid ... two men using long-handled pincers are quietly squeezing the mamillae of a naked woman – she has a high, pale forehead – she remains, calm, serene ... St Gregory is writing a letter – in the corner his triple crown leans against the wall – a delicate humming bird has flown into the room – it is hovering by his ear – whispering something to him that is inaudible to the painter.

'You're still looking for noble savages,' says the German.

HER FACE

Occasionally in the evening I walk around the main square where I buy chocolate from a small booth lit by kerosene lamps. The woman there has the most beautiful Indian face. Every night she's there, haloed by her little pool of brightness. They's why I buy the heavy chocolate. So I can see her face. Invariably I give it to one of the children begging by the cathedral.

Other nights I keep to my room, listen to the BBC or pace the floor. The porter with the Japanese look brings me *maté de coca*, tells me it's only the *saroche* – the altitude sickness – that's unsettling me. We're at 14,000 feet here.

The German thinks I resemble an expectant father walking to and fro. 'What is it,' he asks, 'that is going to be born?'

NOTES

[1] M. Gottdiener and A. Ph. Lagopoulos (eds), *The City as Sign* (Columbia: 1986).
[2] Georg Lukács, *The Theory of the Novel* (London: 1971), 29.
[3] Michel Foucault, *The Order of Things* (London: 1974), 47.
[4] Carlos Fuentes, 'Cervantes or the critique of reading', in *Myself with Others* (London: 1988).
[5] Foucault, *Order of Things*, 49.
[6] Franco Moretti, 'The spell of indecision', in Caryl Nelson and Lawrence Grossberg (eds), *Marxism and the Interpretation of Culture* (Chicago: 1988), 343.
[7] Raymond Ledrut in Gottdiener and Lagopoulos, *City as Sign*.
[8] Victor Turner, *Dramas, Fields and Metaphors* (Ithaca, NY: 1974).
[9] Italo Calvino, *Invisible Cities* (London: 1979).

Local guides – the Pombo family and Roberto Franco.

Photographs by the author.

Rimbaud and Spatial History

Kristin Ross

Rimbaud, it appears, was a topic of discussion between Bertolt Brecht and Walter Benjamin. In his journals Benjamin relates some of his friend's musings about Rimbaud, the poet with whom Brecht felt the closest connection:

> He thinks that Marx and Engels, had they read *Le Bateau ivre*, would have sensed in it the great historical movement of which it is the expression. They would have clearly recognized that what it describes is not an eccentric poet going for a walk, but the flight, the escape of a man who cannot live any longer inside the barriers of a class which – with the Crimean War, with the Mexican adventure – was then beginning to open up even the most exotic lands to mercantile interests.[1]

Brecht's phrase, 'an eccentric poet going for a walk', is an efficient way of summing up and dismissing the various mythic interpretations of Rimbaud as '*poète maudit*' or '*enfant terrible*'. Instead Brecht praises *Le Bateau ivre* as a *historical* narrative, and specifically as a lyric poem that encompasses or expresses the moment of the passage from market capitalism into a far-flung and geographic world system – the whole imperialist heyday of the late nineteenth century. Doesn't the audacity of Brecht's perception lie in its strong linking of two pairs of elements that are not frequently brought together in earlier literary criticism or political thought: namely, lyric poetry and politics, and, secondly, history and space? At the same time that Brecht affirms the narrative, diachronic power of Rimbaud's verse, he is concerned with portraying historical development in terms of a massive, synchronic expansion of spatial movement: the late-nineteenth-century European construction of space *as* colonial space. In Brecht's statement, time and space are not where they should be: history has gone spatial, and the lyric – that unique, evanescent, exceptional moment – tells a story.

Rimbaud's later poetry is marked by a distinct proliferation of geographical terms and proper names: poles and climates, countries, continents and cities – a kind of charting of social movement in geographical terms. A fairly neat division might in fact be established, as Fredric Jameson has suggested, between the erotic microgeography and more or less individual thematics of Rimbaud's early work – the kiss that wanders over the woman's body in 'Rêvé pour l'hiver' – and the move to a global, planetary space in the later works.[2] A vast geography of mass displacements, movements of populations, and human emigrations, dominates the later, mostly, but not exclusively, prose works. But it would be wrong to think that in Rimbaud's case, the move to prose coincided with an objective or political theme replacing a personal, subjective one. Rimbaud's geopolitical perceptions are already apparent in some of his earliest verse, in poems like 'Ce qu'on dit au poète à propos de fleurs'.

This long poem has been read as a parody of and manifesto against a certain dominant brand of aestheticism and rhetorical trickery practised by the Parnassian poets. It was these poets – among them Banville (to whom the poem is dedicated or sent), Mallarmé, Catulle Mendès, and Leconte de Lisle, whom Rimbaud, recently arrived in Paris, was attempting both to impress and to repudiate. The problem with Parnassian poets, Rimbaud makes clear early in the poem, is their excessive concern with mimesis – their dependence on the eye:

> De vos forêts et de vos prés,
> O très paisibles photographes!
> La Flore est diverse à peu près
> Comme des bouchons de carafes!

> Toujours les végétaux Français,
> Hargneux, phtisiques, ridicules,
> Où le ventre des chiens bassets
> Navigue en paix, aux crépuscules –

> [In the fields and forests of your verse
> – Oh, you peaceful photographers! –
> The flora is about as diverse
> As bottle corks and stoppers.

Always this French vegetation abounds,
Grouchy, coughing, silly and sick,
Where the bellies of basset hounds
Wallow through the growing dark–][3]

Whether confined to describing the flora of the immediate suburbs of Paris, or 'free' like Leconte de Lisle, satirized in the next section of the poem as a kind of Great White Hunter –

O blanc Chasseur, qui cours sans bas
A travers le Pâtis panique,
Ne peux-tu pas, ne dois-tu pas
Connaître un peu ta botanique?

[O White Hunter, bootless in a
Panicky Pasture, it
Might really help to recall
Your botany a bit.]

– free to travel to exotic lands to conduct a panicky search, like Chateaubriand and a whole lineage of western writers before and after him, for fresh raw materials with which to revitalize his writing, these poets are guilty of a kind of 'landscapism': they describe what they see. Rimbaud is not alone in making this kind of accusation. Future Communard Eugène Vermersch, in whose London apartment Rimbaud and Verlaine would take refuge in 1872, was also quick to link Parnassian exoticism to an élitist artistic posture and its attendant racism. In his *Les Hommes du jour*, a satiric series of brief portraits of the more visible men and women in Parisian society, written some time in the early 1870s, Vermersch adopts a tone similar to Rimbaud's when he addresses Parnassian poet and future anti-Communard, Catulle Mendès:

Too many, far too many asokas, Monsieur Mendès. What could all this mean to us, the Bhandiras, the Gangas, the Vacu, the devas, the Mangou, the Tchandra Star, the Maharchis, the Cudras, the Malicas? Could it be that you are only writing for the dozen or so of your little friends who lean back in their chairs at your gatherings and swoon at the readings of your verse, and for the young Chinese who follows six steps behind you when you deign to show yourself to the people?[4]

The asoka, apparently an Indian tree, figures in the title of Parnassian Louis Menard's 1855 poem; for Vermersch and Rimbaud that obscure plant became a synecdoche for the work produced by what Rimbaud would playfully accuse Verlaine of aspiring to be – a 'bon Parnassian'. The asoka surfaces in later stanzas of 'Ce qui'on dit':

> L'Ode Açoka cadre avec la
> Strophe en fenêtre de lorette;
> Et de lourds papillons d'éclat
> Fientent sur la Pâquerette ...

> Oui, vos bavures de pipeaux
> Font de précieuses glucoses!
> – Tas d'oeufs frits dans de vieux chapeaux,
> Lys, Açokas, Lilas et Roses!

> [The Ode on Asokas is as bad as
> The Stained-Glass-Window stanza;
> And heavy, vivid butterflies
> Are dunging on the Daisy ...

> Yes, the droolings from your flutes
> Make some priceless glucoses!
> – A pile of fried eggs in old hats,
> Those Lilies, Lilacs, Lotuses and Roses!]

Neither Mendès nor Leconte de Lisle would have denied the accusation of 'landscapism'. Giving voice to what was to become the dominant avant-garde stance in the nineteenth century, Leconte de Lisle situates the 'poetic' definitively on the side of the socially irrelevant: 'The first concern of anyone who writes in verse, or in prose for that matter, must be to emphasize the picturesque side of things.'[5] For de Lisle and the Parnassians, the archaic, the exotic, or the suburban picturesque would automatically procure what was needed to compensate for a world become prosaic to the extent of its scientific and technological progress.

Landscapism was not to be confined to a purely aesthetic debate; a veritable *science* of landscapism, the science of objectal space *par excellence*, university geography, takes form during the era of the Parnassians. University geography *begins* in the 1870s; it is then that the subject is first institutionalized as an academic discipline in France. During this decade the enormously influential French school of geography begins to take shape around the figures of Emile Levasseur, the great initiator who showed the necessity of the instruction of geography as a discipline, Ludovic Drapeyron, founder of the *Revue de géographie*, and, most importantly, Vidal de la Blache, later to be canonized, significantly enough, by Lucien Febvre and other leading thinkers associated with the Annales School of Historiography, as the 'Father of French Geography'.[6] The Vidalian model would exert a virtually hegemonic control over geographic studies until the 1950s.

Febvre's embrace of the work of Vidal de la Blache is not surprising. Annales historians in the 1920s and 1930s established a historiography that brought to the forefront elements most often considered geographic or spatial: climate, demography, the immutable rural life associated with time conceptualized as *longue durée*.[7] History tells us that French geography was born in the 1870s, the bastard offspring of history: Levasseur, Drapeyron, and Vidal were all trained initially as historians, and each turned to more geographic pursuits after the French defeat of 1870. Vidal, writing later about his own metamorphosis, attributes the change to an itinerary well travelled and memorialized by the Parnassian poets of the day: he was seduced into geography, he writes, by his frequent voyages in Egypt, Greece, and Asia Minor where he travelled as a young man to explore ancient ruins.

Vidal was to supply classical French geography with both a definition and a method. The definition was concise and enduring: 'Geography is the science of landscape.' Vidalian geography takes its model from the taxonomic dream of the natural sciences and is resolutely turned towards description. The geographer finds himself facing a landscape: the perceptible, visible aspect of space. When Vidal writes what was to become the master text of French geography, he calls it *Tableau de la géographie de la France*, a title that revealed not only the contents of the book – an inventory of the typical landscapes of France – but the situation of its author as well: the geographer as landscape painter.

The method Vidal provided and which was to spread the renown of the French school can be summed up as follows: the geographical description of any country consists of presenting and describing the regions that make it up. Space is divided into regions which exist as distinct 'individualities', 'personalities'; the role of the geographer is to detail a region's physiognomy and show how its traits result from a harmonious and permanent interaction between natural conditions and old historical heritages. It would be many generations before people noticed that Vidal's regions were not natural 'givens': that Britanny, for example, was not a God-given designation.

What are the implications of Vidal's definition and methodology? First, the definition of the object of study as 'landscape' imposes solely visual criteria and makes of the geographer an interpreter of natural conditions. Vidal defines landscape as 'what the eye embraces with a look', or, in another formulation, 'the part of the country that nature offers up to the eye that looks at it'. One could speak at some length about the sexual metaphors operative in these definitions, about 'space become feminine' and 'offering itself up' to the viewer – all this as preparatory to the more blatant 'penetration' metaphors favoured by later geographers/explorers; here, I want rather to point out an ironic undercutting of Vidal's own fetishization of visual criteria. Radical geographers like Béatrice Giblin have convincingly shown that Vidal's landscapes cannot, in fact, *be seen*; his masterful, almost Parnassian literary style masks the fact that he is *not* concerned with precise localized landscapes – the observed landscape – but rather with the *typical* landscape which he constructs from abstract and derivative cliché formulations.[8] It is precisely this kind of synthetic and derivative mobilization of cliché that Rimbaud ridicules in Parnassian poetry:

> Tu ferais succéder, je crains,
> Aux grillons roux les Cantharides,
> L'or des Rios au bleu des Rhins, –
> Bref, aux Norwèges les Florides.

> [I'm afraid you'd follow up
> Russet crickets with Cantharides,
> Blues of Rhine with Rio golds
> – In short, Norways, with Floridas.]

Here the geographical proper name is in the plural – as in, you've got your Floridas, your Norways – and as such trivializes Parnassian practice as a relation to a series of detached, reified elements: Florida is not a place in all of its particularity, but a hodgepodge of exoticist clichés, textual citations, and trumped-up botanical references. By simply changing the bird, the insect, the colour, PRESTO! We're in Norway.

Both Parnassian landscape and Vidalian landscape pose space as a natural referent. Vidalian geography, composed as it is in the late nineteenth century, is striking in its almost total evasion of ongoing historical developments like the industrial revolution or colonialism, famines or the rise of urbanism. Cities figure very little in Vidalian geography. The methodology of regionalism implies instead a geography of permanences: what in the countryside has been in place for a long time. To conceive of space in this way is to occult the social and economic contradictions of which space is the material terrain; the very concept of 'the region' as it is developed by Vidal implies a homogenous, unitary society at one with its natural milieu and united in its collective will to exist. In fact, 'humanized landscapes' are quite rare in nineteenth-century academic geography; if humans appear at all they must do so in such a way as to reinforce the natural harmony of the region: the native, the peasant is *part of* the landscape, in a synecdochal relationship of décor.

Only when the evolution of capitalist society had created a greatly increased demand for scientific geography were specialist geographers sought. Vidalian geography was to play a large role in physically naturalizing the foundations of national ideology. That the privileged and exclusive status of space as a natural referent corresponds to the needs of western colonialism would become more evident in the decades to follow. Western, Christian colonialism demands a certain construction of space that Vidalian, academic geography was to help provide: natural, which is to say, non-historical – and one where all alterity is absent. Another contribution to the construction of space as colonial space was to come from a surprising source: Saussurian linguistics. (Saussure wrote his first major work in the 1870s.) In order to understand how the Saussurian sign refers back to a doubly determined spatial referent – extra-linguistic and above all *natural* – it would perhaps be enough to recall the canonical example by which each of us learned the explanation of the Saussurian sign. 'I say the word "tree" (the acoustical image, the signifier); the concept "tree" comes to your mind (at this point a tree is drawn on the blackboard), but this is not the *real* tree, which is *out there* (extra-linguistic, spatial, and natural).'[9]

Saussure insisted on the marginal role that denotation – the relation of the sign to the referent – played for his definition of the sign. Consequently denotation played a small and very vague role in his linguistics. The dominance of a Saussurian-informed linguistics over

French literary studies during the past thirty years has been the dominance of a linguistics preoccupied with the problem of signification, the relation of signifier to signified, and not that of reference. Saussure and his followers have given us a 'spatiality' of language – but it is a particular kind of spatiality: one that results from rigorously distinguishing signifier from signified and from giving the former the leading role in what is called the 'play' of language. This is then defined as a purely differential system of relations where each element is qualified by the place it occupies in an ensemble, and by the horizontal and vertical relations it entertains with neighbouring elements. We are familiar with this Saussurian spatiality of language – as well as with its inaccessibility to either geometric space or, more importantly, the space of lived experience, everyday life. If we turn back to Rimbaud's poem, I think we will see another kind of spatiality at work. Rimbaud's linguistics is a linguistics more concerned with the problem of reference ('the silk of seas and arctic flowers; (they do not exist)'; 'Barbare'), of denotation, than with signification. Into the midst of Parnassian stage props, Rimbaud suddenly inserts the problem of the referent:

> Là ...! Comme si les Acajous
> Ne servaient, même en nos Guyanes,
> Qu'aux cascades des sapajous,
> Au lourd délire des lianes!

> [Really, as if Mahoganies
> Were only, even in our Guianas,
> Swings for swarms of monkeys
> In dizzy tangles of lianas ...]

Rimbaud's later poetry is, as I mentioned, characterized by a proliferation of geographical names, but his *use* of geography, is for the most part, distinct from and critical of the Orientalist or exoticist appropriation of place-names prevalent in nineteenth-century French literature. In this passage, for instance, instead of Floridas, Norways, we have not just 'Guianas', but *our* Guianas. The possessive plus the proper name indicates an instance of what language philosophers following Russell call 'definite description' – an instance, that is, of denotation, not connotation. This use of definite description is a referential function; a formulation capable of shifting its referent according to time, speaker, use context – in other words, according to history. The possessive here functions as a shifter, indicating the particular sociopolitical reality of its enunciation – thus, a use of geographical place-names in a historical, non-timeless way.

Two things draw our attention in this stanza. First, Rimbaud's explicit thematic argument against the strict Parnassian limits of what constitutes a proper subject for poetry. By arguing and enacting a definition of the poetic that embraces sociopolitical themes and practical, utilitarian concerns, Rimbaud sets himself not only against the Parnassians, but also against what would become the dominant nineteenth- and twentieth-century avant-garde stance, the one best exemplified by Mallarmé's lifelong concern with hygienically rescuing a truly 'poetic' language of evocation from the hegemonic vulgarity of bourgeois utilitarianism and precision. More importantly, though, 'our Guianas' and the many other examples from Rimbaud's poetry of demonstratives, shifters, proper names, and 'definite descriptions', indicate a repeated insertion of the problem of the referent at a time when poetry was single-mindedly announcing its immunity to changes in denotation. Instead of the Mallarméan problematic of signifier and signified – considered, for example, such spatial experiments as Mallarmé's typographical arrangement of words on a page in 'Un Coup de dés' – Rimbaud's concern is with the referent. Thus his affinity with invective and with the slogan, with all language on the verge of passing over into action. (His affinity as well, I might add, with the performative libidinal politics of the situationists. Deleuze and Guattari and others of the May '68 generation.) Dominant methodological or theoretical concerns have always generated a list of 'chosen texts' which best suit their mode of analysis. Literary theory of the last thirty years – from structuralism to deconstruction – is no exception. The canonization of Mallarmé and Saussure at the expense of Rimbaud goes hand in hand with the priority given to epistemology and aesthetics in recent years over social thought, and the celebration of a romantic 'politics' of textuality – that ludic counter-logic of semantic instability which characterizes much of French theory, and especially French theory readily imported in America, today.

Perhaps the best way to crystallize Rimbaud's opposition to the canonical avant-garde is to recall here, in the context of Rimbaud's poem about flowers, Mallarmé's famous remark about the missing flower: 'Je dis: une fleur! et … musicalement se lève, idée même et suave, l'absente de tous bouquets' ['I say: a flower! and … musically there arises, precise and suave idea, the flower absent from all bouquets']. Poetic discourse 'replaces' the referent; the word 'flower' eliminates the flower. Poetic language speaks of things in their absence rather than in their presence. How different, then, is Rimbaud, in this poem – a poem that asks the question: how does one write about flowers in 1870 without writing about the *fleur de lys*, with all its connotations of French state power and hierarchy? Rimbaud's response is succinct: 'Find flowers which are chairs!' How different, too, the next stanza:

> Dis, front blanc que Phébus tanna,
> De combien de dollars se rente
> Pédro Velasquez, Habana ...

> [Tell, pale-faced one tanned by Phoebus,
> How many dollars are made a year
> By Pédro Velasquez, Havana ...]

Rimbaud's use of a somewhat combative imperative is characteristic: not 'I say' (as in 'I say: a flower!') but 'say it'. The imperative is a shifter; it indicates the historical moment and situation of the enunciation, the speaker and the spoken to. 'Pédro Velasquez of Havana' may or may not exist; what counts is the denotative function of the proper names which allows a set of economic, sociopolitical relations to be constructed – denoted, not represented. In Rimbaud the minimal real unity is not the word, the individual concept, but rather the arrangement, the process of arranging or configuring elements. And the arrangement, as in this passage, is never a neutral exchange; here, it is not only the economic differential that is established but the racial one as well, and this by the use of another proper name, the timeless, mythological 'Phoebus': the Parnassian poet, in contrast to 'Pédro Velasquez', is figured synecdochically by his pale skin, tanned by mythology, by the whole stock of western tradition: a textual tan.

Rimbaud's referent is thus neither the purely natural, a-historical one of Saussure; not is it the post-structuralist 'textual', purely constructed referent of our own critical atmosphere. It is a constructed referent, certainly – but one that allows for historical change. Rimbaud peoples his landscapes, but peoples them in such a way that 'Pédro Velasquez' functions neither as accessory nor décor: Rimbaud's comprehension of space allows social relations to prevail: space as social space, not landscape.

366

At this point we must return to our tale of academic geography in order to point out that the institutionalization of 'landscape geography' and the pre-eminence of Vidal de la Blache took place by way of a significant repression of the work of an anarchist geographer writing at the time: Elisée Reclus. Like Rimbaud, Reclus' political imagination, as well as his personal geography, was marked by his active participation in the Paris Commune; because of that participation he was exiled to Switzerland (his fame as a geographer prevented his deportation to New Caledonia) where he produced most of his major works. He participated in the quarrel that led to the scission between Marx and Bakunin in 1872, and defended anarcho-communism in numerous articles that appeared in journals like *Le Révolté* and *La Liberté*. His geographical informants included fellow anarcho-communists like Malatesta and Kropotkin, who supplied him with information on the terrains of Italy and Russia. In his political writings he advocated a Commune-inspired society organized from the base to the top, and addressed the problems of bureaucracy, autogestion, and the liberty of workers' organizations in relation to the party. His constant preoccupation was the problem of the state and its relation to the individual.[10] In 1879 when the French government granted official amnesty to Reclus, he refused to return to France until *all* Communards were granted amnesty as well.

Unlike his contemporaries Vidal, Drapeyron, and Levassier, Reclus' earliest intellectual formation was not in history but rather theology. While Vidal's decision to become a geographer was fuelled by tours of the ancient ruins of Egypt and Greece, for Reclus it was his voyages in America and to Ireland, where he was moved by the devastations caused by the great famine, that solidified both his socialist convictions and his decision to write geography.

The first to have employed the term 'social geography', Reclus opposed the Vidalian definition of geography as the science of landscape with a different one: 'Geography is nothing but history in space.' As such, his analyses take space into account as a differentiated, non-static, changing ensemble: 'Geography is not an immutable thing. It is made, it is remade every day; at each instant, it is modified by men's actions.'[11] For the most part Reclus avoids the empiricist reification of the notion of space that occurs whenever one postulates in any way an autonomous existence of spatial facts, processes, or structures that would constitute the object of a spatial analysis. Space in Reclus' work is considered as a social poduct – or rather, as both producer and produced, determinative and determined – something that cannot be explained without recourse to the study of the functioning of society. Reclus refutes Vidal's definition of geography as 'the science of places and not of people' by his constant preoccupation with analysing relations of power between empires, states, and peoples. His analyses show, for example, with amazing intricacy, the changes provoked by colonization on indigenous populations and the organization of their space, thus anticipating many of the more modern theories of unequal development. He produced, in short, a kind of analysis that would be repressed and would entirely disappear in the ensuing reduction of geography into a narrow and specialized pursuit.

'Ce qu'on dit au poète à propos de fleurs' concludes with a striking metaphor and a piece of advice:

> Voilà! c'est le Siècle d'enfer!
> Et les poteaux télégraphiques
> Vont orner, – lyre aux chants de fer,
> Tes omoplates magnifiques!
>
> Surtout, rime une version
> Sur le mal des pommes de terre!
> – Et, pour la composition
> De Poèmes pleins de mystère
>
> Qu'on doivre lire de Tréguier
> A Paramaribo, rachète
> Des Tomes de Monsieur Figuier,
> – Illustrés! – chez Monsieur Hachette!
>
> [Look! This is the Infernal Age!
> And telegraph poles
> Will adorn – a lyre that sings a song of steel,
> The splendour of your shoulder blades.
>
> Above all, give us a rhymed
> Account of the potato blight!
> – And, to compose Poems
> Full of mystery
>
> – Intended to be read from Tréguier

To Paramaribo, buy
A few volumes by Monsieur Figuier
– Illustrated! – at Hachette's!]

In the first of these stanzas the poet's body has undergone an amazing
transformation: no longer the detached observer, the 'peaceful
photographer' of the opening of the poem, the poet's body is directly
implicated in the change in production and reproduction. His body has
changed. At stake, here, in other words, is not a mere 'thematic' change
– the substituting of economic questions for aesthetic or picturesque
ones. Instead, in this complex corporeal allegory of technology, the
natural and the technological adhere as tightly to one another as they
do in neologisms contemporary to Rimbaud like 'steamhorse' or
'horsepower': developed technology is fused with the natural, living
creature and from that site will emanate another hybrid, vaguely
Whitmanian formation: a song of steel. The human body is permeated
with apparatus-like elements not unlike the way, for example, the
language of telegraphy is used in popular nineteenth-century scientific
texts whenever the nervous system is described.

These popular science texts are advertised in the final stanza – 'buy a
few volumes by Monsieur Figuier – illustrated – at Hachette's'. Louis
Figuier, author of, among other things, *The Marvels of Science*, was the
leading scientific vulgarizer of Rimbaud's time.[12] His *La Terre et les
mers*, constantly re-edited between 1864 and 1884, was perhaps the
most popularly read 'vulgar' geography in France. Figuier was not the
only major figure to publish with Hachette; Hachette produced the
at-that-time very popular atlases and geographical treatises of Elisée
Reclus, atlases which Jules Verne, who also published with Hachette,
consulted when he wrote his novels. Rimbaud was to follow his own
advice a month later and borrow heavily not only from Figuier, but
also from the most libertarian of Verne's novels, *20,000 Leagues Under
the Sea*, and from Poe's *Arthur Gordon Pym*, when he composed '*Le
Bateau ivre*'.

Historians of French colonial policy generally portray the rise of
French interest in colonial expansion as a rather sudden development
of the 1880s. But if we cannot speak of a full-fledged colonial
movement during the 1870s, we can certainly recognize the existence
of a genuine geographical one.[13] Geography, as the anti-colonialist
geographer Jean Dresch puts it, is not born *during* the triumph of the
bourgeoisie; its development is *part and parcel* of that triumph.[14] In

the decade following the Prussian victory and the suppression of the Commune, 'geography fever' sweeps France. Signs of the new ardour for geography are everywhere: not only in the founding of academic geography by turncoat historians Levasseur, Vidal de la Blache, and others, but in the improvement in the teaching of geography at every level of the school system, and in the number of national and international congresses held in France during that decade. Immediately after the war, pressure groups launched a national campaign to demand the opening of an Ecole supérieure de Géographie in Paris. The mid-1870s saw the appearance of the first French journals – L'Explorateur and the Revue de géographie – devoted entirely to geography; the French societies of geography, which in 1881 were unanimously to applaud the conquest of Tunisia, experienced what can only be described as a meteoric expansion. Before 1871 there was only one such society, based in Paris, with never more than 300 members; ten years later there were twelve important new societies, many lesser ones, and over 9,500 members.[15]

A Belgian geographer writes in 1881: 'No country did more for developing and popularizing an isolated science than France, ever since the war of 1870.'[16] The date and the event, 1870, is crucial. For France's defeat at the hands of the Prussians was popularly thought to have been caused by the French troops not knowing geography well enough. In 1874 when the Revue de géographie begins to appear, the first issue justifies its existence with these opening remarks: 'We all remember those flawed maps supplied to our officers in 1870, which hardly provided the descriptions of the regions which were to be the theatre of such a fatal war.'[17] Not surprisingly, perhaps, the remarks are made by Ernest Picard, Thiers' Minister of the Interior and leading Versaillais strategist during the Commune. Elisée Reclus, in exile in Switzerland five years after the Commune and eagerly awaiting the arrival of the first issue of the Revue de géographie were he hopes to publish some of his work, is appalled to find Picard, the notorious anti-Communard, resurfacing and enshrined in a new form in the journal's preface:

> You must have received Drapeyron's Revue de géographie. I must admit I expected better. That letter of Picard's, who doesn't know a word of geography, placed at the head of the journal like a flag planted on the large mast of a ship; that pretension of wanting to make geography administer politics, a pretension that in the end could have no other motive than to make geography serve political ambitions.[18]

Despite Reclus' prescient metaphor of the geography journal as ship of state, there is nothing, at least initially, that objectively links the geographical societies, with whom Rimbaud was to publish several articles not too many years later sent from Africa, to colonial expansion: their goals, explicitly stated in the bulletins and minutes of the meetings, are to propagate interest in the 'scientific interests' of geography and to aid in the post-war rehabilitation of France. But as the decade advances, the societies function increasingly as propaganda agencies for voyages and explorations; the first French society for *commercial* geography is founded in 1874; Drapeyron, writing in 1875, proclaims that 'the world will belong to the one who knows it best'. Calling for public subscriptions to finance explorers, the rhetoric of the bulletins of the geographical societies begins to show a complete assimilation of the figure of the geographer with the figure of the explorer, and, later, with that of the *commerçant*:

> The end which the Societies of Geography propose to themselves consists in favouring explorations of unknown and still infrequently visited countries in order to draw from them products of the soil and to take there the objects of our industry and at the same time to effect the penetration of moral ideas which will elevate the intellectual level of races relatively inferior up to our own day. But in order to attain that end, a youth much have a relish for voyages and explorations and an exact knowledge of the geographical sciences. This last point is indispensable.[19]

The explorer/geographer, reads another bulletin, is he who sacrifices his life to give 'a world to science, a colony to his country'. In 1881 the *Revue de géographie* expresses the proud belief that its work facilitated French intervention in Tunis.[20] Prizes were offered by the geographical societies for accomplishments which, for the most part, revealed the same 'fantasy of the straight line' that had marked the Baron Haussmann's transformations of Paris a decade earlier: finance capital's new and open Paris, a city of flowing traffic, intra-urban arteries, and bold thoroughfares. A special prize was to be given, for example, to any voyager who could go from Algeria to Senegal by way of Timbuktu. At stake was the persistent dream of a trans-Saharan railroad that would unite the two most important existing French colonies, Algeria and Senegal. One of the most extravagant projects discussed, debated, and planned throughout the 1870s was that of installing a sea in the middle of the Sahara Desert.[21] Placed beside such public fantasies as these, images from Rimbaud's *Illuminations* lose much of the occult difficulty or privatistic surrealism almost automatically ascribed to them.

Another curious project was to found a practical school of higher geographical studies that would undertake a 'round the world' campaign of scientific exploration. To carry out the scheme its promoters hoped to find fifty rich travellers who could each contribute 20,000 francs. Their hopes were based on the astronomical success of a play based on Jules Verne's *Around the World in Eighty Days*; a further bizarre note was added when Verne himself consented to head the organizing committee.

If we look closely at this particular project of the first collective voyage around the world, we see that something has changed. In it we can detect the whole complex dialectic of mass tourism: the vestiges of the romantic ideology of the solitary explorer, who, seeking virgin territory, uncharted worlds, suddenly notices he has brought his whole world along with him in a tour bus. Perhaps no one understood so well as Rimbaud the futility of the flight of the bourgeois tourist from what was his own creation, a futility so well evoked by the Weininger aphorism that 'one can never depart for liberty from a railway station'.[22] This can be seen if we turn now to one of Rimbaud's last poetic works, an *Illumination* entitled 'Soir historique':

En quelque soir, par exemple, que se trouve le tourist naïf, retiré de nos horreurs économiques, la main d'un maître anime le clavecin des prés; on joue aux cartes au fond de l'étang, miroir évocateur des reines et des mignonnes; on a les saintes, les voiles, et les fils d'harmonie, et les chromatismes légendaires, sur le couchant.

Il frisonne au passage des chasses et des hordes. La comédie goutte sur les tréteaux de gazon. Et l'embarras des pauvres et des faibles sur ces plans stupides!

A sa vision esclave, – l'Allemagne s'échafaude vers des lunes; les déserts tartares s'éclairent les révoltes anciennes grouillent dans le centre du Céleste Empire, par les escaliers et les fauteuils de rocs un petit monde blême et plat, Afrique et Occidents, va s'édifier. Puis un ballet de mers et de nuits connues, une chimie sans valeur, et des mélodies impossibles.

La même magie bougeoise à tous les points où la malle nous déposera! Le plus élémentaire physicien sent qu'il n'est plus possible de se soumettre à cette atmosphère personnelle, brume de remords physiques, dont la constatation est déjà une affliction.

Non! – Le moment de l'étuve, des mers enlevées, des embrasements souterrains, de la planète emportée, et des exterminations conséquentes, certitudes si peu malignement indiquées dans la Bible et par les Nornes et qu'il sera donné à l'être sérieux de surveiller. – Cependant ce ne sera point un effet de légende!

[On whatever evening, for example, when the simple tourist stands withdrawn from our economic horrors, the master's hand awakens the pastoral harpsichord; they are playing cards at the bottom of the pond whose face, a mirror, conjures up favourites and queens; you have saints, veils, threads of harmony, and legendary chromatisms in the setting sun.
He trembles at the passing of hunts and hordes. Drama drips on the stages of turf. And the superfluity of poor people and weak people on those stupid levels!
Before his captive vision, Germany goes scaffolding towards the moons; the deserts of Tartary light up; ancient revolts ferment in the heart of the Celestial Empire; on stairways and armchairs of rock, a little world, pale and flat, Africa and Occident, will be erected. Then a ballet of familiar seas and nights, worthless chemistry and impossible melodies.
The same bourgeois magic wherever your baggage sets you down! Even the most elementary physicist knows that it is no longer possible to submit to this personal atmosphere, to this fog of physical remorse, whose very diagnosis is a sickness itself. No! This is the moment of the seething cauldron, of oceans boiling over, of underground explosions, of the planet swept away, of exterminations sure to follow; certitudes indicated with so little malice by the Bible and by the Norns, which the serious person will be asked to watch out for. Yet there will be nothing legendary about it!]

The shifter, 'our economic horrors', establishes the present historical moment of the poem; the simple tourist is indicated specifically and by the whole rhetoric of vision and theatre – the spectacle – which dominates the poem up to but not including the final paragraph: mirror, chromatisms, drama, stages, 'before his captive vision', and so forth. The spectator in the poem is 'withdrawn from our economic horrors', as befits a tourist who has fled the workplace for leisure; but the rest of the poem will erode the possibility of such a withdrawal.

It soon becomes clear that it is a whole spectacular panorama of world history that is being displayed before the tourist's captive vision. The tour guide's weary formulas ring out in the opening paragraph's revival of a waning aristocratic or feudal stage set: favourites and queens, hunts and hordes, you have saints, veils, etc.

The flood of geographical names in the third paragraph announces the triumph of the bourgeoisie: we are once more back to the present historical moment of the poem. Rimbaud presents this triumph less as a movement of social homogenization than one of spatial homogenization, for while the *rise* of the bourgeoisie is indicated by a vertical, ascending topography (Germany goes scaffolding up, deserts light up, stairways, etc.) – all this upward effort and energy results in a chilling spatial platitude: 'a little world, pale and flat', 'the same bourgeois magic wherever your baggage sets you down', 'a ballet of familiar seas and nights', 'worthless chemistry'.

The tension operating in the poem between the temporal homogeneity, the repetition and redundance of 'on whatever evening', and the historical singularity announced by the title; between the spatial homogeneity of 'the same bourgeois magic everywhere' and the convulsive upheaval of the final paragraph; between the figure of the tourist, the detached and affectless observer of spectacular images (or landscapes), and, at the end of the poem, the serious one who will undergo the event – all this becomes apparent with the apocalyptic ending of the poem.

It is as if in the face of the monolithic force of bourgeois spatial conquest, the social upheaval, the 'event' announced by the title, could only be played out on a global scale. If administrative rationalization, if a total colonization of all social and cultural relations, eliminates the possibility of exercising freedom, then nothing less than an apocalyptic reversal of this fate and a cataclysmic break in the continuum of history can set an emancipatory dynamic in motion. The exploded earth doubles a social antagonism which has already, in the preceding paragraph, become 'atmospheric', a 'fog' – that is, climatic or geographic.

The full effect of the geological cataclysm of the last lines can only be felt if we recall once again the dialectically oppposed reaction provided by the example of Mallarmé. Faced with and experiencing the same perceived hegemony of bourgeois platitude. Mallarmé's reply takes the form of a poetics of allusion designed to exclude the real because it is vulgar, designed to disrupt any referentiality outward. Rimbaud's reply to Mallarmé's fetishization of the poetic text, best summed up by the latter's famous dictum, 'Tout au monde existe pour aboutir à un Livre' – 'The whole world is made to end up in a book' – occurs in the last line of 'Soir historique': 'There will be nothing legendary about it.'

NOTES

This article is based on a chapter from my book *The Emergence of Social Space: Rimbaud and the Paris Commune* (Minneapolis: University of Minnesota Press, Theory and History of Literature Series, 1988). Funding from a University of California, Santa Cruz faculty research grant helped me complete it; I thank Alice Kaplan for her helpful suggestions.

[1] Walter Benjamin, 'Conversations with Brecht', trans. Anya Bostock, in *Understanding Brecht* (London: New Left Books, 1973), 106.

[2] See Fredric Jameson, 'Rimbaud and the spatial text', in *Re-writing Literary History*, ed Tak-Wai Wong and M.A. Abbas (Hong Kong: Hong Kong University Press, 1984), 66-93.

[3] All quotes from Rimbaud are taken from the *Oeuvres complètes*, ed Rolland de Renéville and Jules Mouquet (Paris: Gallimard, 1967). Translations are my won, *slightly* altered versions of Paul Schmidt, *Arthur Rimbaud: Complete Works* (New York: Harper & Row, 1976). Other translations from the French are mine.

[4] Eugène Vermersch, *Les Hommes du jour* (Paris: G. Towne, 187–? [n.d.]), 11.

[5] Leconte de Lisle, *Oeuvres diverses*, vol IV (Paris: Société d'édition, 1978), 477.

[6] Several excellent introductions to and analyses of the history of French academic geography have appeared in recent years; my own summary owes much to these works, in particular, Rodolphe de Koninck, 'La géographie critique', in *Les concepts de la Géographie humaine*, ed. A. Bailly (Paris: Masson, 1984); Yves Lacoste, *La Géographie, ça sert d'abord à faire la guerre* (Paris: Maspero, 1982); and articles by Béatrice Giblin published in the radical French geography journal *Hérodote* over the last ten years. See also the American equivalent or 'sister journal' to *Hérodote*, *Antipode*; in particular, Brian Hudson, 'The new geography and the new imperialism: 1870-1918', *Antipode*, 9, 2 (September 1977), 12-19.

[7] In 1922 Febvre wrote *La Terre et l'evolution humaine*, the book which formulated the theoretical positions of Vidal, and subtitled it 'A geographic introduction to history'; it was the first epistemological relection on geography and the history of geography.

[8] See Béatrice Giblin, 'Le Paysage, le terrain et les géographes', in *Hérodote*, 9 (1978), 74-89. See also Yves Lacoste, 'A bas Vidal ... Viva Vidal!' in *Hérodote*, 16 (1979), 68-81.

[9] In the context of an analysis of Zionism, Uri Eisensweig has persuasively argued the relation between Saussurian linguistics and the western construction of colonial space. See his *Territoires occupés de l'imaginaire juif* (Paris: Christian Bourgois, 1980). Eisenweig's argument is relevant beyond Zionism to the larger context of nineteenth-century imperialism.

[10] Thus Reclus's problematic relation with the 'official' Marxism of his time. In his preface to F. Domela Nieuwenhuis's *Le Socialisme en danger* (Paris: Stock,

1897) he writes:

See how that powerful individual Marx is treated, in whose honour hundreds of thousands of fanatics raise their arms to the sky, promising to religiously observe his doctrine! Doesn't an entire party, a whole army with several dozens of deputies in the German Parliament, now interpret that Marxist doctrine in a precisely opposite sense to the thought of the master. He declared that economic power determines the political form of societies, and now his followers affirm that economic power will depend on a party majority in the political assemblies. He proclaimed that 'the state, to abolish pauperism, must abolish itself, for the essence of evil lies in the very existence of the state!' And in his shadow his followers devote themselves to conquering and directing the state! If the politics of Marx triumph, it will be, like the religion of Christ, only on the condition that the master, adored in appearance, be disowned in practice. (pviii)

[11] Elisée Reclus, *L'Homme et la terre*, reissued with an introduction and choice of texts by Béatrice Giblin (Paris: Maspero, 1982); from the original, volume V, p335.

[12] Vermersch provides us with a satirical portrait of Figuier's 'collage' method of composition:

La Cuisinière bourgeoise says: 'To make a jugged hare, take a hare....' Monsieur Louis Figuier says, 'To make a book, take some other books.' He then arms himself with a pair of gigantic scissors and cuts to the right, to the left, in works that are scientific and in those that are not, in newspapers where he makes as much use of the *faits divers* as he does of the serials [*feuilletons*][; then when he has a sufficient weight of these fragments, he makes them into a book. All these bits and pieces, taken from three hundred authors, follow one another without order, without any agency, without connection, contradicting one another and forming an admirable harlequin's costume which parents buy for their children on New Year, but which, fortunately, the children don't read.

[13] Excellent analyses and histories of the French geographical societies can be found in Agnes Murphy, *The Ideology of French Imperialism* (Washington: Catholic University, 1948); and Vernon Mckay, 'Colonialism in the French geographical movement 1871-1881', *Geographical Review*, 33, 2 (April 1943), 214-32. My own description of the societies is indebted to these two works.

[14] Jean Dresch, quoted in Milton Santos, *Pour une geographie nouvelle* (Paris: Publisud, 1984), 19.

[15] Guillaume Depping, 'Le Mouvement géographique', *Journal officiel de la république française* (23 October 1991), 1.

[16] H. Wagner, cited in Numa Broc, 'L'Establissement de la géographie en France: diffusion, institutions, projets (1870-1890)', *Annales de la géographie*, 83, 459 (September-October 1974), 564.

[17] Ernest Picard, *Revue de géographie*, I (January-June 1874), 1. One of a flurry of articles like the following by Levasseur, entitled 'On the study and teaching of geography', suggests that the problem wasn't the maps:

We do not want our country to be the prey of foreigners. We have now understood all the advantages that the knowledge of geography gives.

When the Prussians entered our territory, the public imagined that they possessed marvellous maps, because they are very painstaking about that kind of work, but these maps were only and could only have been the copy of our own maps, with some slight corrections. Their advantage consisted in having them in their baggage and in using them, because the habit of geography has for some time taught their officers of all ranks how important it is to know the terrain on which one is operating. Most of our officers, who neither in school nor in the world learned to appreciate that science, took off without maps and didn't even notice they were missing anything.

Emile Levasseur, 'L'Etude et l'enseignement de la géographie', in *Séances et travaux de l'Académie des sciences morales et politiques*, XCVI (Paris, 1871), 425.

[18] Elisée Reclus, *Correspondance*, Volume II (Paris: Schleicher, 1911), 182.

[19] 'The teaching of geography given by the societies of geography', *Bulletin de Bordeaux*, IV (1881), 213-14 (unsigned).

[20] Drapeyron, 'Le But, la méthode et l'oeuvre de la *Revue de géographie*', *Revue de géographie*, IX (1881), 1-8.

[21] See Murphy, pp70-93, for an entertaining description of this project. To follow the debate, read, for instance, Jules Gros, 'La Mer Saharienne et le Capitaine Roudaire', in *L'Exploration: Journal des conquêtes de la civilisation sur tous les points du globe*, I (1876), 220-4.

[22] Otto Weininger, quoted in Hans Enzensberger, 'Une Théorie du tourisme', in *Culture ou mise en condition?*, trans. Bernard Lortholary (Paris: Juilliard, 1965), 86.

Metamorphoses at
Sydney Tower

Meaghan Morris

In this paper I want to discuss a methodological problem quite
commonly encountered by people working in cultural studies on the
very recent history of the present. Writing about the difficulties of
theorizing popular culture in the United States today, Lawrence
Grossberg puts it this way: 'what do you do when every event is
potentially evidence, potentially determining, and at the same time,
changing too quickly to allow the comfortable leisures of academic
criticism?'[1]

I'm not sure that for my purposes the problem of stabilizing an
object of analysis in an economy of rapid turnover and accelerating
obsolescence is properly posed like that. There is a gesture of
disengagement from a traditional literary practice in the notion of
'comfortable leisure' which, for institutional reasons, seems less
necessary in Australia – where academic critics of *anything* can
presume neither comfort nor leisure as a condition of their work.
Nevertheless, Grossberg's question certainly defines a recognizable
dilemma, and one which is by no means 'new', nor restricted to
'textual' criticism. When we're tempted to fetishize 'The Eighties' as
having been in some way unprecedented with respect to a rate and a
spread of cultural change, it is salutary to remember that in the 1960s
Henri Lefebvre had already formulated the problem of *Everyday Life
in the Modern World* in part by analysing his own abandonment of the
original project of the three-volume *Critique of Everyday Life*, the
first volume of which had appeared in 1946. Lefebvre said of that
volume's 'remainder' that 'this work was never completed or published
because the author soon realized that the momentous changes taking

place in society at the time had transformed his "subject" to the point of making it unrecognizable or virtually non-existent'.[2]

Observing this encounter with mutating and disappearing objects in one of the inaugural texts of the study of everyday life, it would be easy to take off in the direction of an epistemological reverie about the emergence of post-modernity (so-called) as a generalized cultural 'condition'. I prefer to consider instead a mundane but disconcerting experience of a changing object which I've had while working on a localized project in cultural *history*.

I'm writing a book about the politics of Development – with the capital D that connotes real-estate/tourism/leisure-industry or (the phrase I prefer) 'hospitality sector' activity – in Australia between 1972 and 1988. Within this broad framework, I'm analysing particular representations of space, time and movement *at work* in the related practices of tourism, shopping, driving, the use of museums, theme parks and motels. This involves doing quite a bit of comparative research into the histories of specific cases in different regions, and different socio-economic contexts: an urban tourist telecommunications tower, three suburban shopping malls, a country-town motel, a 'Captain Cook' memorial park.[3] I consider all of these sites of analysis to be spaces of women's work in one way or another: not only the obvious labour of shopping, scrimping and saving, staffing and using sites of 'family recreation' (whether one's own or someone else's), managing leisure and holidays and unemployment, but also the work of orchestrating the productivity of *time* in everyday life. Furthermore, most of the places I'm studying are primarily inhabited or invested in some way by white working-class communities, and most of these in turn are now reconstituting themselves as tourist landscapes.

The connective principle for these analyses is a study of the 'ideology' (the narratives and the rhetorics) of Progress in contemporary Australia – how and where 'progress' and 'development' have been mobilized and disputed as values, by whom, for whom, what tasks they perform and what actions they enable, and – since the two terms are in many ways distinct while able to function as synonyms – how they shift in relation to each other, overlapping on some occasions, coming into conflict on others. This study in turn requires the construction of a broader historical framework. Progress and Development are grand narratives both, implicated as they are in modern histories, theories of history, philosophies of becoming, and theories of theories of history which are certainly not unique or 'specific' to Australia. However in both Australian historiography and political rhetoric they have had, and still have, a very intense resonance: the pursuit of competing interpretations of Progress (with Development as its instrument *or* its opponent), has long been understood – and by widely diverging interests – to be inextricable from the project of the European invasion and settlement of Australia.[4] Even today, as the Federal Labor Party enters its fourth term of government by crisis management, and when the word 'progress' is more likely to arouse groans than applause in contexts of public debate about the meaning and the purpose of Development, Progress can still be invoked as a myth of origins – if not necessarily, any longer, of destiny.

During the nine years that I've been working on this project almost every 'place' has changed. Some have renovated their identities, some have won and others lost out in the interlocational competition variously analysed by (for example) David Harvey and Gordon Clark as characteristic of economic restructuring, and which in the Australian context has most often meant attempting to become 'centres of consumption' in Harvey's sense.[5] Here I can only discuss the changing of the place where my whole interest in this project originated, a place in that sense 'foundational' for me, and a place which seems to be, on the surface of things and from the outside in reality, a massive overstatement of an obdurate immutability – Sydney Tower.

Sydney Tower is a tourist-telecommunications monument in the centre of the Central Business District of the city of Sydney. It has the usual revolving restaurants and observation levels, and it rises up out of a pioneering but now rather downmarket shopping mall called 'The Centrepoint'. When Sydney Tower first opened in 1981 it was widely heralded as symbolically inaugurating a downtown revival – which duly eventuated, though not, of course, solely or even primarily because of the Tower – and so it was for quite some time a focus of intense public debate about its aesthetics, and of gossip about its function. In what later turned out to be an inaugural gesture for my own project, I wrote an essay about it.[6] While it may seem self-indulgent to structure my argument now with an account of the problems with that essay – including the parallelism I've just introduced between critical writing and the Tower's history – it can work, I hope, as an economical way to present the problems that this history raises (including the problem of parallelism).

In 1981, I was trying to disengage my own thinking from the

'towering' French semiotic tradition in which I had been schooled; and so I did the obvious, and structured my reading of Sydney Tower around a point-by-point consideration of why it was *not* like the Eiffel Tower constructed by Roland Barthes in his essay 'The Eiffel Tower'.[7] While 'obvious', this comparison was not quite as *arbitrary* as it may sound, or as it 'looks' when you consider the flagrant dissimilarities between the two structures. Long before Sydney Tower was built, it had been planned and promoted in public media as well as in the trades as 'The Eiffel Tower of the southern hemisphere' – 'only higher'.

The reference was, after all, a standard invocation of the historic model of models when it comes to displays of 'modernity' as an engineering feat; it marks, for example, the history of the American skyscraper ('beating' the Eiffel Tower being already the historic mission of the Chrysler Building) and thus of the cloning of *American* skylines around the world. But what interested me was *how* this meta-cliché was deployed in downtown Sydney in the 1970s. Doing a differential analysis by way of an analysis of my own model of models at that time (an essay by Barthes) seemed a good way of going about finding a way not only to write from Sydney rather than Paris in 1981, but also to work through the implications of Barthes' *own* critique of the method of *Mythologies*, in his essay 'Change the object itself'.[8] That is to say: by showing how my Sydney Tower differed from Barthes' Eiffel Tower, I could perhaps change the object 'as it presents itself to speech' – transforming the developers' serial *object* Eiffel/Sydney Tower into a denaturalized, rehistoricized, locally articulated *event*.

Looking back, this project seems to me now not only formalist, but excessively devious. It was also unsuccessful, since in fact I merely replaced Barthes as my model of models with a mix of Foucault on surveillance, Baudrillard on implosion, and feminist theory on voyeurism.

However, in doing that in 1981, I was picking up on a real convergence between local theoretical passions, and the spatial stories then in circulation in the city about the Tower. Looking at the long, opaque stem supporting Sydney Tower's squat gold turret, many believed, and a colleague of mine taught as *fact*, that THEY (the police, the Australian intelligence organization ASIO, the CIA ...) had their offices in there, all the way up to the top. This belief was a tenacious one, in spite of reassurances from the authorities that the stem contained only lifts and scissor stairs, and in spite of the evidence of one's own eyes that there wouldn't be room for much else. As for implosiveness: the media repeatedly represented Sydney Tower as attracting masses (of bodies and money) from outer suburbia, indeed from 'all over the world', to the centre of the city – then worried about the intensified overload, and a possible collapse, of parking and circulation systems. The theme of 'voyeurism' was publicly developed in a ribald rather than a paranoid mode: the great width of the bottom of the turret was frequently considered to have the effect of creating a 'dress', with a resultant discourse on the ambiguity of the Tower's sex, and on the excitements of looking up at it from below.

In producing a mirror exchange between the terms of theory and those of gossip, those of us who were 'working on the Tower' had an intense, if ephemeral, experience of *pertinence* in that work: and I want to make a point about that briefly, that at times there may be a co-*incidence* between the concerns of theoretical work and the terms of more widely circulating public discourses – and this produces an effect that we easily call 'relevance'. One problem with this is that at other times, when there seems to be no such co-incidence, we all too easily assume that the relationship between theoretical debate and 'public discourse' (a very problematic term, I think) is *therefore* one of 'irrelevance'. I'll come back to that, but first I want to describe in more detail the representation of towers and tower history to be found inside Sydney Tower in 1981.

The interior of the turret was vastly and self-reflexively decorated. Each of the two observation decks had a 'gallery' of photographs running round above the rim, and each level had its own theme. The lower deck proclaimed the transformation of Sydney as a locale; old photos of quaint corner shops, pioneer cottages, bullock-dray roads, were played off against the sublimity and modernity of the urban panorama outside. The upper deck was more formalist; it celebrated the history of towers, lookouts, and associated *tourist* activities. The theme linking the two levels (and incorporating infotech toys on both) was the overthrow of one of the great clichés of Australian popular (and academic) historiography, the 'tyranny of distance' (the title of a famous and widely read history of transport and communications in Australia by the rightwing historian Geoffrey Blainey). Inside the Tower, electronic communications were repeatedly invoked as enabling Australia's integration into the age of global simultaneity: no more time lag, no more 'isolation' by vast space from the rest of the world and from each other.

Now this imagery proclaimed the fulfilment of a mission that the Tower's developers had already deployed in the justificatory rhetoric used for over twenty years to 'get the Tower off the ground'. Sydney Tower's *raison d'être* was to stand as an annunciation of modernity: it was to be a structure that would enable Sydney to 'grow up' (as journalists and architects nearly always put it), and thus to become, in its new-found maturity, a 'world city', 'in the real meaning of the word'; it was to integrate Sydney *at last* (if a little late) into the modern age inaugurated long ago by that historic model of modern models, the Eiffel Tower.

As with all such annunciations of modernity and the linear temporality they entail, there could be nothing new in this. Indeed, there seemed to be nothing 'new' about Sydney Tower: it imitated a number of tourist-telecommunications towers existing worldwide (the London Post Office Tower, Toronto's CN Tower), and as soon as the structure was completed local architecture critics were complaining that it was 'an old-fashioned building'. Yet in terms of the history of annunciations of Australian modernity, this very archaism could be said to constitute its *instant* classicism. As David Bromfield has argued in relation to the history of art, architecture and advertising in Perth in the interwar period, 'the modern' in Australia has only marginally been understood as entailing 'the future', 'youth', 'originality', 'innovation', 'rupture', 'the unknown' and so forth.[9] 'The modern' has much more commonly been understood as a *known history*, something which has *already happened elsewhere*, and which is to be reproduced, mechanically or otherwise, with a local content. So Sydney Tower's archaic thrust ethos and failed funk aesthetic put it – along with its Eiffel Tower aspirations – in the grand strategic tradition of Australian 'positive unoriginality'.[10]

At least, that is how it looks if you frame the problem in terms primarily derived from aesthetic debate. For I think there *was* something 'new', or at least symbolically inaugural, about Sydney Tower. This was its self-reflexive celebration of *tourism* as a *means* (not the 'end') of becoming-modern, and thus its double interpellation of Sydney residents as (in Robert Somol's phrase) 'citizen-tourists' – becoming at one with 'foreign' tourists in our gaze at our own city, yet becoming at the same time the potential living *objects* of that self-same tourist gaze. The Tower offered, for example, photographic images of Sydney people, perhaps the very people visiting the Tower, waving at the camera from their/'our' nicely restored wrought-iron balconies, wandering around their/'our' freshly repainted Chinatown, visiting their/'our' zoos and museums. This was a significant beginning, I think, of what has since become a quite explicit (and state-supported, sometimes state-funded) discourse on the necessity of remodelling local culture to meet the needs of a tourist economy: a discourse on changing our manners (learning to say 'have a nice day', for example, in a city traditionally defining its distinction from *other* Australian cities by aggressiveness, rudeness and impatience), a discourse on changing our attitudes to labour (learning that 'service' is a virtue, not a chore), and – since these have been by no means unambiguous developments – eradicating the anti-'Asian' racism of the old working-class culture, not on ethical or humanistic grounds, but because it's anachronistic, and bad for business.[11]

However, the most sinister component in Sydney Tower's self-production as tourist myth *involved* race, and it was to be found in the theatrettes on each level which ran a didactic audio-visual 'display'. If you went from the lower to the upper level, these formed a narrative sequence developing a crudely pop-Darwinist argument about the evolution of towers in human history, and the necessity of Sydney Tower as that history's inevitable outcome. The first display was again about Sydney as a tourist locale, with images of people pointing and waving from boats, streets and houses at objects which were not actually represented – thus creating a poetics of tourist deixis. All of these images, except the last, were in 'candid' snapshot style. The last was a simulated 'primitive' painting of a primal scene, the foundation of the city; 'natives' on the foreshore pointing at a sailing ship in the harbour, Europeans on board pointing back; and on the soundtrack, these words: '*You* can imagine *their* surprise when the first settlers sailed in to this magnificent harbour.' This was genesis: the first white gaze at Aboriginal people, first objects of tourism in a brave new land, and the first ethno-narcissistic gesture: 'we' (for this display did not address Koori tourists) imagine 'their' surprise in gazing at the wonder of 'us', as we gave at 'this' (not 'their') magnificent harbour.

Then, on the next level, you saw 'The evolution of the Tower: From Tree House to Sydney Tower'. This display *began* with a simulated 'primitive' painting, introducing a creation story: caveman is attacked by wild animals and invents the tree house, cavewoman sees a volcano erupting in the distance; she *points*, and as though by spontaneous combustion, the universal language of tourism is born. As primitive images gave way to a 'postcard' mode, a series of model towers 'ascended' from the ancestral tree house, until – in bursts of repetition of a single image – the pure, final form of Sydney Tower was achieved.

The volatility of this narrative progression, *and* narrative of Progress, was considerable given that, for the many decades that Australia was an explicitly racist state, social Darwinism had long been a unifying ideology of national identity. Its volatility would remain considerable in a context where there has been for some years now a very complex debate about, and above all between, Aboriginal people in terms of *their* negotiation of an over-intensifying tourist and art-market interest in them – or (and this is part of the problem) in some of them. So the pop-Darwinist autobiography of Sydney Tower, combined with its positively unoriginal mission, seemed to me to define, therefore, a crucial 'place' to begin my own broader programme of analysis.

So you can imagine *my* surprise when I went back to the Tower in 1989 for the first time in years, and it was almost all gone.

Worse, it was as though none of the representations I had studied had ever been there. I asked questions about the renovations, but no one who was working there had been around long enough to remember the decor of the Tower having ever been any different from the way it is today. So there was a crazed culture critic staggering round the turret saying 'What have you done with the evidence?'

The lower deck had become a cafeteria, and its theatrette had vanished. The old photographs had been replaced by plastic basreliefs with a wildflower motif, in a rectangular design referring not to wildflowers but to plastic cafeteria trays. On the upper level, the 'Evolution of the Tower' remained, but as a story in its own right with no anaphoric reference to Aboriginal people (who are included now only through the toy boomerangs and didgeridoos in the souvenir shop). With them, the whole linking discourse to the history of Sydney as a 'site' had disappeared. There was no narrative (offensive or otherwise) of the founding of the place, and no specific address to Sydney residents. Instead, the images appealed unambiguously to foreign tourists: perfunctory ads for duty-free fur and opal shops, representations of tourist transport systems (trains, boats, hydrofoils, even a picture of a charter bus drawn up right next to a Qantas jet) and of their destinations – anonymous motel swimming pools, distant tropical and rural resorts.

These celebrated neither Sydney nor the Tower, but only the possibility of *going somewhere else*. Instead of promoting itself as the centralizing, spatializing metonym of *The* City, Sydney Tower is now a kind of narrative prelude: it offers a moment of 'overview', not of a spectacle of space to be consumed, but of an itinerary of movements about to be performed. As for Sydney residents, we are simply ignored by the Tower. At best, looking out at our city we can overlook the programmes of tourist pleasure, and gain a vague pride of place therefrom.

I hadn't expected a change this drastic. I had expected, of course, to rethink my theoretical frames of reference and reformulate problems accordingly. I also knew that in 1989 I was looking out on a socio-economic 'landscape' vastly different from that of 1981, when the city was still recovering from the great property market crashes of the mid-1970s. In 1989 I saw a city in the grip of a property boom so extreme that office space had become more expensive than Manhattan's (but still much cheaper than Tokyo's), and a city in which the frenzy of hotel construction was beginning to interfere with the tourist dream it aspired to accommodate. On the ground, between demolitions and new constructions, with the roar of jackhammers pulverising your ears from all sides, central Sydney is no fun to 'tour'; whole guidebooks (let alone critical essays) become dated overnight as buildings and city blocks disappear and mutate.

As for the residents, more are becoming homeless (many low-income tenants were forcibly evicted from housing renovated for tourists during the 1988 bicentenary), while the shortage of affordable housing has become so extreme that another satellite city is about to be founded on the far western urban fringe of a metropolis already sprawling some 50 miles long and 30 miles wide – opening up another phase, no doubt, in a long history of spatial structuring-in of segregation and disadvantage.[12] Furthermore, if, as Leonie Sandercock has argued, the Sydney skyline has always been a projection of the operation of class systems elsewhere, the skyline in construction now is one primarily being created by the emergent class systems of the Pacific Rim, rather than those of the age of the Eiffel Tower.[13]

This knowledge, however, was of no immediate practical assistance in deciding what to *do* with the discovery that my 'founding' site of analysis had changed utterly, and in almost embarrassing congruence with the socio-economic landscape. Here I want to return to Grossberg's question, 'what do you do when every event is … changing too fast to allow the comfortable leisure of academic criticism?' I think it's important to ask first *why* this kind of change is a problem – since, after all, you can argue that such change *itself* should be the object of study, rather than an 'event' construed as a 'text', a text which is in turn construed as a symptom of a general state of culture to be diagnosed by the cultural critic. Studying change, rather than texts or objects or even 'practices' in popular culture, is in part what Grossberg himself is suggesting we might do, and I would agree with his shift of emphasis.[14] Although the tendency to 'read' events as texts as symptoms has been criticized many times before, it does remain a *recurring* tendency – especially, these days, in relation to 'places' and buildings.

But I also have a problem of a different order with 'places', which tend to change at a rate which may be geological in comparison with that encountered by people working on television, music, or fashion, but which is drastic when it happens. This is a problem to do with the status of description or 'presentation' in the *writing* of a cultural study – a problem cognate in some ways with that of the plot summary in film criticism, and also one tied up with difficulties of exchange between different local as well as national cultures in a not quite post-colonial world. Barthes, for example, could define the Eiffel Tower as 'present to the entire world' – a reasonable if by no means unchallengeable proposition, especially if one adds the restriction, 'to the entire world of likely readers of this book' – and this fiction of *presence* (and of stability over time) meant that he didn't have to describe it.

Writing of tourist-tower interiors in Sydney, or, even more acutely, small motels in insignificant towns that most *Australians* have never heard of, I can't assume 'presence', or durability, in quite the same way – any more, in fact, than critics of American cable TV can assume familiarity (even from other critics) with the texts or even the reputations of any but already canonical programmes for analysis – and in this sense, obscurity and proliferation may create similar problems.

But what interests me in the problem of description is not the epistemological and metaphysical issues it can raise, but the technical, and to me minutely political, question of the enunciative strategies (and thus the strategies of reference) involved in *producing* particular descriptions, or in not producing them. For example, if I'm honest about it, the thing that annoyed me most about the metamorphosis of Sydney Tower was the *tense* change it imposed on my original account – because this then involved me in a real shift of register from 'discourse' to 'history' (in Benveniste's sense of those terms) and in the corresponding inscription of a quite different 'subjective' relation to my material. Part of my annoyance at this was due, in turn, to a recognition of a problem of my own legitimacy as a critic now writing history: despite encroachment from economics, 'History' is still perhaps *the* most privileged, and highly codified, discourse of liberal intellectual authority in postwar Australia.

Contemporary cultural studies offers a number of possible ways of circumventing the encounter with this problem.

I could paraphrase various general accounts of the culture of late capitalism, and then read the metamorphoses of Sydney Tower as a local variation of these (the Australian 'modernist' solution).

I could follow John Fiske and find something empowering in the developments I've described.[15] Something like this has in fact been done, not with Sydney Tower (which because of its age is now disinvested of theoretical passion), but with a newer citizen-tourist downtown development in Sydney, Darling Harbour – and a related 'people-moving' monorail that went right through the streets of the city. In the controversy about the monorail's construction, cultural criticism was enlisted to argue that its opponents had a morbid Frankfurt School hostility to popular culture, and that the question of pleasure and user-transformation of the monorail experience could be separated from the debate about why the Labor state that was funding the monorail (under direct pressure from the Darling Harbour developer Transfield-Kumagai) was simultaneously responsible for public hospitals, in the working-class suburbs, with their walls patched together with chicken wire.

Or I could reiterate from my old analysis the notion of *implosion*, taking the now disinvested Tower as an emblem of the post-panoptic collapse of meaning and distinction into the 'dead centre' of the urban core that R.E. Somol discovers in his amusing analysis of the 'singularity of power' in Chicago's State of Illinois Center (an 'urban ruin' which, for a linear narrative of the Progress of simulation, would be well in advance of the jaunty verticality of Sydney Tower), using this example to conform, with Somol, the futility under postmodernism of activism by intellectuals.[16]

But I think that each of these possibilities, whatever their other attractions and disadvantages, have a common flaw. Each is a way of reading a singular *site* as an allegorical exposition of theoretical problems taken as given, and thus as exemplary of general forces already known to be at work in the world. I don't think that it is always a mistake to take such problems as given, or to consider certain forces as 'known', and deeply involved in a local situation. My problem is rather the complicity that is produced between the (fundamentally aesthetic) *problematic* of the exemplary object, the singular site, and what remains, in fact, a planar, continuist and linear concept of historical time – in which the 'inevitable' (whether it be the spatializing 'fix' of late capitalism, the theoretical necessity for empowerment, or the triumph of simulation) realizes itself in *a* time which is not that of the Tower, the 'popular', or late capitalism, but that of the inscribed enunciating subject of the theoretical discourse *in* which that complicity is produced.

It's insufficient, of course, just to assert this, or to cite the classic discussions of the problem (like the Anderson/Berman dispute, or Paul Willemen's response to Jacques Donzelot's essay on 'The apprehension of time') if one simply reiterates as *doctrine* a concept of unequal development, and of differential temporality.[17] I think one needs to argue anew each time *why* a concept of evenly unfolding temporality is a problem, and in my case, this time, it is that such a concept would entail a mirroring in my text of the ideology of Progress that I'm supposed to be analysing.

For example, Somol's conclusion in ' "... You put me in a happy state"; the singularity of power in Chicago's loop' that we must 'abandon the language of struggle' (because 'when one is in quicksand, movement only tends to swallow one faster') depends for its effect on a prior claim that the 'world' has largely 'moved beyond' the techniques of power that once made activism effective. This claim in turn is articulated in classically oedipal, New Generation, terms:

> Foucault's project may well have made sense ... a generation ago, but we are on the side of urban fall-in. Similarly, from our reserved perspective, the currently 'progressive' architects and planners who continue to move away from forty-five are unintelligible to those of us on the down side of sixty-eight. Their nova is our black hole. We remember things in their future, although to them we have yet to be born.[18]

In this kind of formulation (as in most of Baudrillard's work) it is precisely in the present tense of the enunciating subject ('we') that a subject of linear, albeit dystopian, Development is reconstituted – along with a vanguard, albeit cynical, model of intellectual practice.

So one thing I would want to do in response to changing objects is to refuse to be 'sucked in' (in Somol's implosive phrase) by 'singularity' when analysing events or sites. This is one reason for studying *several* 'eventful' places in a particular tourist economy: examining, for example, the relation between their different *relative* rates of renovation or dereliction, as well as a distinctive present, and a local past, in each.

If Sydney Tower, for example, no longer interpellates residents or even domestic tourists, there are now other structures (like Darling Harbour) that do. If Sydney Tower has been generically transformed from a triumphal regional affirmation of an overdue modernity to an ageing simulacrum symbolically inaugurating a promising 'foreign tour', then an analysis of its changes does not necessarily thereby serve as an adequate 'prelude' to going further afield: to asking, for example, why Green Hills shopping mall in the coalfields town of Maitland mutated, at around the same time, from a cheery outdoor 'village square' to a solemnified 'colonial history-effect' enclosure called The Hunter, while 500 miles away the 'colonial history-effect' of the Henry Parkes Motel in the real rural village of Tenterfield should have disappeared in an explosion of High Funk Hot Pink paint – nor to understanding precisely what these changes mean in the lives of the communities inhabiting and using these places, and in the regional economies giving both places and communities shape.

More importantly, I think that the changes at these sites do need to be read in the process of writing *as* cultural studies' a historical discourse which produces these changes *as* 'change', yet which does not thereby lay claim to the legitimacy and authority specific to the developmental traditions either of Australian history, or of avant-garde one-upmanship. In order to consider what that might mean in practice, I want to conclude with a couple of comments on what I see as the related *political* question of 'relevance' in cultural studies.

If, as Grossberg suggests, every cent can be regarded as potentially evidence, as potentially determining and as not only changing very quickly but changing at a *rate* which can seem to be ever-accelerating, how do you *motivate* a particular project of analysis, a specific cultural study? The tower is a useful example here for considering the limits of 'singularity', because if there often seems to be a unique obduracy to towers (and to the tower/landscape relation) in the (institutional) space of *theoretical* discourse, it is in part because of the historical importance of the *figure* of the tower for the 'philosophical imaginary' in Michele Le Doeuff's sense – its history as an image of an 'intellectual *place*', an image of a place for *posing* the problem of place, and of 'the place' of intellectuals, *par excellence*.

I think it is very important now, increasingly so as cultural studies becomes an upwardly mobile discipline in the academy, to bring a concept of differential temporality to bear on our own practice as cultural critics, and on our schemas of theoretical 'development'. Theoretical debates – especially those in highly 'invested' areas of publication like contemporary cultural studies – have their own speeds and rates of change. Sometimes they move very fast, much faster than the rate of change in other public discourses circulating in the media, and in the language of popular struggles. 'Keeping up' with the rate of change in our discipline can lead us to ignore the way that a rhetoric, even a whole 'problematic' (in the popular sense of that term) which is a 'dead issue', 'dated' in one context, can be very much alive and kicking in another. 'Progress', after all, is an obvious case. My view of my own 'place' as an intellectual in Australia is that I need to begin thinking not from a position at the end of decades, indeed centuries, of philosophical argument about theories of theories of history, but from the kind of moment in which people in the path of developments say 'it's sad, but you can't stop progress'.

In a critique of the work of Baudrillard some years ago, Andrew Wernick argued that 'the sales aim of commodity semiosis is to differentiate the product as a valid, or at least resonant, social totem, and this would be impossible without being able to appeal to taken-for-granted systems of cultural reference'.[19] Following from that, I would derive two broad methodological principles for the project I've described: first, that studying such systems of reference and their functioning entails a historical analysis of the enabling rhetorics of public politics (and thus of the 'producers' of tourist culture – developers, planners, politicians, architects – as well as of its 'consumers'); second, that while such a study need not be 'comparative' in the strict sense, it should involve the production of a *connective* analysis of a number of differentially constructed sites and events – the choice of which will no doubt be motivated reciprocally by the thematics of the overall project.

From these two principles I would also derive a third, which is of the order of a self-imposed, but polemical, restriction: there should be no 'morphological' studies of exemplary sites of the production of either 'modernity' or 'everyday life'; no studies of *the* shopping-mall form, *the* motel form, *the* tower form, *the* freeway, *the* theme park, *the* beach, *the* pub.... But given the fascination of towers for intellectuals, as emblematic of our 'place', the 'privileges', differences, contra-dictions, and inadequacies of our speaking position (as though there were always One, the basic fallacy of most polemics on the topic) it is particularly important now to avoid morphological accounts of '*the* Tower' – in which the monuments of urban redevelopment may simply be regarded, in the end, as so many elaborate *mises en abyme* of postmodernist intellectual speech.

Towers, in fact, are in some disfavour these days as representing the privileged place of annunciation not of modernity in general, perhaps, but of General Theory in particular. For Michel De Certeau in *The Practice of Everyday Life*, for example, coming down from the World Trade Center in New York is to leave behind the programmatic, synchronizing, gridding, abstracted, statis-imposing Master power-knowledge of urban theory, and to walk into a space of practice, eventfulness, history – and there is an allegory involved about 'walking away' from a certain 'vision' of structuralism.[20] Yet in reading this text, what always strikes me is that we (at least in Sydney) are not living through a great age of urban master-planning – and that very little of the vicious, vociferous and 'eventful' jostling for power over urban, regional and national (re)development occurring over the past decade has proceeded on the assumption that we are (still less that we ought to be).

It is perhaps worth recalling here Manfredo Tafuri's acerbic comment from some years ago, on work by the then utopian-futurist architect Kenzo Tange (soon to provide Sydney with a four-tower mega-complex), that in such supposedly 'singular' buildings 'the total image is reduced to a mere decorative enhancement of the metropolitan chaos it once aspired to dominate' – or, as Mike Davis puts it in his response to Fredric Jameson's famous analysis of Portman's Bonaventure Hotel – to the status of a monument to the end (and certainly not the apotheosis) or urban reform.[21] It seems to me that the last thing that Sydney Tower could appropriately represent in any history of its changes is an overstated general thesis against 'General Theory' as a doctrinal error; and that, in the midst of an ending of urban reform in the name of '(re)developing' Sydney, it is probably the parallelism involved in becoming a minor embellishment of metropolitan chaos (rather than that of aspiring to the visionary

position of master-thinking) that cultural studies may most need to try
to avoid.

NOTES

[1] Lawrence Grossberg, 'The formations of cultural studies: an American in
Birmingham', *Strategies*, 2 (1989), 144. My thanks to the Unit for Criticism
and Interpretive Theory at the University of Illinois (Champaign-Urbana) for
the occasion to write this paper, and to Lawrence Grossberg for his help and
advice.
[2] Henri Lefebvre, *Everyday Life in the Modern World* (New Brunswick:
1984), 40.
[3] Some of these case studies are discussed in my 'Things to do with shopping
centres', in Susan Sheridan (ed.), *Grafts: Feminist Cultural Criticism* (London:
1988), 193-225, and in 'At Henry Parkes Motel', *Cultural Studies*, 2, 1
(January 1988), 1-47.
[4] Cf. Robert Connell, *Ruling Class, Ruling Culture* (Sydney: 1977).
[5] David Harvey, 'Flexible accumulation through urbanization: reflections on
"post-modernism" in the American city', *Antipode*, 19, 3 (1987), 260-86. A
more pragmatic approach to the political implications of interlocational
competition is given by Gordon Clark, 'Planning in a world of economic
restructuring', *Planning and Developing Australia: Papers Delivered at the
Twenty-First Congress of The Royal Australian Planning Institute* (Melbourne: 1988), 1-25.
[6] 'Sydney Tower', *Island Magazine*, 9, 10 (March 1982), 53-61, reprinted in
Transition: Discourse on Architecture, 25 (Winter 1988).
[7] Roland Barthes, *The Eiffel Tower and Other Mythologies* (new York: 1979).
[8] Roland Barthes, 'Change the object itself', in *Image-Music-Text*, trans.
Stephen Heath (Glasgow: 1979), 165-9.
[9] David Bromfield, *Aspects of Modernism in Perth* (Perth: 1988). This
argument does not imply, of course, that Australian 'modernism' could not
now be re-theorized on the basis of actual local practices. It is rather an
account of the historical functioning of an 'imported' critical discourse.
[10] I discuss this tradition in more detail in 'Tooth and claw: tales of survival
and *Crocodile Dundee*', *The Pirate's Fiancée: feminism, reading, postmodernism* (London: 1988).
[11] For a fascinating account of a large-scale state strategy of cultural
restructuring to meet the needs of tourism in Singapore, see Wai-Teng Leong,
'Culture and the state: manufacturing traditions for tourism', *Critical Studies
in Mass Communication*, 6 (1989), 355-75.
[12] Cf. Frank Stilwell, 'Structural change and spatial equity in Sydney',
unpublished paper (1989), Wolstenholme Library, Sydney University: Margo
Huxley and Kate Kerkin, 'What price the bicentennial? A political economy of
Darling Harbour', *Transition: Discourse on Architecture*, 26 (Spring 1988),
57-64.
[13] Leonie Sandercock, *Cities for Sale: Property, politics and urban planning in
Australia* (Melbourne: 1977).

14 Cf. the extended argument in Lawrence Grossberg, *It's a Sin: Postmodernism, politics and culture* (Sydney: 1988).
15 John Fiske, *Understanding Popular Culture and Reading The Popular* (London: 1989). The second volune, 'Searing Towers', attempts to locate a progressive pleasure in Chicago's Sears Tower.
16 R.W. Somol, ' "... You put me in a happy state": the singularity of power in Chicago's loop', *Copyright*, 1 (Fall 1987), 98-118.
17 Perry Anderson, 'Modernity and revolution', in Cary Nelson and Lawrence Grossberg (eds), *Marxism and the Interpretation of Culture* (Chicago: 1988), 317-38; Marshall Berman, 'The signs in the street: a response to Perry Anderson', *New Left Review*, 144 (1984), 114-23; Jacques Donzelot, 'The apprehension of time', and Paul Willemen, 'Response to Donzelot', in Don Barry and Stephen Muecke (eds), *The Apprehension of Time* (Sydney: 1988).
18 Somol, ' "... You put me in a happy state" ', 115.
19 Andrew Wernick, 'Sign and commodity: aspects of the cultural dynamic of advanced capitalism', *Canadian Journal of Political and Social Theory*, 8, 1-2, 31.
20 Michel de Certeau, *The Practice of Everyday Life* (Berkeley, Calif.: 1984), ch 7.
21 Manfredo Tafuri and Francesco Dal Co, *Modern Architecture* (New York: 1979); Mike Davis, 'Urban renaissance and the spirit of postmodernism', in E. Ann Kaplan (ed), *Postmodernism and Its Discontents* (London: 1988), 79-87.

Notes on Contributors

David Bate lectures in Photography History and Theory at West Surrey College of Art, Farnham. He is on the advisory committee of Camerawork Gallery, London and has exhibited his work in Canada, Estonia and Australia as well as in England.

Glenn Bowman lectures at the University of Kent at Canterbury.

Victor Burgin is a visual artist and writer who teaches in the Art History and History of Consciousness Programs at the University of California, Santa Cruz. He is author of *The End of Art Theory* (London: Macmillan, 1986) and editor of *Thinking Photography* (London: Macmillan, 1982).

Iain Chambers lectures at the Instituto Universitario Orientale, the University of Naples. He is author of *Popular Culture: The Metropolitan Experience* (London: Methuen, 1986) and *Border Dialogues, Journeys in Postmodernity* (London: Routledge, 1990).

James Donald is Senior Lecturer in Media Studies at Sussex University, Brighton. He is author of *Sentimental Education: Schooling, Popular Culture and the Regulation of Liberty* (London: Verso, 1992) and co-editor (with Ali Rattansi) of *'Race', Culture and Difference* (London: Sage, 1992). He was editor of *New Formations* 1987-1989.

Elizabeth Grosz lectures in Critical Theory at Monash University, Australia. She is the author of *Sexual Subversions: Three French Feminists* (Sydney: Allen and Unwin, 1989) and *Jacques Lacan: A Feminist Introduction* (London: Routledge, 1990).

Peter Hulme is the Professor of Literature at the University of Essex. His recent publications include *Colonial Encounters: Europe and the Native Caribbean 1492–1797* (London: Routledge, 1992) and (co-edited with Neil Whitehead) *Wild Majesty: Encounters with Caribs from Columbs to the Present Day* (Oxford: Clarenden Press, 1992).

Anahid Kassabian has recently completed her PhD in Modern Thought and Literature at Stanford University, where she teaches in film and cultural studies. She is the editor (with Lawrence Siegel and David Schwarz) of *The State of the Art: Refiguring Music Studies*, which is forthcoming from University of Virginia Press.

David Kazanjian is a graduate student in the Department of Rhetoric at the University of California where he is researching early forms of US nationalism and colonial, focussing on the ante-bellum US state in its many cultural and ideological forms.

Gail Ching-Liang Low lectures at Staffordshire University and is currently working on multiculturalism and discourses of cultural identity in Britain and American. Her book *White Skins/Black Masks* is forthcoming with Routledge.

Donatella Mazzoleni is a practising architect and teaches in the Faculty of Architecture at the University of Naples.

David Morley is a Reader in Communications at Goldsmiths' College, University of London. He is the author of *Television, Audience and Cultural Studies* (London: Routledge, 1992) and is presently working on a book with Kevin Robins entitled *Spaces of Identity* to be published by Routledge in 1994.

Meaghan Morris is a full-time writer who had worked as a professional film critic and lectured in art and media studies. She is author of *The Pirate's Fiancée: Feminism, reading, postmodernism* (London: Verso, 1988).

Peter D. Osborne teaches at the Media School of the London Institute. He is working on a book on photography and travel.

Benita Parry has written on colonial discourse and the texts of imperialism. She is the author *Conrad and Imperialism* and is working on a study of imperialist discourses.

Kevin Robins lectures at the Centre for Urban and Regional Development Study, University of Newcastle. He is author (with Frank Webster) of *The Technical Fix* (Basingstoke: Macmillan, 1989) and editor of *Understanding Information* (London: Belhaven Press, 1991). He is currently working on a book with David Morley (see above).

Kristin Ross lectures in Literature at the University of California, Santa Cruz. He is author of *The Emergence of Social Space: Rimbaud and the Paris Commune* (Basingstoke: Macmillan, 1988).

Renata Salecl is a reseracher at the Institute of Criminology, University of Ljubljana, Slovenia. She is working on a book of psychoanalytic approaches to nationalism and anti-feminism.

McKenzie Wark lectures in Communications at Macquarie University, Sydney. His essays have appeared in *New Formations, Cultural Studies* and *Impulse*. He is a regular contributor to the Australian magazines *Tensions, Editions Reviews* and *Australian Left Review*.